The Racial State

For Philomena

THE RACIAL STATE

David Theo Goldberg

First published 2002

2 4 6 8 10 9 7 5 3 1

Blackwell Publishers Inc.
350 Main Street
Malden, Massachusetts 02148
USA

Blackwell Publishers Ltd
108 Cowley Road
Oxford OX4 1JF
UK

Library of Congress Cataloging-in-Publication Data

Goldberg, David Theo.
The racial state / David Theo Goldberg.
p. cm.
Includes bibliographical references and index.
ISBN 0–631–19919–5 (acid-free paper) –
ISBN 0–631–19921–7 (pbk.: acid-free paper)
1. Race. 2. Racism. I. Title.
HT1521.G548 2001
305.8–dc21 2001037573

British Library Cataloguing in Publication Data

A CIP catalogue record for this book is available
from the British Library.

Typeset in 10 on 13pt Meridian
by Graphicraft Limited, Hong Kong

CONTENTS

ACKNOWLEDGMENTS

The Racial State has been a long time in writing, a book in process. The idea for the book grew out of gaps in argument and themes addressed in my earlier book, *Racist Culture* (Blackwell, 1993). In particular, *Racist Culture* left the state's assumption of racial order completely under-theorized. As I began to pursue this set of questions, I came very quickly to realize the lack of mutual engagement between state theory and racial theory literatures. Recent thinking around racial theory has begun to address the basic concerns, though in tentative ways. *The Racial State* is my attempt to make the nexus between race and state key to both bodies of literature. I insist on a title already invoked a decade ago because I want to trouble the rampant exceptionalism regarding racial states. My emphasis thus is not *the* racial state, but the *racial* state, its forms and logics, histories and expressions.

I owe enormous debts of gratitude to friends and colleagues, students and support staff, all of whom suffered my obsessive insistence to take on these questions with fabulous generosity of spirit and support, both personal and professional. The book took shape through more conversations than I can recall, through seminars and workshops, colloquia and late-night conversations over cognac, whispered exchanges while listening to lectures and shouted responses over live jazz. I started out testing some tentative ideas with a group of graduate students in a small state theory seminar with the School of Justice Studies at Arizona State University. Pietro Toggia, himself working on a dissertation at the time on the state, or its demise, in the Horn of Africa, pushed me to clarify theoretical positions large and small, locked in dialogue with the likes of Althusser and Poulantzas, Marx and Foucault, Hall and Butler, Pateman and Wendy Brown, Magubane and Bayart, Wolpe and Cohen. Lily Mendoza, and Rona Halualani, working on the colonial and cultural histories of the Philippines and Hawai'i, respectively, brought to my attention much I had overlooked. They were as insightful interlocutors as they were superb students.

A year-long sabbatical leave spent at Berkeley enabled me not only to take to writing the book in a serious way but opened up terrifically instructive conversations with numerous people. Percy Hintzen, then chair of African American Studies, graciously arranged my affiliation with the department and was ever the gracious and hospitable host. Stephen Small welcomed me as a brother. I spent many hours in deep conversation with my landlady, Barbara Christian, a wonderful friend, now tragically only memory in the wake of her terribly sad loss. Tommy Lott served as a sounding board for ideas, deep and delirious, serious and silly, calling me to articulate at hours too late for coherence and places too lively for sustained thought.

While on leave, my call to gather around questions of race and the state brought to life fora I could only have dreamed about in other venues. Thus it was a pleasure and a privilege to organize a workshop on the racial state at Berkeley with Ruthie Gilmore and Gill Hart which included the likes of Barbara Harlow, Michael Omi, Zine Magubane, Don Moore, Caren Kaplan, Norma Alarcon, and Barnor Hesse. I learned a great deal from the engagement, as too from numerous conversations then and since with Barnor. Lewis Gordon at Brown hosted me more than once to talk about my progress to his colleagues, most notably in conversation with John and Jean Comaroff, long-time friends and family, and with Philomena Essed, from whose combined work I have learned more concerning the range of concerns at issue here than from any others. Lewis and Jayne Gordon welcomed us into their house and hearts and family. A talk on genocide to a conversational group at Berkeley hosted by Ian Boal left me thinking about the relation of genocides and ethnoracial states. And a residential research group convened by Angela Davis at the University of California Humanities Research Institute in the Spring of 2000 led me to extend thoughts about race and prison and political economy, pushed by the insistence of Angela and Ruthie, Nancy Scheper-Hughes, Avery Gordon, and Gina Dent. A later residence group at the Institute on race and premodernity pushed me as I was completing the book to specify positions I had long taken for granted. I am grateful in this regard to Margo Hendricks, Karen Bassi, Ray Kea, Sara Morris, Kristi Wilson, and mostly to the inimitable Geraldine Heng.

Two graduate seminars on critical race theory – the first at Berkeley, later one at Arizona State University – challenged me to think more clearly about the possibilities and limits of critical race language. Suzette Spencer's light-hearted though theoretically serious skepticism at Berkeley provided refreshing and energizing fuel for rethinking. And Kim Furumoto at ASU brought me to my senses many more times than my self-image would care to acknowledge. Kim's assistance and insight, care and persistence, theoretical commitment and critical exactitude have proved invaluable, in this project, as in so many others.

Conversations with Michael Keith walking or careening through London's East End have proved as revealing of the interface of race and nation, state and culture in the postcolony as they left me delightfully humored. Michael's dazzling analysis of the political economy of London's racially inscribed culture will contribute significantly to our general understanding of these articulations.

I have presented various pieces of the book along the way, in addition to those mentioned above. Early on in the project, I talked to the Rhetoric Department at UC Berkeley, Sociology at UC Santa Cruz, and the Institute for Law and Society at New York University. I am grateful to Judith Butler, Herman Gray, and Christine Harrington, respectively, for making these fora possible and for causing me to define more precisely the nature of the project. Jeffrey Reiman invited me to American University, Rosi Braidotti to the University of Utrecht, Charles Small and Oren Yiftachel hosted me at Ben Gurion University in Israel, Kent Ono and Wendy Ho at UC Davis, and John Solomos in London. Consequent conversations prompted thinking anew various points in the manuscript. Various discussions with Michael Musheno, Kathryn Milun and Randel Hanson, colleagues at Arizona State University, caused me to rethink ideas already fixed in place.

My administrative life has been inextricably knotted with my intellectual one, and fabulous staff support both in Justice Studies at Arizona State University and at the University of California Humanities Research Institute has literally made possible the completion of the manuscript. Kay Korman protected my time in very trying circumstances and provided whatever I demanded, and then some. I have been fortunate indeed. Doug Feremenga and Jocelyn Pacleb at the University of California, Irvine responded to every request with grace and care. The Institute's wonderful staff – Susan Feign, Rosemarie

Neumann, Debra Massey Sanchez, Natalie Baquerizo, Anita Jackson, Melly Sutherland, and Brian Rowatt – laughingly kept my administrative life afloat even when the ride threatened to get bumpy.

Those who have worked with Andrew McNeillie and Jayne Fargnoli as editors at Blackwell will know the sort of intellectual support they bring to the relation with their authors. Editors are under enormous pressures in these times not just to sign books but to see them quickly published, to reduce their books to the widest audience they could conjure. Andrew and Jayne work exactly in the opposite direction, knowing that serious books sell. Andrew had the courage to sign the book long before a page of it was written. The book might never have seen its end without his patient support. Brigitte Lee has been the ideal copy-editor, sensitive and suggestive without being intrusive.

My son Gabe insisted on my sustained youthfulness when I might otherwise have fled that state all too fast. I hope some of that sensibility is reflected in these pages.

Above all, the book was composed in and through constant companionship and conversation with Philomena Essed who turned over most every idea, insisted at every turn on conceptual clarity, encouraged lightness where heaviness threatened to take over. Her spirit pervades these pages.

Howard Winant's insightful and wide-ranging book, *The World is a Ghetto: Race and Democracy Since World War II* (Basic Books, 2001), appeared too late for me to incorporate references to it below. Those reading *The World is a Ghetto* alongside *The Racial State* will note the overlap in themes discussed and, more pressingly, some of the key terms employed in our respective analyses: race as constitutive of modernity, the racial world system, colorblindness and racial invisibility, and so on. Indeed, I published an article in 1994 bearing the main title of Winant's book. I do want to emphasize nevertheless that the many divergences between the two texts, both obvious and subtle, are at least as significant as any convergence.

Irvine, California

INTRODUCTION: THE
STATE OF RACE THEORY

Racial theory of late has grown awfully weary. It has come to trade in and on a clichéd vocabulary repeated uncritically in journal articles and books, colloquia and classroom seminars, convention panels and collegial conversations. Those of us engaged in critically theorizing racial concepts and racist expressions, formations, and practices should know we're in trouble when the language of analysis assumed all too reflexively turns up unself-consciously on Ted Koppel's *Nightline* and CNN's *Larry King Live*. Making it so superficially onto the world newscasts is a sign not so much of critical acceptance as the blunting edge of appropriation.

In a sense we've been too successful, impressing our students and storming the barricades with an armory of terms that for the most part barely scratches the surface of analytic rigor and critical depth. As with commercial copy, one's publication can only compete for its fleeting moment of instantaneous fame if it incorporates a catchy concept that promotes purchase of the product. We have entered the world of use value, concepts as commodities discardable just as easily as the empty milk carton, and recycled just as reticently. I have taken of late to warning students in my seminars that they will no longer get away with flippant invocations of "racialization" and "sites of contestation," "interrogation" and "narration."[1] The warning produces stunned silence, as though they have been robbed of the only language they have come to know for addressing racial matters and racist conditions. At the same time, concern with and about the latter has disappeared all too quickly before the drunken diffusion of *racial* categories, new domains in the name of whiteness studies, race traitorhood, identity claims, and the romance with hybridity. These are the very domains of analysis the culturalist turn of the past two

1

decades has seductively prompted, for better *and* worse. Liberalism's dance around race relations at mid-century has given way to the infatuation with racial identities in the dying decades of the millennium. The productive possibilities of that turn seem to have run their course. Time, I suggest, to move on.

To move on not by turning back but to begin to address the lacunae, the noisy and bothersome gaps, around which the culturalist turn detoured all too deftly. That turn, it must be emphasized nevertheless, now allows critical theory to re-turn, to address with fresh eyes two decades of sometimes heady but also often suggestively insightful analysis. One of the most telling evasions in these past two decades of thinking about race has concerned the almost complete theoretical silence concerning the state. Not just the way the state is implicated in reproducing more or less local conditions of racist exclusion, but how the *modern* state has always conceived of itself as racially configured. The modern state, in short, is nothing less than a racial state. It is a state or set of conditions that assumes varied racially conceived character in different sociospecific milieus. So, in one sense, there is no singular totalized phenomenon we can name *the* racial state; more precisely, there are racial states and racist states. Yet it is possible at the same time to insist that there are generalizable conditions in virtue of which the modern state is to be conceived as racial, and as racially exclusionary or racist. It is to these questions that I turn in this book.

The Race from State Theory

The history of the modern state and racial definition, as I have hinted, are intimately related. So it is surprising perhaps that the theoretical literature on state formation is virtually silent about the racial dimensions of the modern state. And the theoretical literature on race and racism, given the culturalist turn of the past two decades, until very recently has largely avoided in any comprehensive fashion the implication of the state in racial formation and racist exclusion.

This is not to say that there haven't been micro-studies focused more empirically on the racial experiences of particular states such as South Africa (Greenberg 1987; Wolpe 1988; Magubane 1990, 1996; Posel 1991); or on state implication in policies regarding race, for

2

instance, in the United States or in Britain or in South Africa (A. Marx 1998); or considerable work on the use of state apparatuses like law to advance racially configured projects (e.g., critical race theory, critical feminist theory, LatCrit theory). In contrast to the strong body of recent feminist theorizing about the state (Ferguson 1984; Pateman 1988; MacKinnon 1989; Brown 1995), those thinking about the state in racial terms have tended to delimit their conceptions to the obvious, extreme, and so seemingly exceptional cases like Nazi Germany or South Africa or the segregationist South in the US (cf. Burleigh and Wippermann 1991; Solomos and Back 1996: 49–52). Eric Voegelin's provocatively prescient intervention, *Race and State*, first published in 1933 and recently released in translation, offers the hints of an analytic vocabulary. Yet he reduces the relational scope between race and the state – between "the race idea," "race theory," and the state – not unsurprisingly, to the case of Nazi Germany and the Third Reich (Voegelin 1933/1997; Voegelin 1933/1998).

There has been little recent theoretical work nevertheless – especially since Stuart Hall's timely intervention in the late 1970s (Hall 1978, 1980) or Arendt's and Cassirer's insightful interventions in the immediate aftermath of World War II (Arendt 1951; Cassirer 1946) – focused explicitly on how the modern state came to be racially conceived, on the historical co-definition of race and the state in their modern manifestations, and on state articulation of racially configured and racist commitments (cf. Joseph and Nugent 1994). It is all the more remarkable then that Stuart Hall, of all analysts, writes a genealogy of the modern state around this time that makes no mention whatsoever of the role of race in its conception or institutional emergence (Hall 1984).

One notable exception to the prevailing oversight may be Omi and Winant's book on racial formation in the United States which includes a chapter explicitly entitled "The Racial State" (Omi and Winant 1986: 70–86, revised in 1995). In light of the wide citation of that book in both its editions it is notable therefore that there is virtually no reference to their chapter on the state.[2] Omi and Winant at least raise the question sociologically and outline a theory regarding the racial forming of states. Their chapter is helpful in posing the problem, in drawing attention to the central implication of the state in racial definition and management, and in *outlining* a theory about how the state assumes racially conceived and racially expressive projects. The structure of their proposed theory nevertheless presumes a conceptual discreteness about the state and race that I am concerned here to challenge.

In *The Racial State* I seek to comprehend the co-articulation of race and the modern state. I argue that race is integral to the emergence, development, and transformations (conceptually, philosophically, materially) of the modern nation-state. Race marks and orders the modern nation-state, and so state projects, more or less from its point of conceptual and institutional emergence. The apparatuses and technologies employed by modern states have served variously to fashion, modify, and reify the terms of racial expression, as well as racist exclusions and subjugation.

Thus racial definition is entwined with modern state elaboration from what Dussel calls the "first modernity" in the orbit of Spanish expansion on. Racial definition of modern states is elaborated with the "voyages of discovery" (the very concept bears racial significance) and the debate in the 1550s between Las Casas and Sepulveda over Indian enslavement, through the second "planetary modernity" (Dussel 1998: 11ff.) from the seventeenth century and Enlightenment debates over the constitutions of colonial and liberal states, "national character" and citizenship criteria, to the post-apartheid moment. It accordingly marks contemporary population shifts via extensive migration, policy debates, and legal decisions revolving around colorblindness, the emergence of "fortress Europe" and the American "prison industrial complex." Indeed, racial configuration fashions the terms of the founding myth, the fabrication of historical memory, necessary (as Charles Tilly insists) to both the discursive production and ideological rationalization of modern state power (Tilly 1994). But it is also the case, especially since the racial project and racist exclusions became obvious in the eighteenth century, that the figure of the racial state – and of particular racist states – was fashioned in part by the resistant response of those it most directly and viscerally affected, namely, the racially characterized, marginalized, exploited, and excluded.

In *Racist Culture* (Goldberg 1993), I argued that starting in the sixteenth century racial thinking and racist articulation became increasingly normalized and naturalized throughout modern European societies and their spheres of influence. Race was rendered integral to the emergence, proliferations, and reproduction of world systems. The increasingly sophisticated elaboration of liberalism from the late

4

seventeenth century played a central role in this process of normal-izing and naturalizing racial dynamics and racist exclusions. As modern-ity's definitive doctrine of self and society, of morality and politics, liberalism has served to make possible discursively, to legitimate ideologically, and to rationalize politico-economically prevailing sets of racially ordered conditions and racist exclusions. Classical liberalism (which includes in its range much of the commitments of contem-porary conservatism in the form of neoliberalism) thus was a key element historically in promoting racial reasoning and its racist implications as central to modernity's common moral, sociopolitical, and jurisprudential sense. And it is not farfetched to suggest that racially conceived compromises regarding racist exclusions – ranging from constitutional endorsements of slavery to formalized segrega-tion, colonial rule and its aftermath, affirmative action, immigration and crime policy – have been instrumental in sustaining a consensual dominance of liberalism in modern state formation over the past century and a half.

I am concerned in this book, relatedly, with the connections between race and homogeneity, the state and racial exclusion, with how they manifest conceptually, theoretically, and materially. I am interested then in mapping the ways in which such racially conceived and configured homogeneity came to be promoted, how racial definition prompted and reinforced such homogeneity, and how the commitment to homogeneity shaped race, as a modern project of state conception and practice. And I will be concerned in turn to exemplify the mani-festations and effects of racial homogeneity and racist exclusions, the reach and range of resistances and state responses to them, as well as their instrumentalities, influences, and implications.

In short, this book is about racial states, as a set of projects and practices, social conditions and institutions, states of being and affairs, rules and principles, statements and imperatives. Inevitably, then, it is about the racist expression of states, state-directed racial exclusions, and so about *racist* states. But it is also about the ways in which particular racist states recently have sought to distribute the means and modes of their expression behind the facade of racial dispersal. Racist states have undertaken to deflect resistance by indirection. Con-temporary states have sought thus to dissipate the normative power of critique in two related ways. On one hand, they have rerouted rightful anger at the homogenizing exclusions of racist states into the

5

circuitous ambiguities and ambivalences of "mere" racially characterized, if not outrightly colorblind, conditions; and on the other
hand, they have pursued superficial appropriation through uncritical
celebration of the multicultural. *The Racial State*, then, is about the
tension between racial conditions and their denial, racist states and
their resistance, and about the ways homogeneity has been taken
axiologically to trump the perceived threat of heterogeneous states of
being.

In general, modern states are intimately involved in the reproduction of national identity, the national population, labor and security
in and through the articulation of race, gender, and class. The view of
the state I am suggesting here, and relatedly of the complex, nuanced,
and subtle entanglement (Tilly 1994) of identity processes, cultural
and commodity flows, and state institutions, apparatuses, and functions, is clearly more complex than dominant critical accounts of the
state. The latter have tended to reduce the state and its apparatuses in
one of two prevailing ways. The state is conceived on one set of views
as a purely autonomous political realm. Here it is taken as analytically
distinguishable from civil society or the public sphere, as well as from
the economic processes of the society. On another set of views, the
state is considered an epiphenomenon, a reflection and so effect of
deeper underlying determinations (like the mode of production, class
relations, or the economy).

Catharine MacKinnon (1989) rightly dismisses this epiphenomenalism of the state and of liberal theory's view that the law is
society's text, its rational mind. The law and the state are not simply
rationalizations of dominant social relations. MacKinnon argues that
this epiphenomenalism hides the state's gendered/sexual definition
from view. But in critiquing these forms of Marxist and liberal
epiphenomenalisms of the state, MacKinnon explicitly reinstates
an epiphenomenalism of her own, by making the state reflective of
– reducible to – sex/gender interests. The state in her view simply
rationalizes male power (MacKinnon 1989: esp. 161). This again views
the state and law as nothing else than instrumental to interests set
elsewhere, a set of institutions and texts whose nature is imposed
upon it from outside itself, from a defining condition external, prior
in ontological logic, to the state. Thus MacKinnon, like almost all
Marxist and liberal theorists, fails really to theorize the nature and
definition of state constitution in itself. She continues to share with

these views the image of the state as an unmarked medium, a set of institutions themselves abstractly neutral, autonomously fashioned, that get taken over, invaded and invested with content or interests by groups vying for and expressing power. Autonomy theory and epiphenomenalism collapse, necessarily seeking each other out. Like others, MacKinnon imputes specificity to a state whose constitution is taken to be autonomously defined only by indirection, only by theorizing what it is the state reflects, what it is supposedly an epiphenomenon of.

State Projects and State Powers

I offer here the outlines of a contrasting working account of the state. I will be concerned in the pages that follow to render this account more complex and nuanced both in its historical emergence and its conceptual expression. The state, as I suggest above, is conceived usually either as instrumental to interests set outside itself (economically, popularly, legally) or as representing its own (inherent) interests as a uniform coherent entity. The line of argument I adopt here suggests by comparison that the state is inherently contradictory and internally fractured, consisting not only of agencies and bureaucracies, legislatures and courts, but also of norms and principles, individuals and institutions. This picture is rendered more complicated by virtue of the fact that it must include also those private or semi-private institutions and social agencies contracted by the state that mediate as they represent and reproduce state commitments or interests.

In short, there is no singular modern state, and no singular racial state. Modern states and racial states are deeply intertwined, the conditions of the latter bound up with possibilities of the former, the histories of the former at once accountable in terms of the projected spatialities and temporalities of the latter. Modern states are racial in their modernity, and modern in their racial quality, their raciality. And in that sense any modern racial state is at once a gendered state, and vice versa, its racial and gendered conditions expressed in and through the terms of each other. The modern state is racially conceived and expressed through its gendered configurations, and it assumes gendered definition and specificity through its racial fashioning.

7

Representatives of the state – state workers and agents – in a loose sense form a class, one itself internally diverse, fractured, its members' interests oftentimes inconsistent, but in modern terms invariably racially patterned. Struggles over state formation and control are shaped in part by the powers and positionings of such a "bureaucratic class," and so too by the racial interests they represent explicitly or implicitly. Sometimes such class members are in contest, often in collusion with other contestants for state power, and occasionally they stand aside, seemingly neutral though more than likely biding their time to determine the victor with whom they will collaborate, serve, or compete.

The modern state obviously occupies (or more temporally cast, has occupied) a more or less discrete space. Only a little less obviously, it fashions differentiated internal spaces, ones conceived deeply in relatedly racial and gendered terms. These differentiated spaces are made possible most clearly through policies and laws (for example, the law of trespass, whether or not racial covenants or redlining are tolerated through mortgage and tax policies, but also through welfare policies). They are a product relatedly of the significance the state licenses to such spaces by way of its policies and stances, its bureaucracies and representatives. These various features of the state, fractured and at odds with each other though they often may be, are held together loosely by a logic of the state at odds with itself (if indeed there is a coherent whole it can be at odds with) (cf. Brown 1995: 166–96). This internal fracturing of the state is a product in part of the tension between the state's instrumentality, its serving interests defined external to itself, and the inherent logic of state formation, bureaucracy, and exercise.

It becomes possible in light of this picture to define the state as a more or less coherent and discrete entity in two related ways: as state *projects* underpinned and rationalized by a self-represented history as state memory; and as state *power(s)*. Indeed, one might render this picture more internally coherent by suggesting that the state's capacity to define and carry out projects as well as its capacity to authorize official narrations of historical memory rests on the state's prior claim to power: the power to define the terms of its representations (obviously including legal terms), and to exercise itself and those over whom authority is claimed in light of those terms.

By the "power theory of the state" I do not mean principally the power *of* the state, as though the state invokes power (which of

course it has). In that interpretation the power is co
from – established or existing independent of – the s.
want to insist that the state acquires its specificity as a state
of being constituted in and through powers (a range of powers) w.
the state at once embodies. Power is to the state and the state to
power as blood is to the human body. (I intend this metaphor fraught
with all the nuances and implications imaginable: the discursive relations
between race and blood, kinship and genealogy, historically conceived
– as in blood lines; the relation of blood and body to dis-ease but also
to life lines; the typing of blood; transfusions and infusions; the ritualized practices around blood; on the other side, the corporeal embodiment of a polity that modern political theory conceived; and so on.)
I am conceiving the state thus as a state of power, a more or less
specific codification and definition of power(s), its (or their) institutional specification. The state thus conceived is a state of power the
existence and elaboration of which is a necessary condition, one might
say, of the possibility of invoking the power(s) of the state.

It is in virtue of this specification, the codification of the state, that
the state acquires its instrumental powers. The state qua state has the
capacity to exclude (to which the law is instrumental), and it has this
capacity to exclude whether within or from the state: what would a
state be that were not so enabled? The state has the power by definition to assert itself or to control those (things) within the state, in
short, the power to exclude from state protection. In these senses, the
modern state has readily lent itself conceptually to, as it has readily
been defined by, racial (and gendered) formation. For central to the
sorts of racial constitution that have centrally defined modernity is
the power to exclude and by extension include in racially ordered
terms, to dominate through the power to categorize differentially and
hierarchically, to set aside by setting apart. And, of course, these are
all processes aided integrally by the capacity – the power – of the law
and policy-making, by bureaucratic apparatuses and governmental
technologies like census categories, by invented histories and traditions, ceremonies and cultural imaginings.

The modern state, it might be said, founds itself not just on exclusions, those absences that render invisible, but on the internalization
of exclusions. Thus inclusions, those privileged by and in the modern
state, assume their privileges in virtue of the exclusions the state at
once renders possible conceptually and technologically. Exclusions

accordingly become internal to the possibility of inclusions, the latter predicated upon the realization of the former. State apparatuses sew the variety of modern social exclusions into the seams of the social fabric, normalizing them through their naturalization. So social exclusions in terms of race (complexly knotted with class and gender, not to wax too mantric about the principal forms of the modern modes) become the mark of social belonging, the measure of standing in the nation-state, the badge of social subjection and citizenship.

This power of delimitation through exclusion, and of empowerment through inclusion, interactively definitive of the modern state and its degree of self-determination, offers the artifice of internal homogeneity to a state's population. Here race and nation are defined in terms of each other in the interests of producing the picture of a coherent populace in the face of potentially divisive heterogeneity. Heterogeneity is definitively placed outside the state, excludable in virtue of being the antithesis of homogeneity, of state belonging. At the same time this localism makes possible in racial terms the pretense of a transnational global community (Balibar 1990). European heritage, as racially defined, becomes the modern passport to global access, commercially and recreationally, residentially and geopolitically. The apparent rootedness of modern colonial settlement, ordered and seemingly structured, gives way to the circuits of late modern flows, disorderly and seemingly anarchic. In either case, I will argue, their possibilities are realizable only in virtue of contrasting configurations of racially conceived states at their "center."

In light of this trajectory of analysis, is there the possibility of a post-racial state, and post-racial theorizing? After racial theory, as after theory generally, there is still always theorizing. Theoretical assumptions are depthless and ceaseless, as integral to the processes of thinking and conceptualizing as the terms and concepts through which thinking itself proceeds. And *going* after racial theory, taking it on as a critical project, is as necessary to resistant struggles against racisms as more recognizable material forms. The one entails the other necessarily. The paradox is that a critical racial theorizing is framed, at the surface of its expressibility, by the possibility of it thinking its object, by the very terms it takes as its critical object. It is this conceptual knot I am concerned in this book to tug – not, hopefully, to tighten the strands of a self-absorbed and delimiting theoretical practice but by stripping away the threads to uncover the deep and changing ways modern lives have been racially shaped and ordered at state behest. The questions posed at the outset are those that will continue to haunt us at the close of the book, their underlying assumptions and implications more clearly comprehended hopefully, their contingent necessity admitted, the necessary contingencies of their material conditions challenged. Whether like Wittgenstein's philosophical questions they evaporate in the wake of the analysis remains to be seen less as a function of the analysis as of the materialization of the conditions to which the analysis can only point. But in the end that perhaps is all analysis alone can hope to achieve.

Outline

In chapter 1 I suggest that the deeply racial character of the modern state from the moment of its emergence is a response to a dilemma that is as much the mark as the product of the modern moment. At precisely the time rapidly emergent and expanding social mobilities produced increasingly heterogeneous societies globally, social order more locally was challenged to maintain homogeneity increasingly and assertively. The racial state, I argue, is key to understanding the "resolution" to this modern dilemma. In a sense, the "motility of race" (Stoler 1997) served as a perfect reflection and mold of dramatic demographic mobility, the former the foil of and for the latter.

The following two chapters unfold how, in accounting for the modern state, prevailing political theory in the European mold is at once racially predicated. I am concerned here with how different assumptions about modern state formation articulate different forms of racial statehood, and how different empirical foci of state theorists prompt differing traditions of racial conception in state theory. In particular, chapter 2 distinguishes between two traditions of theorizing the racial state. One tradition, which I call "naturalist," runs from Hobbes and Pufendorf through Rousseau and Kant to Hegel; the other, a revisionary tradition, runs from Locke to Comte, Marx, and Lord Acton. I call this "historicist" or "evolutionary." Chapter 3 exemplifies the distinction between these traditions in the revealing exchange between Thomas Carlyle and John Stuart Mill on "the Negro problem."

In chapters 4 and 5 I turn to a more direct and sustained theoretical elaboration of concepts and distinctions invoked in the first three chapters. Here I discuss different forms of racial rule, most notably under the colonial condition, distinguishing between governmentalities and subjectivities predicated upon assumptions of inherent superiority and inferiority, on one hand, and claims of historical immaturity and un(der)development, on the other. Chapter 6 examines the centrality of law to the shift from earlier dominance of naturalist forms of racial rule to the later command of historicist forms, and the force of law conceptually and instrumentally in shaping modern racial states generally. In chapter 7, I identify the modern state as one conceived in terms of the crucible of whiteness and its critical resistance. It is here that I enter accordingly into critical reflection on the notion of power that such states embody. Within this context I elaborate a theory of the racial state in terms of its representing racially conceived sets of powers. These four chapters thus examine the various technologies and cultural expressions of racial rule, the key administrative technologies of racial configuration in public policy, most notably those concerned with census taking, affirmative action, immigration, and crime. In chapter 8 I argue that a rhetorics of racelessness increasingly has come to mark the past half-century or more. As a central component of the neoliberal conceptual representation of globalization, racelessness serves to extend the routinization of racial states of being as a sort of civic religion behind the facade of privatized preferences.

The book closes by drawing together the principal themes of the analysis in terms of a critical discussion of race and democracy, and the possibilities for reconsidering racial definition and reconceiving citizenship and social life outside the frame of racist exclusions.

NOTES

1 "Racialization" is now liberally used in formal analysis and informal conversation, usually with no attempt to distinguish between its ambiguous meanings. Thus it might characterize in some contexts simply the attribution of racial meanings or values to social conditions or arrangements, or the distinction between social groups in racial terms. In other contexts it is used to impute exclusionary or derogatory implications to social conditions thus characterized. Almost no one now uses it in the manner first used by Fanon, who contrasted "to racialize" with "to humanize" (Fanon 1968: 86).

2   Etienne Balibar, most notably in his focus on issues of nationalism and nation formation, offers useful distinctions concerning race and the state, but he too provides no sustained analysis of the racial forming of the modern state (Balibar 1991c; Balibar and Wallerstein 1991). There have appeared recently a couple of books on the state, race, and culture (Bennett 1998; Lloyd and Thomas 1998). Helpful on the intersection of these phenomena, it is notable that their focus is culturally fashioned and driven. Thus while they theorize aspects of racially conceived states, they fail to address comprehensive accounts of the founding, framing, and forming of modern state making per se.

1

STATES OF RACIAL DISTINCTION

All the best signs . . . are not so different from all the worst.
                            Richard Ford, *The Sportswriter*, p. 265

The history of the human species, for all intents and purposes, can be told as the histories of human migration. It is the history – really, the histories – of movement and resting, regenerative settlement and renewed mobility. With emerging European exploration and expansion from the late fourteenth century on, it is also the history of miscegenation and cultural mixing, of increasing physical and cultural heterogeneity.

By contrast, the dominant view concerned with periodizing the history of growing demographic and cultural heterogeneity in the western hemisphere and among northern countries has reduced the dramatic nature of this heterogeneity to the second half of the twentieth century. Thus proliferating racial heterogeneity among populations and culturally is considered a function of growing global integration following World War II and its attendant shifts in colonial relations, those "winds of change" that swept not just through Africa but throughout colonized and colonizing worlds. These changes produced massive dislocations, prompted large-scale migrations, opened up borders and boundaries, transnationally and culturally, challenged prevailing hegemonies while simultaneously storming the bastions of haute culture. A compelling picture, perhaps, one obviously resonating with the drama of twentieth-century events, economic, political, cultural, and intellectual.

In good part, two reasons account for the dominance of this picture, related to the ways in which liberalism came to be the dominant social expression of modernity's self-representation. The first is that

14

the self-representation of the West's sense of its political and moral progress was fashioned largely around its increasing openness towards – its "tolerance" (as it has been said) of – *religious* differences. These differences emerged for the most part *internal* to European sensibilities, representing family fights of sorts. In one sense, dramatic expansion of the British empire in the wake of the French Revolution was a self-conscious response to the perceived threat of French expansion, a global response to local threat, if some contemporary commentators had it right (Leckie 1808: 10; Majeed 1992: 7). Tolerance and its limits were fashioned for the most part, then, in respect of recognizable differences between those deemed the same, or more succinctly between those recognized at all. Racially configured others were invisible to the application of tolerance in large part until they insisted upon recognition in no longer deniable ways (Goldberg 2001b). The second reason for the dominance of this picture concerns the condescending consideration of external ethnoracial otherness at once promoting and prompted by the colonial condition. Heterogeneity here is externalized to the colonies, the assumption of homogeneity localized to the individuated European nation-state or to Western Europe more generally. Combined, these reasons entailed that tolerable difference was religious, that European states were in an ethnoracial sense internally homogeneous, that they tended to reproduce an internalized ethnoracial sameness. And ethnoracial heterogeneity identified with colonized societies tended to be externalized, to be distantiated if not denied altogether in thought and practice, at least until undeniable with the dying gasps of the classic colonial order.

This picture delimiting significant diversification to the period of the postcolonial, prevailing as it might be, is nevertheless parochial. It occludes the heterogeneity of past ages, the perhaps slower yet steady intermixing of peoples and interfacing of cultures that migrations in the longer view have always produced. Its framing has hidden from visibility the longstanding differences and distinctions flowing through the hearts of colonizing darkness, those capitals of colonial powers at the very height of their imperial spread. And so too it has made less than visible the significance of the notion of "hybridity" at different historical moments. In fact, it clouds over the reasons a notion of "hybridity" has been suffered as a challenge to the presumption of homogeneity, a point I elaborate below.

15

The restriction in the recognizability of heterogeneity, political and theoretical, is tied up with deep-seated presumptions about the modern state. The mis-recognition here is deeply related to the thick ways in which modern state formation has been racially fashioned, with the ways in which modern states have predicated themselves on racial differentiation, and on state-promoted and prompted racist exclusion and exploitation. Developments in theorizing the modern terms and principles of social relation and order, accordingly, are to be understood at basis only against the background history of demographic movements and the challenges they have posed. The emergence and roles of racial states by the same taken cannot be properly comprehended without conceiving them in terms of these movements and the newly emergent social conditions to which they are related.

Thus modern states, especially in their national articulation, ordered themselves not as heterogeneous spaces but in particular as racially and culturally homogeneous ones. G. F. Leckie was explicitly concerned in 1808 about the lack of a "uniform spirit that pervades our [British] provinces, and stamps them as much as circumstances will permit with an *homogenous* character" (Leckie 1808: 16, my emphasis). They have assumed themselves, falsely as a matter of fact, to be constituted upon the presumption, the insistence, of homogeneous group identity, repressively embodying sameness as a value. And so they have acted variously to guarantee, to (rein)force, materially what they have claimed (to be committed to) conceptually and axiologically. In this sense, homogeneity is to be viewed as heterogeneity in denial, or more deeply yet as the recognition of heterogeneity at once repressed. In order to see the implications of this for racial arrangements it will help to rehearse briefly the histories of emergence of modern state formation.

Cities and States

The transformation of medieval city-states into modern states brought increasing urban heterogeneity, even in racial terms. Taking root in the seventeenth century, there was a sharp shift in the conception of the state in political theory, employing new metaphors of space and time. The premodern, late medieval conception of the state, as represented by Machiavelli's *Prince*, articulated an understanding of the state as inward looking, enclosed, self-contained, delimited and limiting, restrictive, and ruled over ultimately by a single authority. Authored in the name of the Prince, the law was authorized by virtue of the authority vested in and assumed by the sovereign ruler, promoted and rationalized by a discourse of Divine Right. The Prince ruled over a localized and delimited domain, for the most part the walled space of a city-state.[1]

The modern conception of the state, by contrast, has been promoted as open and expansive with "naturalized" but permeable borders figured as much in conceptual as in material terms. Modern state boundaries were established as the shifting objects of cartographical mapping rather than physically fixed in place. As such, they necessitated greater centralized modes of administration and ordering. And increasingly they necessitated (self-) surveillance, or at least its suggestion. That the marks of state limits have to be established as much symbolically as physically (by barbed wire and border posts) or legally reinforces the point of permeability, of expansion and contraction, and so also of self-surveillance.[2]

The permeability of modern states is represented straightforwardly in the fact that colonizing capitals like Amsterdam and London began to see significant diversity in their populations as early as the seventeenth century. This visible and increasingly dramatic heterogeneity has been virtually ignored in mainstream historical studies. Well-regarded histories of these cities likewise tend to presume that their significant racial diversity only arrives with global integration following World War II (e.g., Kershen 1997). There is no doubt that these trends accelerated dramatically from the mid-twentieth century on, but to cast it thus is already to acknowledge that there were trends, relatively longstanding trends, already at play, however underplayed by comparison. Notions of hybridity, of physical and cultural mixing, took hold conceptually, in part, in relation to responses to the nineteenth-century tensions such heterogeneity supposedly effected, played out intellectually (in science, philosophy, anthropology) and politically (in law and policy). But of course there has been a relatively long history of European concerns about strangers and strangeness, expressed racially – which is also to say ambivalently and ambiguously – as modern slavery was initiated by the Portuguese and Spanish as early as the fifteenth century (cf. Bauman 1997; Bennett 1998). Racial mixing and hybridity accordingly constituted then, as it continues

17

to constitute in certain circles now, an object of fear and celebration, paranoia and persistence, repression and resistance, a point to which I will return later.

With the onset of modernity, the advent of vigorous transnational commerce, and the rising dominance of Dutch among European imperial and colonial powers, class structure in the Netherlands, and in Amsterdam particularly, assumed plurality and fluidity. This fluidity became especially manifest with the Netherlands consolidating as a nation in the seventeenth and eighteenth centuries. The Dutch were "a people," if it makes sense to refer in the singular to the people of any nation-state in modernity, whose very constitution was a product of immigration, not least within Europe: Flemish and Huguenots fleeing religious intolerance, Sephardic Jews chased out by Catholic terror in Spain and Portugal, Ashkenazi Jews escaping from East European intolerance. Thus two-thirds of Amsterdam's 7,500 Jews at the close of the seventeenth century were Ashkenazi, and German domestic workers arrived in droves in the nineteenth century, many staying to marry Dutch men.

Starting in 1610, the Dutch acquired colonies throughout the seventeenth century. Yet the first inkling of the racially characterized diversification that would challenge the sense of singularity in Dutch society, as elsewhere, in the aftermath of classical colonialism centuries later threatened local tranquility in Zeeland in 1596. A Dutch privateer that had captured 130 slaves off a Portuguese slave ship delivered its hopeless African bounty to port. To their credit the Dutch at the time outlawed slavery (overturned less than a decade later once the profits and "benefits" of slave trading became evident), and the slaves were freed. Within a century the Dutch had become major players in the slave trade, shipping their "wares" from the West coast of Africa to the Caribbean and Brazil.

As the mark of revolutionary transformation began to sweep across Europe late in the eighteenth century, Amsterdam exhibited a sort of local heterogeneity, in classical terms more ethnic than racial in its constitution. By the eighteenth century fully 20 percent of those arrested in Amsterdam were of German background, though there was no indication that they were criminologically discriminated against (Schama 1997: 582). Amsterdam after all considered itself the model of political and cultural tolerance as much as it established itself as the initial center of "planetary modernity" (Dussel 1998).[3] Where there were slaves they would have been house slaves, the occasional symbols of status and curiosity, a souvenir of sorts collected on long travels which might be shown off to family and friends and to impress business colleagues. I think here of Rembrandt's haunting painting of "Two Negroes" (1661), Rubens's four drawings of a "Negro figure," or Van Dyck's early seventeenth-century inclusion of a black woman servant ("The Discovery of Moses") or of a satyr ("Bacchanalia"). Some slaves there were locally, though most got shipped on, and too few people who could be said to be non-white or non-European to be more than objects of curious (in)difference and sometime derision.

It is remarkable thus that Simon Schama could write his masterful history of Dutch culture in "the golden age" without mentioning slavery or blacks. Indeed, Schama excludes any extended discussion of the importance of colonies to or influence of colonial culture on Dutch wealth, forms of desire, and the creation of a "bourgeois aristocracy," points made impressively by Ann Stoler (Stoler 1997).

If racial heterogeneity came slow to Dutch modernity, it touched London life early on. This is more remarkable in light of the fact that it has been downplayed or largely absent from the prevailing histories of that city. The earliest black people were thought to appear in "modern" London (at least on one account) in 1555 (Gerzina 1995), when five West Africans arrived to acquire the English language as a way to promote commerce – slave commerce, it seems. There is evidence though of the employment of black musicians in the English and Scottish courts nearly a century earlier, the appearance of North African pirates as far north as Scotland by the end of the fifteenth century, and two African friars in Edinburgh early in the sixteenth (Gundara and Duffield 1992: 15–18; Fryer 1984: 2).[4] The dramatic modern shift in disposition towards black people is signaled by the fact that at the close of that century Queen Elizabeth had passed an edict requiring all black people to leave England (Gerzina 1995: 3).

The population of greater London, totaling just 200,000 in 1600, doubled in half a century, and spiraled to 575,000 by century's end. A century later yet the metropolis was just short of 1 million (900,000 by the census of 1801), bolstered by the flow predominantly from country to town, and later by Irish migration and Ashkenazi Jews "going and resting" (Josipovici 1993). The latter concentrated themselves in the East End upon fleeing persecution in Eastern and Central Europe. To a lesser degree there were flows also of Germans,

Dutch, and Portuguese. Census counts topped 4.5 million in 1881 and had risen staggeringly to 7 million just thirty years later (Porter 1995: 205). By the latter part of the eighteenth century, the number of black people in London – largely from the West Indies and Indian seamen working for the English East Indies Company – counted at least as much as 10,000 and quite possibly half more than that, a little over 1 percent of the population (Rude 1971: 6–8). Revealingly, as early as April 1721 one London daily was warning that "there is a great number of Blacks come daily into this city, so that 'tis thought in a short time, if they be not suppressed, the city will swarm with them" (quoted in Dabydeen 1992: 31).

Slaves were not uncommon in London also, largely brought back from the West Indies by British planters and mixing with black sailors, students, and musicians. As early as 1696 there appeared heartbreakingly cruel advertisements in the local press for the return of runaway slaves or the sale of black boys as young as eleven or twelve (Gerzina 1995: 5–8). By the end of the eighteenth century, as the abolitionist movement gained ground, these advertisements for the sale of slaves had largely disappeared, the emergent English culture of civility ordering commercial sensibilities regarding blacks (Lorimer 1992: 70). And by the mid- to later Enlightenment there was evidence also of wealthy black men parading undisturbed with white women on Oxford Street, accompanied nevertheless by bemoaning observations of mixed-race progeny, the first inklings possibly of more vociferous concerns to emerge regarding hybridity in the nineteenth century. Thus Philip Thicknesse writing in 1778 complained that "in every town, nay in almost every village, are to be seen a little race of mulattoes, mischievous as monkeys, and infinitely more dangerous" (quoted in Gerzina 1995: 22). Black women were much scarcer, usually brought to London by West Indian slavers bearing in tow their concubines veiled as servants. In larger measure though, David Dabydeen points out in *Hogarth's Blacks* that even more than the demographic presence of black people, London was "visually black." Signboards and business cards imprinted the emblem of a black man as the mark of commerce, the icon of blackness curiously serving as a measure of commercial success (Dabydeen 1987: 18). The growing appeal of this expanding racial exoticism is evidenced by the fact that by the middle of the nineteenth century Topsy wallpaper and dolls were the rage throughout fashionable London (Gerzina 1995: 25).

20

It is telling, then, that both Gareth Steadman Jones (1971) and Roy Porter (1995) can write justly influential histories of London – of Victorian class relations in the former case, a more broadly social history in the latter – without so much as a single mention of blacks or of the influence of colonial commerce and administration of the slave trade upon the life of that capital of finance. Similarly, Steadman Jones's co-edited book with David Feldman (Feldman and Steadman Jones 1989) on the history of metropolitan London is concerned with a wide range of London's demographic and cultural diversity, detailing the importance to London life and "identities" (the title of a section in the book) of Irish and Jews, women and the working classes. Yet perhaps most impressively it has no expressed word whatsoever about black people either narrowly construed as people of African descent or more broadly including Asians. Telling all the more because in a sense the writing of class in nineteenth-century London was at once the writing of race: working-class formation, gender, and blackness were deeply articulated with each other in conceptual and material terms and expression (Gilman 1990).

This exclusionary silence and invisibility are more remarkable in light of the fact not only that by the 1770s London-owned slave ships were transporting close to 10,000 slaves a year in the triangular trade, not nearly as large as Liverpool or Bristol admittedly, but significant nonetheless (Fryer 1984: 36). The silence is more deeply troubling, the influence of Africans on London public performance and musical culture notwithstanding, given the centrality of London in financing the slave trade (by mid-eighteenth century London was handling three-quarters of all sugar imported into Britain). The slave trade was crucial not only to London's economy but to its political life. Many influential politicians were caught up in one way or another in the benefits of slave trading, and West Indian absentee plantation proprietors were able quite easily to buy seats in the House of Commons, a practice that became, well, common. So strong, highly organized, and well-heeled was the West Indies lobby that the abolitionist movement found itself facing significant resistance at the end of the "enlightened century" (Fryer 1984: 44–50).

Arguably, the emergence of a "bourgeois aristocracy" and the liberalism on which it predicated itself and which it served to solidify structured the fabric of British society in the first part of the nineteenth century. By contrast, these forces consolidated in the Netherlands

21

only towards the end of that century. This is reflected most clearly in the temporal gap between the two regarding their respective abolitionist movements and moments. In turn, bourgeois civility came to be fashioned in each society through the dual movement of importing and alienating racially fashioned sensibilities in and from their respective colonies. Victorian bourgeois liberalism, curtaining off its viciousness behind the veneer of mannered polite racism, could be sewn into the fabric of British society only in virtue of a repressively policed restriction on mixed sexuality and progeny abroad. This is not to deny their existence in British colonial conditions, only to emphasize the repressed and repressive conditions of Victorian racial desire. Here the vocal concerns with pollution, hybridity, and degeneration were complemented by fears of moral fall thought to follow from the licentiousness of cross-racial desire. Dutch resolve concerning such questions seemed significantly more ambiguous and ambivalent, relative colonial license underpinning comparative metropolitan closure. Tied to different dominant religious traditions, consequently bourgeois liberalism took hold in metropolitan Holland later and somewhat more tenuously than it did in Britain (Stoler 1995: esp. 125–36).

Two points are worth emphasizing here. First, the obvious lesson of this tale of two cities is that the heterogeneous mix of populations making up the capitals of colonial empires has largely been downplayed, and indeed until quite recently all but ignored. Second, relatedly but more deeply, the occlusion of blacks from the representational historical record of this urban diversity indicates by extension that blacks for the most part were rendered invisible in the daily political life of those cities. This can be seen in sharp contrast to the persistent, one might say insistent, concern with colonized black people deemed administratively problematic by the colonizers.

It is significant then, both as a mark of urban life and of historical scholarship, that accounts of blacks in Britain and the Netherlands (Scobie 1972; Fryer 1984, 1988; Gundara and Duffield 1992; Blakely 1993; Gerzina 1995; West 1996; and Arthur Japin's historical novel, Japin 1997) are exceptional. They are (regarded as) outside of – not properly belonging to – standard historical accounts of those societies, and take this exclusion as their almost exclusive motivating or inspirational focus. Nor is this an excising from the historical record of the traces only of a black Atlantic and its effects, for one finds the silences concerning a "black Mediterranean" equally if not more resounding.

Southern Europe is cut off from African "contamination" both by the Mediterranean, a sea almost never thought of as having an African coastline, and relatedly by the vast white sands of the Saharan desert. The North African coast accordingly is taken more readily "to belong" to the Middle East than it is referenced as a "supra-Saharan Africa." Thus, the historical exceptionalism at work here, it should be clear, is not a product principally of self-determining "minority" separation, an infantilizing celebration of ethnic self-identification. Rather, it is a product primarily of that initial ignoring, the rendering invisible, of peoples designated black so that representational exceptionalism, an emphatic foregrounding focus, becomes the only possibility for writing strangers and outsiders, black people in particular, back into the historical record.

A prevailing problematic of modernity, representative at least in that strand of modernism elaborated through the nineteenth-century positivity of science, has concerned control of both natural and social conditions. But beneath this, perhaps as a Hobbesian-like motivation, lay anxiety – about the unknown, about that which could not be controlled, concerning natural forces beyond control. Heterogeneity may be read as challenge or threat, opportunity or potential problem. For modernity generally, and in the nineteenth century in particular, heterogeneity was interpreted very much in the latter vein, taken to inject into the safety and stability of the known, predictable, and controllable worlds elements of the unknown, the unpredictable, the uncontrollable. For heterogeneity introduces the threat and unmanageability of the unknown, of the diverse, and the uncontainability of that unknown.[5]

Race is imposed upon otherness, the attempt to account for it, to know it, to control it. So to begin with in modernity what is invested with racial meaning, what becomes increasingly racially conceived, is the threat, the external, the unknown, the outside. It is only through the racial configuration of the external, of the other, by implication, that the internal – the self – becomes (and at first by implication, silently) racially defined also. But paradoxically, once racially configured with modernity that threat becomes magnified, especially fraught, because in being named racially in a sense it is named *as* threat. In being so named the threat is reified, rendered real, realized. Race, especially as scientifically understood, appears then to inject control (or at least to claim it), to furnish comprehension (and perhaps

23

comprehensibility) where it otherwise is clearly absent, or to reestablish determination in the face of threatened indeterminacy. The racial conception of the state becomes the racial definition of the apparatus, the projects, the institutions for managing this threat, for keeping it out or ultimately containing it – but also (and again paradoxically) for keeping it *going*.

In the wake of abolition of slave trading throughout the British empire in 1807, and of slavery altogether in 1834, black people seemed freer to come and go from Britain than they had been, although their movement was not always unrestricted. This trend was more obvious in Britain than in Holland owing to the greater global spread of Britain's empire in the nineteenth century, its heavier engagement in the slave trade, the public prominence of the abolitionist movement in comparison to conditions in the Netherlands, as well as to the fact that colonial slavery continued under the Dutch until the middle of 1863. It is in light of this expedited movement that black presence in Britain especially became more obvious, that mixed-race populations began to become more apparent (as they did too in wake of the Civil War in the United States), and to be focused upon more readily as anomalous. The remarkable increase in flows – of populations to and from colonies, of commodities and raw materials, indeed of miscegenation and its offspring – prompted heightened population heterogeneity and cultural bricolage. Coupled with fears and anxieties, challenges to established orders, and manifest changes in prevailing socioscientific interpretation of human differentiation, there emerged concerns, theoretical and political, articulated in terms of the concept of "hybridity."

Hybridity and Homogeneity

Theoretically, the concern with "hybridism" – the static substantivizing of the term indicative of the worry – was a product of the nineteenth-century theoretical shift from mono- to polygenism. If races are separate species, as polygenists claimed definitionally, mating of their members should not produce offspring at all (Nott 1843). "Mixed-race" or "hybrid" offspring were the product of miscegenation, a product significant only on presumption of more or less fixed racial categories. Nominated "mulatto" or "mestizo" variously in the eighteenth and

24

nineteenth centuries, "mixed-race people" increased as a result of greater cross-racial contact, not least following abolition of slavery, migrations in the wake of colonial commerce, and the promise of reconstructed societies. These trends were widespread, in a sense global, given the scope of the colonial mode of production. They marked Britain and the Continent marginally, but the United States, the Afro-Caribbean, and Latin America significantly enough to warrant specific census categories, as well as Southern Africa and the East Indies.

Mixed-race presence offered an obvious challenge to polygenic presumption. If, as polygenesis presumed, races are species, and species are defined by capacity to reproduce only among species members, the existence of mixed-race (or cross-species) offspring suggests failure to meet a crucial condition of the theory. Nevertheless, existence of hybrid offspring prompted revisions in polygenic theory rather than its initial abandonment. The first revision was to insist that hybrids themselves would be infertile; later that more "distant" groups are much more likely to be infertile than more "proximate" ones (Broca 1860/1950; cf. Young 1995: 18). When counter-evidence quickly emerged, predictions were revised to the longer-term view that hybrid offspring eventually – over a number of (unspecified) generations – would degenerate and ultimately die out (Knox 1862; cf. Broca 1860/1950). The failure of this prediction to materialize coincided more or less with the demise of polygenic theory in the face of Darwinian evolution, on one hand, and Darwinist-prompted eugenics, on the other.

Scientific hybridity thus failed theoretically (that is, on scientific criteria). In the wake of Darwin there began a shift – long, slow, and incomplete – away from strictly scientific technologies of race and racism towards more culturalist articulations. Where science continued to contribute to racial thinking it was now less direct, less focused straightforwardly on advancing racial science for its own sake. From the close of the nineteenth century scientific thinking about race became more applied, and curiously more intricately tied up with state technologies of governance. The invocation of scientific technologies developed with a more general purpose in mind – for their own sake or with other object(ive)s at issue – and were adopted or adapted to address questions of race, as in the application of IQ testing. The prevalence of eugenics in the first few decades of the twentieth century may be considered accordingly the tail end of "pure"

25

racial science, scientific racism's more or less last spree. It should be emphasized nevertheless that it was an extension granted new life by the assumption of eugenics in state policy initiatives regarding intelligence testing, immigration restrictions, and in the final analysis genocide. The techniques available from applied racial science, or more precisely from applied science to racial application, suited insidious state missions, mandates, and manipulations all too well.

Those who considered the nineteenth century, and scientific racism in particular, the apex of racist expression have thought the applied turn a shift away also from racist expression as such, a revealing of racism's intellectual vacuity, its essential irrationality, in the wake of racism's failure to exhibit scientific legitimacy. But such an interpretation is misleading. For as the longer-term legacy of Darwin may have signaled a shift from the viability of a scientifically sustained sense of race and racist expression, culturalist and class-centered expressions of racist exclusion began to dominate. The dire political implications that came to be associated with biologically driven racism in the hands of state apparatuses prompted a shift to more palatable popular forms of racial expression. Along with this shift away from physicalist-based notions, the concept of hybridity began in turn increasingly to assume reified culturalist expression (cf. Young 1995: 6). Thus at century's turn Kipling ironically has a Russian speaking in French to a Frenchman refer to "the monstrous hybridism of East and West" in characterizing the effects of British imperialism upon India. Here Kipling reflects the popularly paranoid concern over the degenerating pollution of cultural mixing, as earlier sexual mixing had been considered to result in physical degeneracy (Kipling 1901/1913: 382).

So, in the nineteenth century the concept of hybridity came to represent dominant concerns that white or European-based purity, power, and privilege would be polluted, and in being polluted diluted. If whites were supposedly superior intellectually and culturally to those not white, then on amalgamationist assumptions the mixing of those non-white with white generative capacity ex hypothesi would imperil the power of the latter, would result in their degeneration. Hybridity thus assumed the conceptual expression of anxiety, of white people's paranoia, signaling the ultimate powerlessness of the powerful. Powerlessness precisely in that hybridity poses a challenge to the guardians of purity, power, and privilege, a challenge channeled through desire: the libidinal pull of sexual desire, the lure of forbidden fruit, in the one instance; the exciting, energizing magnet of cultural renewal, and so an implicit judgment concerning the static predisposition of "the pure," in the other. In the faultlines and cracks in power those conceived as racially powerless come to assume a power they are denied by definition.

Nowhere is this more evident than in the case of South Africa in the first half of the twentieth century, that colonially produced hybrid of Africa (a mix of at least ten broad ethnocultural groups), Asia (Indians, Malaysians, Chinese), and Europe (British and Dutch principally, but East European Jews, Italians, Greeks, and Portuguese also, all woven not quite indistinguishably into the invention of whiteness). Thus Afrikaner politicians readily invoked eugenics-inflected phrases concerning "virile" and "vigorous" blacks "flooding" city space, "swamping" whites who were in the minority, and threatening the safety of supposedly vulnerable white women. More than one election was won on the tailcoats of such rhetoric. In 1927 the Immorality Act (sic) was passed prohibiting miscegenation between whites and Africans. Attempts were later made to extend the legislation to prohibit all interracial sexual intercourse, including government commissions of inquiry regarding such legislation in the late 1930s. Yet the fuller restriction manifested only eventually in 1949 with the passing of the Mixed Marriages Act as a cornerstone in the systematic institutionalization of the apartheid state.

Similarly, the South African state revealed itself as the state of exclusively white making – a state of, for, and made (so it would claim) only by whites. It began moving in the mid-1950s against the perceived threat of cultural pollution, stamping out hip hybrid urban neighborhoods in Johannesburg, Durban, and Cape Town that just might prove enticing to white youth (cf. Dubow 1995: 180ff.). White urban youth growing up closely engaged with such neighborhoods, as I did, could be said to be their beneficiaries, the products in part of their cultural contribution (to music, cuisine, a dialect as much as a dialectic of resistance, a medium of political consciousness). The inhabitants contributed to the rich mix of South African culture in incalculable ways, and were direct victims of the state's destructive mission, bearing the terrible brunt of the bulldozing mentality that left scars wide and deep across the landscape, cultural as much as geographical, psychological as much as demographic. One might say that all South Africans, like it or not, were dramatically diminished by these segregationist machinations,

27

black people of course bearing the burdens more directly, materially, and heavily than whites. At the same time, the reproduction of cemented state-regulated consent could never be complete, for its terms were always challenged in the examples of cultures, ways of life, expressions and representations more dynamic, exciting, and appealing than the state would admit, tolerate, or allow.

As negative critique, then, the concept of hybridity becomes an outward expression of the repressed, and in such expression assumes the power of the repressive itself. As the product of two differentiated elements, the hybrid is supposed to fuse them together, assuming features of each into a transformed "third" element. Historically, such elements have stood to each other in hierarchical relations of power, often underpinned if not produced or promoted by state power. As a critical concept, the hybrid thus is supposed to blunt power's point, to shift power's oppressive expression. It does so, however, only by assuming some of the hierarchical aspects of power. As some have pointed out, Homi Bhabha's "hybrid third space" in this respect is tinged with romanticism (see some of the contributions to Werbner and Modood 1997).

On the other side, the denial of hybridity, physiologically or culturally conceived, accordingly becomes the refusal of possibility to the mixed, the repression of heterogeneity, of conditions of possibility for hybridity to materialize. Consider, for instance, the "assault" on European languages maintained to manifest in creolization, and the authoritarian restriction of their use by colonial (and postcolonial) administrations (cf. Stoler 1995: 43). One sees here the threads of a threat hybridity represents to prevailing power, the threat of losing control faced by the colonizers in failing to understand a hybrid language in terms of which critical and resistant formulations might be fashioned, in a sense to their face. Insult added to injury. Hence the multitude of laws against racially defined immigration, miscegenation, cross-racial intercourse (sexual or cultural), racially conceived cultural expressions and practices identified with otherness (like Ebonics as a teaching medium).

There lies barely hidden here an apparent paradox: Precisely at the moment we find greater likelihood of de facto heterogeneity among and between population groups, however conceived or defined, the greater the denial through racial fixity and reification. Where a degree of racial homogeneity could be more or less safely assumed, at least

28

relatively speaking, as in early modern Britain and Holland, the less race seemed necessary as an explicit self-reference. Here race referred to the outside, the strange and exotic at a distance. The more heterogeneous such societies grew, the more racial definition came to mark their self-characterization.

In the face and wake of the colonial condition which helped to produce demographic heterogeneity, the question then becomes why race is invoked in a variety of denials to face off such heterogeneity. The genealogy of hybridity I have offered suggests something of a response, if not to resolving the paradox, then to why it should arise. On one hand, hybridity has been invoked to rationalize (away) and legitimate fears and anxieties that mobilized one side of the paradoxical equation: not least those concerning "species corruption" (White 1972: 14–15) and the associated threats of cultural and sexual miscegenation. On the other hand, hybridity has been pushed more recently as a celebration of the possibilities to which heterogeneity gives rise. Here, however, hybridity serves at once to exacerbate again the very fears, now in culturalist terms and precisely in those (formerly) colonizing societies once considering themselves more or less homogeneous, that the concept and the conditions it references were initially invoked to quell.

We may see this played out in racially marked states like the United States and Britain, the Netherlands and France, Canada and South Africa concerning language and dress, census categories and mixed-race recognition, and perhaps most extremely in immigration policy and opportunity. But one can find versions of this in the academy also, expressed in terms of disciplinarity and indeed epistemologically. I have suggested elsewhere that disciplines are to the academy, to intellectual pursuit, as borders are more broadly to nation-states (Goldberg 1994). The transgressive threats possible in multi- and trans-disciplinarity seem as unsettling to some locally as migration and trans-nationalism seem to the relatively privileged more globally, and for related sorts of reasons. Settled ideas, practices, and institutions are challenged as a result, sometimes at considerable existential cost. The threat is not just that some or other discipline might transform, but that it might turn out to be redundant and disappear completely, that the power and privilege it has secured may be lost. Hence the investment in a conserving resistance. Relatedly, epistemological hybridity suggests new forms of thinking, new categories of knowing

rather than resting (in)secure in settled ways of seeing and comprehending the world. As Bakhtin (1981: 344) suggests, authoritarian
language – epistemologically, disciplinarily, politically – is necessarily
anti-hybrid as it depends upon the singularity and static fixity of
meaning, the insistence of the given and ordered, the silencing of
voice(s) at odds with the authorial power, not least manifested in and
by state institutions.

It bears pointing out here the inherently homogenizing logic of
institutions. In their dominant logical form, institutions are predicated
principally on instituting, operating, and (re)producing homogeneity.
If the state minimally is a collection of institutions, manifesting and
(re-)ordering itself necessarily in and through the logic of such institutional arrangement (I will be concerned later to thicken this picture
dramatically), then one could say that the state inherently is the
institutionalization of homogeneity. Liberal states like Britain, the
Netherlands, Canada, and the US that claim to furnish the structures
for heterogeneity to flourish in this sense actually promote contradictory aims, purposes that pull in competing directions. Hence the
anachronistic language one hears of "managing diversity," of "ordering
difference," of "unifying in difference." The homogenizing imperative
is revealed on both sides of these "hybrid" nomenclatures, for curiously
the active expression is born in the restricting pursuit (managing,
ordering, unifying), the passive in the reified substantivization – the
rendering passive – of what one would have thought to be creative
and energizing (diversity, difference). This homogenizing logic is
internal to administration and governmentality. To run counter to it,
even in an administrative capacity, is to run counter to administrative
or govern-mental logic. The state – and nation-state especially, where
nation here becomes the cultural reproduction of hegemonic con-
sensus to state administrative mandates – is all about institutionally
reproductive homogenization.[6]

On the other side, though, hybridity is conceived as about Becoming, about transformation and so the reiterative undoing of form ("the
permanent revolution of forms," as Young characterizes Homi Bhabha's
view), about flow and flux, a term that apparently "captures" the
logic of history itself (cf. Young 1995: 25). As such, the substantivization of hybridity in the form of reifying resistance – in a movement,
as a (more or less) self-consciously cohering intervention – at once
homogenizes the heterogeneous, fixes the flux and flow, orders the

dis-orderly, renders more or less safe by "capturing" the transgressive expression of the hybrid. Here, at best, the critical conception of hybridity is reduced to the fusional or amalgamational; at worst, any possibility of hybridity is obliterated altogether.

So, like race, indeed, as a sometime proxy for it, hybridity in its ethnoracial connotation assumes a variety of forms. Initially biological in relation to demography, it may connote aesthetically, morally, obviously always politically in any of these senses, as well as in the less obvious epistemological one. Bakhtin reveals, in Young's helpful terms, the "hybridity of hybridity" itself. As I hint at in the preceding paragraph, there are at least two ways in which hybridity may manifest: It may combine otherwise clashing categories, fusing their antithetical senses into new expression and form, the new here possibly assuming renewed homogeneity. Or it may express itself as self-consciously critical, as social unmasking, a studied commitment to undoing the necessary singularity of the authoritative voice, wherever and when-ever expressed (a point turned to some effect by Bhabha in his critique of colonial power, though in romancing the resistive he overlooks the conservationist element inherent equally in any conception of the hybrid and the resistant) (Bakhtin 1981: 344ff.; Bhabha 1994; Young 1995: 20–8).

Colonialism, John Comaroff has made abundantly clear in a scintil-lating rethinking of the colonial state (Comaroff 1998), was about managing heterogeneity, dealing with difference through imposition and restriction, regulation and repression. Seemingly by contrast but in fact relatedly, colonizing states like Britain and the Netherlands proceeded on an assumption of internalized population homogeneity, of ethnoracial sameness and of externalizing difference. They were able to sustain at least a semblance of the charade by purporting nominally to keep the different out and at bay lest they undo by infecting the rationality of brotherhood, thus toppling reason's rule. The creation and promotion of difference is the necessary condition of reproducing homogenized sameness; and (re-)producing homogen-eity necessarily promotes the externalization of difference to produce its effect.

Implicit here is a distinction between two forms of regulation and imposition, the restrictive or exclusionary disciplining of difference and (one might say in the name of) the rule of sameness. The com-bining of racial hybridism with colonialism in the nineteenth century was a "social-scientific" way of managing these related concerns: keeping the Other from polluting and diluting the Same by maintaining the former at arm's length; but at once benefiting from the material and libidinal pleasures exploitation of colonized others made possible. Under the aegis of restricting hybridity physiologically and culturally, otherness, difference, and heterogeneity were reduced to racial management. In the early twenty-first century, by contrast, the regulative force of colonialism has broken down and the unsettling capacity of hybridity can no longer be kept (colonially) marginal by modern modes of control. Indeed, the heterogeneous and hybrid have come to occupy and challenge modernity's centers. Under these altered conditions, hybridity's unsettling capacity has been celebrated and embraced, but also fiercely resisted. Indeed, it has become a contested domain – epistemologically, disciplinarily, aesthetically, culturally, politically.

What I have been suggesting, nevertheless, is that in *both* expressions of racially imposed and racially self-conceived hybridity – the repressive and the resistive – there are always at least delimiting hints of the other. Thus it is not just that heterogeneity is or has been a challenge *or* threat, opportunity *or* potential problem. In the context of racial history, the history of racial theorizing, and the intimate co-definition of race with modern state definition and expression, it has always been both. And necessarily so. Perhaps a concept at once neutering and neutralizing the sexually provocative conditions that are a necessary underpinning of hybridity's very conception cannot help but suffer the anxiety of its ambiguity in this way. It is the value invested in the concept in relation to the material historical contexts in which it is embedded accordingly that will determine hybridity's critical capacity in specific space–time conditions: whether to be shunned or embraced, critically discarded or exploited. In either case, indeed in both given the dialectic at work, state management of racial conditions is crucial, either as medium of homogeneous promotion or the object of resistance.

Thus Anne McClintock's general warning regarding historical agency and colonialism, in quiet criticism of Homi Bhabha, might serve also to warn against uncritical invocations of hybridity. Indeed, it serves as general warning to critical racial studies, most emphatically once race is understood in its various *states* of articulation. "Taking the question of historical agency seriously ('How . . . is authority displaced?')," she writes, entails interrogating more than the ambivalences of form; it also entails interrogating the messy imprecisions of history, the embattled negotiations and strategies of the disempowered, the militarization of masculinity, the elision of women from political and economic power, the decisive foreclosures of ethnic violence and so on. Ambivalence may well be a critical aspect of subversion, but it is not a sufficient agent of colonial failure. (McClintock 1995: 66–7)

So though hybridity continues to be "scandalous,"[7] it is perhaps equally outrageous for an anti-essentialist intellectual politics that it has failed to take seriously the doubleness of hybrid consciousness: not just its in-betweenness but its "caught-betweenness," and accordingly not just the ambivalence it produces but its almost inevitable duplicity. Thus it is never just its transgression that marks racially imposed and racially conceived hybridity as attractive but the type of scandal it stands for, time and place specifically, not least in the context of the history of racially thick and racially reproductive state projects. And this context specificity, as McClintock rightfully insists, is tied up with the specificities of material exclusions, repressions, and subjugations. In short, with the micro-details of racial power and privilege and their articulation with other forms through which the *state* of racial domination is worked.

Ethnoracial, cultural, and national homogeneity is sustained throughout modernity accordingly not because it is the "natural condition," the very assumption of singularity ("it") rhetorically advocating as presumption what it requires repressive acts of material imposition to effect. Such homogeneity is achieved and reproduced, it ought to be emphasized, only through repression, through occlusion and erasure, restriction and denial, delimitation and domination. In the final analysis, such terms and conditions of reproduction are unsustainable without the order(ing) of the state. Here hybridity is conceivable only against the background assumption of racial terms, biologically or culturally comprehended.

It bears reiterating then that, while definitive of the modern condition, the racial state empirically is emphatically not singular. We should take care in not reducing the *racial* state to *the* racial state, a theoretical generality for the purposes of analysis to empirically singular expression. Besides the convenience of the phrase, there is no unique institutional entity that goes by the title of "the racial state." It follows

33

that one can only draw generalizations about the form of states, of racial states, racially conceived and configured states, racism within and racist states, the specificities of which in fact require empirical elaboration. In a sense, the very notion of the *state* (and not just of *the* state, but of statehood per se) is conducive to theoretical reification in the singular. This is a singularity (and a tendency) nevertheless well worth resisting, intellectually as much as politically.

Race extends across modern conceptions of otherness, in some ways defining but certainly pervading them. The racial state, in the generic sense, purports to offer its proponents a way to account for the threat and unmanageability of the unknown, the diverse, the heterogeneous. It seeks to control not least by "knowing" them, by creating their "truth conditions." It pursues thereby turning the heterogeneous into manageable – that is, at once managed – homogeneity. Modernity is commensurate thus with the racial configuration of the threat, the external, the unknown, the outside. And through this racial characterization of the external, of the other, by implication, the internal in the form of the self becomes (and at first silently) racially defined also. So too racial states assume class specific articulation and embody varying expressions of masculinized militarism, policed desire, and state security. The racial state, the state's definition in racial terms, thus becomes the racial characterization of the apparatus, the projects, the institutions for managing this threat, for keeping it out or ultimately containing it.

So if race matters, it is in good part because the modern state has made it, because modern states more or less, more thickly or thinly, embody the racial condition. Modern states have taken shape, in part, in relation to their specific embodiment of racial conditions. In short, the modern state is the racial state, in one version or another.[8] The remainder of the book is given over to making good on these analytic projections, to adding content to the outline of the argument thus far delineated.

Notes

1   Medieval city-states in Europe, exercising considerable local authority, were complemented by a variety of looser and sprawling dynastic-based empires and principalities more or less related to larger monarchies,

empires, or church-dominated domains (cf. Tilly and Blockmans 1994: esp. 12–17).

2 Bhikhu Parekh (2000: 179–80) suggests a contrary contrast between premodern and modern social formations, predicating premodern polities on a homogeneous "way of life" while defining modern states principally in terms of territorial integrity. I am suggesting that the recourse to territory as the basis of modern state definition does not *alone* provide as clear-cut a distinction from premodern polities, especially in the European case, as Parekh would have it.

3 Revealingly, even though they could be citizens of the city, late in the eighteenth century Jews were prohibited from joining a guild in Amsterdam. The shopkeepers' guild in the provincial town of Bois-le-Duc, now in Belgium, complained in 1775 that members were "undercut and disadvantaged ceaselessly by the illegal practices of aliens, particularly of the Jewish nation, who come and go, do not pay any taxes and carry stolen goods, from bankrupt estates into the city." Jews were banned from urban citizenship in that city in 1777, in part as a response to these sentiments, though there is considerable evidence that Jewish inhabitants of Bois-le-Duc grew steadily despite the prohibition, and indeed, a few managed to join the shopkeepers' guild without hiding but no doubt without stressing their Jewishness. These restrictions were dissolved, at least formally, in 1796 when the National Assembly admitted Jews to citizenship in the Batavian Republic, as individuals though not as a people, and restricted urban regulations from overriding national policy (Prak 1999: 22–3, 27).

4 Fryer (1984: 1, 4) notes the presence of a "division of Moors" assigned by the Roman imperial army to defend Hadrian's wall in the third century AD. He also offers evidence of a black trumpeter in the English court in London as early as 1507.

5 The Romantic counter-tradition in modernity (and more recently postmodernity), it might be said, seeks to turn the perceived threat of heterogeneity into a celebrated virtue (cf. Outlaw 1996: 4–5).

6 Not one to use the substantivizing form lightly – it is used much too readily – I think in this case (homogenization) the use is exactly what is called for.

7 McClintock (1995: 299–328, esp. 300–2) never says why hybridity is scandalous, only why some presumably hybridly produced and constituted text in the specific historical contexts of post-apartheid South Africa is.

8 In a series of conversations, Gerry Heng has convinced me that just as the seeds of modern state formation can be traced to the thirteenth century, so too can the fertilizer of racial tending in the entanglements of early modern nation and state manifestation. See Heng (2000) and Mariscal (1998).

2

THE TIME OF RACIAL
STATES

If the black subject and black experience are not stabilized
by Nature or by some other essential guarantee, then it must
be the case that they are constructed historically, culturally,
politically . . .

Stuart Hall (1989/1996)

Charles Mills (1997) argues that the social contract establishing the
basis of modern states really amounted to a racial contract. The
normative and descriptive content of social contract theory, he points
out in summary of a large and largely uncritical body of literature,
accounts for the establishment of European and colonial states. But
they amount also, he insists with considerable at least superficial
plausibility, to a contract to exploit people of color to the material,
mainly economic but also political, advantages of white people. The
racial contract, in short, sustains the state of white supremacy. In
so far as the racially exclusionary and exploitative contractual effects
have been contractually endorsed for the benefit of and among
white people, their legitimation is taken silently and invisibly – in a
sense "naturally" – to be part of the social fabric on contractarian
terms.

   Charles Mills's argument has the virtue of raising insistently the
deep connection between dominant accounts of state formation and
legitimation in the history of Western political theory and racial subjugation. Yet contrary to the hint in his book, he is neither the first
nor the only one to point to such connections (Bracken 1973, 1978;
Popkin 1978; West 1982; Goldberg 1993). More pressingly, though,
Mills's account rests on a number of questionable assumptions. For one,
he presupposes that there are actually two contracts, a race-neutral

36

social contract and then a racial one: "in the social contract's application to non-Europe, . . . it becomes the Racial Contract" (Mills 1997:
42). This suggests oddly that the social contracts that supposedly
established European states historically formed are not racial, did not
fashion and rationalize racial formations, that such racial definition
emerged historically and geographically only with colonial expansion.
This is a view shared by others, like Callinicos (1993: 24) and McLaren
and Torres (1999).[1] It implies, perhaps inadvertently, that race is about
time frozen or past, about Europe's outside, about what Europe is
not. And in that implication it hides, makes invisible, not simply
Europe's own racial identity but the intra-European grounds of racial
authorization and identification.

Second, and relatedly, Mills takes at face value the realist interpretation of social contract theory, the claim that individuals become
modern political subjects of the state as a result of some general
agreement among them. Mills accordingly assumes that social contract
theory accounts for an actual contractual arrangement, implicit and
indirect though it often was, as the basis for modern state establishment
and legitimacy. People on this account are considered actually to have
agreed to the structures of state formation and their stabilizing, securing,
productive, and propertied effects. And such agreement was secured
either explicitly through constitutional creation or implicitly through
enjoying the fruits of constitutional and social implementation. It is
this explicit or implicit contractual agreement that is supposed descriptively and normatively to have established legitimation of those structures and the arrangements following from them.

Simplicity may be the mark of a certain sort of social science and
philosophy. But while simplicity is a theoretical value worth pursuing, complex social phenomena require a more complex theoretical
account than offered here. Racially configuring discourse did not follow
from a social contract but emerged coterminous with modern state
formation. Racial discourse may be seen as such to have rendered
or established – in that sense created – some people in the world,
those without history, as not white and others, supposedly historical
beings or Europeans, as white. These identifications took place within
already existing social formations, even if they were only incipient
modern or emerging absolutist states, not at some creationist contractual originating moment, whenever that might have been. As I show
in later chapters, technologies of governmental administration, such

as the census, helped to diffuse, reify, reproduce, and transform the terms of racial formation.

The modern state, then, both makes and is marked by the conditions and terms, presuppositions and implications, insinuations and effects of "civil" society's racial determination. The modern state is partially produced on the basis of these racial terms and conditions, and it reproduces even as it sometimes transforms them. Those deemed white or European or of European descent considered themselves in light of the ordering fashioned by such racial discourse as different than, often superior to, those not white on a variety of indices. White supremacy accordingly emerges not out of some imaginary "racial contract" but as a complex product of this discursive diffusion, reified in turn by modern state formation.

Now racial expression certainly has been invoked after the fact to rationalize and legitimate already existing economic and political differentiations. But racial thinking also has promoted racially configured exclusions, subjugation, and terror by framing the very ways in which people throughout the world, internal to Europe as well as vacated to Europe's outside, were being ordered and seen. Thus racial discourse made available for exploitation and exclusion those considered or seen as different or inferior. It could be said as a consequence that racial discourse has actually prompted and promoted the exploitation and exclusion of those deemed different, making it conceivable to treat members of the group accordingly. It has done this, though, in varying ways in different social regimes and orders at different times. So just as there is no necessarily identifying coherence to colonial states (Comaroff 1998), so there is no necessary or narrow identity to racial states, a point to which I will return to theorize more fully later.

The social contract tradition, far from being a realist(ic) account, then, is more aptly conceived as the prevailing modern story or narrative form, a gripping and telling myth about state origins, constitution, legitimation, and justification (Taussig 1997: 124–5). It is an account modern political theory in the European tradition has fashioned for itself as a way of coming to terms with – of accounting "magically" for – such social constitution. After all, it was fifty-five men, every one white, who were party to the agreement that fashioned the United States of America, the paradigmatic case of a contractually based state if ever there was one. The constitutional contract was fashioned between but thirteen states at the time, the additional thirty-seven added over roughly a century and half through seizure, conquest, expansion, wheeling and dealing more often than not to the detriment and exclusion of those who already lived in those spaces that became states. Moreover, while the concept of a "racial contract" predicates itself on power *between* racially conceived groups, its presumption of voluntarism completely denies the constitution of power and its effects *within* such groups.

The prominence of the social contract metaphor in political theory no doubt is related to the central importance of contract, materially and metaphorically, to modern social, political, economic, and legal life, an importance the theory in turn has helped to reify (cf. Nedelsky 1990a, 1990b). The social contract tradition historically conceived, as narrative and legitimizing form, is deeply marked in racial as it was also in gendered and class terms (cf. Pateman 1988). As I elaborate below, it was fashioned in and through more or less silent and invisible tropes threading together racial and gendered characterization. The insinuation of these tropes into the terms of the social contract narrative perpetuated the grip of racial discourse on the social imaginary and promoted the legitimation and justification of racially conceived and gendered exploitation and exclusion. The thread of racial tropes, interlaced and fused with those of gender, class, and national citizenship, and in the narrative grip of the contractarian metaphor and its foundational commitments – possessive individualism, property, rights – offered material and legitimizing possibilities otherwise unavailable. Racial and contractual terms accordingly served to reinforce each other in the modern social fabric. This quiet racial configuration of the social contract tradition, of sewing the terms of race silently into the dominant story line of modern state formation and its everyday material practices, in turn has helped to promote, reproduce, and extend the racial character of modern political consciousness. I turn now to elaborate this contrasting picture.

States of Nature and Historical States

The modern state, as initially articulated by Hobbes, was established to seek and promote social stability in the face of the instabilities and insecurities produced by changing political economies (from feudal to bourgeois). Hobbes was deeply sensitive to these concerns, which ultimately formed the basis of his justification for the Leviathan. By the eighteenth century the reason of state came to presume that the modern state was inevitable and permanent. That it may suffer an occasional crisis (economic in terms of recessions or depression – an interesting psycho-economic conflation, political in terms of revolutions or wars) attested only to the conceived irrationality of statelessness, to the insecurities of living without or outside the state. Its power consolidated and centralized, its boundaries clearly delineated (at least in their cartographic semiotic, if not always physically), its coercive capacities relatively unchallengeable (Tilly 1994), the modern state was to be nothing if not permanent. This was a permanence later reflected in the cemented iconography of its representative architecture: solid, later even massive buildings to weather the passage of time.

Where the "permanent state" was found to be in crisis, where its very grounds were challenged, the logic of the modern state required it to shore up its facade of permanence, to alleviate, restrict, and stave off challenges to its authority: revolution, chaos, anarchy, statelessness. A person or people without a state is considered as good as faceless, having no identity, and so a threat to those who do. The modern state therefore found itself required to intervene to reinstitute stability and security in the face of crisis. There is a curious tension then in the very "foundations" of thinking the modern state inevitable and permanent, in a word natural, and the necessity of having to intervene, even occasionally, to make it so. This is a tension revealing the very force such a state at once presupposes as its *raison d'être* and institutes to secure its effect.

Race appears in this scheme of things as a mode of crisis management and containment, as a mode mediating that tension, of managing manufactured threats, and of curtailing while alienating the challenge of the unknown. As representative of the Natural Other (the State of Nature in Hobbes, Pufendorf, Locke, Rousseau), race stands for that which the modern state is not, what the state avoids, what it is to keep at bay. Notwithstanding the differences between them, it is instructive that the principal or only examples these social contractarians respectively cite for the State of Nature are deeply configured in racial terms: American Indians ("the Savage people of America") in Hobbes's case (Hobbes 1651/1968: 187, 378); various "New World" peoples in Pufendorf (Pufendorf 1678/1990); "Indians" in the "woods of America," the Hottentots of "sodania" (Saldahna Bay, about 100 miles northwest of Cape Town), and Africa's "Negroes" in Locke's various writings (Locke 1689/1960: 317–18, 325–6); and the romanticized "noble savage" in Rousseau's (Rousseau 1754/1988).[2]

Hobbes's account reveals that the State of Nature is also and relatedly gendered (1651/1968: 254). Women are taken to have domain over their offspring in the natural state principally because only women know the paternity of their offspring and can seek, without being compelled to the contrary by any law, to withhold that information. That rational law prevails in the contractual state entails that men (generically understood) have moved from the state of relative irrationality, where anarchy allows women to manipulate information regarding life and paternity, into the contractual state, where men's rationality prevails. Hobbes necessarily holds onto a semblance of rationality in the State of Nature, that rationality underpinning the possibility of contracting into modern state creation through the universal laws of reason. Thus it could be argued that the State of Nature is the condition of men's rationality all but drowned in a sea of irrational "force and fraud." The ambiguity of "man" and "men" throughout Hobbes's text – emasculated in its generality, on one hand, gendered in its particularity, on the other – nevertheless remains racially configured throughout.

Carol Pateman (1991) sees Hobbes reflecting (upon) the shift from the pre-patriarchal state to the institutionally patriarchal one. While there is some controversy as to whether the patriarchal state emerges so late, I am suggesting that Hobbes reflects a movement, demonstrably more straightforward, from the preracial premodern state to the racially conceived and racially characterizing one in modernity. I do not mean by this to suggest, contrary to Pateman and Mills, that there was anything like the establishment of a "sexual contract" giving rise to modern patriarchy or a "racial contract" initiating and sustaining white supremacy. I take Hobbes rather to render explicit a rationalizing narrative concerning modern state legitimation, one central to which are the configurations of gendered and raced domination intertwined with and expressed in and through class. Thus the explicit nineteenth-century identification of women and blacks has incipient roots deep in the soil of modern state conception. The elaboration of specific state-fashioned, promoted and rationalized exclusions,

41

exploitations, and subjugations at the interface of race, class, and gender assumed increasing sophistication with the maturation of modern state formation.

If Hobbes represents the transition to modern state and social conception, his views also initiate – incipiently, ambivalently, and in ways more fully worked out later – one prevailing strand in racial conception. This is the claim that there are racial characteristics, fixed by nature, inherent in different racial groups. America's Indians are not just exemplary of the State of Nature; they are naturally, inherently restricted to nothing more than such a state, capable of no more, in contrast to Europeans. One English traveler in 1609 characterized the Indians he encountered in Virginia as "wild and savage people . . . like herds of deer in a forest" (quoted in Ashcraft 1972: 151). Hobbes's particular form of naturalism, of course, is ambivalent. In assuming that those who later became Europeans once faced characteristic experiences as inhabitants of the State of Nature, he must logically presume that Indians too might one day be able to be civilized, to exit into modern state formation.

The naturalizing presumptions here nevertheless are preserved, indeed, reified, in more or less recent historical recountings of the encounter between European voyagers and the indigenous people they took themselves to discover. Discovered lands, so the doctrine of discovery may be led to presume, are those in their more or less pristine state, occupied if at all by those very much still in their "natural," undeveloped condition, indeed, likely incapable by nature of anything more than such a condition. Consider this account of the doctrine of *terra nullius* presumed in James Cook's landing in Hawai'i, January 18, 1878.[3] Day (1955: 3–5) writes of the encounter:

> Nobody in the outer world suspected that any islands were there. . . . Now the world's greatest navigator, an English sea captain on his third voyage of discovery in the Pacific, was cruising that ocean from south to north. What he was now looking for was something that did not exist . . . What he found, he stumbled upon by chance. And on the shores he found, he was fated to be worshipped as a god . . . Cook jotted down in unexcited terms: "All these are looked upon as signs of the vicinity of land. However, we discovered none till daybreak, in the morning of the 18th, when an island made its appearance . . . and soon after, we saw more land . . . entirely detached from the former. . . . On the 19th, at sunrise, the island first seen bore east, several leagues

distant . . ." These islands were thus for the first time observed by Western eyes.

One is moved through history (as a reader) in narrations like this (there are many, and not only about Cook and his "discovery" of Hawai'i); one is placed by, in, and in relation to historical time. As a reader of such texts one assumes history, as a march through time, through (by) identifying with – or more literally being identified with – the European adventurer (here Cook). The "native" is, as Halualani says in her own commentary, simply "there," fixed in time, timeless, a Being in the state of nature in contrast to Cook who represents the Becoming of history. Cook's death, then, is the death of time, his fall – his being pulled back – into nature. The god (Cook, as the narration goes, is identified as a god by the natives he comes across like the fauna and flora of the islands before they turn on and kill him) has to die for history to begin. An interesting twist, actually, for in dying Cook is removed from time, placed outside of history – elevated as a godly figure and thus inserted (back) into nature. As Taussig remarks in a different context, "history only comes into being with the coming into being of the state itself in which, finally, reason has displaced God as the mechanism articulating the particular to the general" (Taussig 1997: 119, 163).[4]

Hobbes and Cook represent the logic of fixing racially conceived "Natives" in a prehistorical condition of pure Being naturally incapable of development and so historical progress. This commitment I call *naturalism*. By contrast, Locke begins another line of racially configured interpretation. This is one that explicitly and self-consciously historicizes racial characterization, elevates Europeans and their (postcolonial) progeny over primitive or undeveloped Others as a victory of History, of historical progress, even as it leaves open the possibility of those racial Others to historical development. This tradition, by contrast, I call *historicism*. It could be said that these two traditions are traceable almost throughout racial conception and theorizing, marking for instance the mid-sixteenth-century differences between Sepulveda's claim of inherent Indian enslaveability and Las Casas's insistence on the saveability of Indian souls.

Charles Mills is not untypical in misinterpreting Locke on this point. Mills reads Locke as naturalizing the inferior condition of "wild Indians" and Africa's Negroes, condemning both to a permanent state of inherent irrationality and infantilization (Mills 1997: 67–8).[5] Yet there is nothing in Locke's corpus to suggest this *naturalized* state of inferiority. Quite the contrary, given Locke's epistemological anti-essentialism, one must presume not that he considered those other than European equal to the English, but that he would deem such inferiority impermanent rather than an essential condition of nature. Locke claims that "wild Indians" and "Negroes" have not *in fact* expended the labor that would give them "the Conveniences" Europeans enjoy (*2nd Treatise*, #41), not that they are naturally incapable of such rational design and so perennially condemned to such natural state. An American colonist, the Reverend John Bulkley, for instance, invoked Locke to legitimate expropriation of Indian land. He did so on the basis not of "first occupancy" but of the ascendancy of the "God-fearing" and so "morally dignified" productive labor of "the people of New England" over the presumed laziness of the indigenous inhabitants (Huyler 1995: 176).

This historicized conception in Locke's text is consistent too with his celebrated anti-Aristotelian condemnation of a state of natural slavery (*1st Treatise*, #1) combined with his justification of enslavement as a function of avoiding death in the face of defeat resulting from a just war (*2nd Treatise*, #23–4). Accordingly, in formulating the *Fundamental Constitutions of Carolina*, Locke notoriously included the rule that freemen "shall have absolute power and authority over his negro slaves," the masculinist definition of mastery hidden only slightly beneath the more obvious racial conception of the slave state (Locke 1824: 199). That Locke thought the expeditions of the Royal Africa Company, in which he held stock, equivalent to *just* wars sufficed in his mind to legitimate the slave trade. In a sense, he considered America's Indians and Africans equivalent to minors, children not yet fully developed, but nowhere does he refer to either as idle, inherently irrational and inhuman, and so enslaveable (contra Mills 1997: 67).

It bears noting then that Locke later in the *2nd Treatise* characterized children, whom he calls minors, as those in their "Nonage" (*2nd Treatise*, 365, #69). This is the very term by which John Stuart Mill more than a century later referred to nations he supposed historically yet too immature to rule themselves. It is not that Locke condemned American Indians and Africans forever to the State of Nature while modern states are reserved for Europeans and their progeny. Rather, like children, "minors" in their "Nonage," Native Americans and Africans are

44

considered not yet ready historically for the self-rule modern "contractual" states make possible.[6]

Thus, in evading for what principally are philosophical reasons the standard biologized conception of racist commitment, the *"ancien régime"* of race rule, so to speak, Locke initiates a new line of interpretation. It is one that though less remarked has remained at least as popular since, perhaps precisely because more nuanced and easily hidden, harder to pin down and tougher to dismiss. So, Locke initiated a tradition of racial argumentation that runs clear through John Stuart Mill and Auguste Comte in the empiricist tradition of the nineteenth century. But it equally marks the technological progressivism and streak of historicist developmentalism in Marx, as it does also contemporary monoculturalists and conservative liberals.

I do not mean to suggest that this historicizing of racial thinking so much displaces or occludes the essentializing fixity of naturalizing racial natures that we find in Hobbes. For the latter is elaborated by the likes of Rousseau and Kant, acquires novel form in polygenism, and is expressed ambivalently by Dinesh D'Souza and the Bell Curve apologists in contemporary terms (D'Souza 1995; cf. Goldberg 1997: 175–226; Murray and Herrnstein 1994). The two strains of racial thinking coexist uneasily and sometimes awkwardly, the more nuanced historicizing conception becoming more explicit, even dominant with the twentieth century, as the earlier balder strain came under harsher scrutiny and critical attack.

In his *History of Navigation from its Original to the Year 1704*, for example, Locke characterizes only the people of Africa in racial or color terms (as "black," "near black," "Moor," or "tending to Moor"), and refers to them exclusively from the time of the European expeditionary voyages onwards. Those of Arabia or the East Indies, by contrast, he characterized regionally. Thus, he wrote,

> The natives [of the West African coast] are for the most part black, or else inclining to it. All the commodities brought from thence, are gold-dust, ivory, and slaves; those black people selling one another, which is a very considerable trade, and has been a great support to all the American plantations. This is all that mighty continent affords for exportation, the greatest part of it being scorched under the torrid zone, and the natives almost naked, no-where industrious, and for the most part scarce civilized. (Locke 1824: 414–17)

Here Locke's racial historicism overlaps with Hobbesian racial naturalism, for the lack of industry is exactly Hobbes's principal description of the State of Nature, influenced as he was by Montaigne's earlier characterization of "cannibals."[7] Racial historicism, even an historicism that purports to avoid conceptual essentialism, can be equal to racial naturalism in its biased presumption, its ignorant projection, and its violent denials of any virtues but its own.

In the middle of the eighteenth century, the heart of that age of Enlightenment, Rousseau takes up once again the Hobbesian tradition of naturalized racial characterization of the State of Nature, and relatedly the possibility of modern state governance. Rousseau, it is true, has a considerably more benign view of the State of Nature than Hobbes, and he accordingly views its inhabitants somewhat more appealingly as precursors of modern European "man." American Indians, Rousseau's (hopelessly false, as it happens) anthropological exemplification of "natural man," nevertheless are destined to savagery, supposed nobility notwithstanding: "Both metallurgy and agriculture were unknown to the savages of America, who have always therefore remained savages." Rousseau repeatedly emphasized this inherent incapacity for civilization on the part of those he deemed "savages" of various stripes: "for the many years that the Europeans torment themselves in order to acclimate the savages of various countries to their lifestyle, they have not yet been able to win over a single one of them, not even by means of Christianity; for our missionaries sometimes turn them into Christians, but never into civilized men."

Rousseau exemplified his claim of inherent inferiority by reference to a "Hottentot" man. This Khoi man had been extended all the European luxuries by Simon van der Stel, then Dutch governor of the Cape, whom he served faithfully, even traveling to the East Indies on VOC business. He returned to abandon his European finery, service, and master, fleeing back to his "natural" habitat in the "bush" (Rousseau 1754: fn. 16, 106–8). Destined racially to their natural state, "savages" fail to belong in the "civilized" state of self-rule, no matter how much education may be devoted by Europeans to their upliftment. Only civilized Europeans thus are self-determining, free to place "their common power under the supreme direction of the general will," to be members in other words of the sovereign, self-willed, and so free state (Rousseau 1759: Book I, ch. 6, 148). The battle-cry of enlightened eighteenth-century revolutions that Rousseau did so much to orchestrate is haunted by the echoed screams of slaughtered savages. "Liberty, Equality, Fraternity," but only for and among those not inherently incapacitated. The Rule of Man and Race Rule combined in the Rule of Law silently, invisibly to effect dispossession, dislocation, denial, and denigration.

The racially conceived and characterized State of Nature in each of the historical cases discussed, whether "grounded" on rationalist or empiricist, naturalist or historicist presumption, is taken to be predicated precisely on a lack. It assumes the incapacity to fulfill rational and civilized needs and drives, a failure to deliver the goods. It is instructive to note here that the racial references invoked by classical social contractarians to exemplify such lacks in terms of the State of Nature metaphor are taken up from the culture of racially conceived modernity they found about them. They are not created by a contract or by contractarians' reflections upon contractarian arrangements, as Charles Mills's argument may be read to suggest.

So the modern, if transforming, conception of the state is racially defined, as it is engendered, from its inception, not least because it is embedded in an already almost pervasive dominant culture of racially configured othering and infantilization. The State of Nature in the likes of Hobbes, Pufendorf, Locke, and Rousseau is racially figured as the space of the racial Other, of the irrational or prerational and uncivilized being. Largely hypothetical, the State of Nature was thought nevertheless to have some empirical validation in the historical record of "primitive" people. Where those mired in the State of Nature were considered capable of it, they may escape into political statehood precisely by pursuing the civilizing mission of Europeanness. Those inherently incapable would be condemned to a permanent state of "savagery," and so to regulation by those in control of modern, "civilized" states. Such regulation might assume the form of direct or indirect colonial rule, or alternatively to permanent exclusion from the space of "civilized" rule and representative governance.

The modern state, in contrast to these more or less thick representations of the State of Nature, was understood as the space of white men. Towards the end of the eighteenth century, Immanuel Kant, in a deeply naturalizing vein, is unself-consciously bold (and all but bald) in insisting notoriously that citizens of the modern state could only be white men of property.

> The only qualification required by a citizen (apart, *of course*, from being an adult male) is that he must be his own master . . . and must have some property . . . to support himself.

To which Kant adds in a footnote,

> The domestic servant, the shop assistant, the laborer, or even the barber are merely laborers, not artists or members of the state, and are thus unqualified to be citizens. (Kant 1970: 74)

If Kant feels obliged to remind his reader what he presumes them to take as the obvious and unquestionable gendered condition of citizenship, he is only slightly more veiled, because more deeply presumptuous, in his racial characterization. Domestic servants, shop assistants, laborers, and hairdressers silently specify for the most part the labor of black folk as well as women, as much in the late eighteenth century as contemporarily. Olaudah Equiano, the first African in London openly to call for slavery's abolition, not uncommonly worked as a hairdresser, domestic servant, and shop assistant between becoming a freeman in London and a principal abolitionist spokesman at about the time Kant was penning these words.[8]

It is worth emphasizing here that race (like gender) is assumed silently in the quiet insistence upon seemingly neutral descriptors. Set apart as lacking agency (because lacking no doubt the grounds of historical elevation to rationality), the (gendered) other of modernity is deleted from state protection and right (though hardly from state regulation). Self-mastery – the gendered characterization carried in the choice of words themselves – is predicated on the presumption of rational capacity, which blacks and women Kant took to lack to far greater degrees than white men.[9] Lacking the necessary degree of rational capacity to underpin self-determination, blacks and women accordingly lack the possibility of self-directed labor and so of self-mastery. Reduced rationally to working for white men, blacks and women are incapable accordingly of modern state citizenship. It must follow, *of course*, that to imagine it otherwise presumptively would be to take on that irrationality rendering one at once illegitimate and so unqualified for citizenship. The struggle of women and people characterized as not white to acquire voting rights in the first half of the twentieth century as a consequence was as much about clearing away these insidious background presumptions as about the formalities of legal change.

The prevailing narrative about the "progress" of modern states to maturation, I am insisting, is a less remarked but at once equally bald progression in state racial configuration. As much as the modern state has been about anything – about increasing bureaucratization and rationalization, about increasingly sophisticated forms of democratization and social control, about the rule of law and the control of capital – it has been about increasingly sophisticated forms and techniques of racial formation, power, and exclusion.

The modern state, it follows, has been about keeping racially characterized others more or less "out," and about regulating otherness in spaces increasingly determined, defined, and rationally regulated by the state. The means and modes, styles and reasons of such racially predicated exclusion have varied across time and place, space and state. The spaces of racially conceived others throughout (one could say provocatively "for") modernity accordingly are threatening and fearful, more or less abstract objects of regulation and control. These spaces predict if they do not already preconceive the loss of rationality and serve to exemplify the brutishness and barbarism thought to follow from the abandonment of or the failure to achieve civilization. This reveals an often overlooked reason also why the prevailing narrative of modern state formation and claimed justification should assume social contract form. In predicating the logic of modern state expression so heavily on claims of rationality, social contract theory at once marginalizes those deemed irrational while reinforcing itself by way of the contrast. Race qua otherness is as necessary and "natural" to the logic and historical development of modern state formation as modern technologies of state governmentality are to racial formation.

The Racial Obsession of Modernity

It follows from the logic of my argument, and contrary to Charles Mills's notion of "the racial contract," that though historically important to the articulation of modern state formation, the social contract narrative is logically contingent. It is contingent also to the development and expression of racial terms. It is simply a narrative in that sense, an historically important one to be sure, but lacking any inherent power. By contrast, one could say as a reversal of the line of analysis I have adopted here that race is integral to – a constitutive feature of – modern state formation. The tropes of social contract and race developed in part independent of each other. But they have served at the same time historically to reinterpret and reinforce, to institution- alize, each other's terms. This interpenetrating contingency of social contract and race nevertheless furnishes further indication of the cent- ral importance of race to modern thinking about the polity.

Hegel's contrast of the maturity of the modern European state of his day with the supposed immaturity of those societies identified with racially conceived others offers further evidence of this emergent centrality. Hegel's, of course, is by no means a contractual account. Yet his theory of the state, his claims of Africa's supposed irrationality and immaturity as well as Arabs' apparent barbarity and lack of civil- ization, perhaps offer the most obvious and extreme exemplification of this claim to the maturity of the modern state based on reason's rule (Hegel 1821/1944: 79–102; 1952: 247; 1975: 176–89, 218–20).

Hegel's conception of the state thus illustrates the points I have been emphasizing. First, his views extend the tradition of naturalistic interpretation regarding the modern racial state. Second, his account points to the widespread and variously articulated theoretical grounds of modern state racial configuration. Indeed such non-contractual state conceptions – as we will see, John Stuart Mill's utilitarian conception is another – poses for Charles Mills's account serious questions about the historical necessity of a "racial contract," literally or as a trope, for the reproduction of state-based racial formation. Hegel's view suggests also a third point emergent in my argument here: that race is integral to, a central feature – indeed, an obsession – of, the historical development of European-influenced and inflected modernity.

Accordingly, it is Reason's rule, on Hegel's account, that marks the politics of the modern state as one of self-determination and autonomy, of the control of one's own destiny, the historical moment at which the rule of God gives way to the power of the state, religion to politics. But it also licenses the extension of the rule of self-promoted rationality over the projection of the irrational, rationalizing thus the colonial project as one of modern destiny. So modern states expand their scope of authority, legitimacy, power, wealth, and control not only over their citizens – in the name of freedom, autonomy, self-determination, and self-direction – but also over those racially considered incapable or not yet capable of self-rule. The colonial project, necessarily racially configured, is accordingly an expansion of modern state definition.

It follows that colonialism, from the point of view of the state, was about policing, securing, and controlling the outside of the colonizing (European) state power. Of course, there were multiple motivations for such control, not least economic. For the early modern state, for the Renaissance state in transition, race is an instrument in establishing exploitable labor. With the emergence of settler (and ultimately settled) states, as Fanon suggests in *A Dying Colonialism*, racial formation takes on forms different (because conditions, interests, and so on are different) than racial expression in colonizing parent states. Quite literally, the state forms differ. Racisms in colonies assume state forms different from those in the European metropoles, just as there are differences in state racisms in and across the various colonial empires (French, British, Spanish, Belgian, Dutch, for instance) (Comaroff 1998), and even as metropolitan desires in colonizing societies were fashioned through the racial experiences in settled societies (Stoler 1995). Hence also the postcolonial differences between them.

Once again, though now in contrast to Hegel, views of colonized states and their relation to the colonizing ones cannot be reduced singularly to their naturalistic forms. Here the "new historicism" in conceiving racial state formation is borne by the likes of Marx, of all people. Unlike Hegel, for whom African and Asian societies were inherently fixed as irrational or barbaric, Marx thought of "Asiatic" states as historically undeveloped, even as his projections and predictions were fueled by a historical teleology underpinned by Western chauvinism: European states offered Marx the model of historical progress.

> [T]hese idyllic village communities [of Asia] had always been the solid foundation of Oriental despotism . . . they restrained the human mind within the smallest possible compass, . . . enslaving it beneath traditional rules, depriving it of all *grandeur and historical energies* . . .

> England, it is true, in causing a social revolution in Hindustan was actuated only by the vilest interest, and was stupid in her manner of enforcing them. But that is not the question. The question is, can

51

mankind fulfil its destiny without a fundamental revolution in the social state of Asia? If not, whatever may have been the crimes of England she was the unconscious tool of history in bringing about that revolution . . .

England has to fulfil a double mission in India: one destructive, the other regenerating – the annihilation of old Asiatic society, and the laying of the material foundations of Western society in Asia. (Marx 1973: 306, 307, 320)[10]

Thus for Marx, as for Auguste Comte, it is not that "backward societies" racially conceived are inherently irrational and so naturally incapable of self-development and progressive governance. Rather, it is that they have languished in "primitive" and confining social arrangements that have undermined their capacity for evolution. If there is a virtue to colonialism for Marx – the preference of British over Turkish or Persian or Russian conquest (Marx 1973: 320) – it was that it stripped away those confining limits to rational administrative conditions of modernization. Colonialism thus enabled, in Marx's mind, the sort of productive capacity necessary for the historical "destiny" of socialist revolution. Comte, by contrast, recognized more readily the necessarily destructive character of imposed colonial rule. However, he recommended, naively, that non-Western peoples, liberated from the colonial yolk, "spontaneously" recognize the superiority of Western, and particularly French, governmental capacity and socioeconomic productivity, and choose to emulate the model.

While I have concentrated throughout this account on the ways state theory has been racially fashioned and has reinforced racial conception and exclusion, it should be emphasized that such "racial fabrication" (Goldberg 1997) has not been without resistance, in representation as in action. Thus Hawai'ians' execution of Cook represents an instance of broader forms of indigenous response to the arrogance of European invasion, broken promises, dashed hopes, and failed treaties throughout the Americas (Todorov 1984). Phyllis Wheatley's poetry (1773), Ignatius Sancho's letters (1782), or Equiano's autobiography (1789) are early instances of the racially repressed writing back.

Two related points bear notice here, however. First, the modern obsession with race, as we have seen, was deeply predicated on an appeal to Reason, to a deeply racial sense of rationality, that representational expressions of resistance felt bound to emulate. Reaction suffers having to employ the very same terms and conditions of denigration and subjugation as a condition of their being understood, as proof of their rationality initially denied. Second, and consequently, the terms of racial fabrication are likely reproduced in the expression of resistance. Racial identification is either embraced or denied when one so characterized says, "That's not me!" For in the "that" racial identification ironically is reified, as it is in the personal distancing from the attendant racial characterization. The reifying nature of racial characterization tends to trump whatever resistant echoes might be trumpeted in its name, even in its anti-essentialist and historicizing forms. This is especially so where the cementing power of the state is behind the forms of racial expression.

It bears rehearsing here that Locke's "new historicism" regarding racial matters was prompted principally by his anti-essentialist commitments, Comte's by his empiricism, and Marx's by his background judgments regarding technological impoverishment. In short, the respective commitments to racial historicism are theoretically embedded and motivated. But it is also the case that openness to empirical evidence in the case of Comte (and later Mill), as well as greater experience of colonial conditions and administration, prompted acknowledgments of (if only) instances of intellectual and creative contributions among and from those judged inferior. The new historicism then was as much a product of (empirically) recognizable counter-presumptive capacity on the part of those considered racially inferior – such as Phyllis Wheatley, Benjamin Banneker, Olaudah Equiano, and a little later David Walker (not to mention recurrent slave revolts and the Haitian Revolution that consumed the last decade of the eighteenth century) – as it was theoretically prompted.[11]

The broader tension between the naturalist and the historicist models of racial conception in relation to social configuration and state formation is played out in all its nuanced complexities in a remarkable exchange between Thomas Carlyle and John Stuart Mill at the middle of the nineteenth century. Embedded in the exchange are competing conceptions of race and racial conceptions of the state, contrasting judgments of capital and colonialism, and contesting visions of social life. It is to an analysis of this exchange as embodying the issues at hand that I now turn.

NOTES

1 "Racism emerged as the ideology of the plantocracy" (McLaren and Torres 1999: 50). Mills himself seems to vacillate between different claims. So later in the book he writes, "The Racial Contract . . . underwrites the social contract, is a visible or hidden operator that restricts and modifies the scope of its prescriptions" (72); and "the Racial Contract is the real meaning of the social contract" (74), which seems to suggest that the racial contract is implicit in the very conception of the social contract, a necessary condition of the latter's possibility.

2 Locke's knowledge of the Khoi-Khoi may have sprung from stories he picked up about "Coree the Saldanian" who had been kidnapped by a captain of the English East Indies Company and transported to London in 1613, nineteen years prior to the birth of Locke and Pufendorf. Coree later returned to Saldania, where he served as a broker between the English and Khoi-Khoi in cattle trading. His refusal to trade with Dutch ships led to his public execution at Dutch hands in 1627 (Fryer 1988: 12–13).

3 I owe this example to my former student, Rona Halualani.

4 Halualani goes on to argue, persuasively, that Cook and the ensuing European settlers came in this narration to be conceived as native to the islands as the natives are simultaneously made strange. This, she says, is a "fated" inversion that opened up the possibility for non-Hawai'ian settlers to this day "legitimately," at least in terms of the law, to claim Hawai'ianness.

5 "In the Lockean state of nature, in the absence of a constituted juridical and penal authority, natural law permits individuals themselves to punish wrongdoers. Those who show by their actions that they lack or have 'renounced' the reason of natural law and are like 'wild savage Beasts, with whom Men can have no Society or Security,' may licitly be destroyed. But if in the racial polity nonwhites may be regarded as *inherently* bestial and savage . . . then they can be conceptualized as carrying the state around with them" (Mills 1997: 86–7, my emphasis). In a more carefully argued book of essays published shortly after *The Racial Contract*, Mills (1998: xiii) still insists on the naturalist interpretation: "since its emergence as a major social category several hundred years ago, race has paradigmatically been thought of as 'natural,' a biological fact about human beings and the foundation of putatively ineluctable hierarchies of intelligence and moral character." In bewildering exculpation of James Mill of any racist expression, Majeed writes "[James Mill] never expressed a belief in *inherent* racial differences as accounting for different forms of society" (Majeed 1992: 138, my emphasis).

6   Thus Locke writes of children, but he could equally have had Indians and Africans in his sight, as his identification of children with "Brutes" makes evident: "To turn him loose to an unrestrain'd Liberty before he has Reason to guide him, is not allowing him the priviledge of his Nature to be free; but to thrust him out amongst the Brutes and abandon him to a state as wretched and as much beneath man as theirs. This is that which puts the *Authority* into the *Parents'* hands to govern the minority of their Children" (*2nd Treatise*, #63). "The subjection of a Minor places in the Father a temporary Government, which terminates with the minority of the Child" (*2nd Treatise*, #67).

7   "In such condition there is no place for Industry . . . and consequently no Culture . . . ; no Navigation, nor use of commodities that may be imported by Sea; no commodious Building . . . ; no Knowledge of the face of the Earth; no account of Time; no Arts, no Letters; no Society" (Hobbes 1651/1968: 186). In 1575, Montaigne had written in "Of Cannibals," that they have "no manner of traffic; no knowledge of letters; no science of numbers; no name of magistrate or statesman; no contracts; . . . no clothing; no agriculture; no metals" (Montaigne 1946: 206).

8   Similarly, in the Netherlands of the mid-nineteenth century, citizenship excluded "all women, minors, madpersons, beggars, prisoners, the dishonored . . . and all persons who did not have full use of their freedom, their minds, or their possessions" (quoted in Stoler 1995: 120–1).

9   "The Negroes of Africa have no feeling that rises above the trifling . . . not a single one was ever found who presented anything great in art or science or any other praiseworthy quality, even though among the whites some continually rise aloft from the lowest rabble, and through superior gifts earn respect in the world. So fundamental is the difference between these two races of men, and it appears to be as great in regard to mental capacities as in color" (Kant 1764/1960: 110–11).

10   Auguste Comte, writing at roughly the same time, is equally driven by a model of idealized Western (indeed, French) teleology imposed upon the rest of the world. His vision of a "universal State" is to be achieved by progressive evolution, "spontaneous incorporations" into Western forms of productivity and governance. Non-European races and their representative states are backward, capable of development, not inherently inferior: "Mere differences in intensity and speed are mistakenly cast as radical diversities, each with its own laws, in such a way as to rebuff any truly general conception, and thus any sound explanation" (Comte 1852: II, 405, quoted in Todorov 1993: 31).

11   Cedric Robinson (1997) furnishes a sustained history of the nature and extent to black intellectual, social, and political resistance in America. It is worth noting also that Howard Winant is representative of contemporary

commentators on racial theory in recognizing a shift from racial naturalism to predominantly culturalist conceptions of race, but restricts that shift to the aftermath of World War II.

> [B]efore roughly World War II, before the rise of nazism, before the end of the great European empires, and particularly before the decolonization of Africa, before the urbanization of the U.S. black population and the rise of the modern civil rights movement, race was still largely seen in Europe and North America (and elsewhere as well) as an essence, a natural pheno-menon, whose meaning was fixed, as constant as a southern star. (Winant 1994: 113)

It could be said accordingly, as Ann Stoler (1997) and Paul Gilroy (1993) suggest, that essentializing histories have continued deeply to mark anti-essentialist commitments.

3

THE STATE OF
LIBERALISM'S LIMITS

his Epic be a mighty Empire slowly built together, a mighty
series of Heroic Deeds – a mighty Conquest over Chaos . . .

> Thomas Carlyle, "The English," *Past and Present*
> (1843/1888: 196)

As [mankind] range lower and lower in development . . . [rep-
resentative] government will be, generally speaking, less suitable
to them.

> J. S. Mill, "Representative Government" (1861)

Shifting Grounds

In 1849 *Fraser's Magazine*, the popular London literary periodical, published an anonymous attack on the nature of black people under the
title, "Occasional Discourse on the Negro Question." The vicious essay
turned out to be written by Thomas Carlyle. Outraged by the incivility
of its language, if not distressed by the intransigence of the sentiment
it expressed, literate liberals in Britain and the northern States in the
American Union openly objected to the attack. Chief among the responses was a particularly impassioned essay, published again anonymously, in the following issue of *Fraser's* under the title, "The Negro
Question." This time the author was England's leading public intellectual of the day, John Stuart Mill. Four years later, fueled no doubt by
his increasingly acrimonious feud with his former mate Mill, Carlyle
published in pamphlet form a revised and expanded version of the
attack under the more pointed and painful title, "Occasional Discourse
on the *Nigger* Question" (August 1971, my emphasis).

57

This semi-anonymous exchange, almost too sensitive to touch in their own names, offers a particularly revealing window to the excesses and limits of nineteenth-century racial discourse, issues of race rule, a raced labor supply, and the racial reasoning of the state.[1] It exemplifies the parameters of Victorian racially conceived sentiment, explicitly racist in one direction, seemingly egalitarian in the other, as Eugene August (1971) hopefully has it. Indeed, while it represents imperious tensions (Cooper and Stoler 1997) within colonial racial configuration and racist derogation – colonialism's vicious recourse to neoscientific racism, on one hand, and liberalism's polite racism, on the other – the exchange reveals at once implications of the distinction I elaborated in the previous chapter between "naturalistic" and "historicist" reasoning in the history of racial discourse.

But the tense conflict between Carlyle and Mill illustrates as well the long reach of colonial discourse embedded in elements of contemporary postcolonial racist expression. Carlyle on race was to mid-nineteenth-century Britain what Dinesh D'Souza or Charles Murray is to early twenty-first-century America, offering a totalizing rationalization of the sorry state of black folk in the most extreme, and thus eye-catching, terms. By contrast, Mill's singular contribution to "The Negro Question" – just as his "On the Subjection of Women" was his seminal contribution to "The Woman Question" – nevertheless marks the implicit limits to racially conceived egalitarianism, perhaps as Thomas Sowell, Clarence Thomas, or Ward Connerly ironically do for the contemporary moment. Such difficulties are especially acute for a liberalism committed unstintingly to a conception of formal equality. This suggests at once the challenge facing liberalism on the question of race and racial governance more generally.

The sociohistorical background to the exchange between Carlyle and Mill concerned the fading prospects and conditions of the British plantation owners in the West Indies, though the questions of race addressed have to be understood in terms of the colonial condition more broadly. Emancipation of slaves in the British empire in 1834 curtailed the supply of desperately cheap labor and cut into the artificial profit margins enjoyed by the West Indies sugar planters. In 1846 the British parliament ended plantation subsidies, thus forcing plantation owners in the islands, those increasingly disaffected white British subjects, to compete unprotected on the world market. Recessionary conditions and "commercial panics" in Britain in the closing years of the 1840s

(Wood 1964: 10) dampened demand for colonial goods, further deepening the crises in Britain's colonial economies. Carlyle's voice was that of the disenchanted colonial "aristocracy" abroad and (more ambiguously) the distressed English working classes and Irish peasants closer to hand, combined under the racially promoted aggrandizement of whiteness; Mill's by comparison was that of "enlightened" Victorian abolitionism. Here then are to be found the two prevailing pillars of nineteenth-century racial theory, legacies and media as I have suggested of longer traditions. Carlyle represented the bald claim to "the Negro's" inherent inferiority articulated by racist science of the day. Mill, on the other hand, was the principal spokesman for the European's historically developed superiority, though (as Afrocentrists like Molefi Asante and their critics like Mary Lefkowitz both should note) he temperately acknowledged the influence of ancient Egyptians on the Hellenic Greeks.[2]

More broadly, however, this tension between the biological and historicist conceptions of race and racial governance reflects as it serves to solidify broader social shifts in the wake of the French Revolution, the promotion of and reaction to Enlightenment principles, and the emergence of vigorous and ultimately successful abolitionist movements. In short, the contest over conceptions of race is tied up with world historical events, material and intellectual, which suggested as they represented newer forms – concrete categories – of conceiving racial others. The shifts in prevailing racial conception are threaded through shifts in political economy, from slave-based economies to the industrial revolution, colonial expansion and solidification, and they are determined in part by the discovery of mineral resources in the colonies. The latter, in particular, was seen to necessitate a steady, administratively manageable, and inexpensive labor supply. Thus, the imperatives of exploitability prompted by but also requiring a sense of quasi- or subhumanness are tied nevertheless to administrative requirements demanding recognition of (legal) personhood for contractual purposes and legal management (Comaroff 1998). The vicious naturalism underpinning Carlyle's negrophobia makes way bit by begrudging bit, at least for the moment, for the veiled Victorian politeness of Mill's historicist racism.

Carlyle's Critical Caricature

Carlyle's negrophobia is interesting intellectually only because its vituperative language directed at black people was an expression of more than just bald prejudice, though it was clearly that. Thus, his objectionable language (revealing of equally objectionable presumptions) regarding people of African descent was expressed against the background of a critique of the conditions of the working classes in Britain. Carlyle's negrophobia accordingly was tied up with a critical account of laissez-faire capitalist political economy prevailing at the time.

The failure of the potato crop due to extended drought had devastated Irish peasants, and the mid-century recession had caused massive unemployment among the English working classes, represented in Carlyle's discourse in the forlorn figure of the "Distressed Needlewoman." Carlyle contrasted these desperately sad figures with the stereotype of the lazy, "sho' good eatin'" Negro.[3] He assumed that the capitalism of his day causally connected the alienation of working people in England and Ireland to the emancipation of shiftless and workless Negroes in the colonies.

Carlyle thus predicated in this essay what might otherwise be deemed an insightful reading of unregulated capitalism that he had developed for example in *Past and Present* (1843) on a set of deeply racist premises. In the spirit of the early Marx, Carlyle criticized laissez-faire capitalism for reducing *human* relationships (the paradigm for which he assumes to be between whites) to the "cash contract" (August 1971: xvii), between employer and employee. Capitalist "Lords of Rackrent" (or landlords) lost all interest in the impoverished Irish peasant or English seamstress once the latter were unable to afford the rent. The latters' freedom, under laissez-faire liberal capitalism, reduced to the liberty to die by starvation. Carlyle accordingly predicted that the importation of English workers into the West Indies in response to planters' demands for workers who would work would render the Negro inhabitants as free to starve as their British counterparts.

Carlyle attributed the underlying cause of this general condition to the demise of paternalistic control by the British state, which he considered superior on all counts to the inherently inferior natives of the islands. Those in a situation of superiority, whether individuals or their governments, had a paternalistic obligation to effect the well-being of the inferior for whom the former were responsible. Carlyle insisted that the feudal serf was (materially) better placed than the Irish peasant, English needleworker, or "Negro" of his day. He concludes that "the Negro Question" was to be answered by turning

Negroes into a relationship of loyal serfdom to the benevolent feudal-like lordship of their white masters. White men, wisest by birth(right), were destined by nature and God to rule, Negroes to serve; whites ought to try to convince Negroes to assume their God-given role as servants, failing which masters would be obliged to turn to "the beneficent whip."

Likely unaware first hand of any black people, Carlyle's "nigger" of the "Nigger Question" was the stereotypical figure of "Quashee," a polygenic form of black lowlife – lazy, laughing, rhythmic, musical, dance-loving, language defective (August 1971: 12). "Horse-jawed and beautifully muzzled" (August 1971: 4), "Quashee" was the Carlylean equivalent of "sambo," etymologically linked to squash and so to pumpkin. Carlyle characterized "Quashee" as working only at eating pumpkin – Carlyle's mean metaphor for any juicy tropical fruit like watermelon, cantaloupe, mango, or papaya – and drinking rum. Yet Carlyle insisted on finding "the Negro," "alone of wild-men," kind, affectionate, even lovable, and pointedly not the object of his "hate" (August 1971: 12). The abundance of tropical fruit in Carlyle's view reduced the need on the part of West Indian natives to work. Carlyle's solution was to compel "the Negro" in the islands to work by restricting to the laborless the right to own fruit-producing land or to enjoy its abundant products (August 1971: 9).

In order to sustain this degraded image of the inherently inferior "Nigger," Carlyle (like his counterpart D'Souza a century and half later) was driven to reduce the debilitating effects of slavery's experience for people of African descent. Carlyle accordingly insisted that the debilitations of slavery were "much exaggerated" (August 1971: 13). Slavery, and so mastery too, were considered "natural" conditions; slaves, as Aristotle once put it, are slaves by nature. Blacks are born to be servants (Carlyle's euphemistic bow to the abolitionists, August 1971: 22) of whites who "are born wiser . . . and lords" over them (August 1971: 32). Indeed, Carlyle insisted that there is a slavery far worse than that of Negroes in the colonies, "the one, intolerable sort of slavery" (as though enslavement of black people is not). This, he remarked without a hint of irony, is the "slavery" throughout Europe of "the strong to the weak; of the great and noble-minded to the small and mean! The slavery of Wisdom to Folly" (August 1971: 14). Thus Carlyle diminished the horrible experience and effects of *real* slavery historically by reducing them to less than the "Platonic" manifestations of a metaphorical Nietzschean servitude of the strong and wise to the weak and ignorant. Of course, it says little for the strength and wisdom of the European wealthy and wise that they should be so constrained by the weak and witless, a point to which Carlyle in all his critical power seems oblivious.

Carlyle emphasized that it was European governance through its creativity, ingenuity, and productivity that developed the colonies from their supposed prehistory of "pestilence . . . and putrefaction, savagery . . . and swamp-malaria" (August 1971: 28); that it was the English (or "Saxon British," August 1971: 27) who supposedly made the West Indies flourish and without whom the islands would reduce to "Black Irelands" (August 1971: 33) or "Haiti" with "black Peter exterminating black Paul" (August 1971: 29). Yet Carlyle repeatedly contrasted the conditions of "Negroes," those "Demerara Niggers," with the conditions of English laborers, white working women, and Irish peasants. Fat from the abundance of land, the consumption of fruit, and lack of labor, the character of the Negro was measured against, if not silently considered the cause of, working peoples' plight in the mother country and the colonies. White working women and Irish peasants were perhaps racially salvageable in ways black people were not, revealing in particular English ambiguity and ambivalence towards their Irish brethren.

Carlyle's discourse nevertheless reveals beneath the racially conceived overlay of this contrast a class-induced ambivalence. Thus he identified also the Distressed Needlewomen, Irish peasants, and English working classes through a nineteenth-century version of the discourse of an underclass (or lumpen) poverty of culture with "the Nigger" of the West Indies (August 1971: 20–1). Most of the 30,000 Distressed Needlewomen, he objected, were really "Mutinous Servingmaids" unable "to sew a stitch," and defying their inherent need for a master: "Without a master in certain cases, you become a Distressed Needlewoman, and cannot so much as live" (August 1971: 21). Carlyle further reduced this equation of posing seamstress and free "nigger" to the infantilized condition of babies and the animalized conditions of dogs and horses (August 1971: 23, 12), all of whom needed accordingly to be cared for, looked after, mastered by "philanthropic Anglo-Saxon men and women" (August 1971: 23). Equal in quantity to an entire English county, black West Indians "in *worth* (in quantity of intellect, faculty, docility, energy, and available human valor and value)" amounted to but a single street of London's working-class East End.

In Carlyle's view, then, the working classes (most notably, working women) along with Negroes especially were born to serve, to have masters. With little wit of their own, they would flourish only in servitude, in being told what to do and looked after. Carlyle concluded from this claim of inherent servility that the "Black gentleman" be hired "not by the month, but by a very much longer term. That he be 'hired for life.'" That, in other words, he be the slave he was to "Whites ... born more wiser than [he]" (August 1971: 21–2, 33, 34–5). Ironically, and against the naturalist grain, such lifelong servitude was to be enforced through might and fright (August 1971: 26–7, 29, 31), for if "the Saxon British" failed to assert their dominance some other colonial power would (August 1971: 35). The colonial imperative was as much about relations of power, domination, and "the education of desire" (Stoler 1995) internal to Europe as it was straightforwardly about imposing European will upon those it at once defined, dismissed, and desired as its other.

Lest it be thought that Carlyle's intervention was exceptional either in the extremity of its language or the substance of its claims, there appeared almost forty years later a book-length appeal to return to the conditions of slavery in the West Indies by the Regius Professor of Modern History at Oxford, Anthony James Froude. A close friend of Carlyle's, an experienced colonial observer, and a classical scholar of considerable repute, Froude visited the West Indies in 1887 with the view to writing a rousing defense of British colonial retention. Basing his arguments on the Carlylean presumption that West Indians are inherently incapable of exercising self-government because little more intelligent than animals,[4] Froude's *The English in the West Indies* (1887) served as the rallying cry for the English *ancien* colonial *régime* (James 1968).

Mill's Racial Rule

It was the call to reinstitute slavery headed by Carlyle to which Mill principally objected in his response. This perhaps is predictable, given Mill's longstanding and well-known commitment to abolition. Mill's critical concern with Carlyle's racist sentiment was only secondary

63

and much more understated. Moreover, not only did Mill not object to colonial domination, he insisted upon it albeit in "benevolent" form. After all, Mill worked for the better part of his working life administering English colonialism.

Thus Mill opened his letter to the editor of *Fraser's* by emphasizing that abolition was "the best and greatest achievement yet performed by mankind" in "[t]he history of human improvement" (August 1971: 38–9). Slavery was wrong for Mill on utilitarian grounds in that it produced much more pain than would liberty and equal opportunity, and it is for this reason that Mill considered slavery inherently inhumane (August 1971: 48–9), a view derided by Carlyle under the mocking title of the "Universal Abolition of Pain Association" (August 1971: 2).

In contrast to Carlyle's critique of laissez-faire capitalism, Mill offered a defense of laissez-faire principles as embodying economic freedom and underpinning a liberal social order. Mill however qualified these laissez-faire principles by insisting that all people, black and white, enjoy equal opportunity: "[Carlyle] . . . will make them work for certain whites, those whites not working at all . . . Does he mean that all persons ought to earn their living? But some earn their living by doing nothing, and some by doing mischief" (August 1971: 42–3). Mill continued:

> let the whole produce belong to those who do the work which produces it. We would not have black labourers [in the West Indies] compelled to grow spices which they do not want, and white proprietors who do not work at all exchanging the spices for houses in Belgrave Square [a London residential neighborhood inhabited by aristocracy and haute bourgeoisie] . . . *Let them have exactly the same share in what they produce that they have in the work.* If they do not like this, let them remain as they are, so long as they . . . make the best of supply and demand. (August 1971: 44–5, my emphases)

Mill's quiet qualification of class by race – black laborers, white proprietors – was tied to his denial that every difference among human beings is inherent, a "vulgar error" he rightly imputed to Carlyle (August 1971: 46).

In objecting to Carlyle's racist hierarchical naturalism, however, Mill inscribed in its place, and in the name of laissez-faire and equal opportunity, an imputation of the historical inferiority of blacks. Mill implied that this assumption of inferiority, because historically produced and contingent, was not always the case (Egyptians influenced Greeks) and might one day be overcome. Yet Mill's superficial bow to what has become an Afrocentric cornerstone barely hid beneath the surface the polite racism of his European-elevated history. Contingent racism is still a form of racism – not so bald, not so vituperative, and polite perhaps, but condescending nevertheless even as it is committed to equal opportunity. Equal opportunity among those with the unfair, historically produced inequities of the colonial condition will simply reproduce those inequities, if not expand them, as the experience especially of African Americans will attest.

The very title of his response to Carlyle – "The Negro Question" – indicates Mill's presumption that (to use Du Bois's terms) blacks are a problem to be solved by utilitarian application. Mill pointedly was not committed to arguing thus that people of African descent in the New World faced problems – least of all that those problems were imposed by their masters – and that such problems might best be resolved through the utility calculus. This interpretation is borne out by placing Mill's response to Carlyle in the context of the former's views on development, modernization, representative rule, and race. These were views Mill developed most fully in terms of India and his experience in the English East Indies Company but which he generalized to Africa and the West Indies also. So to confirm that these premises indeed underpin Mill's liberal egalitarianism it is necessary to engage his views on the colonies.

Mill worked as an examiner for the English East Indies Company from 1823 until 1856 and then, like his father, as chief examiner until his retirement to politics in 1858. Thus he was central in and ultimately responsible for all bureaucratic correspondence between the British government and its colonial representation in India. (Mill was involved in writing 1,700 official letters to India over this period.) It was in the context of India (and the "Asiatic" countries more generally), then, that he worked out his views on colonial intervention in those "underdeveloped" countries. Like Marx and Tocqueville at roughly the same time, Mill considered such societies stagnant and inhibiting of progress, and he generalized from this context to other areas.

In *The Principles of Political Economy*, Mill wrote that "Colonization is the best affair of business, in which the capital of an old and wealthy country can engage." It would do so in order to establish first, a better government: more complete security of property; moderate taxes, and freedom from arbitrary exaction under the name of taxes; a more permanent and more advantageous tenure of land, securing to the cultivator as far as possible the undivided benefits of industry, skill, and economy he may exert. Secondly, improvement of the public intelligence: the decay of usages or superstitions which interfere with the effective employment of industry; and the growth of mental activity, making the people alive to new objects of desire. Thirdly, the introduction of foreign arts, which raise the returns derivable from additional capital, to a rate corresponding to the low strength of the desire of accumulation: and the importation of foreign capital, which renders the increase of production no longer exclusively dependent on the thrift or providence of the inhabitants themselves, while it places before them a stimulating example, and by instilling new ideas and breaking the chains of habit, if not by improving the actual condition of the population, tends to create in them new wants, increased ambition, and greater thought for the future.

Mill picks out for application of these principles India, Russia, Turkey, Spain, and Ireland. The West Indies and African countries were not recognized as having yet remotely in sight the capacity for self-development.

The difference between a developed and undeveloped country, between those more or less civilized, was defined by Mill in terms of the country's capacity to enable and promote representative self-government and individual self-development. In short, in terms of its capacity for autonomy and good government. "Good government" would enable a society, as Mill once said of himself, "to effect the greatest amount of good compatible with . . . opportunities" with a view to maximizing wellbeing and so happiness. Mill attributed the success of such promotion fundamentally to economic development that apparently would enable opportunities.

Civilized countries like Britain, on Mill's reading, limited government intervention in individuals' lives; those less civilized he thought should be ruled by those more so with the view to promoting their capacity for self-development. Liberal individualization was consonant with economic, political, and cultural modernization. This would require greater restriction in the ruled country on people's freedoms and so more government regulation, a view shared explicitly by Tocqueville in the case of French colonies (Tocqueville 1843: 105; Todorov 1993: 193). Mill considered progress a function of education and enlightened institutions but also of people of "similar civilization to the ruling country," of Britain's "own blood and language." The latter – Mill, in a state of classic English self-denial, mentions Australia and Canada – were "capable of, and ripe for, representative government." India, by contrast, was far from it, for India had stagnated for many centuries under the sway of "Oriental despotism." In India's case, and even more perpetually in the case of the West Indies and African colonies, "benevolent despotism" – a paternalistic "government of guidance" imposed by more advanced Europeans – was the rational order of the day. Bhikhu Parekh (1994: 89) usefully suggests that, for the order of Mill's thought, India in particular and the East in general serve in much the way "the state of nature" did for contract theorists. This is a point one could usefully generalize for nineteenth-century racial historicists like Marx, Tocqueville, and Comte also.

For Mill, thus, the justification of colonization was to be measured according to its aid in the progress of the colonized, its education of superstitious colonial subjects in the virtues of reason, and the generation of new markets for capital accumulation through the fashioning of desires. The purpose of education was to inform: both to provide the informational basis to make rational decisions and to structure the values framing practical reason in ways conducive to the colonial ends Mill deemed desirable (cf. Koundoura 1998: 74–6). Mill considered progress to consist in being socialized in the values of liberal modernity, that is, in the sort of social, political, economic, cultural, and legal commitments best represented by the British example. As a colonized country exemplified such progress, the colonizing country progressively would give way to the colonized's self-governance.

This differs somewhat in its rationalization, though not in its outcome and effects, from the position of Lord Acton, Mill's other political critic. Acton held that "those states are substantially the most perfect which, like the British and Austrian empires, include various distinct nationalities without oppressing them. Inferior races," he insisted, "are raised by living in political union with races intellectually superior" and "exhausted and decaying nations are revived by the contact of a younger vitality" (Acton 1862/1996: 31). Lord Acton's "benevolent despotism," like Mill's in this respect, amounts to a colonialism with a human face. The world was to be directed by the most developed and capable nations whose self-interests nevertheless (in Mill's but emphatically not in Acton's case) would be mitigated and mediated by the force of utilitarian reason. Mill insisted that states be isomorphically identified with a singular nationality (Mill 1861: 298). Acton, it is true, strenuously objected to this "modern tendency to found the state" upon a "monistic idea" like "the greatest happiness of the greatest number," insisting that the identification of states with singular national configurations would "destroy limited government and the pluralistic bases of true liberty" (Acton 1862/1996: 28). Nevertheless, it is evident that for all the critical distance Acton takes from Mill he shares with him a commitment to the new racial historicism.

Mill was blind to the internal tensions in his indices of progress. The ideal conditions for the generation of new markets and the fashioning of new desires for the sake of capital accumulation, we have at least two centuries of evidence to suggest, are likely inconsistent with genuine self-determination, autonomy, and self-governance. Colonization is straightforwardly consistent with developing new markets and desires – it is after all a central part of the historical *raison d'être* for colonialism – in a way in which it is historically, if not conceptually, at odds with self-determination. Mill thought different socioeconomic imperatives face the "advanced" and "backward" nations: improved distribution of goods (not wealth) for the "advanced," better conditions of production for the "backward countries." So before worrying about distribution of goods among the people of the "backward countries," he considered improving production paramount, and in any case (re)distribution of wealth was never an issue.

Mill's "benevolent despotism," relatively benign and masked by humane application perhaps, nevertheless sought

> to make provision in the constitution of the Government itself, for compelling those who have the governing power, to listen to and take into consideration the opinions of persons who from their position and their previous life, have made a study of Indian subjects, and acquired experience in them.

Thus Mill recognized the relation between knowledge and power, specialized information and administration, as the underlying imperative of colonial governmentality. Knowledge of the Native was instrumental to establishing the conditions for developing the colonies in a way they would continue to serve the interests of the colonial power.

It may seem curious that Mill implied that the Natives themselves would not be consulted in accumulating knowledge about local colonial conditions, for he did insist that qualified Natives be appointed to all administrative and governmental positions "for which they are fit," though without "appointing them to the regular service." Mill's utilitarian reason for this restriction was that Natives were not to be "considered for the highest service" for "if their promotion stopped short while that of others went on, it would be more invidious than keeping them out altogether." And as Europeans, rationally superior, were to be the appeal of last resort, Natives' ascension was naturally delimited. James Mill (John Stuart's demanding father) seemed to project onto the Natives of the colonies the same utilitarian paternalism with which he treated his son, and John Stuart never did manage to shake this paternal(istic) framing.

However, even in their administrative advance, the Natives (here Indian) were to be "Indian in blood and colour, but English in tastes, in opinions, in morals and in intellect." Blood may run thicker than water, but it was to be diluted by a cultural solution. Cultural colonialism mediates racial inferiority, culture replacing biology as the touchstone of racial definition. Accordingly, English was to be the language of administration, the local vernacular to be used only to convey rules and regulations to the local population. Thus, far from "creating the conditions for the withering away of their rule," Mill (even if inadvertently) was instrumental in identifying and administering the sort of conditions that would perpetuate indirect rule, Lugardian (post)colonial control from afar without the attendant costs.

Mill's argument for "benevolent despotism" failed to appreciate that neither colonialism nor despotism is ever benevolent. Benevolence here is the commitment to seek the happiness of others. But the mission of colonialism is exploitation and domination of the colonized generally, and Europeanization at least of those among the colonized whose class position makes it possible economically and educationally. And the mandate of despotism, its conceptual logic, is to assume (almost) absolute power to achieve the ruler's self-interested ends. Thus colonial despotism could achieve happiness of colonized others only by imposing the measure of Europeanized marks of happiness upon the other, which is to say, to force the other to be less so. Mill's argument necessarily assumed superiority of the despotic, benevolent or not; it presupposed that the mark of progress is (to be) defined by those taking themselves to be superior. And it presumes that the ruled will want to be like the rulers even as the former lack the cultural capital (almost ever?) quite to rise to the task. Mill's ambivalence over inherent inferiority of "native Negroes," even as he marked the transformation in the terms of racial definition historically from the inescapable determinism of blood and brain size to the marginally escapable reach of cultural determination and historical development, has resonated to this day in the liberal ambivalence regarding racial matters.

Liberalism's racially mediated meliorism and commitment to a moral progressivism, as much evident in Lord Acton or Tocqueville as in Mill, translates into an undying optimism that its racist history will be progressively overcome, giving way ultimately to a standard of non-racialism, to contemporary colorblindness. Colonialism, as Todorov concludes in Tocqueville's case but this applies equally to Mill, "is merely the international expansion of [their] liberalism" (Todorov 1993: 202). Yet this standard non-racialism (sic) is imposed upon the body politic at the cost of the self-defined subjectivity of the traditionally dominated. Liberalism's response to matters of race in the face of the fact that race matters amounts to denying or ignoring race, paternalistically effacing a self-determined social subjectivity from those who would define themselves thus without imposing it on others.

This erasure in the name of non-racialism rubs out at once the history of racist invisibility, domination, and exploitation, replacing the memory of an infantilized past with the denial of responsibility for radically unequal and only superficially deracialized presents. Racelessness is the legacy. Divested of a historically located responsibility, the relatively powerful in the society alongside and indeed through state rule are readily able to reinstate the invisibility of the subject positions of the presently marginalized: Savages become the permanently unemployable, the uncivilized become crackheads, the lumpenproletariat the underclass. Distressed Needlewomen become sweated labor, poor Irish peasants turn into distressed defaulting family farmers, and, well, "niggers" become "Negroes" or blacks scarcely disguised beneath the seemingly benign nomenclature. For every Mill or Acton of yesteryear today there is a William Bennett or a Gary Becker, a Shelby Steele or Thomas Sowell, and for every Carlyle or Froude a Dinesh D'Souza or Charles Murray. I return to elaborate this logic of racelessness in chapter 8.

Suffice it to point out here that Carlylean commitments, the set of naturalistic presumptions and projections about Africans and the African diaspora advanced in support of extending slave-based colonialism throughout Africa and the West Indies, received their most complete critique at the hands of a Trinidadian intellectual. John Jacob Thomas was a noted Trinidadian philologist, teacher, and educational administrator who wrote a trenchant and comprehensive refutation of James Froude's history of *The English in the West Indies*. As C. L. R. James is quick to note (James 1968), Thomas's response is a classic example of intellectual resistance: the quality and analytic rigor of its critique offer a much more direct refutation of Froude's Carlylean naturalism than Mill is able to conjure. Ironically entitled *Froudacity: West Indian Fables*, Thomas contrasts his own analytic rigor with Froude's "extravagance and self-abandonment whenever he brings an object of his arbitrary likes or dislikes under discussion," most notably in discussing "Negroes" (Thomas 1889/1968: 63–4). Thomas repeatedly draws attention to Froude's complete absence of historical method and lack of empirical evidence in support of his most demeaning observations. Pointing out in contrast to Froude's implicit degenerationism that whites newly arrived in the West Indies often had married local blacks to advance the former's local influence, Thomas observes with a wry humor that "the blending of the races is not a burning question," that the social implications of miscegenation could be worked out easily enough if left unperturbed by racist consideration. The esteemed Professor Froude, "unreflective spokesman that he is of British colonialism," Thomas concludes, not only has "forgotten nothing, but . . . learnt nothing also" (Thomas 1889/1968: 69–70, 72). As James reminds us, Thomas offers as fine an example as one could conjure of the empire writing back, the repressed returning to haunt the big house.

Between Mill's "Negro" and Carlyle's "Nigger," then, lies the common thread of racist presumption and projection, bald and vicious, on the one hand, polite and effete, on the other, but both nevertheless insidious and odious. Better in utilitarian terms to have a Mill or Tocqueville, perhaps, for at least one gets the sense that it is possible to enlighten and thus transform such a person. That after all is the premise, and the promise, of liberalism's rule. With a Carlyle one knows clearly and openly what resistance to racisms is up against, what it has to confront and in some circumstances to avoid; with a

71

Mill, a promoter of abolition is at once a barrier to it. This exchange between two leading English public intellectuals of their day, and then later between the haughty Oxford Professor of Modern History and a "mere" Trinidadian school teacher, reveal in the final analysis, then, that structural and discursive transformations necessary for resisting racisms are deeply bound to and by subjective expression. Ultimately it makes abundantly apparent that a combined commitment to changing minds and to changing conditions is crucial. An emphasis on attitudinal change alone is tantamount to "the neutrality" of a regressive tax on the racially defined poor; structural change absent a transformation in consciousness, on the other hand, is likely to leave even those economically equal socially segregated (Goldberg 1998). The state is implicated in any comprehensive consideration of these questions because the modern state has always been implicated more or less closely in the material and discursive conditions of their formulation.

It should be clear from this line of analysis that the conflation of reasoning about the state in political theory with the reasoning of the state – those reasons the state mandates as its governmental authorization, by, with, and in its name – mutually reinforces racially factored inscription and a pattern of racist exclusion. It is this doubling – writing about, and writing about the writing of, racially configured, racially reproductive and racist states in their governmentality – that I now turn to pursue and elaborate.

NOTES

1 August includes in his little volume an editorial in a London newspaper of the day, *The Inquirer*, protesting Carlyle's claims.

2 Bhikhu Parekh acknowledges that Mill rested his claim to European superiority on a "non-biological explanation," on grounds of a "quasi-historicist utilitarianism" (Parekh 1994: 88, 93). It might also be noted that Mill's crediting of Egyptian influence on Hellenism may have been spawned by the likes of David Walker's *Appeal in Four Articles*, first published in 1830, and Maria Stewart's "Address at the African Masonic Hall" in 1833.

3 This is Fanon's cutting characterization in *Black Skin, White Masks* (1968: 79).

4 "There was a small black boy among us, evidently of pure blood, for his hair was wool and his color black as ink. His parents must have been

well-to-do, for the boy had been to Europe to be educated. The officers on board and some of the ladies played with him as they would with a monkey. He had little more sense than a monkey, perhaps less, and the gestures of him grinning behind gratings and perching out his long thin arms between the bars were curiously suggestive of the original from whom we are told now that all of us came . . . he could not be made into a white, and this I found afterwards was the invariable and dangerous consequence whenever a superior negro contrived to raise himself." Froude's words are quoted in the remarkable refutation by the Trinidadian intellectual, John Jacob Thomas, in 1889, *Froudacity* (Thomas 1889/1968: 66–7). I am grateful to Tony Bogues for bringing Thomas's exemplary critique to my attention, and for so generously making the text available to me.

4

RACIAL RULE

On the periphery . . . people . . . learned quickly enough that
Progress in the abstract meant domination in the concrete . . .
                                        Nairn (1977: 335)

Naturalism and Historicism

The two traditions I have identified in conceiving and writing about
racial states, while conceptually distinct and seemingly mutually exclusive, coexist historically. The naturalist conception, the claim of inherent racial inferiority, dominated from the seventeenth well into the
nineteenth century; the historicist or progressivist commitment concerning itself with contrasting claims of historical immaturity displaced
the dominance of naturalism in the second half of the nineteenth
century but far from eclipsed it. It is revealing that the rise of what I
am calling the historicist conception, for those societies in which it
actually attained prominence, is more evident in the administrative
expression of colonial rule than in popular culture or even in prevailing
intellectual commitments. Popular culture and intellectual fashion came
to embrace racial historicism, if at all, more slowly, begrudgingly,
ambivalently. Indeed, one could say that each tradition has licensed
various embodiments and expressions throughout the twentieth century
– in fact, as I have hinted, continues to – and in that sense each is
internally diverse. It is too easy to think that greater familiarity of
those of European descent with those who are not would prompt the
shift from naturalism to historicism, for such growing familiarity just
as easily promoted contemptuous dismissive segregationist sentiments
as progressivist sensibilities or egalitarian commitments.

74

These two traditions of racial conception are linked to two broader traditions of state formation, namely, to coercion and capital-based states. Particular states have emerged and matured out of specific histories that emphasized capital accumulation or coercion as the principal basis of state creation, expansion, and structure. As Tilly (1994: 8) argues, cities have tended to be containers of capital, states cells of coercive power like the military and later the police. By extension, I want to suggest that those states in Europe and their satellites that tended to emphasize coercion in their emergence, national unification, and elaboration – Germany under the diplomatic direction of Bismarck's iron fist, for instance (Breuilly 1992), and later apartheid South Africa – were likely to have been prone to a naturalist conception of racial formation, of racial superiority and inferiority. Here racial rule was considered imperative, if not the product of a Divine hand then the logic of Nature. The racially dominant were seen to set laws, impose order, and maintain control because destined by their blood or genes to do so. Dilution of their blood or genes was considered at once transgression of nature, with dire consequences. It follows that colonial rule, (imperial or self-determining) expansion, governmental imposition, and state control might be motivated as manifest destiny or natural law and effected principally at the crack of the whip, the point of the sword, or the barrel of the gun.

By contrast, those states growing out of financial centers and founded predominantly on capital formation and circulation – England, for example, or France – tended in the history of their development to have inscribed in their racial administration, implicitly or explicitly, a historicist or progressivist set of presumptions. Racial rule here was seen as the outcome of history, domination ordained by the hidden hand of historical development, the "fact" of historically produced superiority. Likewise, their colonial legacy would tend to be predicated on developmentalist assumptions, committed at least on the face through a long slow process of "progressive development and maturation" to colonial self-rule.

These links, it must be stressed, are a matter of emphasis and nuance. So I am not suggesting that there were not those in coercive-based states committed to racial historicism, or those in capital-directed states rationalizing claims to superiority and practices of subjugation on naturalist grounds, just as there were resistant voices to both in either state form. But again there is no natural relation between the force or vehemence of resistance and forms of racial disposition. A naturalist might just as well dismiss intellectual contributions by those regarded racially inferior as "mimicry of the parrot"[1] and physical resistance as the "restlessness of the natives." And they might equally respond with vehement repression as with an attitudinal shift to historicism. The progressivist, in turn, might respond to resistance with further liberalizing reforms or with an inclination to naturalist rationalizations for more repressive subjugation, an ambivalence already reflected in the conceptual ambiguity of "progressivism."

In similar vein, those committed to naturalist principles on some issues or for some racially conceived groups might be found to express themselves in historicist terms on other issues or regarding different groups. So, for example, in 1857 Chief Justice Taney of the US Supreme Court declared in his majority opinion in *Dred Scott* that "it has been found necessary, for their sake as well as our own, to regard [American Indians] as in a state of pupilage." Because he saw them effectively as members of foreign nations, he claimed American Indians could acquire United States citizenship. Blacks, Taney argued by contrast,

> had for more than a century before been regarded as beings of an inferior order, and altogether unfit to associate with the white race, either in social or political relations; and so far inferior they had no rights which the white man was bound to respect; and that the negro might justly and lawfully be reduced to slavery for his benefit.

Taney concluded that black people were excluded intentionally from being considered citizens under the US Constitution, unprotected by constitutional rights, immunities, and privileges (*Dred Scott* 1857: 403–7; Bell 1992: 20ff.). From the 1880s until at least the 1930s, not unrelatedly, American Indians were regarded in the US as assimilable while people of African descent were considered segregable because the two groups were seen to occupy different rankings on prevailing racial hierarchies. The former were deemed open to evolutionary progress, of being whitened precisely, in the way the latter prevailingly were not.

The distinction between naturalism and historicist progressivism likewise accounts, at least in part, for the vacillation regarding slavery and social integration by US civic and political leaders like Jefferson and Lincoln. Lincoln's is a case of espousing initially a naturalist commitment (inherent inferiority) and acting on (later expressing also) historicist assumptions precisely in the name of a racial political progressivism. Lincoln's debates with Stephen Douglas in 1858 make clear his sense of "Negro" inferiority.[2] But his commitment to expatriation of blacks to Liberia, in keeping with the prevailing emigrationism of the day, at least implicitly acknowledged blacks' capacity for self-governance.[3]

Thus, in drawing the distinction between racist naturalism and historicism I am mapping dominant trends preparatory to delineating different forms of racial rule in the contrasting styles of state formation. The naturalist tradition is most evident in the intellectual trajectory regarding racial studies running from pre-Adamism through polygenism to eugenicism and the likes of *The Bell Curve*. It informs state formation in the "cruelty" of Spanish colonial rule even as the Spanish crown struggled in the sixteenth century with establishing laws recognizing the "equality" of colonial subjects (Merivale 1841/ 1928: 3–4). "The great principle of the Spanish law respecting the Indians," writes Herman Merivale in his extraordinarily revealing lectures on colonization in the early 1840s, "was that of preserving them in a state of *perpetual minority*" (1841/1928: 6, emphasis in original). Similarly, Jefferson notoriously insisted that "the difference [between black and white] is *fixed in nature*," indeed, that

> the blacks . . . are inferior to the whites in the endowments both of body and mind. . . . The [Roman] slave, when made free, might mix with, without staining the blood of his master. But with us [Americans], [w]hen freed, [the black slave] is to be removed beyond the reach of mixture. (Jefferson 1781/1955, my emphasis)

What makes Jefferson's insistence more troubling than those of most contemporary or later racial scientists is precisely that he stood in a position to act on it politically. Jefferson could invoke the state apparatus at his disposal to effect his proto-segregationist imperative even though in fact he proved reluctant to do so (cf. Appiah, in Appiah and Gutmann 1996: 42–7).

In terms of state expression, then, the naturalist tradition is exemplified in the extremity of early Spanish expansion in the fifteenth and sixteenth centuries (Mariscal 1998: 8); in seventeenth-century English colonization of the Irish (Canny 1973; Lloyd 1999); in the vicious violence of Belgian colonization of the Congo, most notably under Leopold II; in Nazi apocalyptic megalomania; in slavery, and the Jim Crow segregationist South; as well as in respect of apartheid South Africa. In a speech in 1932 Hitler, for one, foamed forth that the "economically privileged supremacy of the white race over the rest of the world" can be understood only on the basis of

> a political concept of supremacy which has been peculiar to the white race as a *natural phenomenon* for many centuries . . . The settlement of the North American continent was . . . a consequence not of any higher claim in a democratic or international sense, but rather of a consciousness of what is right which had its sole roots in the conviction of superiority and thus the right of the white race. (Hitler 1990: 96, my emphasis)

In like fashion, a Southern white leader could claim more or less publicly unchallenged at the height of imposed segregationism that

> [t]he Negro's skull is thicker, his brain is smaller than the white man's. . . . This accounts for the fact that while Negro children at school often compare favorably with whites, adults do not.

And a newspaper editorial in Maryland at the time insisted that black people develop

> a greater respect for toil – manual toil. . . . What the negro needs is to be taught and shown that labor is his salvation – not books. The state appropriation is intended to encourage that teaching. (Both quotes in Litwack 1998: 102–3)

These were claims to be echoed a half-century later by H. F. Verwoerd, principal architect of explicit apartheid. As Minister of Bantu Affairs in the South African government, Verwoerd infamously asserted in 1952 that blacks should not expect to be educated for positions they would have no hope of occupying.[4] We should note in these remarks the fear of black capability, in South Africa as in the American South, hidden just beneath the (imposed) surface presumption of inherent intellectual inferiority. Here we find an acknowledgment that collapses the productivity of discursive force with ex post facto ideological rationalization characteristic of racist naturalism.

The new historicism, as we have seen by contrast in the liberalizing hands of John Locke and John Stuart Mill and the developmentalism of Comte and Marx, marks British rule in India and Egypt. The model, incipient in the claims of Las Casas about the convertibility of indigenous Indians in the sixteenth century, fueled the commitments of British and French abolitionists in the late eighteenth and nineteenth centuries. But it also underlay French assumptions about assimilation or association in governing its colonies in Southeast Asia and Africa (cf. Lorcin 1999), the explicit "developmentalism" of British colonial policy from the 1940s on, as well as the ethno-immigrant model of race relations in the US associated above all with Robert Park and later Gunnar Myrdal's *An American Dilemma* (cf. Omi and Winant 1986: 16–24). And racial historicism similarly informs contemporary neoconservative commitments to racelessness, in the US, South Africa, Britain, and Europe, as I argue in chapter 8.

It should not be thought, nevertheless, that I am claiming that the historicist is relatively more benign (because somehow more "progressive") than a naturalist mode of racial governance. Naturalist forms, it is true, tended to be more viscerally vicious and cruel, historicist ones more paternalistic. But by the same token the naturalist tended to be bald, bold, and direct concerning racist presumption and commitment, the historicist ambiguous, ambivalent, indeed, hypocritical. With the naturalist accordingly the battle lines could be more directly drawn, the historicist tending to politeness, coded significance (the very implications of "progress" tending to hide assumptions about inferiority), and tolerance as veils for continued invocation of racial power. But as with all tendencies, these are trends only rather than hard and fast rules.

Merivale's comprehensive lectures on colonialism were delivered between 1839 and 1841 at the University of Oxford, academic center for preparing candidates for British colonial administration. Contrasting his own brand of incipient racial progressivism with the naturalism of the Spanish, Merivale generalized one anonymous colonial observer's conclusion concerning "the case of Australian Aborigines" to the effect that "native peoples" are as "apt and intelligent as any other race of men I am acquainted with: they are subject to like affections, passions and appetites as other men." As soon as they are declared British subjects, Merivale's observer continued, they should learn "that the British laws are to supersede their own" (Merivale

1841/1928: 500–1). Such rules must apply, as Merivale insisted citing the support also of Sir George Grey, colonial administrator in Australia and the Cape of Good Hope, both to

> violations of the eternal and universal laws of morality: such as cannibalism, human sacrifice and infanticide [but also] to customs less horrible, yet, from the greater frequency of their operation, perhaps still more injurious and incompatible with civilization: such as the violent abuse of the authority of husbands over wives, and barbarous ill-usage of the weaker sex in general, and some of the features of slavery among [the colonized themselves], if not the practice itself. (Merivale 1841/ 1928: 502)

Protect them from themselves, by making them other than what they currently are, by undoing their uncivilized conditions.

Amalgamation and Assimilation

That "natives' uncivilized conditions" can be undone entails that such conditions are not considered inherent but the product of custom, climate, and habit. "[N]ative races," Merivale emphasized, "must in every instance either perish, or be *amalgamated* with the general population of their country. By amalgamation" he intended "the union of natives with settlers in the same community, as master and servant, as fellow-laborers, as fellow-citizens, and, if possible, as connected by intermarriage." Every "native," he stressed, should potentially be regarded as a citizen at the earliest moment possible (Merivale 1841/ 1928: 510–11, my emphasis). Merivale later summarized the range of empirical documentation he assumed available at the time evidencing "improvement" of "the inferior races" – Africans, American Indians, South Sea natives, Australian Aborigines – once influenced by their European "superiors" (Merivale 1841/1928: 549–53).

Colonization, astonishingly in this historicizing view, was sought to provide the virtue of protecting colonized women from the savagery of colonized men. This twist is replete with Anglicized irony. Racist protection against sexual invasion usually has assumed the fashion of white men claiming to protect white women against the projection of voracious sexual appetites of black men. It has hidden behind this presumption the sexual proclivities of white men's desire satisfied by the rape of black women, real and fantasized. Merivale's enjoinder to racial upliftment effected by means of "amalgamation" was evidently to be pursued through white men marrying black women. Intermarriage, he apparently thought, would produce racial upliftment, biologically as much as spiritually and culturally, through generational enhancement. Far from being the "predestined murderers" of the colonized, he concluded that colonizing whites "are called to assume ... [the latters'] preservers" (Merivale 1841/1928: 549). Here the polite Victorian hope of racial improvement sprang eternal through the gendered domination of racial intermarriage and interracial offspring. Haym remarks, not unrelatedly, that sexual interaction was as important to the effective running and extension of empire as the more obvious concerns of government and commerce. "In the erotic field, as in administration and commerce, some degree of 'collaboration' from the indigenous communities was helpful to the maintenance of imperial systems" (Haym 1991: 2). The euphemism notwithstanding, sexual domination – homo- as much as heterosexual, as Haym reveals – has proved a central practice if not condition of racial rule.

Merivale added another liberalizing advantage of the intermarrying "mixture of blood," namely, a "considerable check on the prejudices of colour ... for which there can be no substantial reason where slavery does not exist" (Merivale 1841/1928: 538). This is all the more curious in light of Merivale's ready admission of the destructive force of "our profligacy, our fraud, our extinction, our invasions, the terror and the hatred which Europeans excite at almost every point of the earth where they are brought into contact with unsubdued races of inferior civilization" (Merivale 1841/1928: 561). It is useful to see Merivale, accordingly, as representing the bridging shift from naturalist to historicist presumptions, adding social and cultural influences of amalgamation to the biological, and without reducing the former to the determination of the latter.[5]

All this may seem a far cry perhaps from the deadly presumptions of Leopold's Congo or Hitler's Reich, of subjection in the segregationist South or apartheid South Africa. What is evident here, it must be stressed however, is not that the historicist assumptions are somehow more appealing than or morally superior to the naturalist's, more benign because less physically vicious. As the tone of Merivale's insistence suggests, historicists have been moved to make such a claim in the name of a variety of "racial realism." "Amalgamation," as the later assimilationist experience of American Indians from the 1880s on revealed rather tellingly, could be as devastatingly destructive of a people, as violative of forms and conditions of social being, as any extremes of physical violence.

"[A]malgamation, by some means or other, is the only possible Euthanasia of savage communities," concluded Merivale in an astounding turn of phrase. "Amalgamate, or perish" is but one historical remove from "perish through amalgamation." And that step is all but explicit in the exhortation to euthanasia. The paranoias of degeneration had not quite fully taken hold so that intermarriage could yet be conceived as a mode of racial upliftment, as much physical as cultural, biological as civilizational, the one in fact not so distant from the other; 1840, it seems, is not all that far in some respects from 1990.[6]

The policy of *assimilation* clearly rests on historicist grounds, and it rules by historicist design. Assimilation emerged in the 1880s to dominate French colonial policy and US "internal colonialism" regarding Native Americans as well as Canadian policy concerning First Peoples. French or Anglo "civilization," as the case may be, "represented the apex of development." Peoples "less fortunate" than Europeans should be provided the "universally applicable principles" of "colonial development and good government" (Lee 1967). "Everywhere," writes Roberts of French assimilationist policy, "political development was to be as far as possible Europeanization." And yet "[a] good law," Condorcet insisted, "is good for all men, just as a sound logical proposition is sound everywhere" (Roberts 1929: 100ff.). Colonial assimilationists were confident of their possession of universally just laws, building the policy on the assumption that natives should become civilized through their acquisition of the rule of law and the custom of the colonizers, by ceasing, that is, to be native. Education was the principal mode. The first act of French colonizers like Galleni once they had established themselves in a colony was to found a school, free to natives, conducted solely in French and emphasizing French culture, history, values, habits. Local elites were created and elevated, for the dual purpose of mediating French culture to the mass of the local population and assisting in the running of local government. The children of the elite were sent to university in France, in strict proportion to the number of jobs available to them in the colony, so as not to foment rebellion on the part of a local "literate class" with too much time on their hands (Crocker 1947: 52–3). Indeed, it turned out to be just this literate class of largely European-educated middle-class elites that provided the intellectual inspiration for the nationalist anti-colonial movements at the middle of the twentieth century.

Similarly, US officials, most notably between the 1880s and 1930s, tore American Indian children from their rural reservation environments where they were likely to learn indigenous custom and rebellious habits, shipping them off over the plaintive and painful protests of their parents for adoption by white families and assimilation into white schools.[7] Stripped of family and culture, in a sense deracialized, they could be recreated, racially reconfigured – as white. Out of indigenous context not only did they look white but they were "reinvented" as white in terms of custom, habit, culture, practice. It could be said that official American disposition towards "the racial question" from the later 1880s to the aftermath of World War II was a mix of naturalist assumptions concerning "negro" segregation and historicist commitments concerning Indian assimilation.

These examples suggest a distinction in colonial disposition also regarding governance of the racially different. The French were disposed to treat many of their colonies effectively as provinces or *départements* of France, worldly extensions of the body politic. The British saw their own colonial policy evolve to embrace developmentalism, a concern with the economically and educationally determined development of the colonized society to ultimate self-sufficiency and self-rule. Even the troubled, ambiguous, and ambivalent history of US policy regarding indigenous populations can be read through the struggle over sovereignty.

This is not to deny or underrepresent the force of local resistance in prompting the demise or shift in the scope or forms of racial rule. Such transformations in no way would have been initiated or have struck so deep in the absence of the racially subjugated and repressed striking back. Power is never ceded or shifted without resistance, in the limit case even where the repression is internalized. I mean only to emphasize that all of the dominant and dominating political projects listed here are underpinned by or represent or reflect historicist assumptions, commitment to which was more or less explicit and conscious. Those modes of racially inscribed governance tied to naturalist commitments, by contrast, were moved to treat the societies considered racially inferior either as free space for the (profit-)taking – as space needing to be cleared of the supposedly inferior inhabitants, as sources simply of wealth provision directly as a consequence of raw material or mineral provision – or indirectly due to (artificially) depressed labor costs. As a result, rule was to be imposed directly just as the space of the racially distinct and differentiated was to be kept at a distance, to be maintained as lands or spaces apart.

The claim to universal principles as ideals to be pursued or emulated that underlay both progressivist racial historicism and naturalism hides from view the fact that, touched by Africa or Asia, South America or the South Pacific, Europe could never be the same again. This was especially so in the historicist case, though the internalization of naturalist-provoked violence had telling effects too. In seeking to assimilate Africans and Asians, indigenous Indios and Pacific Islanders – economically and culturally, religiously and intellectually, socially and politically – Europeans would be forever transformed. Little did the English, French, or Dutch, in (former) colonies as in their metropolitan "homes," realize how profoundly Empire would alter them, what libidinal forces it would loosen and license, what consumptive desires it would liberate, what fashion – clothing and jewelry, art and body art, music and literature, food and drink – it would spawn, what habits of the heart as much as heartless darkness it would engender, what modes of spirituality, religiosity and flights of fancy it would suggest. Seeking to impose values and practices upon the colonized from without, from social contexts and political arrangements radically different, European colonizers failed to understand how deeply altered they would be whether at close hand or from the "safe" distance of European centers.

It follows that the naturalist and historicist traditions of racist commitment always contained the seeds, the incipient presumption, of each other. Only the historicist window would allow (for) such provocative developmentalist possibilities, but no sooner allowed, acknowledged, and embraced than the naturalist warnings echoed through European consciousness and culture. "Look, Mama, a Negro." Dare not touch. Fear of contamination, the terrordome of a "black/ brown/red/yellow" world. And no sooner touched by the whip of naturalism than the plaintive dignity of slave songs and narratives, the pull of native wealth, the tastes, tales, and fictions, the lure of silks and spices, landscapes and spaces – in short, the irrepressibility of forbidden fantasies and practices – raised the teleological possibility of humanist historicity. Dance with the orangutan and an orangutan one degenerately just might become. So human hope for the orang-utan, at least developmentally, progressively, there must be.

Naturalizing Order, Historicizing Governance

The differences between the naturalist and historicist traditions, how-ever, are clearly revealed in their respective considerations regarding both miscegenation and access of those not completely of European descent to offices of governmental power. Racial naturalists almost always have been committed to anti-miscegenation laws. For the natur-alist, miscegenation prompts the fear of degeneracy or cultural and physical pollution, the bringing down of the superior by socializing with the inferior. Rape of black women by white men, nevertheless, if not formally condoned, was more widely engaged than acknow-ledged. It obviously effected for white men release of sexual frustra-tion, the raw expression of libido or power, or in some cases sexual practice by young white men for their impending marriage to white women (cf. Haym 1991). Racial historicists, by contrast, might – Merivale's amalgamationism notwithstanding, one might think would – frown socially upon mixed-race partners and offspring though not necessarily preclude their possibility legally. Here, racial taboos on intermarriage or miscegenation mirrored interclass taboos. As such, they were (to be) socially discouraged rather than legislatively pre-cluded. The distinction is borne out by policy differences between pre-apartheid British rule in South Africa, where miscegenation was socially discouraged but not outlawed, and the apartheid regime that banned all sexual relations between whites and other racial groups between 1950 and 1988.

Similarly, naturalists tended to deny access to offices of governance to those considered racially inferior. Historicists, by contrast, were likely to encourage such access within strictly delimited parameters and for more or less well-defined purposes: maintaining control, guar-anteeing a steady supply of migrant labor at minimized costs, securing racial and social peace, hands-on preparation of the historically less developed for ultimate self-governance, and so on. Again, the apartheid regime maintained strict educational segregation at almost all levels, whereas the British in India or in their African colonies provided mixed schools not least for children of local elites. Many a European and US university has been advantaged by the likes of Achimota's legacy.[8]

Now the civilizing mission of colonial missionaries obviously must have presupposed, at least in principle, the presumption of racial (including cultural) progressivism. If it were to prove possible to convert the colonized to Christianity, and in conversion to introduce the infidels to the virtues of civilization, to the habits and manners of righteousness, and to the promise of "the heavenly city," this must presuppose not only convertibility and comprehension on the part of the momentarily inferior. It must presume in addition the very *possibility* of progress, advancement, civilization. The civilizing mission, as John and Jean Comaroff have spelled out in fascinating detail regarding the Tswana of Southern Africa, involved "methodically" transforming everyday life of the natives, their modes of "personhood and production, . . . habits and homes, . . . notions of value and virtue" (Comaroff and Comaroff 1997: xvi). Ironically, as this civilizing project necessarily presupposed the possibility of historical development and cultural, social, and intellectual progress on the part of natives considered racially naive and immature, it presumed the claim to transcendental value at once economic and epistemological, legal and moral. Transcendental value was represented in the universal currencies of money and the word, productive labor and sanctified truth, industry and knowledge, rational legality and moral virtue. The assumption is ironically universalist, for these imposed aspirations to universal ideals were always no more than embodiments of European, Christian virtue and practice, morality and truth.

We can see at work here the twin sides of colonialism: historicist and universalist, educational and forceful, developmentalist and destructive, pious and power-mongering. If the naturalist version of colonial racial rule governed by unswerving principle, the historicist ruled through the pragmatics of political, moral, cultural (in short, racial) imposition, local in effects and global in reach. Historicists struggle always with the tension between "obvious" racial differentiation, heterogeneity, and heterodoxy and their seemingly necessary drive to the civilizing imperative of a created homogeneity, a structured sameness. If naturalist logic was differentialist and ultimately

86

segregationist, the historicist's was assertively assimilating and in the end integrationist. Colonialism, it could be said, was always negotiating, if mostly all too unhappily, the space between required conformity and rebellious dissent, the latter a tradition found throughout the history of Christianity, as the Comaroffs are quick to comment regarding Protestantism (Comaroff and Comaroff 1997: 7–8). Indeed, colonial rule is stretched repeatedly between the rule of law and the rule of force, extravagant excess and modest self-sufficiency; between promoting and prompting conspicuous and "careful" consumption, radicalism and civility, consensual consort and violence. "A hand of iron beneath a glove of velvet," implored Arthur Girault of French colonial policy, "must always be the rule in our relations with the natives" (quoted in Roberts 1929). The impositions of developmentalism are not so far a cry from the terrors of destruction.

In their colonial applications, historicism or progressivism was to naturalism as the velvet glove was to the iron fist. The former was inclined to be soft and smooth, proceeding through the imposition of education and ideology, subtle coercion and calculating manipulation, but bristling to the critical touch. The latter tended to be vicious and vindictive, bald in design and ends, cruel and forcefully commanding in its means, sometimes driven to transgress genocidal limits, and tolerating no opposition.

In both colonial and postcolonial worlds dominated by racial conception, racist exclusion, and racially tinged resentments, the naturalist conception has been more prone to critical attack, to moral disapprobation, and ultimately to governmental and state distantiation. This was so precisely because of the extremities of violence and cruelty to which the naturalist conception "naturally" lent itself, both as discursive progenitor and as ex post facto rationalization. Dehumanize people in group terms – "racialize" them, precisely as Fanon would first use the term (Fanon 1968) – and they are rendered more disposed to dehumanized abasement. Render *them* abject and there is little to prevent their dehumanized dismissal, their "moral eviction," to invoke Zygmunt Bauman's characterization of Nazi treatment of Jews, among others. Indeed, to nothing within the scope of naturalism per se. It turns out that naturalism is little disposed to auto-critique, to moral self-reflection. What critical objection it faced historically was likely to come as much from historicist quarters as dismissive outrage on the part of the subjugated, at least until well into the twentieth century. Witness Mill's polite liberal disapprobation of Carlyle in chapter 3 above.

The racist predispositions and presumptions of progressivism or historicism, as we have seen by contrast, are more nuanced and hidden, less self-assertive, more worried about appearing so. But the dominant effect of this trajectory has been not the dismissal of racist commitment and expression as such but the replacement – one might say displacement – of naturalism by racial historicism, of one form of racist articulation by another. The perpetuation of racial commitments and racist exclusions has been veiled behind this shift, preserved anew in the vocal dismissal of the bald and extreme in the name of the polite and subtle, of the presumptively unsustainable in wake of the enlightened. Enlightened racism is camouflaged beneath its liberal historicist enlightenment. This is a point I will return to elaborate in chapter 8 for it concerns the very meaning and legacy of racelessness (for instance, colorblindness) as underpinning more or less contemporary state policy.

Racial Subjection, Ambivalent Rule

It is possible to map out the different forms social subjection assumes under the two models. By subjection here I have in mind the sense both of the making of the social subject and the modes of racial domination, of racial rule. The naturalist and progressivist conceptions are alike in viewing as agents those defined as white and those occupying the position of colonizers. For the naturalist, whites and colonizers are considered agents of biological or inherent destiny; for the progressivist, they are agents of history. So both traditions assume or inscribe a teleology, the former reductively determinist, the latter the product of a logic of temporality. For the naturalist, Europeans are living out the superiority of their biology or inherent nature, for the historicist they are satisfying the teleological logic projected in "the end(s) of history." The naturalist and progressivist differ more deeply regarding the social subjectivity of those considered colonized, not white, and non-European.[9] The naturalist takes the colonized and those rendered racially inferior to have no (or little) agency. For the historicist, the agency of the colonized, those categorized non-white or non-European, is undeveloped. Such agency has to be promoted by developing their potential for self-determination, saving natives from their (pre)historical selves, the effects of their undeveloped or uncivilized conditions.

I stress here accordingly the ways in which racially embedded presumptions about social subjectivity and racial rule mutually reinforce each other. Both the naturalist and progressivist presuppose a notion of universal subjectivity, a subjectivity closed off by the naturalist to those considered not white while potentially reachable for all in the historicist or progressivist view. The historicist thus claims to recognize, by presuming actually, an abstract, neutered, universal agency in the personhood of the colonized, a potential agency not yet actualized among the differentiations of their social specificity. That ambivalent tension identified above between the assumption of an embedded universalist nature hidden beneath historically undeveloped, particularistic ways of being is reasserted here in the historicist conception of social subjects. Peeling away the specificities of native ways of uncivilized existence through education was supposed to reveal the possibility of the universal subject, presumed in the example(s) of European high culture and modes of governance. Amalgamation, as Merivale would have it, was to help kill off the savage dispositions (or to help the colonized kill off the specificity of their own subjectivities) through the sanctity of intermarriage, the attendant mixed offspring, and the cultural upliftment supposed to follow.

This way of casting the issue reveals at once the deeply gendered character of racial subjection and the rule of racial subjects. Until well into the twentieth century white women were fashioned in racial terms as the media of national reproduction, in at least three ways. First, they were the bearers of future generations of citizens and citizen creators, providing care as nurses for military or administrative agents of the colonizing state. Middle- and upper-middle-class women served also ideologically to reproduce the body politic in ethnoracial and national terms, via their principal positions as governesses and teachers. Working-class women by contrast serviced the economy largely by working up the raw materials from the colonies into commodities for both domestic consumption and global circulation, while expected also to reproduce new generations of workers. Non-European women in the colonies served as domestic labor for the colonizers as well as field hands, in many instances effectively nurturing young white children while all the time considered fair game for satisfying the sexual proclivities of their masters. They were simultaneously objects, almost incessantly, of a Malthusian discourse of population control through family planning and more extremely sterilization (cf. Stoler 1995). As slaves, African, Asian, and Indian women assumed added value on two related counts: as commodities to be bought and sold at "fair value" on the market, and as the reproductive bearers of additional profit, the generators of potential slaves or indentured servants. Black women especially were seen as the means to surplus value in a triple sense, then: as making commodities, as making babies, and as themselves commodified objects for possible trade (Davis 1981; Anthias and Yuval-Davis 1989: 6–11).

Colonizing, as Helen Callaway makes clear, was considered man's work, the work of white man's regulative control, to be exact. The colonies, it was emphasized repeatedly, "were no place for white women" (Callaway 1987: 4–5). European women – "nice girls" as the characteristic infantilizing identification with African "boys" employed as servants and workers would have it (Callaway 1987: 6, 23) – were more or less excluded from British colonies in Africa until the early twentieth century. Even in the dying decades of direct colonialism, white women were admitted to the colonies only begrudgingly, whether or not seeking to accompany their husbands serving as colonial agents. Indeed, lower male ranks in the colonial service were required to sign a contract restricting marriage in their first three years of foreign service, so as not to be distracted from the duty of Empire (Callaway 1987: 20).

The colonies thus were male clubs of a kind, at once the laboratory, factory, and stable of white men's making, their fantasies forcibly serviced by the local population, men and women of color alike. Colonization in effect was about European men teaching their like to be men, to do men's work, to exercise power and to serve country, king (no doubt preferably), and God (undoubtedly masculinized). Here the traditional tension between Kantian duty and utilitarian instrumentality got resolved neatly in service of the imperial imperative, the sense of superiority and the civilizing mission tenuously and ambivalently combined as European men's prerogative. White women were seen as getting in the way of completing the "rough" work colonization necessitated and its vast profits required, too squeamish in the face of the necessary violence, too soft and tearful before health and hellish hazards, too sensitive even for the hardships of difficult administrative decision-making. But – and this is all too little stressed – white women were regarded the bearers or symbols of too much moral conscience, in the way then not only of white men expressing unmitigated power but of fulfilling their most extreme sexual fantasies. They were, as one-time governor of the Gold Coast, Sir Alan Burns, remarked all too priggishly, "intruders into what had been essentially a bachelor's paradise, where a man could dress as he pleased, drink as much as he liked, and be easy in his morals without causing scandal" (quoted in Callaway 1987: 19).

In those colonizing states where naturalism clearly gave way to historicism as the dominant colonial disposition towards the close of the nineteenth century (most notably among the British, French, and Dutch), increasing numbers of women began to appear in colonial service. A gendered form of historicism, it might be said, paralleled the racial variety. It is illustrative of this point that European women were all but absent from what I have characterized as naturalist colonial orders such as Belgium's Congo Free State. European women came to occupy positions in the colonies ruled by an historicist vision first as nurses and later as teachers, secretaries, doctors, welfare officers, and in the dying moments of colonial rule as junior-level administrative officers, exceptions like Margery Perham and Flora Shaw (Lady Lugard) dramatically proving the rule (Callaway 1987: 6–7).

In general, and perhaps prompted by their own experiences, white women showed greater sympathy than men to the plight of the colonized, a more charitable spirit to the local children and women with whom they were likely to have more contact, and stronger support for their educational advancement (Callaway 1987: 4). If colonial practice was predicated upon a mix of Kantian duty and utilitarian calculus, women's moderating influence, not to make too much of it, turns Kohlberg's masculinist model of moral developmentalism on its head. I do not mean to deny in this white women's privileged position regarding colonized women and men, the benefits white women accordingly enjoyed, the possibility of their class elevation as a result of relations between madams and maids. Nor for that matter to pass over in silence the "preexisting hierarchies of power," gendered precisely in their inscriptions of domination, that met European imperializing missions (McClintock 1995: 5–7). Yet precisely because of these preexisting forms of gendered domination on both shores of the colonizing ocean, ambivalence surely marked colonial relations between women on each side of the racial divide more deeply than it did the dominant master–slave relation between white men and black people. European women, it is safe to say, engaged in a less totalizing, more tenuous embrace of whiteness than their male counterparts. Not unrelatedly, I have to think that the colonial desire of white men for black women, admittedly motivated by and reinforcing their own sense of power, sparked the sort of hesitation one finds towards slavery in the likes of Thomas Jefferson. What does it say, after all, about white men's sexual desire and about white men's character more generally, whether or not rationalized (away) at the time as biological instinct or drive in the absence of European women, that it be satisfied by those recognized only as animals?

This ambivalence is deeply configured in racially cohering terms, gender differentiation notwithstanding. If ambivalence is a constitutive mark of the modern condition, as Zygmunt Bauman has argued forcefully (Bauman 1991), modern ambivalence is clearly revealed in relation to race. In governmental terms modernity has been about undertaking to impose order, to assert and manage with the view to guaranteeing the conditions that make order as much possible as invisible. Order is projected as the antithesis of nature. Nature, as Bauman remarks, "means . . . nothing but the silence of man" (Bauman 1991: 6). Conceived in naturalistic terms, those classified or considered not white are reduced to silence – both incapable of speech and in the end of being spoken about. In Kantian terms they are merely phenomena, objects, lacking the capacity for rational autonomy that is the authorizing mark of noumenal beings. Silence and invisibility – neither heard nor seen – are mutually reinforcing. Being written into the official record as not white is at once to be whitened out, so to speak, to be made part of the natural landscape, the silent backdrop in relation to which life is lived, taken for granted or passed by while being ignored.

There is an inherent unsatisfactoriness attendant to the constitutive ambiguity at work here conceived precisely from the point of view of imposed order. In this arrangement, those not white are taken on one hand to inhabit a nature that places them as such beyond (the very possibility of) order. On the other hand, they are supposed to be ordered through nature, for they are (pre)conceived as inhabitants of a natural order controllable by enacting the laws of nature. Nature is that about which – in the face of which – "man" is driven to silence as

much as it is the metaphor for silence itself. Those conceived racially
as nothing more than the products of nature accordingly inspire awe,
in the way in which nature can. Nature in this formulation stands in
stark contrast to – the dark or underside of – humanity. Thus nature
is not just that about which man is driven to silence but about which
there cannot be anything to say. It is beyond knowledge because
beyond speech.

The "cannot" here itself is ambiguous, indicative of the ambivalence
at work. It falls between the "cannot" of inherent inability or incapacity
and the "cannot" of imperative impossibility, of commanded incapacity. The ambiguity embedded here, in other words, is a particular
expression of the classic modernist tensions between fact and value,
nature and norm, description and prescription. It is this ambiguous
ambivalence that marks modernity, that fractures the world of the
past half millennium and that has been called into question so sharply
of late. Race accordingly is not just part – an aspect – of that modern
world but *emblematic* of it, as much the exemplary condition of the
modern as one example of modern practices and conditions among
others. As much synecdoche of the modern as an instance, an index as
an outcome. Thus the "constructedness" of race, about which so much
has been made in recent racial theorizing, is more complex than most
contemporary analyses all too glibly make out. For modern racial
order, as I have outlined its conditions of possibility here, is as much
"discovered" as it is (re)produced; it is as deeply the "product" of some
presumed laws of nature as the outcome of law's imperiousness.

The shift from naturalism to historicism or progressivism is the
(re)admission of those deemed not white into a history not simply
naturalistic. It represents the elevation of those who had been considered objects of nature to subjects of history, of being placed not before
but in time even if as inhabiting a time not yet modern. Here, in
contrast to racial naturalism where those regarded as racially inferior
are restricted to spaces before or frozen in time, the racially differentiated are defined in terms of inhabiting an earlier premodern time. In
either case those not white are placed outside: outside time or outside
the space(s) of modern time. Thus for modernity the space of race is
that of *the outside* – the external, the distant. The trick of race in either
case then was to turn imagined conditions, those conditions (re)created
and (re)produced, into the presumed and discovered, the given because
natural.

Classifying schemas, of course, have been central to modern modes of administration precisely because classification is all about imparting order to and imposing it upon the world. In some ways, modern modes of thinking became consumed with classifying mentalities. The modern condition as a consequence caught itself between worlds always more than any order(ing schema) can "capture," on one hand, and the incessant drive for – the imperative of – control, on the other. All those concerns with racial classification schemas marking modern social thought from the late seventeenth century onwards accordingly are about the insistence on epistemological order in the face of the unknown, of control in the face of the anarchic – in general, of order in the face of disorder. Thus modern states – the state of imposed order naturalized – are not simply consistent with racial classification schemas but perfectly conducive to – in a sense dependent upon – them. Modern states invoke the classifying of races as offering structure to worlds seen as if by nature (recall the state of nature). They order worlds otherwise altogether unstructured, un- or deformed, indeed, worlds considered as incapable in their "natural" form of structure. Colonial order accordingly was as central to elaboration of racial classification schemas as such schemas were to the material order of the colonies.

Classification, as Bauman argues, is at basis about setting apart, about cutting things off from each other into discrete containers, about *segregation*. Classification thus involves those acts of inclusion and exclusion so central to the experience of racism (cf. Bauman 1991). In seeking through classification to impose order upon an otherwise unformed world – or one seen and experienced as lacking form – the social world becomes mapped onto the natural, the natural is filtered through, alchemically transformed into, the social. And in the process the modern order of nature ironically comes to offer a model for the social.

Race is the perfect medium for this collapsing of the social, the historical, into and upon the natural, of value into (claimed) fact, of "seeing" – really conceiving – social conditions and relations, identities and subjectivities in natural terms. Racial naturalism, as such, emerges as the seemingly fitting ordering of the social in terms of the natural, the "natural" veil of the socializing of the natural. Racial historicism may be read in this light as trying to have it both ways, reading the historical against lingering naturalist assumptions. It follows that racial naturalism almost perfectly suits modernity's twin mandates of order

94

and control. Almost but not quite, for racial naturalism refuses to take into account two ultimately undeniable and related considerations. First, it refuses to acknowledge that the modes of objectifying imposition it presupposed and promoted rub up against the abilities and capacities, needs and wants of those supposed in the naturalist classificatory schemas not to have any, or to have them but not in quite the forms they would actually manifest. And second, it flees from the unhinging phenomenon of the fantasies and desires of those for whom the classifying forms were supposed to guarantee order and control. Those distantiated in virtue of their racial distinction are at once rendered desirable in virtue of their difference; those fashioned as somehow fantastic are at once constituted, ambiguously and ambivalently, as the objects of fantasy, pursued as much as fabricated, desired as much as denied, in those terms.

Thus, modernity's ambivalence strikes at its very "foundations," its core. Modern consciousness increasingly comes to recognize the heterogeneity it was so deeply implicated in prompting. To this recognition it responds, however, with various epistemological and practical interventions in seeking to reimpose order. On the one hand, there is a recourse through repressive state assertion to insist on the implications of a naturalist order by materially imposing it through law and policy, through classificatory modes and material control. The long history of racially exclusionary immigration policies throughout "Western" societies is ample testament to the point. On the other hand, there is begrudging revision of the categories in view of which the racial outsider could claim to be known. The revision prompts shifts from naturalist to historicist or progressivist or evolutionary terms, from the stasis of "Being" to the developmentalism of "Becoming," from objects of natural order to subjects (though not – at least not yet – as citizens) of the state, from racial subjection through technologies of the whip, sword, and gun to racial management via the funneling technologies of education, opportunities, and access.

Racial order, at the very heart of the modern state machine then, suffers the ambivalence of modernity multiply. Racial order imprisons modern subjects under the control of classifying schemas always delimiting of possibilities. It thus splits selves and subjects between the "can" and "ought," between possibility and impossibility, requirement and liberty. But in this, the tension between racial naturalism and historicism perfectly represents the ambivalence of broader modern tensions, exacerbated by the order of race: between determinism and freedom, structure and indeterminacy, form and formlessness, the before of history and its end. The ordering of the state accordingly by, in, and through race is at once representative of modernity more generally as race serves centrally to define and refine the modern condition.

For the racial naturalist the engagement with the racially subjugated is one of strict, unmediated exploitation. The racially inferior are seen as surplus value, both as usable labor and discardable detritus. In this, they are considered both laboring means to the production under-pinning the possibility of profit and as objects themselves from which profit can be elicited by being traded as commodities themselves, bought and sold on the market, much as garbage has become both a bother and a commodity. For the racial historicist, the racially imma-ture are inserted into historical development. They accordingly are promised progress, a promise at once undermined by racial imposi-tion in being progressively postponed to a future never quite (to be) achieved. Historical progress is to come, as Homi Bhabha has revealed so insightfully (Bhabha 1994: 86–92), through mimicry of the Euro-pean, a "colonial mimesis in which to be Anglicized is emphatically not to be English," where the colonized can be "almost the same, but not quite" – "not quite/not white." The colonized are inserted into global markets perpetually as laboring means, promised equality as economic players but perennially shortchanged as political and social equals. The effect is that those deemed racially undeveloped and imma-ture are reproduced almost inevitably as unequal – as exploitable labor in the colonies, as discardable in the postcolony, and in both as ab-usable migrants employed to take on work no one else will – or apparently needs to. Behind the promise of racial progressivism, as Nairn hints at in the epigraph to this chapter, in the name of its proffered utilities, lies the rule of a racial domination no longer natur-alized perhaps, but modernized nevertheless. It is to a consideration of racial governmentalities associated with naturalism and historicism respectively that I now turn.

NOTES

1   This is David Hume's characterization of eighteenth-century "evidence" of "Negro" intellectual contribution.

2 "I have no purpose to introduce political and social equality between the white and black races. This is a physical difference between the two, which in my judgment will forever forbid their living together upon footing of perfect equality, and inasmuch as it becomes a necessity that there must be a difference, I, as well as Judge Douglas, am in favor of the race to which I belong, having a superior position" (Lincoln 1863/1953: 16).

3 By 1864 accordingly Lincoln had backed away from emigrationism and could be seen creeping carefully towards black enfranchisement.

4 Booker T. Washington's insistence on vocational training for blacks, on which he founded the Tuskegee Institute, perhaps reveals the internalized ambivalence in responding to such presumptions.

5 Harriet Martineau's *Dawn Island*, written in 1845, provides a literary expression of this shift, in her terms from the racial extinction of some groups so "savage" they are incapable of being saved from themselves to those groups whose racial salvation is the benevolent product of European civilization. See Brantlinger (1995: 43–4).

6 The view that racism is reducible to the naturalist assumption, I have argued, has dominated the secondary literature on race and racism. Charles Mills, as I have pointed out in chapter 2 above, represents a widespread assumption in this regard. It follows that it is unproductive to look to the secondary historical literature for evidence of the historicist expression, for the secondary literature tends to replicate and thereby reinforce the naturalist presupposition. It is at once blind to and blinds analysts from seeing the revisionary force of the historicist interpretation. For one example among many, cf. Bolt (1971).

7 I am informed that this still occurs in South America, most notably, in Suriname. Government-sanctioned practice in Australia was even more vicious, if this is imaginable and as recent evidence there has revealed. Thus Aboriginal children were abducted by white adoptive parents or orphanages with the view to bringing up the children to believe they are white.

8 Achimota is the highly regarded British-founded school for Ghanaian elites that assumed significance in the wake of World War II. The Freetown Grammar School served similarly in Sierra Leone.

9 Historically, Europeans and whites were considered synonymous, as much represented accordingly in formal state classifications as assumed informally in the culture. Thus prior to the 1960s, the official state designation for whites in South Africa, for instance, was "European" and "Non-Europeans" for blacks – "Coloureds," Africans, and indeed Asians inclusively. In good part in the face of the insistent pressure of Black Consciousness in the 1960s, the designation shifted to "Whites" and "Non-Whites," the insult of negation nevertheless remaining in place.

5

RACIAL STATES

Written law is the law for civilized nations; customary law is for
"brutes."
        Bentham, *Of Laws in General*, p. 153 (Majeed 1992: 147)

Exterminate all the brutes.
        Kurtz, in Conrad's *Heart of Darkness* (1901/1991)

In states that are racially conceived, ordered, administered, and regulated,
the racial state could be said to be everywhere. And simultaneously
seen nowhere. It (invisibly) defines almost every relation, shapes all but
every interaction, contours virtually all intercourse. It fashions not just
the said and the sayable, the done and doable, possibilities and imper-
missibilities, but penetrates equally the scope and quality, content and
character of social silences and presumptions. The state in its racial
reach and expression is thus at once super-visible in form and force
and thoroughly invisible in its osmotic infusion into the everyday
(Essed 1991), its penetration into common sense, its pervasion (not to
mention perversion) of the warp and weave of the social fabric.

States of Racial Rule, States of Racial Being

The racial state accordingly is as much a state or condition of being as
it is a state of governance. Actually, we should speak more accurately
here of racial states, for (as I have argued) the forms and manifest
expressions are multiple and multiplicitous, diverse and diffuse. Racial
states, one might say, are places among others where states of being
and states of governance meet. For instance, race has long enabled

citizens both to deny the state's implication in violence and where acknowledged to deny any personal implication or to abrogate responsibility. In the vein of racial naturalism, it is common to hear claims like "they are not really people, so it cannot be violence after all, for there are no victims at all." Racial historicists, by contrast, often rationalize that "racism is a thing of the past, so contemporary racial inequities must be due to individual, or even group, inadequacies." It has become all too common to hear the complaint that "neither I nor my family had anything to do with slavery, so why should I be responsible for remunerating slaves' progeny?" (Darity 2000). Citizens of racial states thus are able to trade on the ambiguity between condition of being and form of governance, at once benefiting from (the historical and contemporary effects of) reproducing racisms and distancing themselves from any implication in them.

It is important to recognize here that the racial state trades on gendered determinations, reproducing its racial configurations in gendered terms and its gendered forms racially. Bodies are governed, colonially and postcolonially, through their constitutive positioning as racially engendered and in the gendering of their racial configuration. As I have argued, white men enacted the "dirty" governance of colonialism; white women, excluded from the formalities of colonial governance almost altogether, in very large part were excluded also from the colonies, or from those colonial spaces least like Europe. Largely ripped from traditional forms of labor, "non-European" men were put to work manually in both historicist and naturalist regimes, where they were employed at all, under grueling, debilitating, ultimately crippling conditions. Under historicist regimes, the more educated indigenous middle and educated classes of men would be employed at lower levels of local colonial administration, their sons ultimately becoming the nationalist leaders of the decolonizing movements a half-century or more later. Black women, black women of mixed origin, and Asian women likewise were racially devalued and driven to lesser or deskilled work in domestic or manufacturing or agricultural arrangements. And they were under constant threat of sexual invasion and exploitation by white men (and often by men generally), as too were young boys not classed as white, though to a lesser extent than girls and women (Haym 1991).

It is revealing to think of the military in this context as a state institution. While self-evidently defined and ordered by men for, in, and reproductive of the interests of men, the military has served different racial interests in different states and at different times. In Israel, for instance, it is *the* state agency through which youth are socialized and trained, opening up and closing down social possibilities for Israeli (and most notably Jewish Israeli in contrast to Arab Israeli) youth over their lifetimes. Thus military positions less available traditionally to women and non-Jews – intelligence gathering or visibly heroic and physically demanding leadership roles – close down available professional possibilities later in life. Who gets conscripted and to what positions reveals something about the interfacing exclusions effected by an institution so powerful and central to state identity. In South Africa until the late 1980s only white (presumably heterosexual) men were conscripted to the military, serving the imposed definition of national security within its national borders and without in terms of the discursive confines of apartheid. In the United States, the racial and gendered complex of the military became more contested in light of Truman's desegregating order in 1947, of the growing insistence recently of (at least some) women to be institutionally incorporated and the implications for institutional culture and practice. But the racial identity of the military has become more questioned also in the wake of the tacit equation in some quarters of the contemporary American state (like the "new" South African one) with blackness (roughly one-third of US military personnel now are African American). Military engagement colonially and postcolonially has also prompted a form of domestic politics. So, many less advantaged Filipino and South Vietnamese women sought social elevation through engaging and servicing American soldiers at and around bases in the Philippines and South Vietnam, practices American men were quite happy to encourage.

Theoretically, all this entails that the military is no longer simply, if it ever properly could be conceived as, an exclusively repressive state apparatus. It plays also a more or less defining role for state socialization in regimes of racial patriarchy. This in turn reveals intersections more complex, nuanced, and subtle than Althusser's well-worn distinction between repression and ideology warrants.

So racial violence perpetrated in the name of and by the state invariably assumes gender-specific expression, and state-shaped racially figured labor policies and practices are almost always contoured to reproduce a state of gendered effects. The promotion of migrant labor flows by the colonial state in South Africa in the late nineteenth century through the imposition of hut and poll cash taxes drove black men from the land to seek work in mining, secondary industry, and urban domestic settings. Rural women were left to tend for children, agriculture, and the rural homestead, with devastating effects on family units. Urban black women were driven mainly into domestic labor, menial manufacturing jobs, managing shebeens (illegal home bars), or prostitution, reduced almost invariably to servicing whites and men. The statutory restriction of mixed marriages throughout the southern United States until 1968 principally affected black women, effectively restricting them from claiming paternity support for the children fathered by white men as a result of rape and coercion.[1]

Defining States, Refining States

There is a deep tension here between the state as a set of institutions representative of specific political interests, or a site around which the struggle for such political representation takes place, and the political as more diffuse, as infusing all social relations and subject formation. Theoretically, this tension emerged explicitly in the wake of the 1960s. It manifests most clearly in the swirl of views around Althusser and his followers regarding repressive and ideological state apparatuses as well as the interpellation of subjects, renewed deployment of Gramsci's analysis of hegemony as social reproduction through popular consent, and Foucault's critical interventions concerning subjection, normalization, and governmentality.

The modern state was never simply an epiphenomenon or conduit of capital. This is especially so when one considers the state in its colonial – colonizing or colonized – form, or more broadly in its racial shape and ordering. Racial states most broadly construed, as modern states generally, often have served capital's interests, more or less self-consciously, and certainly always have expressed its gendered interests. They have done so not least by regulating the (racially ordered and deeply gender-differentiated) labor supply and by policing the gates and terrain of bourgeois access and style, substance and aesthetics, the shapes and roles of families. Thus they have ensured economic wellbeing for some and social law and order diffusely. Capitalist states have drawn heavily on these racial possibilities. They have

101

concerned themselves virtually throughout their formation accordingly with three conditions that have deep racial definition: first, with regulating migration and immigration, not least with the labor supply and labor costs in mind; second, with shaping social, and particularly sexual, interaction with the view to sculpting the face of demographic definition; and third, with controlling crime, predicated primarily in relation to property rights.

Capitalist states – or more carefully, states that operate in the terrain of capitalist economic formation and a more or less expansive capitalist world system – nevertheless are not simply reflective of capital's interests. Indeed, one could make the matter more complex still by insisting that capital's interests are never single, and often not unitary, either intra- or internationally.[2] Capitalist states are capitalist, as Poulantzas points out, not for their class composition – not simply for representing the interests of the capitalist class. They are capitalist rather for occupying a particular "objective" structural position in virtue of reproducing an historically specific and internally contradictory mode of production, locally and globally (Poulantzas 1969: 73; Holloway and Picciotto 1977: 4–6).

There are times states have insisted on representing or mobilizing interests antithetical to those of capital. Particular states, for instance, have insisted upon working protections and improved living conditions for the working classes over bourgeois objections. Many states regulate im/migration even in the face of labor shortages that would drive wage rates and so labor costs up. And many support greater leisure as a mode of social control in the face of pressures to extend the working day, while recently some economically developed states have moved at least nominally to equalize wage rates across race and gender.

A state can be called capitalist, then, primarily in the structural sense of enabling the reproduction of capital overall, of mediating in some general and contingent sense the contradictions capital and its fractious factions almost inevitably generate. So states are not in any narrow sense functional for capital's reproduction, or for the extension and expansion of accumulation. Rather, capitalist states constitute at most the terrain of struggle over the range of selected strategies (what Jessop calls "strategic selectivity") for capital's reproduction and accumulability locally and globally, short and long term. They offer the field for fashioning the sort of underlying hegemony, the (re)production of consent, that would sustain overall such reproduction and accumulation across classes (Jessop 1990: 9–10).

Thus, as Comaroff concludes, "the history of governance is irreducible to the history of political economy or vice versa" (Comaroff 1998: 338), though they do, and interactively, set horizons and so define the range of possibilities available for each other (cf. R. Williams 1981: 83–9). States of governance and political economy offer for and in relation to each other the limits of conceivability and possibility rather than the specificities of their discretely or mutually produced outcomes. State institutions seek to control capital's resources to their own political ends, just as the representatives of capital undertake to bend the state to its instrumental concerns. They do so not least by attempting to massage the contradictions within and between capitals and their fractions so that these tensions remain productive rather than implosive.

Where Marxists like Poulantzas theorize the state as "relatively autonomous" from infrastructural material production, then, they still maintain the primacy of the mode of production in setting the limits of social conception and comprehension. State derivation theorists, for instance, insist that the political and its expressions are derivable from the forms capital and the economic assume at any historical moment (Holloway and Picciotto 1977). This is preferable perhaps to liberal political theorists such as Habermas, Offe, Rawls, or Kymlicka who claim to theorize the political in almost complete absence of discussion regarding capital formation and accumulation. Yet in shaking social theory loose of these moorings, in undoing the hold of the base–superstructure metaphor on thinking the social, "relative autonomy" should not give way to thinking of material production, politics, and economics totally autonomous or independent of each other. Rather, the shift makes the causal connections multidirectional and historically specific. Thus it no longer is necessary to maintain determination of the state by the interests of capital "in the last instance." There are historical moments when the forces and resources of capital have been deployed by design to reproduce the conditions of sustaining the racial state – the racial conditions of the state – either generally or in a historically specific form like apartheid even to the detriment, short or long term, of capital's interests.

The *relative* autonomy of state and capital, accordingly, concerns their autonomous logics. These in turn prompt the possibilities of state and capital defining themselves in and through each other, their strategic deployment in relation to each other, their strategic selection of elements from each other necessary for their existence and survival or to craft outcomes each defines in its best interests. But relative autonomy here concerns also the relative "need" to define themselves through – and so by means of the terms of – each other (cf. Jessop 1990: 83–4). Neither economic nor political spheres are inherently privileged, though both at least are necessary, and mutually so. To these historically specific and so contingent purposes, the state and capital (and to these one could add law and culture) look to mediating terms to effect a language of mutual comprehension and deployability, and of common practice. They are, in short, terms of reasoning – logics – that make it look like they are at one, of a piece, engaged in common projects that are seemingly the product of common sense. People after all do not live out their economic, political, social, legal, and cultural lives discretely but interactively, in interconstitutive and mutually determining terms.

It must be insisted relatedly that the racial state is racial not *merely* or reductively because of the racial composition of its personnel or the racial implications of its policies – though clearly both play a part. States are racial more deeply because of the structural position they occupy in producing and reproducing, constituting and effecting racially shaped spaces and places, groups and events, life worlds and possibilities, accesses and restrictions, inclusions and exclusions, conceptions and modes of representation. They are *racial*, in short, in virtue of their modes of population definition, determination, and structuration. And they are *racist* to the extent such definition, determination, and structuration operate to exclude or privilege in or on racial terms, and in so far as they circulate in and reproduce a world whose meanings and effects are racist. This is a world we might provocatively identify as a *racist world order*. But more about this in due course.

Racial Subjects, Racial Selves

Althusser's work on ideology and interpellation made it possible to think anew about subject formation in relation to the state, a question that had largely been buried within the Marxist corpus and political theory more generally. It was Althusser's insistence on the importance

104

of this question that rendered recuperable Gramsci's concern with hegemony, thus refocusing the problem of ideology at the interface of the social and the self. These concerns were rendered central for racial theorizing in a genuinely new way by Stuart Hall's timely interventions in the late 1970s. Hall first demonstrated the importance of notions like "articulation," "societies structured in dominance," "hegemony," and the historical contingencies of "racial formation" and "racializing" for thinking about race. And it was Hall who insisted on the importance of Gramsci in theorizing race and ethnicity (Hall 1978, 1980, 1986/1996).

Stuart Hall, I am suggesting, was formative in rendering fruitful for racial theorizing central and non-reductive aspects of contemporary Marxian conceptualization. Yet he demonstrated also the productivity for understanding race of notions Foucault had shown to be key in thinking the social (Hall 1996). Until the late 1970s racial theorizing in the critical tradition had been dominated by Marxist interventions, on the one hand, and race relations theory, on the other (cf. Zubaida 1970; Rex and Mason 1986; Miles 1993). One of Foucault's theoretical motivations in mobilizing a notion of governmentality in light of concerns about modernist political theory was precisely the presumption, prevailing for liberal and Marxist political theory alike, that repression was institutional, imposed politically by the state, from outside the subject, in a sense from above. Foucault encouraged a shift to thinking about the interiorization of surveillance and discipline, the auto-production of security in part by citizen-subjects themselves. "Governmentality" made it conceptually possible to demonstrate the effectivity of social power upon, through, and by subjects in their self-making without reducing such power to the often questionable assumption of institutional state imposition.

Racial rule is caught always in the struggle between subjection and citizenship, as Comaroff (1998: 329) characterizes the contradiction of colonialism (Cooper and Stoler 1997). In the case of racial governance, this (set of) tension(s) is "resolved" pragmatically though always contingently in different directions for racial rule naturalistically predicated than for the historicist. Under naturalist regimes – those defining their marginalized subjects as inherently inferior – this dilemma between social belonging and its conditions of enactment tends to be fashioned in terms of the terror of abject subjection, of physically threatened and imposed violence. This is a belonging conceived only as property relation, whether enslavement, debt peonage, coercive contractual work, or nominally waged labor.

For historicist racial regimes, by contrast – those conceiving their racially identified subjects as historically differentiated in maturity and development – the tension is played out formatively in favor not principally of physical terror but rather the (never to be?) fulfilled promise of citizenship. Here social belonging does not privilege some form of property relation but the deferred longing for a common humanity ideologically fashioned. If for racial naturalism the inherently inferior could never qualify for citizenship, for racial historicism racial subjection was effected through the holy grail of legal citizenship and its attendant rights (Comaroff 1998: 339). Citizenship was a status and standing not only never quite (to be) reached for the racially immature but for whom the menu of rights was never quite (as) complete. Even *within* naturalist and historicist scope, the multiplicity of the dimensions as well as the variability in styles of rule imply that the modes of racial rule and regulation are never fixed, given, or singular, but multiple, shifting, site-specific, temporally and discursively defined.

So subjection is internalized and to that extent seemingly self-designed and fashioned. The racial state, thus, could be said to strive for a racial subjection which, though usually perceived as externally imposed upon subjects, actually is self-fashioned and promoted. "Racial subjection" seeks as such to turn imposition into self-assumption, assertive charge into autonomous, self-imposed choice, harness into hegemony. Thus, there is no clear-cut contrast between state and individual, between asserted institutional power and capillary governmentality. Foucault shows, in short, that the distinctions between the state as institutional power and power vested in and through the state of being, between "what is within the competence of the state and what is not, the public versus the private," are fictions of modern sociodiscursive formation (Foucault 1991: 103).

All modern states – not least the colonial, as Comaroff comments, but one could extend the point to cover the racial state more extensively also – exercise themselves in good part by way of the capillary, by local instrumental and institutional forms of coercion, physical and symbolic forms of violence. They trade on various more or less implicit modes of discipline and surveillance, and on hegemony as the fashioned and diffuse production of consent (Comaroff 1998: 338).

106

This represents a project of governance that, even where relatively effective from the point of view of racial rule, was never quite complete. One might say it never could be complete, for subjection in both (and related) senses of the term promotes its resistance; imposition from the outside – the external – calls forth at least redefinition internally, in terms of the already (pre)existing sum of defining conditions of the self, and at most outright, explicit rejection, denial, dismissal. The self accordingly is always caught – split – between the past and the present, the self itself (so to speak, as already socially defined and conditioned) and the social, between self-assumption and imposition, in short, between "my"-self and its other. This is especially so in the context of race: race as socially (and state-) imposed and as taken on "freely," assumed as a project, as a self-making.

One little-emphasized implication of Foucault's focus on governmentality, on the logics of (self-)governance, and on the interiorization of state power and subjection, I want to suggest then, has been to collapse the artificial distinction between ambiguous meanings of the public: as civil society and as state power, of individuals acting "in public" and of the "res publica," of economy and society, and state formations as discrete entities somehow acting upon each other rather than as mutually and depthlessly defined. In the sense I am suggesting, economy and society, private and public spheres are co-constitutive of the possibilities even of their distinction. Kim Crenshaw shows that segregation in the United States, historically and contemporarily, is sustained by the legally maintained and managed distinctions between formal and informal racial distinctions, and between public and private discriminations (Crenshaw 1998: 286). In a deep sense, then, the "publics" of public spheres, public goods, public sectors, and public culture are not as distinct or as discrete as the obtuse literatures constituting them often would have it. Race, I am insisting, makes it less easy to sustain (as discrete and distinguishable) the seams between civil society, public sphere or sector or goods or culture, and governmentality. Race is co-defined by such domains in the particularity of its local expression and significance. What makes this more complex, though, is that race simultaneously serves to cohere these domains, to imprint upon them their seeming specificity, the mark of their common state(d) definition.

It follows that race is more than simply threaded through the fabric of modern and modernizing racial states. States are drawn into racial frames of reference, into the rings of racial globalities, in entering into the circles of modernity, in becoming modern states. Race then is not a premodern condition but a quintessentially modern one masquerading in the guise of the given and the ancient, bloodlines and genetic pools. States have acquired their modernity more or less and partially through racial assumption, through being drawn into the terms and forms, shapes and spaces, temporalities and rhythms of racial world ordering and world racial definition.

The historical trajectory of the colonial state developed in relation to European discovery, pacification, commerce, and rational administration of non-European peoples (Comaroff 1998: 323ff.), of those deemed without history and culture. By contrast, the genealogy of the racial state, as I have surveyed it in previous chapters, is more complex. Obviously it includes, precisely because implicated in, the colonial trajectories identified so insightfully by Comaroff. But the racial state cannot be delimited to its obvious colonial form. There are two conceptual reasons for this beyond the clearly political one that to do so would be to bury responsibility for the racial state in and with a colonial past that even where transformed leaves its traces, more or less firmly imprinted, upon the present.

First, as I have insisted, the racial state trades in its emergence on the shaded space between the state as lived condition and the more formal mode of governance, between subjection in the sense of existential constitution and subjection as a mode of governmental imposition and political constitution. Gramsci captures this connection between the political sphere, civil society and coercion in his classic formulation of the state: "state = political society + civil society, in other words hegemony protected by the armour of coercion" (Gramsci 1971: 263). The state as institutional governance depends for its functionalities on the embodiment and reiteration in everyday practice of micro-informal expressions, of assumed states of being, a fact upon which dispositions to resist have long traded, as James Scott notes (Scott 1998: 6). The racial state accordingly is the embodiment, the exemplar par excellence, of the shift in theorizing the political from institutional forms to governmentality, from politics as domain and discipline to politics as disciplinary practices embedded in the everyday. Thus it must be presumed to outlive its colonial expression not least because in penetrating the everyday the racial state was destined to "survive" its institutional forms.

108

Second, and this by way of periodization, the racial state at least in its emerging form as a set of assumptions about the nature of being and living was deeply implicated not only in fashioning and effecting the outcome of the colonial imperative but in making it conceivable. In short, the presumption of the racial state, as we have seen in earlier chapters, opened up the possibility of thinking the colonial project at all. As sets of institutions, and as ways of thinking and institutionalizing the governance of societies racial in both their metro- politan and their colonial expression, racial states emerged materi- ally out of, as they were elaborated in response to, the "challenges" of colonial rule. And so conceptually they gave rise to conceiving the possibility of the colonial, while they emerged institutionally in elabor- ating rule in the colonies and – though less visibly but at least as presumptively – to mark the nature and scope of metropolitan soci- eties in Europe too. Racial states accordingly have shaped the possible and marked out the impossible in the latter also. The charged atypicality of the Irish or Jews in the European context, for instance, is compre- hended and sustained only by identifying each respectively with and in terms of the conjunction of blackness, (European) femininity, and the lumpenproletariat, as chapter 3 above revealed in Carlyle's case.

The (racial) state, in its institutional sense, must be seen thus not as a static thing but as a *political force* fashioning and fashioned by *economic, legal,* and *cultural forces* (forces of production, of sociolegality, and of cultural representation). It is a player not just in productive, distributive, circulating, and consumptive patterns and tensions, and in their reproduction. It has been central to political contestations over control of the materialities of society but also (and especially) of its own instrumentalities, its means and modes of rule and repres- entation, of social supervision and control, over the style and substance of social governmentality. In short, the state is a contestant in the markets of representation, of who speaks for whom and in and on what terms.

Racial Governmentalities

In their particularities, then, racial states oversee a range of institutional, definitive, and disciplinary practices. They are engaged in definition, regulation, governance, management, and mediation of racial matters they at once help to fashion and facilitate. For one, racial states *define* populations into racially identified groups, and they do so more or less formally through census taking, law, and policy (the scope, styles, and effects of which I engage in chapter 7 below), in and through bureaucratic forms, and administrative practices.

Second, racial states *regulate* social, political, economic, legal, and cultural relations between those racially defined, invariably between white citizens and those identified as neither white nor citizen, and most usually *as* black (or more or less *with* blacks[3]). These are relations more often than not tense and internally fraught, exacerbated by their racially imposed character. The racial complexity may be intensified by the fact that their shape is determined in part by the externalization of tensions, ethnically or nationally or in some other sense politically defined, within and among those competing for the benefits, privileges, and profits of whiteness. Historical examples of these intrawhite tensions abound: between northerners and southerners in the US, between Afrikaner and those of British background in South Africa, or between Flemish and Walloon, Dutch- and French-speaking in Belgium.[4]

Relatedly, racial states *govern* populations identified in explicitly racial terms. The identification legally and administratively of groups as inherently inferior or historically immature, as native or indigenous to colonized spaces, is taken invariably to entail – *to require* – their management and oversight. Such regulation commands not just what the racially regulated can do but where they can and cannot go, what educational institutions they can access, with whom they can fraternize, and where they can reside. But it commands also under what conditions the racially marginalized are profiled and criminalized – which is to say, subjected to surveillance and suspicion, punished, imprisoned, placed on probation, and paroled.

Fourth, racial states *manage economically*. They oversee economic life, shape the contours of racially conceived labor relations, structure the opportunities or possibilities of economic access and closure. To these ends, racial states will intervene to secure the conditions for the reproduction of capital not least by ordering resources and attempting to ameliorate tensions threatening the conditions for capital's expansion externally and internally. Thus states will open or stem the flow of the racially figured labor supply in response to the needs of capital, but delimited also by political demands and worries. In the naturalistic extreme, racially identified groups are treated much like the natural resources found in the environment, no different than the objects of the landscape available for the extraction of surplus value, convenient value added to raw materiel. And as I have insisted, racial governance accordingly assumes different forms under naturalist and historicist presumption: most notably, slavery, segregation, and forced labor in the former mode; assimilationism, indirect rule, and developmentalism in the latter. Thus the racial state participates in, as it promotes, racial rule – whether locally or at a colonial distance. It rules not just through labor regulation but by insisting on managing most if not all forms of exchange, commerce, intercourse, raw materials, production, trade, markets, labor circulation, distribution, and redistribution. At the extreme, then, the racial state is a peculiar sort of totalitarianism, seeking (only more or less successfully) to pervade all social forms, institutions, and expressions.

These considerations again reveal the irreducibility of the political to the economic. States may enact policies, rules, and instrumental modes of operation conducive not to the maximizing of surplus value, short or long term, but in the name of some politically driven logic like maintaining security, or white supremacy, or "principled" racial segregation irrespective of the duplicate costs it entails. In fact, it is specious to think that the cost–benefit calculation can be divided so discretely between the economic and the political. The fine line between the two likely collapses in the face of the calculation, just as it is manufactured by and in the interests of those whose power is identified artificially on one or other side of the dividing line.

Finally, racial states not only regulate but also claim to *mediate* relations between those (self-)identified as "white" or "European" and those declared "non-white" or "Native." Such mediation manages disputes and conflicts over land, labor, and mixed-racial intercourse, socially and sexually. As adjudicator, the state claims a nominal neutrality. Yet its actions historically have been largely partial. In reproducing a racial system, a mode of being and governance, the actions of racial states are representative mostly of those belonging to the ruling racial class, whose racial status as privileged – indeed, as ruling – the state in its racial configuration has helped to define, refine, and promote.

In a remarkable admission, Judge William Harper reveals in a South Carolina case of 1835 the intricate ways in which racial definition and regulation, governance and potential mediation run together. While claiming the mantle of legal neutrality and impartiality, Judge Harper's judgment subtly reveals the contorted but calculated depths of racial configuration and management:

> We cannot say what admixture of Negro blood will make a colored person. The condition of the individual is not to be determined solely by distinct and visible mixture of Negro blood, but by reputation, by his reception into society, and his having commonly exercised the privileges of a white man . . . it may be well and proper, that a man of worth, honesty, industry, and respectability, should have the rank of a white man, while a vagabond of the same degree of blood should be confined to the inferior caste. It is hardly necessary to say that a slave cannot be a white man. (Quoted in Williamson 1995: 18)

While raising the challenge of mixed-race manifestation to the logic of race manufacture generally (Small 2001), Harper's remark at once tellingly acknowledges the importance of race making and ranking to modern social management and disciplinary control, of population definition and a relatively engendered inter- and intraracial privileging. As early as 1681, for instance, the state of Maryland had legally restricted slavery to those not white, and defined race according to maternal lineage, signaling early on the centrality of gender to racial reproduction.[5] In the case of racial states this racial privileging has almost always historically prevailed. It raises the question accordingly whether the racial state is *necessarily* representative of the interests of the ruling racial class – defined as whites, Europeans, or those of European descent – and thus inherently implicated in racial subjugation and exclusion. In short, is the racial state inherently a racist state?

Racial States and Racist States

Racial states employ physical force, violence, coercion, manipulation, deceit, cajoling, incentives, law(s), taxes, penalties, surveillance, military force, repressive apparatuses, ideological mechanisms and media – in short, all the means at a state's disposal – ultimately to the ends of racial rule (Comaroff 1998: 324–6). Which is to say, to the ends of reproducing the racial order and so representing for the most part the interests of the racial ruling class. And as Judge Harper so bluntly reveals, this entails in the history of fabricated racial configuration that racial rule by definition serves the interests of those conceived as white. "Whiteness" then is not some natural condition, phenotypically indicative of blood or genetic or intellectual superiority, but the manufactured outcome of cultural and legal definition and political and economic identification with rulership and privilege. If we go by history – and in this instance what else is there to go by? – then in class terms whiteness definitionally signifies social superiority, politically equates with control, economically equals property and privilege.

This equation of racial states with privilege and power requires qualification. Clearly, the racial powers and privileges of whites are magnified or tempered by class position, gender, even the standing of and within a nation-state. Thus those otherwise considered (as) white in the scheme of common sense who occupy social positions of disprivilege or disempowerment become referenced precisely as less or other than white. They are characterized with the likes of "white niggers" or "half-niggers," as "temporary Negroes" (Dollard 1937/1988), "hunky" (Hungarian), "dago" (Italian), "polak" (Poles), "spicks" and "kikes" (Jews). The characterization in an 1898 debate over the disenfranchisement of Italians in the US exemplifies the power and (dis)privilege at work in racial identification: "according to the spirit of our meaning when we speak of 'white man's government,' [the Italians] are as black as the blackest negro in existence" (quoted in Cunningham 1965: 34; Barrett and Roediger 1997: esp. 9).

It follows that the racial state is at once implicated in the possibility of producing and reproducing racist ends and outcomes. Race has been invoked normatively in institutional terms and state contexts almost always to hierarchical purposes. This fact deeply delimits the taking up of race as an organizing theme to anti-racist ends. It is not simply the invocation of race per se that is fraught with this danger, for as historically contingent on social determinations race conceptually is open to the ends of anti-racist mobilization. Rather, it is the deep historical implication of race in state structure, its relative penetration of state definition, organization, and determination that delimits its resistant potential even as it renders strategic racial invocation essential. It means that race can be mobilized to anti-racist purposes at best only as a short-term and contingent strategy. We have witnessed the limits of affirmative action recently in just these ways, for instance. The effects of anti-racist race mobilization have

113

tended to be ambivalent and ambiguous. In invoking the very terms of subjugation, in "standing inside them" (Goldberg 1993) to transformative purposes, racial invocation likely reinscribes elements of the very presumptions promoting racist exclusions it is committed to ending. Hence Sartre's struggling over what in *Antisemite and Jew* he nominates "anti-racist racism," the conceptual contradiction hinting at the pragmatic tension.

We might usefully bear in mind here the distinction Etienne Balibar insists upon between "*(official) State racism*" and "*racism within the State,*" between what Balibar characterizes as the "exceptional state" and "exceptional moments" of the normal state (Balibar and Wallerstein, 1991: 39, Balibar's emphasis). A state may license racist expression within its jurisdiction simply by turning a blind eye, by doing nothing or little to prevent or contest it, by having no restricting rules or codes or failing to enforce those on the books. By contrast, a state like Nazi Germany, apartheid South Africa, or Jim Crow Louisiana may assume racism as a state project, definitive of state formation, articulation, in a word, (national) state identity. As I have argued, between the two instances lies a myriad of racially articulated expressions both licensed and practiced by state mandate. One set of examples concerns the racial characterization of the criminal classification system (i.e., activities or profiles associated with a devalued racially identified population treated more harshly than otherwise comparable activities or profiles of those not so devalued). Another covers civil service job classifications (e.g., white prison guards of predominantly black prisons in states with a long history of racist structures most notably in the criminal justice system; white truck drivers and black manual workers; white male bosses and black female clerical staff).

In these many micro-expressions, as well as more explicitly at the macro level, the racially conceived and reproducing state is characteristic of, not exceptional to, modernity. Modernity is defined by racial conditions even as it characterizes those conditions as abnormal or exceptional. So while *racist* states may seem exceptional, their very possibility is underpinned by the normalcy of the *racial* state. But there does remain a difference, captured by Balibar's distinction, in degree if not kind between states in and through which race is sewn into the social fabric by way of racial routinization and those where racist exclusion is explicitly defined as *the* principal (and "principled") state project.

114

Racial invocation by the state and definition of the state by race, it follows, almost invariably restricts the range of critical intervention and transformative potential to a dualistic and mutually exclusionary choice. On one hand, it elevates the narrowing naturalization of the assimilationist or integrationist; on the other, it begrudgingly spawns the separatist (in the Black Nationalist contrast to the segregationist). Ranging between the promisingly reactive and a reactionary politics, race-based anti-racism may be pragmatically necessary in some historical moments, but it clearly reifies under the weight of its own logic into racial essentializing once those historical openings close down. It is for just this reason that both Angela Davis and Philomena Essed strongly urge political mobilization around common *political* interests rather than preexisting or prefashioned common identities. Here, the common identity is to emerge out of the mobilization rather than essentialistically (and so exclusionistically) giving rise to it (Davis 1998: 319–20; Essed 1996: 109–10).

Racial Penetration, Racial Routinization

In Foucauldian terms, the state not only invades the body of subjects. It goes a long way in making bodies what they are, and by extension who they are. It is thus instrumental in subject formation. The more the racial state is implicated in fashioning the form and content of subject formation, the more it penetrates into everyday social life, and the greater the hold of race over the social horizons of the conceivable. Consider how the racial state defines, manages, and regulates family formation: who can form a family racially, who can belong to a family, who can marry, how the offspring will be defined and designated racially and so what the life opportunities are for them. Women thus are implicated in reproducing the nation-state's population, its citizenry (though even this might become contested technologically before too long). Again, examples are numerous: The 1950 Mixed Marriages Act in South Africa prohibited not just interracial marriage but any interracial sexual activity. The Serbian men who impregnated while raping Bosnian and more recently Kosovan women of Muslim background were self-consciously pursuing a policy of diluting the "national stock," at once mockingly reducing Muslim men to a sense of impotence. Anti-miscegenation laws abounded throughout the colonial and then state legal codes of the American South until they were called into question in a 1948 California case, *Perez v. Sharp*, and then ultimately rendered completely unconstitutional in 1968 in the appropriately named *Loving v. Virginia* (see Furumoto and Goldberg 2001).

The racial state sets limits on social possibilities, or enacts them, not just formally through law but through *routinization* (Omi and Winant 1995: 85; Comaroff 1998: 331ff.; Hesse 1999: 122ff.). Rendering these practices normal by their routine repetition hints at their presumed naturalization; they are taken as given and therefore (in the collapse of social imperative into the natural) coterminously unalterable. Besides sexual routines, permissibilities, and prohibitions, the examples are more or less pervasive. Consider birthing practices licensed and prohibited. Similarly, birth certificates define what and how one is named and thus recognized legally and administratively (Scott 1998: 3–4), how such recognition or its failure furnishes social standing.

Nevertheless, racial routinization in states that are more or less racially predicated runs deeper still by invading all aspects of sociomaterial life. It colors childrearing (members of "races" regarded as "alien" or of "lesser value" in Nazi Germany were forced into abortion, castration, and sterilization), schooling, recreational activities like sports, and recognizable religious practice. It manifests through marriage licensing and annulment, technical training and higher education; through spatial design and control, especially urban planning, apportioning residential and labor spaces, and relatedly property ownership; as well as through laboring conditions. In the extreme instance, again, the Law for the Reduction of Unemployment introduced by Hitler in 1933 extended marriage loans to citizens the conditions for repayment of which they could satisfy by producing children. As Burleigh and Wipperman (1991: 46) note, this law was designed to effect three principal outcomes: to multiply a "pure" German population, to reduce unemployment of men, most notably, by forcing women to return to their traditional maternal roles. As examples such as these reveal, racial routinization is reproduced in temporal templates, marking life by a racial brush from early childhood, for example, through health practices such as inoculation injections; driving, drinking, and conscription ages; as well as voter registration and voting rolls. And racial routinization is licensed materially in the card of identity registration that serves as the codification and so condition of these social acts and duties, responsibilities and rights, all of which are more or less racially thick.

The routinization of race silently in social life is reproduced also through criminalization, taxation, retirement, death, burial, and inheritance formalities, all factors the state regulates or oversees, manages and mediates. In short, the modern state has come to enact racial configuration in virtually all, or at least all significant, social practices and conditions, markers and indices from birth to death and burial, from the personal to the institutional. The more penetrating racial categories are in a state's lexicon and bureaucratic practice, the more such practices routinize racial reference and social shaping.

Thus all these domains and practices, conditions and regularities, codes and orders come at various moments in modern states to be racially conceived and enacted, ordered and structured, produced and reproduced, color and culture coded. They constitute regulative and regulated regimes in good part through state administrative apparatuses like the census, tax forms, passports, lending and banking practices (Scott 1998). In short, the exercise of racial states in the merging of their institutional forms with – their penetration into – daily life renders the trace of the state's racial dimensions relatively invisible. Racial regulation is reproduced through routinized governance of/ over family, civil society, labor and markets, private and public morality, ownership, public monuments and parades, open and closed ceremonies, common and commonly restrictive and restricted social practices in living and in death (Comaroff 1998: 337–8). In racial states, as Benjamin Disraeli commented over a century ago, all comes to be race. And in the twist of their most extreme manifestations, in the penetrating institutionalization of race, race comes to be all.

One should be careful here, however, as Foucault and those he has influenced have emphasized, not to reduce all subject formation and subjection to the political, directly or indirectly to the state institutionally conceived. This is a position one might call politicism or statism in the face of economism. Subjection in both senses is at least multiply, and most likely over-, determined, often (though *pace* Foucault also not completely) internalized. So social subjection (mostly) becomes self-regulating and self-directing. The institutional state assumes as its necessary condition the state or condition of being, of lived culture and cultural life, the imposed becoming the self-chosen, the fabricated the given, the historically fashioned the state of things, the social the natural. If there is anything approaching a "national character" perhaps this is all it amounts to, the (informal) codification of the cultural characteristics and values of a dominant or majority group whose definition is state related or directed. Again, imposition may be more or less violent, more or less coercive, more or less subtle. Coercion is more the former in the case of naturalist racial regimes, sustained principally by repressive apparatuses, while more the latter in historicist ones, reproduced largely by ideological and discursive apparatuses though underpinned always by the threat of repressive violence.

Racial Assertion and the Nation-State

Race and nation

These remarks raise the distinction between race and nation. Race may be thought of as the social or cultural significance assigned to or assumed in physical or biological markers of human beings, including the presumed physical or physiognomic markers of cultural attributes, habits, or behavior. Nation, by contrast, is the significance of cultural markers as assumed or assigned (imagined) indicators of common originary belonging, where race (or ethnicity, as cultural socialization) might be one of those (imagined) markers assigned significance or dominance in picking out members. Where this is so, race and nation overlap, more or less isomorphically.

It is worth observing that race (or ethnoracial identification) has a thickish history of being legislated – directly, baldly, and in its own (mostly unmediated) terms. Nation has not been so legislated, at least not directly and unmediated. Thus the restrictions of immigration law historically have been predicated in terms either of ethnoracial identification or state origin. Here the reference in some laws to "national origin" is actually to where people were born, or the citizenship they hold. This difference between race and nation has to do with the very basis of their conception. So it is thought possible to legislate race directly, in its own terms, in ways nationhood is deemed not so amenable to legislation (in contrast to nationality, which really is the legislation of state belonging and potential access to state rights, privileges, and resources). This difference in legislative amenability may have to do with the privileging of a presupposed physical optics thought to make racial identification accessible in ways the cultural references of nation are not (or less so). The former is imagined to have a

118

"substance" available to the latter only through some more readily questionable idealist metaphysics. German law, for instance, establishes German national belonging only in virtue of marking nationhood in racial terms. German origin is defined as the claim to German blood. Belonging to the nation is a matter not just of being born in Germany but of being born to parents whose blood or genes awkwardly are considered "to run German," who in that sense are "racially" German.

Racial assertion

The German citizenship codes make clear that it is the business of the state to state, of authorities to author the law, to assert themselves (Comaroff 1998: 340, 342). Historically, it has been the business of racial states to assert themselves – to state their conditions – racially. It has been their business to generate the possibilities of their boundaries in no more or less than racial terms. I will argue in chapter 8 that the institutionalization of race by the state, its routinized assumption in the structure of state institutions, has made it possible for contemporary states to assert themselves racially without explicit invocation of racial terms. The racial state, then, is never complete, always (as Comaroff says of the colonial state; 1998: 341) on the make, a work in progress, a Sartrean project. This is necessarily so in the case of racial states not simply because race is, as the cliché says, socially constructed. It follows multiply and interactively from the very interface of the state and race.

The state is a condition of assertion. As a prevailing form of power it is, and necessarily, the effect of constant reassertion. This reiteration is required in so far as the state provides the principal modern institutional sites through which social status is claimed, and the gains of status quickly dissipate if not guarded, in the absence of their reassertion. The state then can never not speak itself, for as soon as it stops stating itself, so to speak, it ceases to be a state. Likewise, in so far as race in its status claims is dialogical and ideological, discursive and illocutionary, it presupposes for its enactment its assertibility, its required capacity at every moment of being stated. Thus, in the face of its own social silence race ceases to reproduce itself; it cannot reproduce and replicate *sans* the state, in the absence of its more or

119

less invisible institutionalization. But once institutionalized in and through the state, the state now racially conceived cannot speak, cannot state itself, other than in the terms of race. So modernity's race to the state became at once the stating of race, its institutional assertion. Race stated, in short, is the state raced.

To say this, however, and once again paradoxically, is to give the racial state perhaps too much coherence. For, as I have argued above, the state may be thought of as the phantom of governance and authority, a territorial placeholder for sets of often competing and more or less local institutional interests and powers. In this sense, the state provides media and a measure of scope for the assertion and authorization, legislation and legitimation of institutional power(s). The latter two institutional practices offer to the former two a semblance of coherence, a singularity of style and voice, a common language and mode, the shadow of an institutional sphere in the face of prolific heterogeneous messiness. They offer, that is, the artifice of national, cultural, expressive unity – comm-unity – in the face of fractured disunity and anarchy, the artifice of homogeneity in the face of proliferating heterogeneities.

Comaroff distinguishes between colonizing states in Europe that concerned themselves in their metropolitan conditions with "manufacturing homogeneity" and colonized states devoting themselves to "managing difference," regulating the threat of heterogeneity, of anarchy (statelessness) (1998: 329). Fabricating homogeneity in the metropoles, at home, it might be said, was predicated upon displacing heterogeneity to the outside. Colonized states thus were initially shaped to represent racial otherness as exteriority. Conceived as embodiments of material states, they were considered in naturalist terms to lie outside the civil(ized) societies of metropolitan order. As the colonies became increasingly sewn into a world capitalist system (offering raw materials, consumptive agricultural products, mineral wealth, and markets) and as colonial governmentality took shape over time (offering employment, opportunity, adventure, excitement, and the exercise of power), managing heterogeneity shifted from the semi-avoidance of exteriority to the regulative and ordered intimacy of "containerization" (Tilly 1994). The shift transformed unknown objects of adventurous discovery and examination into elaboration of a logic of colonial rule, first through imposing direct rule and later mediated via indirect management of more peripheral units in a growing global order. The colonial state accordingly turned "savages" dialogically and governmentally first into "colonial subjects," by subjecting them to colonial rule and regulation, and then again into "units of labor." And in doing this, the colonial state transformed "savages" ironically into legal persons (cf. Baker 1998).[6] The ambivalence of colonial subject-ivity is revealed here, for "legal persons" were extended little more than formal personhood. These are persons for or really "before" the law, regulable units or administrative entities rather than fully human beings.

The modern state may be conceived accordingly as a container. It has enabled the internal dynamics of modernity to be played out by offering not just a backdrop for pressing modern tensions but struc-tural constraints on their explosiveness, and so on the scope of their effects. These are the tensions between futurism and nihilism, revolu-tionary zeal and conservative denial; between technological imper-ative and anti-technological commitment; between a retrospective *ancien régime* and a prospective avant-garde; between repression of the new and its celebration; between fixity and the given in tension with flux and change, speed and motion. The modern state is tied then to a fixed mode of managed accumulation with the logic of production largely dictating the limits of circulation, exchange, and consumption.

In their racial framing, thus, the freedom of the modern state (and perhaps this is the state condition generally) is necessarily illusory. It is predicated always and necessarily on an unfreedom both for those ruled and for those ruling. Racially ordered and manifested freedom – the freedom of whites, historically speaking—accordingly is no free-dom at all. Power, generally, and racially predicated and ordered power particularly, requires always its own reproduction, its reiter-ated assertion, freedom's necessity a logic of determination that at once discounts the freedom such necessity dictates (cf. Butler 1997b).

Relatedly, as states have increased their scope and range, their growth in institutional determination and (formal) authority over the lives of their inhabitants – both citizens and non-citizens, those in and out of the state alike – de facto control, efficiency, and effect have dimin-ished (Comaroff calls this "the Minogue Paradox"; 1998: 336). There is, one could say, a point of diminishing returns, a marginal effectivity of rule. The more repressive, the more likely resistant. And the more cemented, the more internally cracked. This is especially so regarding racial repression and rule. States, as Weber famously insisted, are

121

those institutions effecting a monopoly over the legitimate means of physical force. Thus the greater state insistence on effecting and exercising such monopoly, the more visible. The greater the violence states promote in everyday life, the more they have to resort to threatened or explicit violence as the mode of rule. And the more violence becomes a norm, the readier those within and without the state are loosened if not licensed to resort to forms of personalized and anonymous violence. This is especially exacerbated by racial terms for race, while making institutionally visible the perpetrators, picks out the objects of violence in emphatically identifiable ways.

In becoming systemic and institutionalized, racial violence effectively renders its perpetrators individually irresponsible, in both senses of the term. If racial violence is normalized as a given of daily life, individual responsibility is abrogated either to invisible social forces (ancient histories of antagonism, poverty of culture, etc.) or to errant individuals. The perpetration of racial violence in the state's name is clouded over, mediated, rationalized away by those reserving (relative) humanity or progress to themselves while cast(e)ing off or out as in- or less human the objects of the violation and as exceptional the particular perpetrators. Racelessness, or colorblindness as a particular expression, as we will see in chapter 8, is the project to reinstitute the relative invisibility, the anonymity, of racial rule in the wake of its postcolonial and globalizing excavation.

Laying Down Racial Law

Racial states attempt accordingly to assert themselves, to regulate through the rule of race, to impose race upon a population so as to manage and control, divide and rule. In these attempted assertions, though, racial states paradoxically divide by rule and so destabilize the very order they supposedly are designed to produce. In subjecting to (and through) race, states race subjection and so too cohere the response, reaction, and resistance by the terms through which they seek to repress. In insisting on the universalizing rationality of raced regulation, racial states delimit rationality to that of race, thus racially inscribing rationality and circumscribing reasonableness. In insisting on racial order, they impose racial violence upon the very violence they claim to be staving off, thus rattling the order they are seeking to reproduce. In the final solution, to rule racial brutes that are brutish by state assumption – brutes, as Hobbes at the dawn of the modern state insisted, are those the modern state must necessarily exclude from its domain – the brutes must all be exterminated, materially or symbolically. And to do this in the name of – executed by – the written law of the state.

Modern states – and here racial states once more are the norm of modern statehood, not the exception – speak through the law, in legal codes and terms. The institutionalization of race in and through the state is a form of legal reasoning, as I elaborate theoretically in the following chapter. It consists in the claim to displace brutish custom, to substitute for the idiosyncrasy and variability of everyday practice the systematicity and normativity of written codicils, and the assertion of atemporal order. Yet the extermination of all the brutes in the name of the law, and the project to institute racial arrangements through law, can only be effected brutally. In seeking to exterminate brutishness – the self-professed racial project par excellence – the state necessarily reveals at once its racial conception and becomes nothing short of brutal.

As much as anywhere else, the Congo Free is the place where, in the name of racial naturalism, "exterminating the brutes" was both asserted – stated – and literally acted out. The Congo provided, after all, the ethnographic example for Kurtz's notorious exhortation in Conrad's *Heart of Darkness*. Leopold II, the self-possessed Belgian monarch, hatched his brutal colonial designs in 1877 on the Congo Free State upon which he proceeded to impose direct dictatorial rule as a personal possession, principally effected for his selfish entrepreneurial ambitions and profitable ends. To legitimize Belgian domination of the Congo basin in the name of "free trade," Leopold skillfully manipulated the Berlin Conference on African colonies in 1885, and by extension invoked to his own purposes Bismarck's reputation in Europe.

From the outset Belgian imposition upon the Congo implicated both the Belgian state and people, monetarily and in terms of personnel, socially and legally. The Congo Free State furnished Leopold massive personal fortune in the raw material of ivory and most notably natural rubber (fueling the bicycle tire industry). This wealth in turn funded a large public buildings works in and around Brussels, including the Royal Museum for Central Africa (Goldberg 2001a), all glorifying Leopold's monarchy. Leopold's administration of the Congo had been under constant critical attack from as early as 1890 when the African American historian and activist, George Washington Williams, after visiting the Congo and witnessing abuses himself, wrote Leopold, the US President and Secretary of State in protest of the conditions he found there (Cookey 1968). Led by E. D. Morel, a British peace activist, a massive international campaign against Leopold's colonial rule in the Congo took off in 1903. It brought to light the enormous abuses, terror, and death executed at the hands of Leopold's agents in the Congo. And perhaps more pertinent in local Belgian politics of the period, it revealed Leopold's financial manipulation of the state coffers to his own colonial and local purposes. In 1908, faced by increasing international ostracism and growing debt, the Belgian government wrestled direct colonial rule of the Congo from Leopold's firm and direct grasp.

The Congo Free State – a more arrogant misrepresentation in naming a state does not exist – was ruled directly from Brussels, through the arms of a small number of European personnel, contracted bureaucrats, and mercenaries from Britain, Romania, and America, in addition to the majority of former Belgian military men. Guy Barrows, an American administrator in Leopold's employ, reports that in 1896 there was a total of 1,678 Europeans residing in the Congo, of whom a mere 335 served to administer a territory of 700,000 square miles populated by nearly 20 million indigenous people. The overriding mode of racial rule was depopulation along with the active deforestation caused by careless rubber-sap tapping. Rubber production in the Congo grew from 135 million tons worth half a million Belgian francs in 1890 to 5,500 tons worth nearly 50 million francs in 1904 (Nelson 1994: 84). But the human cost was almost inestimable. Between 1885 and 1920 it is projected that 10 million people died, murdered randomly and invariably on a whim, actively starved by state agents in the name of state policy and rubber collection, or left to rot from disease and decay, lack of food and declining birth rates. No woman was young enough to avoid rape (one especially infamous administrator, the cruel Major Lothaire, traveled nowhere in the territory without carrying with him a harem of around forty women, randomly killing or licensing the killing of countless Congolese). Men were removed of hands for failing to deliver impossible quotas of raw rubber. Children were orphaned because their parents were engaged in or happened to be in the vicinity of rebellious activity. Genitals were strung publicly from washing lines as warning signs and sick spoils, skulls marking the boundaries of claimed colonial estates. The crazed character of Kurtz was an accurate, if amalgamated, ethnographic narration of Euro-Congo culture.

In the Congo Free State law existed only to administer the "natives." The state's Civil and Penal Codes were "confused collections of orders and decrees" by various officials, exercised with limitless latitude and abject abandon. Appeal to administrative rule was tolerated for whites only, and clearly no black person could bear witness against a white man (Burrows 1903: 270–5). An English steamer captain employed by the Congo Free State writes that, though he had observed few atrocities by whites himself, he had heard many reliable stories "of revolting atrocities committed by State officials, who if they were not acting under the orders of a superior, at least escaped any punishment, and were decorated by the King on their arrival in Brussels." Captain Andrew Jones adds that even though eventually outlawed, "the flogging of women was a common practice . . . like all the State laws it exists on paper only for their [colonists'] own protection" (appendix to Barrows 1903). The "atrocity business," as Barrows remarks, "was placed in the hands of the State" (Barrows 1903: 173). In the name of "bringing civilization to the Congo," an explicit assertion to this day publicly circulated in the name of the Belgian state at the Royal Belgian Museum for Central Africa in Tervuren, written law is no less brutish for its claim to technological advance. Indeed, we could say that it does no more than advance (the extremities of) racially imposed brutishness and brutality in the name of naturalism.[7]

Leopold's rule in the Congo arguably offers the initial example of intense genocidal practice that has come to mark the twentieth century. This was rule through racial terror, the active pursuit and more or less conscious and executed design of extermination. By contrast, the affair surrounding the flogging of Phinehas McIntosh in the British Bechuanaland of the 1930s exemplifies under the title of historicism and the civilizing mission of racial progressivism a different if relatedly ambiguous form of laying down the racial law.

Phinehas McIntosh, a young working-class and nominally white man, by all reports "lived native" in Serowe, a large village and capital of Bangwato, covering about half of the then British Protectorate of Bechuanaland (now Botswana). But for the British administrators who lived in a separate compound, Serowe at the time was residentially mixed. A notoriously rowdy troublemaker, prone with his friends to drunkenness and physical abuse especially of local inhabitants, McIntosh was not untypical of British residents who took local mistresses as concubines (Stoler 1990). If he was untypical, it was in assuming the life of a local, in custom, dress, language (he spoke Setswana fluently), living arrangements, and social relations, actually, in all but the color of his skin. He acknowledged the children he fathered with a Serowean woman, and eventually respectfully recognized the authority of local rule.

Tshekedi Khama was a Chief who served as Regent in the area, standing in for his nephew, Seretse Khama, a minor who would later preside over Bechuanaland/Botswana. Tshekedi Khama acquired his administrative office in accordance with the British policy of indirect rule promoting decentralization. The policy of indirect rule was codified in the 1920s at the hand of Lord Lugard in light of his long colonial administrative experience culminating as Governor of Nigeria (Lugard 1922/1965: esp. 199ff.). Accordingly, local leaders were to be appointed to administer largely rural provinces in terms of customary law in matters affecting only "natives." Customary law in this instance was a collection of local rules and customs across different groups fashioned into an administratively coherent and manageable amalgam from the colonizers' perspective (Mamdani 1992). These local leaders were to be subjected in turn to the commands of colonial officers at whose behest they ultimately served. Tshekedi Khama answered most immediately to the authority of Bechuanaland's Resident Commissioner, in this instance Charles Rey, a military man of considerable arrogance, unsatisfied ambition, and little tact.

In 1933, after many brushes with local authorities, an unrepentant McIntosh was brought before Tshekedi's court ostensibly on charges of social nuisance and insubordination but as much as a result of concern over his frivolous sexual socialization with "native" women. Phinehas was sentenced at the outcome of the hearing to a flogging, two strokes of which were administered before Tshekedi dismissed him. Colonel Rey, livid at the prospect of a "white" resident being "subjected" to local law and corporal punishment, and incensed at the "evil of interracial sexual intercourse," nevertheless was delighted finally to be handed grounds for ridding himself of a Regent he had long found to be a nuisance. Rey had been trying to develop mineral mining in the territory as a basis for its economic self-sufficiency by employing local labor at exploitative rates. This was a policy vehemently opposed by the sometimes obstinate but always deliberate and occasionally cunning Tshekedi. The latter was justifiably more concerned with improving the living conditions of his wards. Rey attempted to circumvent Tshekedi's capacity to derail his policies by instituting rule through proclamation, which Tshekedi properly opposed by seeing it as eroding the expressed intent of indirect rule to empower local self-determination.

Rey instantaneously arranged for the British navy to exhibit a show of imperial force. Within days, a battalion of seamen had traveled 1,000 miles by train from their ships near Cape Town to invade poor, desert dusty, landlocked and militarily helpless Bechuanaland, arriving fully armed with the most modern of military weaponry. The displayed power of British military might was hilariously necessary to reinforce the vaunted rule of British law. Tshekedi was found in the ensuing formal enquiry to have overstepped his authority in seeking to exercise local customary rule over a European. In a series of ensuing rulings by appeals courts the justifiability of the Foreign Jurisdiction Act of 1890 was reiterated, giving to colonial authorities the "unfettered and unlimited power to legislate for the government of and administration of justice among the native tribes in the Bechuanaland Protectorate." This was a power deemed unmitigated by any subsequent treaty.[8] Tshekedi was banished from his province for a year, before being reinstated, and Phinehas McIntosh together with a close white compatriot was banished to Rhodesia for life (ironically, without the benefit of a hearing McIntosh had received from Tshekedi). Tshekedi allowed him to return a few years later to live out his life in Serowe (after marrying a local white woman), where they became neighbors and fast friends. Colonel Rey retired to the Cape, bitter at the metropolitan British establishment, and was replaced by a Resident Commissioner with considerably more administrative experience in indirect rule who recognized the woeful ways of Rey's attempts to rule by proclamation.

We find in this fascinating episode a different style and substance of racial rule than under Belgian despotism. Law is taken relatively seriously, at least as the principal mode through which power is exerted and exercised. Racial rule, if only in its initial exercise, was effected not so much upon the heads and bodies as through the hand of those ruled racially by themselves, with sometimes ironic implications ("white" treated as "native," "black" treated as if "white," law imposed through force, force effected through the rule of law). The threat of physical force was reserved to prop up the sense of dominance where it was seen to falter or where British authority was as much as challenged, rather than to be assumed as the resort of first, faultless, and deadly recourse.

The McIntosh case reveals at the same time that the localism of indirect rule in provincial localities was encircled by the overriding and unquestionable authority of rule by colonial imposition. It was contained by surrounding it in a commanding rule from the colonial capital (in this case Cape Town and Pretoria) that, in turn, was folded hierarchically into metropolitan rule from Europe. Thus local "native" rule was at least partly shaped and authorized by the generalizing hand of colonial administration. The distinction Mamdani draws between tribal and racial regimes – the former local and rural, ruled by customary law long in the making, the latter centralized and urban and ruled by an imposed Native Authority – collapses under the weight of racial imposition. Tribal governance was transformed into nothing more than a modality of the racial – historicist rather than naturalist, to be sure, but racial nevertheless (Mamdani 1992: 37ff.) Mamdani's "decentralized despotism" amounts to no more than centralized containment through local dispersal, with both local and centralized rules assuming multiple and varied expressions across space and time, as Comaroff's (1998) entire argument is designed to reveal.

The racial state, then, is a genus of forms and processes, an analytic generality the specificities of which differ case by case. Colonies of Britain, Belgium, France, the Netherlands, or Germany differed in their particularities, as indeed in racial specificity they differed from each other as well as from those of Portugal or Spain. It is because of these overdeterminations – in number and nature, in variation, and in the variety of their interaction – that one could begin to differentiate not only between particular expressions or institutions of racial rule but also their forms. In their spatio-temporal specificities regarding racial rule, the US differs not just from Canada but also from those societies with which it has been most compared, namely, South Africa and Brazil (contra A. Marx 1998), a contrast I will further elaborate in following chapters. Colonized states and metropolitan ones differed almost as much between as from each other, as too have the postcolonial from their colonial manifestations. So "the racial state" as a category offers no more than a template for rule, the contours rather than the content.

States of Racial Violence

The McIntosh case reveals that in its visible assertibility racial rule developed into a form of crisis management (cf. Lowe 1996: 174). It is in moments of perceived crisis that the routinized obscuring of racial rule evaporates to leave evident behind it the force upon which it is necessarily predicated. It renders evident, in addition, the (threat of) violent physical enforcement that racial rule is driven to invoke so as to reinstate the threatened order. The Congo (and perhaps this is generally the case for naturalistically driven racial regimes) was perceived in its otherness as inherently threatening, as state crisis constantly under construction. The virtually ceaseless states of emergency under mature apartheid exemplify this notion of rule through racially fashioned crisis also. With historicist racial regimes the overriding pursuit has been to rule through routinization, to normalize racial governance through the order of law, resorting to naked force only when the threads of racial order have torn at the seams of the social fabric as the administrative routines failed to contain(erize) the racially dominated "in their place."[9]

If crisis is the dominant medium of the visibility of racial rule, power is its mode, its defining condition. Power may be considered a potency, the capacity to act (Habermas 1986: 75–6). In social terms (as Arendt says), power is the capacity to act in concert (Arendt 1986: 64). The social power to act, however, is not to be defined simply in terms of capacity; it is more fully the potency to affect the standing of other people. Social power accordingly is not merely a capacity but a relation of relative capability, at basis a political relation. It is the active shaping of people's social standing, or the social positioning and possibility so to shape. The state affects social accessibility and status by way of its institutionalized apparatuses. It does so not only in class terms but interactively also in racial and gendered ones. Race in particular delimits acknowledgment of the grounds of such social (in)accessibilities, attributing them to the force of individual or group (in)capacities (Sartre 1960/1976: 720).

129

It follows that the state is (an institutionalization of) the exercise of power. It is, by both design and effect, the institutionalized elevation of the interests – political, economic, legal, social, cultural – of some to the exclusion or devaluation of others. State power thus is exercised and embodied in the name of and through the institutionalized apparatuses of the state in behalf of some (always more or less contested) interests to the exclusion of others. These interests may be narrowly those of the group directly holding and exercising political power, or more broadly of those whose class interests are represented by administrators of the state apparatus (or some combination). They may be exercised in concert with the logic of systemic imperatives mandating the terms of its own reproduction. In modern terms, I have argued, such institutional commitments, interests, and imperatives have been advanced through the order of law, underpinned by the threat of force.

Race is an especially convenient form of conceptual social cement here. For just as the state is an expression of power, so it is possible to reconceptualize race in terms of power. Race covers over the "magical" nature of the modern state, making its fetishistic characteristics appear all too readily as naturally given, as sacred and so unchallengeable (Taussig 1997). Thus even the historicist conceptions of race appear naturalized. Race is conceived as a container or receptacle of power, a medium through and in the name of which power is expressed. All too often race is projected as a rationalization for, an epiphenomenon of, power's expression the determinants of which are otherwise established (for instance, economically). While not always inaccurate, I have been arguing by contrast that race is itself the expression of relations of power. It is the embodiment and institutionalization of these relations.

Jewsiewicki and Mudimbe (1995) argue that it is not some naturally preexisting nation in the name of which state creation is mobilized. Rather, states instrumentally invent nations as a form of generalized socialization. By the same token, I am claiming, states are instrumental in inventing races both as a form of socialization and as technologies of order and control. States fabricate races, imputing to them a semblance of coherence. They do not create races artificially from whole cloth, however, but pick up the threads for designing the racial fabric from various sources, scientific and social, legal and cultural. States then are fundamental to weaving race into the social fabric,

130

and indeed the fabric of the modern state is fashioned with racially woven threads. States thus are endowed or endow themselves with "races"; they adjust and adopt races to governmental purposes. While states are instrumental in the institutional conceptualization of races, racial conceptions define and refine state formation.

That race is a marker, an expression, indeed, constitutive of modern relations of power makes it especially amenable to the expression of state power, one might say, to the central defining condition of modern statehood per se. Through race there is displaced from the modern state, covered over, the raw expression of state power. Such power, nothing more than created, is projected through racial terms as the given order of things, seemingly intractable and so established by natural or teleological law. The consensual rationalization of modern statehood acquires the anchor of racial naturalization; and the givenness of race, its teleology, becomes legitimated – reinforced – through the veneer of consensual agreement of citizens to the state and state fabrication. Those rendered racially inferior or different are locked in and away. The almost conceptual vacuity of race (Stoler 1997) enables configuration of transnational extra-state identities – for example, "the white race" or diasporic Pan-Africanism – as well as the reification and magnification of local, intrastate racial exclusions (cf. Balibar 1990). These two movements do not simply pull away from each other. Rather, the elasticity of race pulls them back as they stretch apart into a taut, mutually reinforcing racial order.

Now violence is conceived usually as the invocation and use of instruments (in the case of the state, state apparatuses) to implement the effects of power's exercise at the expense of those upon whom it is exercised (Arendt 1986). But we might think of violence more extensively also as the dispersal throughout the social of arrangements that systematically close off institutional access on the part of individuals in virtue of group membership, and indeed that render relatively hidden the very instrumentalities that reproduce that inaccessibility. This is violence not just in virtue of wrenching life's possibilities from some in order to elevate those of others, though it is clearly that. It is violent the more so in refusing to acknowledge the sources of the inaccessibility, attributing them through the forces of racial subjection to the individualized or group capacities or their relative absence of those who lack access. It follows that racial conditions of life as we have come to experience them throughout modernity – the racial

131

state in that broader sense of the term identified above – are inherently violent. So racial states in both their institutional and existential senses are not simply the exercise of power but equally states of violence. And the more violent the racist imposition, the more likely will it be that effective resistance will have to respond violently to some degree also. Here the violence of resistance is generically that of breaking the conceptual and social strangleholds, the yoke, of "given" and naturalized relations and conditions that have been enacted and reified historically in the name of race.

Thus, on this conception, not only were colonial conditions in the Congo violent, or colonial administration in Bechuanaland or India, but also those colonizing regimes licensing the instrumentalities of exclusion and refusing to do anything about them. The same point extends to the racial regimes in the United States, southern *and* northern, but also to the federal government that not only failed to curtail lynching but through constitutional law enabled the implementation of the "one drop rule," the institutionalization of the "separate but equal" principle, and segregated social space.

A Racial World Order

Finally, racial states are elaborated, reproduced, extended, and sustained – in short, they exist over time – in virtue of their relative positioning in the establishment of a complex global arrangement. Race was discursively fashioned as its elaborating definition helped to imagine and create a world known even by its protagonists as colonization (Merivale 1841/1928). Bodies were racially produced, constituted as bearers of political and economic, legal and cultural power and meanings. They were constituted as perpetrators and objects of racial violence in relation to their insertion into a world process of racial states, conditions, and arrangements. Belgian military and missionary men flocked to Central Africa. Indigenous people were dehumanized and delimbed as they or their relatives were Christianized. Phinehas McIntosh found himself in a British Protectorate at the southern end of Africa, stripping himself largely of his Scottish identity even as British colonial administrators insisted on his racial belonging. He was flogged at the orders of a local indigenous official, Tshekedi Khama. Khama's authority, in turn, was derived in large part from the colonial system

132

of governance that at once disciplined and denigrated him. His rule, as we have seen, was subjected to the might of a landlocked British navy whose unquestioned power was about to be challenged by a more extreme form of racist state formation in the name of Nazism. And European women traveling in the colonies at the end of the nineteenth century could see their patriarchal homelands as free by comparison despite the fact that they still lacked the vote (Grewal and Caplan 2001).

We find in these examples and countless others like them the representation of a worldly web of racial arrangement, relationally produced over time, positioning not only people(s) but nation-states in terms of the fashioned hierarchies. As Balibar notes, Wilhelm Reich characterized this as "nationalist internationalism."[10] These meanings and the institutional arrangements upon which they depend and which they recreate have shaped the outlines of possibility for their inhabitants.

As much as power was cemented racially in state formations within a global ordering, resistance to any part of the racial ordering of states, affairs, and people ultimately has had to assume proportionate global reach. Not only was the abolitionist movement transnational in organization, so too the debate in America concerning post-slavery prospects for freed slaves conjured global movements. Thus the American Colonization Society, founded in 1817 by the likes of Jefferson, insisted on African repatriation (as did Lincoln famously later) because the racial differences between whites and blacks were deemed so naturalistically deep as to prevent "the races" living peaceably together. The Society was infamously instrumental in founding and funding the free state of Liberia. On the other side of the divide, the African Civilization Society, led by the likes of early "black nationalists" Alexander Crummell and later Edward Blyden, likewise looked to Africa as post-abolition salvation for freed slaves. Crummell in particular argued that emigrating American blacks had the responsibility to "civilize" Africa into the virtues of Christianity and commerce (Crummell 1861/1996; Blyden 1862/1996).

Anti-colonial and anti-racist campaigning, most notably in the wake of massive migrant mobilization, has recognized the global scope of racial conditions. Racial states anywhere are shored up in larger or smaller ways, more or less directly, by their connectedness to racial states everywhere. Resistance movements have understood the need to respond to racist conditions in appropriately global terms. The campaign led by Morel against Leopold's regime in Central Africa grew from London but certainly looked for support to America and Europe. Tshekedi Khama journeyed to London to petition the king concerning the appropriate forms of colonial rule in Bechuanaland. Colonial subjects, upon studying at the likes of Oxford and Paris, Amsterdam and Heidelberg, Moscow and Louvain, returned to their homelands to lead nationalist decolonizing movements in the name of Pan-Africanism and Negritude. Both sought and secured international connections, reflected not only in the Conference on Race in 1911 but also in the international sites of the various Pan-African Conventions (New York, London, Paris, Manchester). Among the earliest mobilizations at the fledgling United Nations was the Convention Against Genocide in 1946 and the first of many Declarations on Race followed just two years later.

There is a negative implication to this globalizing of racial conditions, however, well worth closing this chapter by noting. At the turn of the nineteenth century emergence of Afrikaner nationalism enabled the British to think themselves free of discriminatory spirit. We see here how the interconnectedness of what I have tentatively identified as a loosely ordered racial world systemic process has served not merely to mobilize racist structures, nor simply to sustain racial resistance movements. Relations between the civil rights movement and the anti-apartheid struggle, between Black Power and Black Consciousness, jump to mind. This racial world system equally shores up racially exclusionary conditions globally and locally. It has enabled denial of their own implication in racial state formation and conditions of those claiming greater racial tolerance, displacing their implication behind the veil of those more extreme expressions. The international anti-apartheid campaign reproduced this logic: conservatives and liberals alike in Europe and the United States could declare themselves against apartheid and for colorblindness, against racism and at least ambivalent about affirmative action, at once blind to the relation. It is to the implications of these questions of law, violence, and globalization for more or less contemporary manifestations of racial states that I now turn.

NOTES

1 I do not mean to make too much of this, in light of Stephen Small's careful empirical research revealing that the white men fathering mixed black offspring were usually poor and hardly in any position to extend advantages to their children, other than their nominal whiteness, even where unusually they might have wanted to (Small 2001: 28).

2 "[T]he state . . . does not have this unity, this individuality, this rigorous functionality" (Foucault 1991: 103).

3 For instance, the legislature of the State of California in 1850 prohibited the conviction of a white defendant in criminal proceedings on the strength of testimony offered by a black, mulatto, or American Indian witness. In *People v. Hall* (1954), the murder conviction of a white man was overturned on appeal on the argument that, as a member of "the Mongoloid race," the principal witness, a Chinese man, was identifiable with blacks and so his testimony was ruled inadmissible because unreliable (see Goldberg 1997: 39).

4 Anthony Marx (1998) has argued recently that political elites resorted to racist exclusion, most notably in the form of de jure segregation, to consolidate whites in the face of intrawhite conflict (Civil War in the US, the Boer War in South Africa), national instability, and potential demise in power. So de jure segregation apparently was fashioned to unite whites in these societies. By contrast, Brazil suffered no internalized conflict among whites, and so no need to resort to segregation of blacks as a way of uniting a divided nation identified with whiteness. In Brazil, discrimination accordingly assumed less overt forms. Marx takes racial formation in these societies to be imposed more or less top down by elites seeking to ensure solidity in their nation-building in the late nineteenth and twentieth centuries. He adds in a nod to nuance that formal exclusion prompted resistant racial identities among people of color which were necessary in turn for protesting such exclusion and mobilizing for inclusion and resource sharing. Here again Brazil is differentiated from the other two instances, for in the former lack of formalized racism is deemed to result in the relative lack of resistant race-based identity formation.

Marx conceives the state minimally and traditionally in a Hobbesian vein, as using race instrumentally to the ends of stability and security (Marx 1998: 4, 13). He accordingly offers no account of race and race making beyond what elites and resisters are taken superficially and obviously to do in relation and response to each other. So he fails to show how race is used, what it stands for materially and symbolically, what work and conditions in different contexts it is able to effect beyond the

135

bald unification of whites in the face of their own potential conflict. Accordingly, he suggests a totally reductionistic sense of race as functional to social definition, determined by a mix of economics and politics, the effect of which is to force an artificial similitude between the US and South Africa in order to save the thesis. Superficially both the Civil and Boer Wars were conflicts for control over territories and wealth. By contrast, however, the Civil War was not an *ethnic* conflict among whites that necessitated state imposition of segregation to resolve. Nor in a more subtle reading of their respective histories are either simply reducible to black–white bifurcation, even as that racially created division has dominated both. Indeed, as I have argued above, the state was implicated in modern race creation from the outset, as race was mobilized to mold modern state definition in different ways at different times. And if ethnic tensions among whites in the making of modern states supposedly are resolved through a broader black–white bifurcation, how is it that Belgium fails to fit that model?

5   Irish Nell, a white indentured servant of Lord Baltimore, married Charles, a Negro slave, shortly before this, bearing him children after passage of the law. A great granddaughter in turn contested her enslavement in the eighteenth century on the basis of the law, finally prevailing in 1787 (Hodes 1997). Indeed, Jefferson realized the economic importance of black women to the reproduction of slave labor: "I consider the labor of a breeding woman as no object, and that a child raised every 2 years is of more profit than the crop of the best laboring man" (Thomas Jefferson, letter to Joel Yancy, January 17, 1819, in Jefferson 1953: 43). Cheryl Harris (1995: 279), following Ron Takaki, wrongly attributes the quote to a letter Jefferson wrote to John Jordan in 1805.

6   Charles Mills (1998: 187–9) calls this "subpersonhood." He insists, again, that the creation and elaboration of the category of subpersonhood is a product only of what I have identified above as the naturalist tradition. As he says, *"for these beings* [subpersons], *a different set of normative rules applies; natural law speaks differently"* (Mills 1998: 188, his emphasis). A little later Mills insists that Kant, "preeminent Enlightenment theorist of personhood and the founder of the modern concept of race," places Native Americans at the bottom of his hierarchy of races, a rung beneath blacks. But nothing Kant says bears this ordering out. Quite the contrary, Kant's characterization of "Negroes" – as "stupid" with "no feeling rising above the trifling" – is in clear contrast to his sometime, if begrudging, praise for "the savages of North America" whom he insists are not one of "the four original races" but derivative from the "Hunnic (Mongolian or Kalmuck) race" of northern Asia (Kant 1775/1950: 17–18). Thus he says of the latter that "Among all the savages there is no

136

nation that displays so sublime a mental character" for "they have a strong feeling for honor" and are "truthful and honest" and above all driven by "valor" (Kant 1764/1960: 110–12).

7 By 1887, it should be noted, naturalist presuppositions in the case of the Congo had already been placed in question. Thus, Jerome Becker, a Belgian military representative and colonial agent in the Congo Free State, could claim in historicist terms that, "I ask any one who knows anything about Africa to look over the land, and ask himself if there is not abundant proof of the *improvability* of the native" (Becker 1887, 1: 140; quoted in Fabian 2000: 237, my emphasis). For these reasons along with his association with Arab traders to whom he "remained loyal" even when the Belgians mounted a campaign against them (Fabian 2000: 18), Becker was ostracized from Belgian rulers and resigned from colonial service.

8 *Tshekedi Khama and Another v. The High Commissioner*, in William (1935: 31). For the detail of the Bechuanaland episode, I have relied upon Crowder (1988).

9 While devoting relatively few pages to the use of military force and only late in his large book, Lugard nevertheless recommends that a soldier shoot quickly to kill a single or few insurrectionists as a show of power. He promotes the willingness to use force rather than sparing immediate life at risk of revealing weakness and facing the need for a much larger response later (Lugard 1922/1965: 580). For an elaboration of "principles of imperial policing," see Gwynn (1934). Since its establishment over fifty years ago, the state of Israel has had in effect a legal state of emergency designed for the most part to deal with its internal "Arab question," legislation that enables "the Israeli cabinet to supersede the legislative process" (*New York Times*, April 7, 2000, p. A10).

10 Balibar understands this to begin with Nazism (Balibar 1990: 287). I am suggesting that it is initiated at least with colonial formations in the nineteenth century.

6

LEGISLATING RACE

We must find a form of government that puts law above man.

Rousseau

More than forty years have elapsed since the men of the Anglo-American United States shook off the yoke of our Kings: the yoke – the fouler yoke – of our lawyers [lawmakers], is even hugged by them, and remains still upon their necks.

Bentham (1820/1995: 126–7)

It is the monstrous, yet seemingly unanswerable claim of totalitarian rule that, far from being "lawless," it goes to the sources of authority from which positive laws receive their ultimate legitimation, . . . that far from wielding its power in the interest of one man, it is quite prepared to sacrifice everybody's vital immediate interests to the execution of what it assumes to be the *law of History* or the *law of Nature*. . . . The discrepancy between law and justice could never be bridged because the standards of right and wrong into which positive law translates its own authority . . . *are necessarily general* and must be valid for a countless and unpredictable number of cases, so that each concrete individual case with its unrepeatable set of circumstances somehow escapes it. . . . The law of Nature or the law of History, if properly executed, is expected to produce mankind as its end product; and this expectation lies behind the *claim to global rule* of all totalitarian governments.

Arendt (1951: 461–2, my emphases)

Law's Order

Racial states, as modern states in general, are bound by necessity to legal expression, though not in any singular sense. Modern states have taken themselves to be conceived and constituted, managed and maintained through the rule of law (Kriegel 1995). As modern states paradigmatically understood, racial states are no exception. Their very modernity is ordered through the racial configuration of law, and the legal fashioning of racial definition and articulation.

Shedding the cloak of religious determination, the modern state socioinstitutionally came to represent the theoretical presuppositions first of Nature and then of Rationality. As I have demonstrated in earlier chapters, the modern state, qua modern, assumed the mantle of reason, thus establishing itself as principal or supreme Authority: textual, political, legal, at once as telos and interpreter of History. Modern reason, in the name and under the authority of science, has traded on classification and taxonomic schemas, purporting to guarantee the predictability and so control of particulars by folding them under the generalizability of laws. Modern state authority thus has sought as its "foundation" the stature of scientific reason that the state undertakes to undergird and license, to reflect and represent. In the waning part of the nineteenth century, legal positivism came to voice this blending of state assertion with the epistemological commitments of scientific positivism (MacKinnon 1989: 162).

We find a suggestion here of law's importance to state practice and institutionalization. In authoring the law, the state seeks its own legitimation through law's claims to justification. Law, legal discourse, and legal consciousness assist in proliferating state control and discipline across the landscape and population, in disseminating the marks and effects of the state and state reason, its modes of comprehension and logic, and in contrasting state civility with primitivist anarchy (cf. Goodrich 1987; Merry 1990). Law fashions state identity and order over increasingly diffuse regions, people(s), and activities. People are united in the face of their apparent anonymity by legal instrumentalities, discourse, and the legal consciousness their diffusion through the population (seeks to) promote(s), even as law defines and divides those it unites in contradistinction to those falling outside of the defining criteria. Modern (liberal) legality's imposed uniformity,

139

seeming neutrality, and supposed impartiality (Giddens 1985: 99) help to paper over these deep contrasts and divisions across space, place, people, and classes. Modern law accordingly promotes as it serves the "'national fantasy' of homogeneity" (Comaroff and Comaroff 2000a; Berlant 1991).

The proliferation of law deflects any critical or resistant social focus from the state itself, or from state authority and raw state power. Where prevailing social arrangements and relations of power are identified by Reason and represented in their codification through the authority of Law, they are resistible only at risk of irrationality, at risk that is of identification with (or as) "the Primitive."

Law has assumed increasing social centrality, a sort of foundational artifice, with the rise of modern states. The state of modern governance, as many have been quick to point out, has been a product of increasing populations, rising heterogeneity, expanding anonymity and alienation in the face of failing familiarity and fading kinship communities. Where social intimacies have given way to privatizing cultures in the face of rapid individualization, modern law has offered an abstracted connectivity, a more or less anonymous link between fabricated similarities the law in part has helped to fashion through its own classificatory logics. This capacity of modern legal logic to order similarities, to be the architect of likes, has served well the nationalizing drive to a fantasized homogeneity. For central to modern legal logic is not just to recognize but to create the very likenesses across difference that modern law claims to treat alike. Those falling outside of the assimilative categories – and the categories of legal similitude necessitate for their very recognizability the category of the outside, of outsiders – are cognizable only as strangers or criminals. If the subjects falling within law's scope are disciplined to act or be alike, to be the objects of law's authority, those outside are marked by the force of criminalization or varieties of other racio-national and ethnoracial exclusion. This logic of legally mediated racio-national alienation has served settler colonial societies in their drive to state formation, and postcolonizing states in managing what they consider the challenges (and threats) of postcolonial migrations.

So, despite its idealized claims to fairness, objectivity, impartiality, and thus integrity, and of the rightfully successful claims of groups to advancement through law's ideals, there is something inherently alienating and dehumanizing about modern (liberal) legality (a point driven home by the work of critical legal studies (Fitzpatrick and Hunt 1987; Kairys 1998)). In its imperious insistence upon universality, modern (liberal) law opposes particularity and proceeds from a stance of anonymity. As Kant emphasized, a person is moral not in terms of any specificity but in virtue of exemplifying the abstract moral law. Here law's efficiency is a function of its abstraction, the appeal of its capacity to be blind to particular conditions or status. There is a subtle sense, then, in which modern liberal legality is indiscriminate, deeply committed both to a specific ordering of social relations and to the denial of such commitment. Modern (liberal) law's objectivity and impartiality thus are achieved by the distancing technology, and ultimately by this (moral) blindness, central to its mode of applicability (Bauman 1998).

Depersonalized and dehumanized in legal abstraction, people are reduced to mere objects, alien and anonymous. In giving standing to people in terms of their group status, through the concern to right states of injury, for instance (Brown 1995; Engel 2001), the law shapes and in shaping reifies and limits the categories in virtue of which the state or claim of injury may be manifested. Modern law's contours of identification are necessarily the identification of (limiting) contours. In its elaboration, then, modern law is especially disposed – one might say, constitutively so – to work its way through interfacing group categories such as race and gender. Feminist legal theorists have revealed astutely how patriarchy has been, inter alia, a legal project and process. The simultaneously cohering and distancing categories of race and gender tend in turn to reify and exacerbate law's limitations, as critical race theorists have insightfully identified. This conceptual integration of race with gender through law accordingly enables the couple to be insinuated or collapsed into, and so to work their way quietly and amorphously through, the law (Bauman 1989: 189; Crenshaw 1995b; Harris 1995; Weisberg 1993). Through law, race and gender have become routinized in state institutions, penetrating into civil society and its institutional frameworks.

Laws of Racial Rule

Now law plays a central role in the shifts I have been mapping from racial naturalism to historicism, early modernity to high modernism, the absolutist state to the modern one (Giddens 1985). The authoritative influence of legal positivism, in particular, served to structure these shifts. As the most fitting expression of modern rationality, law (as Hobbes quickly understood) was central to modern state formation, and to elaboration of the modern state's self-conception. It is unsurprising therefore that modern law has been invoked as a technology of racial rule, promoting racial categorization and racial identification, thereby exacerbating law's abstraction. Under older naturalist regimes, those more expressive of absolutism, however, it was a means simply to shore up, to whitewash, to legitimize physical violence imposed upon bodies as the preferred, more direct and primary mechanisms of racial rule and social control. Here law served violence, rendering acceptable the reign of racial terror by the state, state agents, and state members (cf. Baxi 2000: 547). With historicism, the recourse to law shifts. Law becomes the primary means of racial order, (the threat of) violence now the means to ensure legal enforcement. Racial rule from the late nineteenth century becomes first and foremost rule by and through law. Under historicist challenge thus even naturalist states – southern states in the US, Nazi Germany, apartheid South Africa, increasingly and certainly after 1908 the Belgian Congo – find themselves challenged to invoke the rule of law to racist purpose. Racial rule comes to assume the rule of law.

European expansionism was initially promoted principally through physical force trailed by the legitimizing light of the law. Local homogenization in Europe and among Europeans far afield was figured through the projection of naturalized racial difference led by physical force and then legally codified. In the broad, European self-elevation was effected through degradation of the colonized, materially and ideologically. Where the Spanish empire struggled in the first decades of the sixteenth century over proper moral treatment of its colonized, this moral soul searching quickly gave way to legally legitimized physical repression. Bentham's advice to the fading Spanish crown at the beginning of the nineteenth century concerning the closing of its colonial ventures which required the assertion of physical repression intimated the legal shift that would follow a century later (Bentham 1820/1995). In the overlap of naturalist and historicist commitment, Portuguese Angola in the later nineteenth century, not unlike American Indian policy in the US at the time or Australian Aboriginal policy fifty years later, legally mandated assimilation while violently committing to native extermination or separation. The elevation of racial historicism was not simply coincidental but co-constitutive with the rule of law as the principal medium through which racial dominance was henceforth to be maintained. The racially elevated and devalued were codified in and through law, the integral processes of elevation and evaluation juridically produced and reproduced, managed and maintained.

This distinction between naturalist invocation of legality in a sense after the fact and historicist law as socially constitutive may be further nuanced by distinguishing between legitimation of repression *by* law and racial governance *through* the rule of law. Naturalist regimes have sought to impose order upon a racially conceived social formation by using law to effect and legitimize raw force, to render that force more palatable. Law is invoked rationalizationally to distinguish modern civilization from those natural (and so uncivilized) states taken to lack positive written law. Here law, most notably in the natural law tradition of early modernity, comes to assume what Baxi in another context characterizes as "the face of fate" (Baxi 2000: 551). Historicist regimes, by contrast, resort to law not so much instrumentally as constitutively, ruling racially through law, shaping race in the terms of legality, threading race through law into the very fabric of the social. Here lawlessness becomes not so much a transgression (or enactment) of nature as a failure to live up to one's historically delineated potential. The distinctions between naturalism and historicism, modern racial rule legitimated by law and enacted through law thus nuance the classic Weberian definition of states as the agency of legitimate force.

It follows that the command theory of law could be considered characteristic of colonized contexts in more direct and less mediated forms than colonizing metropolitan formations. Assumptions of the "rights of man" and broadly speaking of a constitutionalism embodying abstract principles of right and legality tend to delimit imposition of raw governmental force in the way conjured by the command theory. As Upendra Baxi (2000: 541) aptly remarks, "Colonialism and constitutionalism were always strangers." Perhaps it could be said that the unmediated commands of colonized legalities make possible the more mediated legalities of the colonizing metropolitan ones. Colonized contexts often rendered the subjugated population inherently unqualified for protection by application of such normative principles. "Negro slaves," for example, were explicitly excluded from protection in the Constitution of the Carolinas largely penned by Locke, while in British

143

India or French Algeria law applied to its colonizing and indigenous inhabitants differentially even as inherent equality of the rights of man was abstractly recognized. In the first case, law legitimates its own inapplicability in the Lockean lack of Negro slave protection; in the second, law itself produces the categorical differentiation in its racially driven applicability.

Colonial legality and the thin sense of "justice" it embedded are, to borrow Baxi's terms, "at best *paternalistic* and at worst *accessories* to imperial domination" (Baxi 2000: 541). In investing this power of differentiation in the law, law at once is placed above "man," as Rousseau insists it ought to be, and deflects responsibility for the subsequent injustice that follows from the men that effect it. As John Stuart Mill makes clear in an article on "Civilization" written for the *London and Westminster Review* in 1836, modern constitutionalism has been predicated upon two central commitments, articulated as basic rights, the first to private property (Fitzpatrick 1999) and the second to free expression (Passavant 1999; Mill 1836/1963: 49, 53). In marking the constitution of modernity, each becomes a sign also of incapacity, of an inherent or historical human lack.

The lack of private property and the projected impossibility of civil speech serve as measures of racial inability, inherent or manifest. Where and when taken as inherent, these projected incapacities are codified into law as negations, as the necessary denial of legal extension to the natives. When deemed historical incapacity, the absence of temporal acquisitions of the basic requisites of civility, rights to property and expression are delimited, circumscribed in space and time to those moments and places convenient to the ruling "burdens" and fears concerned with maintaining racial privilege, identified in terms of maintaining order and morality. Private property and the right to speak thus become productive of social formations, as Paul Passavant insightfully reveals in regard to speech, constitutive conditions and markers of ways of world-making and being at different moments in time. They furnish the axes in modern cartographies of liberty, mapping the "moral geographies of civilization and barbarism" (Passavant 1999: 65–6; Mill 1836/1963: 46–9) they at once serve to define and refine as the very conditions of their own possible promotion. Rights to property and speech – the rational power to "calculate" over the otherwise irrepressible pull of impulse, as John Stuart Mill puts it (Mill 1836/1963: 48) – inscribe the borderlines between civilization and savagery, extensions of Europe and peoples without or before history. Those lacking or preceding history serve not only as the ghosts of things past, that which civilization is not and its laws are designed to delimit if not exclude, but also the specter that threatens always to haunt the future. It is perhaps partly because of the insistent extension of such legal rights and protections in principle to all "legitimate" metropolitan residents in our postcolonizing period, therefore, that we have witnessed an increasing shift, since the civil rights and independence movements, to privatization of racist expression. I will have more to say about this drive to privatizing discrimination later.

Modern state rationality has depended on law's powers, which are as much *productive* and *constitutive*, then, as they are *sanctioning* and *restrictive*. This distinction cuts across as it complements that between law embedding conceptions of *justice* (and their applicability) and enacting modes and procedures of *governance* (cf. Baxi 2000: 544). Of course, governmentalities and principles of justice can coincide, complement each other, or collide. Where racial distinction is embedded in or reified by the law, its effects are exacerbated, producing what one might call "racial justice." Racial justice ambiguously references those peculiar forms of injustice we have come to witness all too often. A state constitution might be suspended (or not extended) in relation to some racially defined population (Palestinians most recently, for instance), or their differential treatment might be written into constitutional terms. Even where the law is racially silent, it might easily extend established social effects long embedded in or lingering from past sociolegal formations. Thus the neutrality of the law is no guarantee of equal treatment, as we have now come to see all too often. Many have followed Anatole France's lead in commenting that those finding no other place to sleep than under, say, Manhattan's bridges are subject to law's forceful prohibition in ways de facto inapplicable to the residents of overlooking penthouses. Oftentimes forms of governance, whether racially explicit or silent, squeeze out or reduce the range of permissible responses to historical or contemporary racist acts or structures, institutions or implications.

The law regulates the processes of social formation it reflects. It makes possible the production not only of commodities but also of their signifying powers, the possible and legitimate public meanings that commodities and social processes carry (Coombe 1996). Law regulates in addition their distribution and consumption, imposing order upon socially coded objects, signs, and meanings. Thus, even where racial signs and meanings are established outside of legal domains, seemingly beyond law's reach, the law undertakes to contain and constrain, refine and order those meanings within law's logic and definition. So law's force is underpinned by state authority and power, as well as by social investment, just as state authorization manifests in the logic of the law. And yet, as I have suggested, the law also calls subjectivities into being. This is law's *constitutive* role in daily life, at work in consciousness formation and cultural creation. So those committed to racial classification need constantly to shore up the categories in and through the law (even as the law helps to establish, shape, and authorize these categories). Law accordingly assists in shaping identities, meanings, and so the social world. It promotes identities and meanings, and it offers a medium in and through which identities and meanings circulate.

So it does not help in any straightforward sense, as MacKinnon insists in respect of gender (MacKinnon 1989; Brown 1995: 128–34), to commit to expanding law's universality. The universality of law is constituted *necessarily*, not merely extended or restricted, through the particular determinations for which the generalizations of race, gender, and class stand. Given the universality of law's formalism, law's applicability necessitates its customization. Social considerations of race, gender, and class mark particular conditions that sociolegal universals reference either not at all or only partially and incompletely (Siegel 2000: 87; Volpp 2000a, 2000b).

Lest this picture seem overdeterministic, it must be qualified by emphasizing that state racial subjection and subjectification, at least as much as sexed subjectification, are rarely (performatively) complete, rarely exhaust the (self-)identification, (self-)formation, and (self-) definition by the subject generally, and by the subject in particular as raced. Social formations and structures offer the contexts and conditions, the limits of possibility (if not always conceivability) in, and in terms of which, identities and agencies might be conceived and considered, manifested and expressed. So, the state may license and promote racial or gendered identities like "white" or "male," and their co-articulation. And yet racial subjects obviously may express their identities – more or less complex and more or less intersectionally articulated – in ways transgressive of state license, individually or collectively, though across the political spectrum ("race traitors" or "keep America white" groups, "passing" persons or activists persistently desegregationist in racially segregated circumstances, mixed-race or strictly color-coded couples or families, and so on).

The color of constitutional cruelty

Thus there is no racial regime and regimentation without law (and more or less no modern legal formation without racial representation, explicitly or implicitly). If for naturalist regimes law is in the service of a more or less brutally imposed racial order, effecting a "constitution-alized cruelty" (Baxi 2000: 544), for historicist state formations racial order is already manifest in the shaping of the legal terms itself.

So the surge of the spectatorial blood sport of lynching throughout Dixie from the 1890s to the 1920s, while complexly prompted, can be seen in this light as a naturalistic reassertion in the face of a critical insistence on historicist legalism. Reconstruction was the attempt in part to shift racial order in the South from a primarily forceful to a principally legal mandate. Segregation was a spatial schema that once more mixed force with legality, though in varying order. If lynching could be rationalized as "taking law into their own hands," law by implication comes to be represented in the acts of lynching them-selves. This is especially the case in the absence of any other response or resistance to such acts on the part of legal representatives. The forces of "law and order" not only turned a blind eye to acts of lynching in this period but were often directly implicated in the acts themselves. Lynching after all was seen by the perpetrators and im-plicated bystanders precisely as acts of (re-)instituting a threatened (or even lost) law and order. The decade of the 1890s averaged one lynching in the South *every other day*. Certainly, no participants, direct or indirect, active or passive, were punished for their acts. And the participants were varied, ranging from the anonymous few working in the dead of night to the many cheering spectators notoriously "captured" in photographs and postcards.

Understood thus, lynching is the racial violence of vigilante rule, the manifest masculinist expression (Wiegman 1995) of segregationist space in the face of the historicist challenge to a seemingly raceless rule of law. It is the privatizing of the insistent imperative to law and order, or more strongly still the collapsing of the public and private into each other, the invasion of the state's instrumentality by self-proclaimed agents and the execution by state agents of private agendas. State and society do not simply mirror each other in the repetitive practices of lynching's sanctioned terror but invoke and enact each other's modus operandi. Race becomes the medium of this collapse, at once making it thinkable and rendering it legitimate, placing the all too transgressive taboo of castration barely out of conscious view even as it makes the violence of those sexual acts conceivable. The fact that James Bird's vicious lynching at the hands of three white supremacists in 1998 (he was dragged to death chained to the back of their truck), or its copycat act in South Africa, could be taken to be the basis of "racial healing" or "reconciliation" among the still racially segregated residents of Jasper, Texas, or Johannesburg, indicates the continued dialogic tension between naturalist "anomaly" and the contemporary rhetorical hegemony of historicist racial rule.[1] But it also signals the reinscription of the distinction between public and private spheres that more recently has become the terms of extension of racial states, as I argue in chapter 8 below.

In its sanctioning capacity, then, law both opens up and closes down forms of representation, spaces of accommodation and transformation, possibilities of expression, truth claims, and legitimation. While the law closes off areas of contestation (to state power and its expression, to the privatized expressions of civil society, indeed, to thought itself), it simultaneously opens up areas of subversion, of counter-formation in the face of social formation and reification, of counter-hegemony in the face of hegemonic totalization. It thus offers a venue, conceptual and material, in and around which mobilization might take place to effect the representation of interests, the legitimation of social standing, extensions of rights (as interest, claim, liberty, and power) to social resources (Goldberg 1995). As we will see in a variety of examples in chapter 8 below, in offering such possibilities, though, the law shapes and mediates not just public meaning but the scope of economic expression, cultural signification, and political practice.[2]

Racial Restrictions

I have been suggesting that race has marked modernity and its development constitutively, that the racial state is in this sense the paradigmatically modern social formation. It is not simply that modern states have invoked race as technologies or instrumentalities of governance, though that clearly has been quite common. At the basis of the possibility of such invocation, rather, racial configurations have ordered the making of modern states, their formation and elaboration, their founding and shaping, as modern state technologies have helped to fashion racial conceptions and concerns, classification schemas and population controls. Thus the narrowing of social heterogeneities in the name of racial conception is not something simply or merely ordered by state instrumentalities, most notably law, though this is not to deny such racial instrumentalities on the part of the state either. Underlying the very possibility of such homogenizing effect is that the modern state is inherently constituted through racial formation, though not in any given or singular form. The very terms of race are disposed to homogenization, and its malleability in meaning makes it especially open to political arrangement. Modern state imperative is directed towards the fantasy of homogenization precisely because modern state formation is constitutively marked from its inception by self-defined racial design, by racial restriction. Modern state architecture is racial by definition as modern racial conception in the final analysis is state mobilized or maintained, managed or mediated. In the absence of state prompting or promotion, articulation or ambivalence, invocation or implication, (explicit) racial conception would become marginal at best. But that would imply the end of the peculiarly *modern* state.

The line of argument I have pursued here reveals that, through law, the modern state narrows heterogeneity in form as it sharpens the particularity of social distinction. The abstraction from particularity and to general principle necessary to law's conception and application at once makes possible civil rights protections – that abstraction away from the *discriminatory* particularity of race – and the impossibility of (fully) addressing the particularities, the specificities, of racist exclusions, derogations, (dis)privileges, and (in)opportunities. The almost "universal *lingua franca* of [modern] law, of rights and constitutions," as Comaroff and Comaroff note (2000: n. 22), fashions the means through "which human beings, divided by irreconcilable distinctions of one sort or another, might render commensurable, and hence negotiable, otherwise inimical values, demands, and expectations." Law's formal narrowing of heterogeneity accordingly leaves to the non-formal – the private – realm those distinctions and hierarchies that formality is unable to tolerate.

So, unlike the more vicious naturalist racial regimes, liberal legality does not seek to obliterate the distinct but fashions a space outside, beyond its self-authorized realm, for such distinction to be enacted (cf. Siegel 1998: 31). That the emergent legal emphasis on privacy in modern constitutional law is coterminous with the legally mediated shift I have been noting from racial naturalism to historicism is not a superficial coincidence. The-soon-to-be-Justice Brandeis's famous essay on the constitutional place of privacy that he penned with Stewart Warren (Warren and Brandeis 1890) opens the possibility for thinking exactly the extension of privatized racial privilege and power in the shift to formalized constitutional colorblindness first marked by Justice Harlan's equally famous dissent in *Plessy v. Ferguson* (1896). In the discourse of privacy, the modern state in fact has managed to order a lexicon by which it has enabled distinctions in substance and content while denying them in form.

Racial distinction in law's lexicon

There are at least three senses in which the state molds a language, a grammar and a vocabulary, through which it rules. The first, of course, concerns the language of the law itself, and the assumptions under-pinning the terms of its expression. The law is an abstract set of codes that mediates heterogeneity, fashioning the artifice of administrative and administered homogeneity. It offers not merely the treating of like alike that forms the basis especially of liberal systems of justice, but the making of difference into sameness so as to be able to treat "like" alike, through the language – the *lex*icon, as Comaroff (1998: 343) points out – of the law. Here law's language becomes the medium of symbolic, cultural, commodity and capital circulation and exchange, the producer and arbiter of difference, the maker, mediator, and man-ager of disputes. Nevertheless, in order to effect such mediation the de facto differences occluded by law's homogenizing imperative become repressed, to sometimes devastating effect.

Consider here the shape and operation of the "reasonable man standard" in the law. One can trace genealogically the transformation from the "reasonable man standard" represented in the Anglo legal tradition through the image of the not-quite generic "man on the Clapham omnibus" into the "reasonable person standard" of that "com-muter on the Simi Valley Expressway." These figures are embodiments of much the same (if not identical) presumptions about the normative commitments that conflate to produce the content of that standard considered at once civilized and citizen – the cultivatedly disinterested "exemplary person" (Lloyd and Thomas 1998: 6) of the modern democratic state: white, suburban, middle class, and male, but also Western and modern, possessed of property and the capacity to speak rationally.

It is against the normative commitments of such a standard that one must understand the dominant dismissal of the "irrationality" of the jury deliberations and decisions in the O. J. Simpson criminal trial (Goldberg 1997; Cornell 1995: 14–15), or the effect on jury outcomes in moving criminal trials from inner city to suburb, or off Indian reservations into non-Indian jurisdictions (Brigham 1996). Unarmed Guinea immigrant, Amadou Diallo, was shot at forty-one times in the vestibule of his apartment by four white New York policemen as he reached for his wallet to show them identification. The murder trial of the policemen was moved to Albany in upstate New York nominally to escape the glare of New York City publicity, a move that substantially provided an almost all-white, female, completely middle-class jury. The police were acquitted of homicide, even dereliction of duty or reckless endangerment. The jury must have considered the more or less indiscriminate police firing of their guns as Diallo deliberately reached for his wallet a rational response – an instance of rational discrimination – in the face of standard stereotypes of black criminality. Such examples, for they are many, furnish faces both racially and gender hued to the abstraction of state power and powerlessness, to agents exercising and objects of the law. They demonstrate the ways in which the supposed neutrality of formalized state power, of its definition and expression, is fashioned in (but also through) law as a generalization of particular group conceptions, dispositions, commitments, and interests.

Second, the state rules through an administrative lexicon, of which the law is a more particular, perhaps more ritualized expression. The state's administrative language likewise supposedly seeks to fashion homogeneity in the face of differentiation, imposing order in the face of distinction and tension, repeatability when faced by multiplicity, the reiterability of precedent and past example in the face of dissonance, commonality before contrasts. Census classifications, as we will see in chapter 7, are a case in point. But they reveal at once that any classification into racial groupings works logically and symbolically by an at least implicit, and often explicit, set of contrasts. The failure to fit – to fit in, in the sense of finding a place inside the categories of the administrative linguistics, both its vocabulary and its syntax – entails at once also being cast out. The failure to fit (in) amounts to being a social outcast, named if at all as stranger or terrorist and racially as not white, the generic anomaly to whom in one's particularity and specificity the language fails to refer. To fail to be referenced by the lexicon is to fall outside the law, to be unadministered save as the object of expulsion and abjection, removed or at least removable in the state's name to a place beyond its borders or to institutionalized holding pens such as prisons. These are the only sorts of ways modern law knows to name generically those the law cannot leave nameless.

The third sense of the lexicon through which the state rules is the broadest sense of language itself, the spoken and written word. This includes the language of intercourse and ideology, pedagogy and politics. In the racial collapse of civil society and public sphere, state arrangement of everyday statements and state meanings shape the signs of civil exchange. This is the state's determination over the scope of social and political meanings, its policing the parameters of sense and sensibility, fashioning the horizons of significance through signification. Here the state, always only partially successful because internally incoherent itself with multiple agencies and constituencies, serves to limit what can be said and thought, to patrol meanings and feelings, social commitments and habits while limiting antithetical responses. It is as if the state affects itself, fashions and projects itself, as a coherent entity through this linguistic self-assertion. The limitations are proposed and circulated, if not enacted, through the literal language and logic of bureaucracy and pedagogy (what I have elsewhere nominated "administrology"), through the medium of public language and education, the linguistic mediation of official discourse in administrative and legal documents, radio, television, and newspapers. And of course such limitations are restrictive, though sometimes as much in a productive (dare I say progressive) as a conserving direction, and not always so easily distinguishable.

Thus the imposition of European upon indigenous languages by colonizers in the interests of the assimilative project sought by design or implication to annihilate indigenous culture. European languages and their derivatives like Afrikaans were considered superior, the bearers of the values of civilization, of rational thinking, to which in the historicist mode the native ought to aspire. Which is to say that it was thought the native ought to be encouraged to shed his nativity, in part through language acquisition. As the "natural" reproducers of the racio-national condition, not just biologically but culturally (and so linguistically also), women (at least in a much more lingering way) for the most part were considered incapable of shedding their nativity, thus exacerbating the ambiguity between racial naturalism and historicism, inevitability and transformability, stasis and progression. Where racial states tolerated administrative bilingualism they were almost inevitably dual European languages, or European and European derivative vying for precedence rather than a European and an indigenous language. Thus we find English and Afrikaans in contest in South Africa after the Anglo-Boer War, or English and French in Canada, or the struggle over English only in the face of contestation from Spanish in parts of the United States. And where colonizing states enabled or promoted the use of indigenous languages for administrative purposes, as in the case of indirect rule in Africa, it was through the imposition of a single indigenous alternative across multilinguistic indigenous usage. Here the concern was to fashion administrative homogeneity in the face of multiplicity, an artifice of uniformity – cultural, political, legal, and administrative as much as linguistic, indeed, the former through the latter (Lugard 1922/1965; Mamdani 1992). The English-only movement in the US has sought to restrict by law the language of formal education and state administration to English, thus recognizing the cohering instrumentality of legal power.

In streamlining state management through linguistic and administrative means, racial states, colonizing or otherwise, already prefigured the language of response and resistance. They forced the terms even of resistant reference into the narrowing confines of comprehension and comprehensibility, making racially ordered subjects in the language of rebellion assume the lexicon of their nemeses, of those subjecting them. So the language of racial struggle becomes black *nationalism* or civil *rights*, homogenizing customary law or colorblind constitutionalism, racial essentialism or racelessness (cf. Comaroff 1998: 345). This sociolinguistically confining and refining sociolegalism, while providing paths to "progression" and interest advancement for those formerly or otherwise racially excluded – most notably (though in some broad sense not only) educated elites and political or economic opportunists – nevertheless narrows the choices of resistant response to a rejected extremism or an imposed legal culture long representing dominating interests. And it places once more just beyond reach the possibilities of an unmarked social condition, whether racially acknowledged or raceless, for it makes those not white never white, as Lewis Gordon insightfully puts it (Gordon 2000: 32), but always "whitelike," legally as much as linguistically. As naturally not white they are white never naturally, aspiring always only in spite of themselves. "Passing" on this set of assumptions is as much a transgression of some projection of natural law as it is of positive law.

Racial Sovereignty

Law, then, is a generalized and generalizing apparatus of power deeply implicated in establishing state sovereignty, consolidating and reifying lines of power in modern state formation (Giddens 1985: 98–9). State sovereignty, taken to be the defining and refining condition of modern state formation, is fashioned dialectically in relation both to external powers and threats – most notably, control in the face of invasion by others – and the manufacture of internalized threats. Thus the very thinking of the state of sovereignty is predicated on the dream of a legislated homogeneity, of sameness across populations and the relative externalization of threats and the different.

Race thinking here offers the (pre)conception, a projection, of a naturalized, originating population homogeneity. As such, race has made available a ready (but *not* necessarily naturalist) means for defining and refining internal state homogenization, a homogenized state formation thus ethnoracially and racio-nationally differentiated from external states and conditions. Throughout modernity race at once has erected barriers to threats from external state sources racio-nationally differentiated while connecting states in global systems of racial homogenization and differentiation. State homogenization and national definition came to be molded through racial configuration, sewing racial definition into the seams of state sovereignty.

To play on Balibar's terms, then, homogenizing racial definition has offered to individual nation-states superpower fantasies, if not quite always such status, exacerbated by the powerful possibilities of racially encapsulating suprastate global forces such as NATO or the G7 group of economic power houses (cf. Balibar 1990). The sentiment of racial comfort artificially promoted by this prevailing sense of homogeneity has also offered the possibility of privileged global movements between states for the human and economic capitals considering themselves racially identified. It cannot pass without commenting that every current member state of the G7 not much more than half a century ago was marked for the sake of its own drive to social domination, internal or external, more or less deeply and assertively by racial articulation under one interpretation or another.

It follows that Nazi German exceptionalism is a function not of state racial definition and racially mandated violence, which were widespread throughout the world system of colonial regimes and settler societies. The exceptionalism of the Nazi state, rather, has to do with the extremity and unmitigated violence of its racist expression, its mostly unmediated racial assertion and its willingness expressly to purge itself of those defined by "scientific" and positive law as the racially impure. Japan and China at the time, as well as the US and Canada, South Africa and Britain, Latin America and Australia, embedded elements of such definition without being moved to express themselves either in law or policy, national philosophy or demographic profile quite so explicitly, self-confidently, or extremely.[3] Allied states were far more ambivalent about state racial definition, and indeed about invoking race as a totalizing deterministic for world order. This ambivalence was exacerbated by the depth of the mid-century global crisis. Nazi exceptionalism, not unlike that of apartheid, accordingly had to do rather with the holdover or reinscription of naturalist insistence in the face of the emergent hegemony of racial historicisms.

Gilroy (2000) thus is right to emphasize fascism's formal expression as a pivotal point in calling into question the racial programs of state formation. Nevertheless, like others, his historical periodization overplays the moment, for as I have been suggesting the crisis marks less an anomaly and challenge to the history of modern racial state formation than it does both the logical outcome and the death throes of a world order predicated largely on naturalism and the shift to a global regime premised on the institutionalized fabric of racial historicisms. It is not that naturalist commitments die or disappear altogether, as we will see later, so much as they furnish the necessary counter in contrast to which historicism at once can claim success and clean hands.

Racial historicism, it might be said, is the mediation between naturalism as the extreme, classical expression of racist embrace and universalism in epistemology, morality, and legality that is considered a central mark and commitment of modernity (cf. Fitzpatrick 1999: 39–40). Historicism makes it possible for proponents of modernity to hold onto the privileges of racial configuration of state and civil society without abandoning the expressed commitment to universalism. Here law and order become key components of this mediation, for those social arrangements or states considered racially less well developed are exhorted to modernize precisely by adopting the mandates of a legality considered to be rationally configured. Race at once serves as premise ("less developed societies"), administrative medium (classification schemes), target of state intervention ("racial progress"), and teleological object of categorical evaporation (legally fashioned colorblindness or racelessness).

If the category of "civilization" served as the standard for naturalist assessment of the racial hierarchy of colonizing states, Fitzpatrick and Darian-Smith (1999: 5–10) usefully point out that the notion of "human rights" has come to operate as that proxy in the historicist register of globalized postcolonial state positioning. The point is not that the concept of "human rights" must necessarily anchor such a racial register – Western democracies historically, if not inevitably, supposedly have come to respect them, "Third World" states to violate their observance. Rather, it is that any such universalizing concept is available to particularistic conception, design, content, and purpose in the claim to universalism. Fitzpatrick and Darian-Smith characterize this as the logic of "universalized particularity."

The historicist exhortation to "traditional" or "less developed" societies to modernize through the legal or constitutional assumption of human rights is marked by a deeply Hegelian irony. Those societies once marginalized as static are implored to become dynamic by those standard bearers of a world-historical telos who in their self-enthronement have become the embodiment of stasis, invariance, totalization, absolutism (Fitzpatrick and Darian-Smith 1999: 10). The logic of late modernizing legalities necessarily trades on rhetorical tensions at once dismissed and embraced. At the same time, the universalizing thrust of a concept like "human rights" is available to those historically positioned as wanting by racist representation to demand equal treatment. This availability and demand, it has to be admitted, have enabled and effected social movements in many ways successful in turning racist arrangements into racial ones, and racial social orderings into raceless, non-racial, post-racial, and indeed occasionally anti- and trans-racist ones.

The latter litany points back however to the depth, and perhaps even to the intransigence, of the general concern. The logic of universalized particularity is not simply local to the notion of "human rights" but to any claim to universalizing political conception. Thus, too, the call for racial equality, important as it has been in moving from the horrors of naturalist presuppositions and political frameworks, has foundered not so much on the racial qualification as on the ways in which equality assumes a conceptual particularity in its (silently or implicitly racial) qualifications and localizations. The tensions between equality of process and outcomes, the ambiguities surrounding equal treatment *before* the law, and the potential gaps between the equalities of existential conditions and processual treatment have steadily undermined or undercut commitments and claims to universalization, not to mention "racial progress."

The tensions here are exemplified in an especially acute way in thinking about the social threads tying together the racially driven discourses surrounding immigration, affirmative action, and criminalization, most notably but not only in the US. This trilogy, of course, is mutually implicated precisely through racial configuration. Nevertheless, I will address the centrality of immigration law to the definition of states of white racial rule in the following chapter, and so will limit my brief remarks here to affirmative action and criminalization.

On one reading, affirmative action is at odds with historicist commitments of colorblindness or racelessness. Racelessness in state commitment or rhetoric did not come all of a piece. It manifested piece by piece, in contest with invocation of race to undo past racisms, and affirmative action at least in its most controversial concerns regarding admission, employment, and funding preferences sought through explicitly racial terms to address the legacy of racist exclusion. On a counter-interpretation, however, affirmative action is a later historicist version of educating those for whom there are no inherent barriers to the degree of economic or moral self-determination. Understood thus, affirmative action is to be seen as the extension of historicist commitment. The social dominance of historicist discourse accordingly restricts the terms of struggle between proponents of racelessness with their vehement attack on race-based preferences and policy promoters of affirmative action to a contest over the shape and content of historicism. That race matters deeply to the resolution, whether directly or by implication, is testament to the framing power of race in setting the terms and limits of thinking the social.

Affirmative access and restriction, socially delimited through racially coded law and policy, is chained dialogically to the racial contours of criminalization. In one sense, racial presumption positions those not privileged by white heritage as presumptively social outsiders. Policies and legislation concerning immigration and criminalization not only become colored by racial estrangement, they are mutually implicated in some ways. Modern state mandates to homogenization promote policies of racially restricted access, the racial delimitation of surplus populations, and the racial production of surplus value in terms both of profit and populations (see Goldberg 2000b). In the face of such circumstances, modern states trade on racially promoted social elevation and racially contoured privilege. While prisons have served as modern institutions of social control in wider ways, they have been integral administrative apparatuses of racial definition and reproduction, racial conception and control, racial privilege and value – explicit and extended, assertive and implicative.

It should come as no surprise then that racially driven increases in prison populations, in North America or South Africa, Europe or Latin America, should spiral at exactly the moment explicit racial privilege and power as well as demographic homogeneity as a result of (im)migration are called into question. As Zygmunt Bauman (1998) suggests, the threats to presumptive safety and certainty that follow the magnification of global capital flows, economic and human, prompt recourse to law, order, and the instrumentalities of spatial control. Disprivileged historically, populations defined as not white are (re)configured as anxiety-promoting threat or surplus, devalued or revalued as potential sources of violating the social compact and of socioeconomic and cultural regeneration.

The terms of racial legality, and of a law that refuses to face up to the historical implications of racial configuration in the wake of racial erasure, are thus always ambiguous. Modern states are modern in virtue of legislating race. Written into law, race rules in, through, and by legislation. But inscribed in law, racial order in a sense becomes required by law. Every modern state is defined, then, if not explicitly by racially driven formalities, certainly by implication into a modern world system fueled by its terms; every attempt to go beyond race is weighted by its legacy, every gesture at universalization by race's particularities. No escaping modernizing racial positioning from within or without precisely because modernity and modernization are defined by, in relation to, and in terms of the index measuring the progression of states of whiteness. In this, racial legality mirrors – and is deeply related to – the condition of law as patriarchal, so well conceptualized in the past two decades by feminist legal theorists. White by law, modern state formation authorizes itself in the name of the imperatives of whiteness. Modern states are states governed by a patriarchal whiteness, at once masculinist states of white being, states ruled by those self-nominated white and representing the interests of white privilege and patriarchies.

Racial progress, by one measure, is determined by the distance traveled from the rule of racial naturalism. By another measure, though, it is always the distance traveled in relation to white patriarchal yardsticks. The sustained critique with which I am engaged throughout the book is predicated on a difficult underlying concern, namely, to consider what social arrangements generally, and sociolegalities in particular, might look like that took as their central commitments not the reproduction of homogeneity but the generative possibilities of heterogeneities. I turn now to elaboration of the lunge to white states – which is to say, the rule of racial patriarchies – and their implications, shadowed at all times by heterogeneous resonances as the possibility of a counter-normative ideal.

NOTES

1 In the wake of the lynching, for instance, residents made much symbolic capital of tearing down the century-old fence that divided the black cemetery from the white one. Jasper continues to be deeply residentially segregated.

2 Rosemary Coombe's work on trademarks, commodification, and the law has been especially helpful in thinking about law's productive capacities (Coombe 1993, 1996).

3 Regarding race and Japan, see Weiner (1994); on race and China, see Dikötter (1992). On race and Latin America, see Graham (1990); Whitten and Torres (1998); De la Cadeña (2000); and Grandin (2000). In general, see Bennett (1998).

7

STATES OF WHITENESS

Some States have allowed facts other than physical character-istics to be presumptive of race. If one was a slave in 1865, it is to be presumed that he was a Negro. The fact that one usually associates with Negroes is proper evidence to go to the jury as tending to show that the person is a Negro. If a woman's first husband was a white man, that fact is admissible evidence as tending to show that she is a white woman.

Stephenson (1909/1910, 2: 41)

It is not a fact that in Canada or Australia there is any contempt for the coloured races as such. The two countries are faced with the problem of keeping their civilizations intact and their blood pure while huge migratory populations are knocking at their doors. Their political systems are democratic, giving the same right to every citizen, and they have made no allowances for the incorporation of an alien laboring class such as to be found in South Africa. If immigration were to be allowed without restriction they would be submerged entirely in a few years by the mobile proletariat of Asia, people who have no intimate acquaintance with political institutions in their own countries, and who have a marked tendency to coagulate in large masses that disturb the social balance. And inevitably there would be the racial feuds, embitterments, and exasperations which destroy the felicities of life wherever the races live freely side by side.

Palmer (1919: 558)[1]

These leaders [of the white mob] were perfectly willing . . . to recede to the level of race organization, if by so doing they could

160

buy lordship over other "races." And they knew from their
experiences with people gathered from the four corners of the
earth in South Africa that the whole mob of the Western civilized
world would be with them.

Arendt (1951: 207)

I have argued in previous chapters for thoroughly rethinking the
history of racial identity creation and identification in terms of
modern state formation, and the emergence of modern states in
terms of racial conception and framing. This refashioning of socioracial histories suggests a response to the controversy over whether
racial thinking marked premodern conceptions of self and society,
and by extension whether there is racism in ancient or medieval
worlds.

Clearly, discrimination of an ethnocentric variety pervaded premodern worlds. I have argued elsewhere that such ethnocentrisms in
some ways served as precursors while failing to amount to modern
forms of racist exclusion and subjugation (Goldberg 1993: 2–5, 14–
40). In the modern but not in the ancient or medieval worlds, there
no doubt is an explicit sense of racial distinction, and racial nomination throughout modernity has underpinned a range of individual
and socially organized discriminations, exclusions, and oppressions.
The crucial point, however, is that the significance of race and the
racist exclusions and oppressions that racial distinction is taken to
license are modern state projects. Racist exclusions and oppressions
are authorized and legitimated by state commission, and often made
possible by state omission. Racial identity is conceived, authored, promoted, and legitimated in good part by state action and speech, and
institutional racist exclusions throughout modernity more often than
not have been prompted and legitimated as state commitments. This
is not to deny that state promotion of race distinctions and exclusions
is favored because they often are already circulating in civil society.
Once cemented silently into the fabric of state definition and pursuits,
however, racist effects are sustained by their routinization in social
and state practice, and by state silence and omission. This is absent
from premodern state formation. There is no evidence of racial or
racist state projects at work there.

Generally, it could be said that the more rigid and formal the racial
classification system in a society (whether considered prevailingly

binary as in the United States or tripartite as in South Africa), the more state creation of racial terms is likely and explicit state management would be required. The less formal and more broadly proliferated the racial categories (as in Latin America, and Brazil in particular), the less state implication would seem explicitly necessary in forming, fashioning, and fueling the racial categories.

Of course, social and political imposition as well as legal definition are in considerable part behind defining blacks or whites, First Nations or Indians, Hispanics or Anglos, as "a people" (Hickman 1997), as a group with a more or less coherent identity. Each of these groupings form social collectives – for instance, in the US, South Africa, Britain, or Australia – the *racial* underpinnings for which are very largely state mediated and managed, fabricated and fictioned, displayed and displaced. Racially conceived states are invariably molded in the image of whiteness, to reflect the interests of whites. But *"being black"* or "Indian," for instance, should not be thought of as simply reactive, either in a forced or resistant sense. Blacks, like Jews and Indians, are formative in creating themselves as "a people" before and through and after state imposition and resistance. Black folk fashion an identity in relation but not reducible to the identity created "for" them informally in social culture and more formally through state formation. Black identity – as social identity more or less generally – is one created and recreated for itself in negotiation with the definition and meanings of blackness extended to it by broader social forces and relations. In turn, the sense of a more or less self-fashioned social identity diffused throughout the group influences the more formal state definitions over time.

Racial distinction is adopted as a state practice very early in modern colonial regimes. More or less formalized racial differentiation and identification as well as racist subordination and subjection, however, "elevate" to the level of coherent and designed state projects only by the closing decades of the "enlightened" eighteenth century, though they are clearly in evidence centuries earlier. Why racial historicism took hold in some colonial powers such as Britain around the middle of the nineteenth century and a little later in France and the English diaspora but not – or not so firmly or only much later – in others, such as Germany and Belgium, has to do with a host of more or less directly determining considerations. The distinction follows from different traditions of coercion in state formation, the determining conditions of capital, as well as with emergent traditions of public morality and the local vigor of abolitionist movements.

The differences between naturalist and historicist socioracial commitments vary with the presence or absence in a state of internal governmental and administrative confidence, with the influence of religious liberalism, with utilitarian powers of capital, and with the visibility and literacy of expressed forms of resistance. The larger and more administratively elaborate the empire at the time, the more heavily engaged in the slave trade, the more likely the colonizers would be dependent paradoxically upon the colonized. And the more heavily colonizer and colonized interfaced with each other, the more difficult it became for those dominating to deny the humanity and historicity of the dominated. The Haitian Revolution (1790–1804), for instance, shattered the complacency of the naturalists. It encouraged a number of slave rebellions throughout the Caribbean and in the adolescent United States, and a steadily swelling stream of writing in the form of an emergent black nationalism. More immediately, as Laurence Thomas (1993: 129–30) has noted, it became increasingly difficult for a slave master to deny the humanity of slaves cooking for his family or caring for his children, or indeed upon whom he was imposing his sexual demands.

Principles and practicalities of governance, racial conceptions and theories, social, political, and economic conditions as well as legal articulations and disciplinary reflections thus weave together to produce specific expressions and manifestations of racial states. The late nineteenth-century complex of material conditions and racial conceptions is illustrative. The slave emancipations by the latter part of the century almost throughout the European sphere of influence sat uneasily with the discovery in various colonial sites of precious metals like gold and diamonds and the attendant push for cheap sources and control of local and migrant labor. Labor demands and the threat of job competition in the wake of abolition and industrialization, alongside fears about spatial pollution and moral (not to mention biological) degeneration, existed in tension with the civilizing missions, calling forth often uneasy alliances between church, capital, and state. As the panics over moral and physical degeneration evidence, the shifting intellectual tensions between naturalistic and historicist presumptions – between claims to inherent inferiority and cultural difference in racial othering – cut across these materialities. Segregationism is one outcome, prevalent at least formally across a wide swath of settler states at the close of the nineteenth century, of the intersection between such sociodiscursive forces.

Segregating States

Segregationism manifested more or less at the same moment in the American South and in South Africa, in British and French colonial cities.[2] Formalized segregation was a dominant response, in theory and policy, to the interactive conditions of labor demands and political imperatives, changing demographies and legalities, political realities and moral paranoias, shifting discursive terms and disciplinary presumptions. As the Palmer epigraph illustrates, it was a locally specific, if internationally sustained, reaction to the perceived threats of population proliferation, economic and sexual competition, fear of lost authority, however nebulous, and the challenges of social heterogeneity. Segregationism, then, responded to these concerns with the force of sociospatial imposition promoted, if not sometimes prompted, by legal imperative.

Systems of segregation

The Anglo-Boer War in Southern Africa (1899–1902) marks the moment in which these shifts became explicit, indeed, more or less self-consciously contested. The war, fought nominally over continued British colonial rule in the region and so over local settler independence and control of newly discovered mineral sources, was really about the shape of the racial state, and of racially shaped empires, across a changing global map, as Hannah Arendt (1951), if in somewhat problematic terms, makes clear. It was a war – perhaps the first explicitly – between north and south, in global terms, between Anglo-American capital in contest for control with emergent local settler capitals and self-determination, and between naturalist and historicist commitments in racial rule. It reflected the struggle between what at the time was perceived as a hopelessly unsalvageable *ancien régime* of racial rule and an emergent developmentalism taking itself as representing enlightenment. It contrasted the inefficiencies of a physically debilitating and economically inefficient labor supply sustained by

164

terror and the costly technologies of sociospatial segregation with the promise of an industrialization requiring a proximate, skilled, and more or less steady and stable labor supply. The war accordingly represented the contest between completely color-coded and colorblind social arrangements, between racially configured peasantry and over-lords, on one hand, and racially conceived, if denied, demands for proletarianization and embourgeoisification, on the other. More deeply, however, the Boer War sounded the imminent death knell to British colonial aspirations and perhaps the warning bell to colonial regimes more generally that racial colonization would face open challenge and ultimately insurrection, from settlers as much as from indigenous populations, though for diametrically contrasting reasons. The ten-sions outlined above would soon explode openly onto the world stage. In short, the Anglo-Boer War rendered the shape and content of racial states open, and openly contested, questions.

I am taking the war that closes a century of racial imperialism and opens one of formalized and informal segregations and their anti-racist challenges, then, as a visible marker of a deeper set of global shifts, first in racial conception of state formation and more broadly in social arrangement. The Boer War signals the initiation of a long and slow evaporation of global colonialism and the equally tortuous emer-gence of economic neo- and postcolonialism under the supposedly benign banner of racelessness. But it evidences more immediately the explicit centering of spatial arrangements as a technology of racial configuration, most notably in the form of de jure segregation and migrant labor arrangements. The moment of the Boer War accordingly reveals a shift in state technologies of racial rule. State transformation (Tilly 1994) once again is tied up intricately with racial reconception.

Prior to the late nineteenth century, race was considered the outside of Europe or European domain, European *exteriority*, what Europeans or those of European descent considered themselves not to be, the negation of civilized rule and being. Towards the close of the nineteenth century, this dominant concern in conceiving racial con-ditions becomes *internal* to state formation. Racial governmentality loses the pointed focus of colonial exteriority, thus becoming at once more diffuse. It now concerned the shape and nature of the state itself, the conditions of being of and within the state, the character of its population.

Racial rule in the twentieth century thus concerns itself dominantly with immigration and local urban arrangements, with controlling racial conditions internal to state formation. Concerns about race turn increasingly to the nature – the state – of *the urban*. Initially, this is a shift in racial focus from conceiving race as the outside of civil(ized) society – as its negative space, as the natural landscape of the state of nature – to keeping out those considered racially uncivilized (at least relatively speaking): Out of the state (as in immigration restrictions), out of urban areas (migration restrictions and pass laws), out of white neighborhoods (residential restrictions and removals), in short, out of white space. Over the longer *durée*, however, it has involved a slower shift to the guarded internalization of race, and so ultimately to a new racial governmentality of *containability* and *containment*, to enclosing race within. And these enclosure acts (Dumm 1993) have served to render race the centerpiece of social life, the diseased heart of dark- ness, even as they have sought at once to render racial conditions invisible in their commitment to make social conditions raceless.

Shifts from exteriority to containability in the technologies of racial rule are those first from the invented discovery of racial outsiderness to keeping racially conceived others out, and then when this proved unsuccessful (for push–pull reasons) to keeping in "dangerous," racially defined populations. Such shifts are not unlike the modes of administering other perceived pollutants of the social body, like lepers and the insane. Governing those characterized as lepers and the insane shifted from islands of insanity and leper colonies to immunologically isolated institutions locally located within urban centers. In the case of race, these transitions may be exemplified in the emergence of spatial segregation in the US at century's turn.

Servicing segregation

In 1900, the prevailing social setting and experience of blacks in the United States was "southern and rural"; for whites it was "northern and urban" (Massey and Hajnal 1995: 531). In 1880, less than 13 percent of blacks lived in towns and cities, while roughly 28 percent of whites did. The typical black urban resident at century's end lived in a ward 90 percent white, and was more likely to share a neighborhood with a white person than a black neighbor. Ninety percent of blacks lived in southern states while 75 percent of whites

166

lived in northern states, mainly in urban counties. White *exposure*[3] to blacks outside the South was limited, and Jim Crow laws orchestrated contacts in the South. In 1900, then, the physical distance between blacks and whites was a function of the fact that they tended to live in different states and counties. Most blacks tended to reside in relatively few states, the average black American living in a state the population of which was 36 percent black (Massey and Hajnal 1995: 531; Hirsch 1993: 65–6). If *evenness*[4] of racial distribution across state lines were a value, nearly two-thirds of blacks would have had to change their state of residence to achieve it. In southern states a majority of blacks lived on the land in counties significantly black. By the same token, as Massey and Hajnal reveal, if cross-county racial evenness were to have been sought, it would have required nearly 70 percent of all blacks changing their county of residence.

As black migration led to greater racial interaction across state and county lines, blacks became progressively segregated within cities. The more black urbanization expanded, the more racial segregation and restriction of black residents within cities were extended. Thus, by 1930 the spatial location of segregation already had transformed perceptibly from region to neighborhood. Black urban residents tended to live in wards 40 percent black. From 1890 to 1930 black residence in New York surged nearly tenfold from 36,000 to 328,000, in Chicago over twentyfold from 14,000 to 234,000. Chicago neighborhoods just 10 percent black in 1900 were swept by the cold wind of segregation into neighborhoods 70 percent black just thirty years later (Massey and Hajnal 1995: 533–4; Hirsch 1993: 66).[5]

Already in 1940 ethnic white neighborhoods were far from uniform in their ethnic composition. Neighborhoods in which blacks lived tended much more to be overwhelmingly black (Denton 1994: 21). Identifiably "Irish" areas of cities included just 3 percent of the total Irish population, and most of New York's Italians did not live in Little Italy, for instance. By contrast, 93 percent of black people lived in neighborhoods that in the categorical formation of race in the United States can be characterized as majority black. The historical (re)production of contained Chinatowns reinforces the ethnoracial logic at work here (cf. Goldberg 1993: 198, 201). The conditions for the reproduction of European immigrant ghettoes in US cities, accordingly, have never existed in the way they have in the twentieth century for black ghettoes. European immigrant segregation ebbed as

167

their migration flow waned, and as we shall see they were transformed through "assimilation" over time into *being* white. Black segregation within the boundaries of confined urban space, by contrast, increased not primarily as a result of black housing preferences but of conscious white avoidance and state design (cf. Denton 1994: 22). Means of segregating enactment and enforcement included physical violence, intimidation, and the creation of a dual housing market by way of racial covenants, tax breaks for housing development, state-funded project housing, and so on. So white exposure to blacks was still self-determinedly minimized through ensuring black isolation and containment in urban ghettoes (Massey and Hajnal 1995: 533–4). As Denton concludes (1994: 22), cities became instruments for European immigrant group advancement, but blocks for blacks, their containing isolation, not only residentially but educationally and economically also.

Carceralities of state formation

These newly emergent forms of racial confinement were social spaces, state enabled and sustained, mandated and managed, surrounded symbolically and materially by racially conceived and created sanitizing boundaries. In their interiorities, they are, as Michael Taussig has so provocatively put it in another context, magical and implosive maps of anarchy and containability, "freedom and imprisonment." We may think of them as terrains of repressive liberty, spaces in which the inhabitants are left largely to do almost whatever they find personally profitable or appealing so long as such acts and their material implications, if not quite so straightforwardly their symbolism, are confined within quite strict spatial constraints.

The power of race is magnified here by the fact that it is so obviously everywhere and nowhere. The boundaries of such spaces are visibly identifiable through race as seams of the social fabric. The extent and degree of their material effects are evident to all and yet causally ungraspable. That the causes seem so invisible, so ethereal, makes the racial nature of the spaces seem less real too. Responsibility for their production and reproduction, I will argue more fully in the following chapter, evaporates with historical memory behind the veil that comes to be called colorblindness. Their boundaries in any case are "a cordon that with money and influence could be broached any time

168

despite its brutal disposition" (Taussig 1997: 56–7), and indeed from both sides of the divide.

These late modern states of confinement differ, as Taussig rightly insists, from that of the panopticon, both actually and metaphorically. *Panoptical carcerality* rests upon an internalized gaze promoted by initially placing the all-seeing social eye at the institutional center. By contrast, the *carcerality of containment* encircles the source of anarchic difference and more or less abandons the spatial internalities to their self-chosen excesses. If panopticism is predicated on the presumption of the self-internalized logic of control, it necessarily fails where increasing numbers of the subjected population explicitly and self-consciously reject the presupposition. The logic of containment is a response to the rejection by the subject population to the given premises of racial rule. It seeks thus to cut off any consequent anarchic influence and implication from effecting or influencing those outside the spaces of confinement. The sought amputation nevertheless is anyway and necessarily incomplete and partial.

The state is deeply implicated in reproducing, if not always initiating, the segregating spatial presuppositions of confinability. De jure segregation enabled the containability that flows from spatial segregation, the latter at once materializing the former. The strategy of containment is implicit within and hidden behind the legal formalities of segregation, though its material possibilities were pursued self-consciously only in the wake of segregation's formal demise.

Formalizing segregation

There is a significant shift in the United States from the pre-Civil War to the post-Reconstruction state conceptions of race. As both Gotanda and Crenshaw indicate, where prior to the Civil War race was taken as a marker of material *status* distinctions, the post-Reconstruction segregationist interpretation marked race in terms of *formal* differentiations constructed by governmental apparatuses (Gotanda 1995; Crenshaw 1995a). This change in racial signs is clearly evidenced in Supreme Court rulings. Thus, in *Dred Scott v. Sanford* (1857) Chief Justice Taney could insist that, because black people were almost universally considered by white people to be inherently inferior, "negroes" were clearly diminished in material and legal status. "Status race" mixes presupposition and perception with material conditions,

169

the former taken to legitimate relative standing as regards the latter, the latter reinforcing the former.

By the late nineteenth century, by contrast, the state had become much more self-consciously instrumental in its creation of racial categories – as we shall see, for instance, in census counts – leaning increasingly on the claimed neutrality and objectivity of formal racial distinctions. These formal racial distinctions were taken as proof that the state is neutral in its formal treatment of the differentiated groups, considering the groups de jure equal even if de facto dramatically unequal. So the *Plessy* court argues formalistically in 1896 that

> A statute which implies merely a legal distinction between the white and colored races – a distinction which is founded in the color of the two races, and which must always exist so long as white men [sic] are distinguished from the other race by color – has no tendency to destroy the legal equality of the two races . . .[6]

Material elevation and devaluation in reality not only hide behind formal equality in the law but the status differentiations marked by race – in particular, the presumption that whiteness is (a) property (Harris 1995) – are promoted and sustained by the claim to formal equality.

> If he be a white man, [sic] and assigned to a colored [de facto third-class] coach, he may have his action for damages against the company for being deprived of his so-called "property" [i.e., his "reputation" of belonging to the dominant race, in this case the "white race" – and so "belonging" in the first-class carriage]. On the other hand, if he be a colored man, and be so assigned, he has been deprived of no property, since he is not lawfully entitled to the reputation of being a white man.[7]

Nowhere in the decision does the *Plessy* court resort *directly* and *formatively* to status differentiations to sustain racial distinction. Formal distinction is assumed the basis for racial groups identifiable from all others having access, equally, to their own racial railway carriages.

> The power to assign to a particular coach obviously implies the power to determine to which race the passenger belongs, as well as the power to determine who, under the laws of a particular state, is to be deemed a white, and who a colored, person.[8]

Reputation, a status distinction if ever there was one, is derivative of the formal distinction between racial groups established in the legislated classification schemes.

Formal equality of course is supposed to veil substantive inequality, and thus may be said to legitimate it. The legal consciousness which the US Supreme Court helps to promote, sustain, and diffuse as the national common sense becomes instrumental in the reproduction of a broad though always challenged consent in the racial status quo. So, the judiciary is implicated in ideologically legitimating in the name of the state the differential quality of social facilities to which each group has access: first-class carriages or schools or university classes in the case of whites, third-class facilities literally in the case of blacks. And yet the judiciary serves not only an ideological function. Through its coercive instrumentality, it helps initially to make possible, to promote and extend, the racially differentiated quality of such social facilities.

This process of formalizing racially segregated space, first and foremost instrumentally and then ideologically, is born out also in colonial cities in the first decades of the twentieth century. Urban spaces like Dakar and Johannesburg, Leopoldville and Algiers were formally divided between Native and European cities. It is revealing to conceive of this conscious division of urban space, alongside the policy of indirect rule that dominated at least British colonial policy at this time, as a means of institutionalizing and extending racial segregation for settler colonial societies.

Cultivating Whiteness

In the colonies, all Europeans presumptively were more or less white. This presumption is revealed by the contrast of the moralizing phrase "he's gone native." The "gone" in "gone native" is of course ambiguous. Literally, it meant the person referenced had become native, had assumed the codes and mores, the lifestyle, of the indigenous. More extensively, though, it also indicates a moral judgment expressed about the person having "gone," having abandoned Europeanness or whiteness. This identification of Europeanness and whiteness reveals that whiteness here is considered a state of being, desirable habits and customs, projected patterns of thinking and living, governance and self-governance. So, in claiming the person gone in this latter sense,

171

not only is the judgment expressed that he or she was lost but also that the person had lost his or her way (of being), indeed, had lost his or her mind, and so had become irrational. At the same time, rendering the characterization in the present tense – "going" native – indicates the possibility of a return to one's senses, to rationality, and to the virtues of European calling.

Now if all Europeans were supposed prima facie white in colonial settings, it was not quite so "at home." Working-class English, for instance, migrated to the colonies and became white where they might not be so fully regarded in English cities like Manchester, Birmingham, or London. The transformative logic at work here mirrored that of the European immigrant experience to the United States, where immigrants "got caught up in this racial thing" (Barrett and Roediger 1997: 3, 15). As Malcolm X famously remarked, the first word non-black immigrants learned upon disembarking in America is "nigger." Colonies elevated the European proletariat to the property of whiteness by making at least the semblance of privileges and power, customs and behavior available to them not so readily agreeable in their European environments.

The urban English working class at "home" in the latter half of the nineteenth century, however, were quite explicitly identified with immigrants and degraded races. As we witnessed in chapter 3 above, Thomas Carlyle led the way in equating the English urban working classes with degraded West Indian slaves. By the end of the century there was widespread equation of Britain's urban poor as much with "savage tribes" of Africa as with East European immigrants, most notably "Hottentots," "Bushmen," and "pygmies" (Bonnett 1998). In 1902, Rider Haggard captured a widespread bourgeois sentiment in bemoaning the effects of migrations from countryside to city, from the rural sites of "real" Englishness to cosmopolitan degeneracy, as leading to "nothing less than the deterioration of the race" (Haggard 1902). Built into whiteness accordingly is a set of elevated moral dispositions, social customs, and norms from which the working class, like immigrant and black "stocks," are taken to be morally degenerated (Bonnett 1998). Whiteness, then, is deemed definitive and protective of the well-bred national stock, defended against the perceived internal threat of working-class mores, tastelessness, and lack of social standing as much as from foreign invasion, whether Continental[9] or colonial.

172

This "motility" of racial characterization and identification, as Ann Stoler (1997) puts it, reveals at once the racial mobility of the European working and immigrant classes. Racial motility makes evident accordingly not simply the cliched constructedness of whiteness but more pressingly the relative lack of fixity in racial derogation and elevation. Working and immigrant classes might be devalued from or promoted into the relative privileges, powers, and properties associated with normative middle-class whiteness according to the political, economic, and cultural demands and interests of place and time. Built into this racial motility as an inherent presumption, then, are an implicit critique of racial naturalism and the embrace of racial historicism. In principle anyone could assume the standards of whiteness, though in fact not quite. Whether or not would depend on one's group history, legacy, education, and capacity for self-determination. John Stuart Mill, as we have seen, initiates the polite liberal Victorian embrace of historicism, from status to formal race, and from color-bound degradation to race-neutral indifference and status as well as property maintenance in the name of formalized racelessness.

The racial urban

Embedded in these shifts – from status differentiations to formal(ized) racial divisions, from racial rule imposed from the northern metropoles to the viciousness of its local settler variety, from slave driven to proletarianizing economies – is, as I have hinted, the relative shift in focus from race as a largely rural to race as a prevailingly urban concern. As the twentieth century unfolds, racial concerns lie less with agricultural labor supplies and stock theft, with skirmishes over slave rebellions and wars over broad territorial claims or control. Rather, they are directed to urban ecologies, to migrant and immigrant influx into cities, to town turf, manufacturing and mining labor supply, protection of skilled white workers, school access, housing stock, and a sense of social elevation. The concerns over race increasingly become those about the nature and discipline, aesthetics and morality of public space, about who can be seen where and in what capacity. Thus the moral panic over miscegenation was driven not simply by the disturbed imaginary of mixed sex, with the feared moral degeneracy of black bodies consorting with white, though it was clearly that. Increasingly such panic was expressed as anxiety regarding mixed offspring, and so the make-up and look, the peopling of and demographic power over public space.

These transformations in concern are reflected clearly in the dramatic emergence of intellectual and academic interests in the disciplines of urban sociology and anthropology in the first decades of the new century, initially fashioned around questions of race and culture. The change in comprehending race from biology to culture is exemplified in the work of Franz Boas in the early decades of the twentieth century. Boas claimed to show a shift in shape and size of skulls in the offspring of immigrants moving from the European countryside to American cities as a function of changing environment and diet.[10] This reconceptualizing of race as culturally conceived accompanies the transition from a colonial to a metropolitan set of foci by the 1920s. The new racial urbanism, its intellectual variant reflecting significant social shifts, is exemplified most clearly in the work of Robert Park and the Chicago School. From this point on, the mainstream social science of race increasingly attends to questions of urban poverty and its effects on urban ecologies alongside the individualizing social psychology of intelligence and attitudinal testing. At the same time, racism is identified as a concern about pathological individual prejudice.[11]

No longer a product of or reducible to a social setting considered the outside of white space – colonies, plantations, or rural counties rather than cities – those deemed racially other were to be conceived and comprehended in different terms than before. Where black people in particular had been the object of scientific fascination, considered as different in their very physical constitution, as natural products of naturally different and distinguishable environments, they could – indeed should – now be observed close at hand. Blacks became viewed as products of urban arrangements the determining conditions of which were not unrelated to the very conditions producing the observers' metropolitan ecologies also. The focus thus shifted, slowly and imperceptibly at first, but by the 1930s quite evidently, from measuring bodies and heads to the racial mappings, sociologically and psychologically, of urban spaces, of "the city beautiful." Not unrelatedly, the colonial condition in Africa, Asia, and the Americas came under fire more or less at the time the governance of colonial cities was called increasingly into question. Here "urbanity" assumed the general "measure" of civilization, standing for fine breeding, well-mannered

174

gentility and cultivation, and the capacity for rational deliberation. Those not white, or capable of being considered or made white, failed for the most part by default.

Restating whiteness

It is clear, then, no matter for the moment the specific differences between national experiences, that from the later nineteenth century on there is something distinctively new in the manifestation of whiteness. The decades leading up to and the decades following the close of the century mark a qualitative shift in the production and conception of whiteness. From roughly the sixteenth century to abolition in the later nineteenth century Europeans and those of European descent were self-elevated as (relatively) privileged and powerful, (more) civilized and superior, whether as a function of blood or historical progress. Superiority and power, civilization and privilege were taken as givens, as mostly unquestioned, a simple fact of racially predicated life. The state of course had a role, looming increasingly large across time, in enabling and establishing, maintaining and managing the possibility of this mania. The state was instrumental in defining and refining, projecting and policing who should count in the class of the privileged, propertied, and powerful and who could not, in defining whites and blacks (or more generally and negatingly non-whites), their possibilities and prohibitions. But there is a sense in which the state was taking itself simply to codify the nature of things, making explicit what was in any case taken for granted, as the state of being. Thus Justice Taney could write, well along the way of this project and with just a hint of self-doubt, that

> [Negroes] had for more than a century before been regarded as beings of an inferior order, and altogether unfit to associate with the white race, either in social or political relations; and so far inferior that they had no rights which the white man was bound to respect; and that the negro might justly and lawfully be reduced to slavery for his benefit . . . This opinion was at that time fixed and universal in the civilized portion of the white race. It was regarded as an axiom in morals as well as in politics, which no one thought of disputing or supposed to be open to dispute; and men in every grade and position in society daily and habitually acted upon it in their private pursuits, as

175

well as in matters of public concern, without doubting for a moment the correctness of this opinion.[12]

By the mid- to late nineteenth century, in the aftermath of slavery, whiteness had very clearly begun to be challenged – in colonial and settler societies, if not yet quite so emphatically and more slowly in the metropoles. With abolition and the changed conditions it represents, with the tearing apart of the world that slave-based colonization reflected and the increasingly assertive resistance to racial subjection and domination, confidence in the positions of whites, in their givenness, waned. In the face of these challenges, whiteness no longer could be so safely assumed, white superiority so easily taken as a given of nature. Whiteness, in short, needed to be renegotiated, reaffirmed, projected anew. To be sustained it had to be reasserted; to survive, inevitably in altered form as the conditions for its sustainability had altered, it had to be insisted upon. Its re*state*ment required commensurably altered terms. It is from this point on – from the point at which labor needs shift, racial conceptions transform, capital formation and modes of accumulability alter, moral dispositions and cultural conceptions turn – that state racial design is reconceived.

From this point on, then, whiteness explicitly and self-consciously becomes a state project. To say that it is a state project is not to say that the state had been absent from earlier racial manifestations nor that whiteness was now a product only of state definition. Rather, it is to say that from this moment the state explicitly, deliberatively, and calculatingly takes the lead in *orchestrating* the various instrumentalities in the definition and materialization of whiteness. From the closing decades of the nineteenth century the making of whiteness flows in and through and out of the state.

This reformation of whiteness is factored around the state(d) project to manufacture people – indeed, peoples – in the mold of whiteness. Being white was considered to carry certain properties. It was not only that one either naturalistically had them or not, but they could be manifested – discovered or developed – in one, depending on one's breed, one's national geographic origins, one's breeding. In the long wake of slavery and the demise of slave labor, in and for the sociospatial sake of segregation, whiteness had to be made – explicitly, by design – much more self-consciously as a project of the state. And once made, it had constantly to be restated, maintained, and remade.

176

Slavery gave way to segregated space. Segregated space was more nebulous at its social boundaries than slave space. So segregated boundaries had to be established and enforced as much through defini- tion of identity as directly through marking space on the ground itself. Add immigrants and migrants, miscegenation and intermarriage, and the borders become even more porous. With the remaking of white- ness through segregation and segregation through the renegotiation of whiteness came the well-documented transformation of ethnic immigrants like the Irish and Jews, and the working class generally, into whites (Roediger 1991; Saxton 1992; Allen 1994; Ignatiev 1995; Sacks 1995).

Under colonialism, as I pointed out in the previous chapter, racial rule in the colonies was about managing heterogeneity while in the metropoles it was about maintaining and securing homogeneity. In the closing decades of the nineteenth century, heterogeneity in the metropoles – including American towns and cities – was becoming palpable, and so undeniable. Thus emerged a shift to reestablishing and reimposing the artifice of homogeneity in the name of whiteness. This growing heterogeneity – the product of migrations from south to north, and east to west – alongside the increasing authority of historicism as an assumption about racial otherness undercut the easi- ness with which white superiority and natural homogeneity could be assumed.

Homogeneity thus was reestablished symbolically, categorically, through the cohering artifice of whiteness, the refashioning of who could belong and who does not. Whiteness became not just a racial but the national identity. In Australia, at the same time, white workers more or less violently mobilized against Asian labor immigration by demanding wages "fit for white men." The new Federal Parliament responded in 1901 by enacting the White Australia Policy that excluded all non-European migration for the most part until 1973 (Castles and Miller 1998: 57, 76). Vance Palmer offers evidence in the epigraph to this chapter that this was a policy receiving strong support from Britain. As Balibar has made clear, then, race gave to nation both its specificity and its globality, both its criteria of exclu- sion and exclusivity and its universal connectivity (Balibar 1990).

This culture of racial manufacture and remaking is revealed most clearly in the spectacle of racial contrast of Europeanness and Africanity, of civilization and presumptive primitivity recirculated between world fairs and international expositions in "European space" as the century closes. Consider the state culture of whiteness-by-negation as revealed in the case of the Royal Belgian Museum for Central Africa. The Museum, established by King Leopold in the wake of the wildly successful International Exposition he sponsored in 1897, was fashioned around the "authentic" display of a displaced African village recreated in the suburbs of Brussels. Here Europeans could find themselves in the mirror of their negation, of what they took themselves not to be (Anderson 1991; Goldberg 2002a).

Racial borders

More broadly, then, modern colonial and settler states were involved initially in shaping the ebb and flow of migration and its conditions from European metropoles to the colonies, and policing the counter-flow in more restrictive terms, especially in the case of permanent residential settlement. As Hegel indicated in 1821, colonial migration was seen as a solution to Europe's perceived overcrowding and over-production problems (Hegel 1821/1972, Addition to #248, p. 278). By the end of the nineteenth century, metropolitan states had become concerned to restrict counter-migrations identified precisely in ethnoracial terms not just from the colonies but from the southern and eastern peripheries of Europe to the opportunity-filled centers of "the West" also. The overriding concern was to preserve the artifice of homogeneity, sociobiological as much as cultural.

This concern with polluting the body politic, as I have elsewhere called it (Goldberg 1993: ch. 8), is exemplified by the English immigration restrictions imposed the day after war was declared on Germany in 1914.[13] The Aliens Restriction Act of 1914, extended after the war by the Aliens Restriction Act (Amended) of 1919, denied entry to Britain to anyone deemed by the Home Secretary to be contrary to "the public good." Targeted were Germans obviously, but also Austro-Hungarians, Turks, and increasingly Africans first from German colonies and then more generally, including Afro-Caribbeans. The British restrictions were modeled on the Natal Act of 1897, which devised a method "to place certain restriction on immigration" pioneered by the colonial regime of Natal, then a colony in Southern Africa, later a province in the Union of South Africa. "Racially neutral on its face," the Act necessitated "knowledge of a European language which an immigration officer judged to be sufficient" (Dummett and Nicol 1990: 118ff.). It was designed to exclude all but Englishmen and its rationale, mimicking the formalizing logic of "separate but equal," was widely adopted throughout the colonies, as it would later be in Britain itself.

Concerns with racial hygiene, eugenic population formation, and "well bred races" (Voegelin 1933/1997) underpin also the terms of the increasingly restrictive immigration laws in the United States. The Immigration Restriction Act of 1924 limited European immigration to 2 percent of already present national stocks as evidenced by the 1890 census count. The Act thus privileged Northern and Western Europeans over those from Eastern and Southern Europe, especially Jews, even as it studiously avoided reference to any specific European national or racial groups. It was not so careful with those of Asian heritage, however, explicitly extending the existing exclusion of Chinese, formalized in the Congressional Act of 1882 forbidding the naturalization of "Chinamen," to extend also to all Japanese immigration.

A series of US naturalization cases between 1890 and 1925 bears out in fascinating if painful detail the judiciary's struggle over racial admission and belonging, and so explicitly over the scope and character of whiteness. The courts found themselves torn between preserving the conceit that in 1790 "the United States were a more or less *homogenous* people who . . . had come from what has been termed 'Northern Europe'"[14] and the interpretation of laws obviously at odds with rapidly expanding heterogeneity. That national admittance is filtered in the name of naturalization already predisposes the process to racially fashioned principles. The naturalization cases grapple openly and tortuously with whom are to count as white, and therefore naturalizable as American citizens. The language of exclusion is explicitly and for the most part unapologetically racial, the significance heightened against the background of America's imperial expansionism at the time.

In 1790, Congress had delimited citizenship to "free white men." This was extended in the wake of the post-Civil War amendments in 1870 to "aliens of African nativity and to persons of African descent." The prevailing deliberations in the wake of this amendment and the increasing heterogeneity effected by rapidly expanding immigrant populations thus concerned whether those outside the Western European frame should count as white. Court after court pained over initial Congressional intent in its naturalization restrictions to free white men, and did so explicitly in the context of prevailing scientific theories of race.

Significantly, there is almost no troubling of who might qualify as African or of African descent. I have found but one contentious court claim to naturalization on the basis of invoking African heritage, and significantly no court appeals by the immigration and naturalization apparatuses of the state that an already naturalized citizen should have their naturalization revoked because of a misrepresented claim to African descent. Africans or those of African descent apparently could be assumed self-evidently – "naturally" – classifiable as such. The District Court of Eastern New York troubled briefly in 1938 over whether to grant naturalization to a man "half African and half Indian by his mother and fully Indian by his father" on the basis of his being "of African descent." The Court ruled that because the petition would be denied were the man one-quarter white and three-quarters Indian the same logic must be applied in this case.[15] While the 1870 amendment resulted in increased Afro-Caribbean naturalization, the courts nevertheless continued to reveal and reify the degraded status of people of African descent. "To refuse naturalization to an educated Japanese Christian clergyman and accord it to a veneered savage of African descent from the banks of the Congo would appear illogical . . . yet the courts of the United States have held the former inadmissible and the statute accords admission to the latter."[16] As the San Francisco Board of Education insisted in 1906, it

> is determined in its efforts to effect the establishment of separate public schools for Chinese and Japanese pupils . . . for the higher end that our children [sic] should not be placed in any position where their youthful imprecisions may be affected by association with pupils of the Mongolian race. (Quoted in Stephenson 1909/1910, 8: 700)

The artifice of American homogeneity was refashioned accordingly both (and relatedly) through the reinvention of whiteness and the making of pan-ethnoracial formations. In assuming Americanness immigrants became white, and took on whiteness in being Americanized (Barrett and Roediger 1997: 6, 27). Those Americans determined to be not white were likewise herded over time into administratively contoured racially referenced groups.

180

In an 1894 challenge to Japanese exclusion from citizenship, the Massachusetts Circuit Court ruled that the 1790 Congress intended to exclude "the Mongolian race." Later language identified "the Mongolian race" as "Asiatic" or "Oriental." By white was meant only "the Caucasian."[17] Japanese, as too Koreans and Filipinos[18] and "the race of people commonly known as Hindus,"[19] did not qualify as members of "the free white race."[20] In 1919, the California District Court however reversed the exclusion of a Hindu man, citing similar instances in Georgia, southern New York, northern California, and the state of Washington.[21] The Supreme Court nevertheless closed this line of cases, ruling in 1923 that a Hindu, even one of "high caste [and] although of the Caucasian or Aryan race, is not a white person within the meaning of the naturalization laws."[22] That the Court resorted to the narrowed restriction of legal significance ("within the meaning of the naturalization laws") reveals not simply the well-noted making of "whiteness by law" (Haney-Lopez 1996) nor additionally law's imperiousness (Dworkin 1988). It makes evident equally the self-conscious implication of the state in fabricating and fashioning racial homogeneity, in recreating the artifice of a national community by whitening out[23] those deemed not to fit the presumptive national profile (Lowe 1996: 13).

At the same time, there are court rulings that render this teleological homogeneity much more troubled and ambiguous. In an interesting example of judicial race resistance, if not quite race traitorhood, in 1910 the Massachusetts Circuit Court, acknowledging the dramatic extent of race mixture, refused to allow that there is any such thing as "a European or white race" or indeed any "Asiatic or yellow race which includes . . . all the people of Asia." To its credit, the Court refused "to deny citizenship by reason of their color to aliens" though it limited the refusal to those "hitherto granted it." In the context of its decision the Court nevertheless affirmed the definition of whiteness by negation, characterizing as white any person "not otherwise classified as . . . Africans, Indians, Chinese, and Japanese." Whites were left "as a catch-all word to include everybody else." Armenians thus were to count among whites, actually on the evidentiary authority of the most prominent anthropologists of the day,[24] as were Persians whether living in Persia or having long migrated to India.[25]

Syrians, it seems, were the courts' ultimate poltergeist. Determined both by the Massachusetts District Court in 1909 and the Oregon District Court in 1910 to be white,[26] the South Carolina District Court objected in 1913. Explicitly denying citizenship to Syrians, the Court ruled generally that "all inhabitants of Asia, Australia, the South Seas, the Malaysian Islands and territories, and of South America, who are not of European, or mixed European and African descent" would be "exclude[d] from naturalization." Whites were characterized principally on "geographic" grounds as any "fair-complexioned people of European descent." They explicitly included Celts, Scandinavians, Teutons, Iberians, Latins, Greeks, Slavs, Magyars, Lapps, Finns, Basque, Albanian, "mixed Latin, Celtic-Iberian and Moorish inhabitants of Spain and Portugal" as well as "Greek, Latin, Phoenician, and North African inhabitants of Sicily," "mixed Slav and Tartar inhabitants of South Russia," and "all European Jews . . . of Semitic descent." Alongside Syrians, whites excluded Chinese, Japanese, Malays, and American Indians, exclusions already noted in 1910 by the *Balsara* court.[27] The South Carolina District Court twice reaffirmed exclusion of Syrians in 1914, citing *Shahid* as precedent. The Court rejected the related claims that the decision should turn on perceptual criteria of skin color or other morphological considerations and that whiteness be defined as being of *Caucasian* descent. The correct basis of determination, the Court insisted, is that of "*European* descent."[28] Syrians, it concluded, because "certainly Asiatic," clearly are not.[29]

Syrians objected, claiming humiliation on the at best awkward grounds that in being denied their claim to whiteness they were relegated to the inferiority of a "colored race." The District Court reconfirmed its earlier finding that Syrians are not racially European, adding also the excludability of "Parsees" and "Persians," "Hindoo" and "Malay." It nevertheless encouraged the applicants to pursue that matter to the Supreme Court to "[settle] . . . this most vexed and difficult question."[30] In 1915, the US Appeals Court obliged, overturning the District Court rulings. The Appeals Court pointed out that "Syrians, Armenians and Parsees," many of whom had already been naturalized, had been considered and treated self-consciously by US immigration law over the previous fifty years as white.[31]

We find in the complex of these examples, then, the tensions over racial definition within and between state agencies. As Stephenson summarizes his remarkable survey of US race laws for the period:

> Under the shadow of [US] statutes and the constitution, the legislatures
> and courts of the states have built up a mass of race distinctions which

the federal courts and Congress, even if inclined to do so, are impotent to attack. (Stephenson 1909/1910, 2: 37)

The Justice Department, and indeed in some cases the Congress, occasionally are at odds with the judiciary over the scope of whiteness, and even at times over its fact. These cases reveal a struggle, one internalized within the courts, over the face of America, over the boundaries of belonging and the homogeneity of the national constitution, of who could claim a home and claim to be at home. They highlight the ambiguities and ambivalences over the definition of whiteness cracking at the smoothed surface of national commitment just as racial belonging and excludability were taken as givens of national order. Thus, the renegotiation of whiteness recreates no straightforward homogeneity but a troubled hierarchy of internally differentiated and differentially privileged "white races" (cf. Barrett and Roediger 1997; Jacobson 1998). But these cases reveal also, contrary to Anthony Marx, that even though racial boundaries in the United States were most clearly articulated in the dualism of black and white, racial rule in America from the mid-nineteenth century on was never simply binary.

Ambiguous boundaries

If the redefinition of whiteness in the wake of abolition and (im)migratory movements was contested, the reconceiving of blackness was contested and complex also. The one drop rule furnished perhaps the most extreme administrative fix for racial definition, a sort of bureaucratic plastic surgery in the face of these increasingly evident social cracks that came to mark the US following the Civil War and the segregationist attack on Reconstruction. Neil Gotanda reveals that the principle of hypodescent consists of two related decision rules, one of "recognition" and the other of "descent." The former insists that a person will be black if his or her black or African ancestry is visible. The latter claims that a person will be black if known to have a trace of black or African ancestry (Gotanda 1995: 258). Clearly, the rule of descent is designed to plug the hole thought to be left by the rule of recognition.

Now if white supremacy could no longer safely be assumed as a given of nature, it had to be reset in place by the state, reified in the edifice of social structure. And the one drop rule was taken as the cement. Social order was to be resettled by administrative fiat, homogeneity reestablished by state imposition, white supremacy recreated by decree. Just as the onslaught of lynching at the time might properly be read in part as "the denial of the black man's newly articulated right to citizenship and, with it, the various privileges of patriarchal power" (Wiegman 1995: 83, 90), so the one drop rule would provide segregationism with its principle of administrative operationality. "Separate but equal" was to be reduced to rote application. At the very moment the racial state, in the US as elsewhere, seemed in more or less unsalvageable crisis, it was able to reinvent itself through definitional (re)assertion. The slave state is dead; long live its racial legacy.

Or so the story has gone (cf. Hickman 1997 for a clear example of this prevailing position). Even at its height, at its most authoritatively insistent, ambivalence marks "one drop" statability. Ambivalence, in this scheme of things, one might say is that space between arrogance and self-doubt, between power's self-denial and its immobility, between the celebrated assertion of privilege and the sheer despair over power's conceits. If Louisiana was at the center of white assertibility, segregationism, and hypodescent, racial definition, design, and order (ing) were in question there almost as much as in sites less amenable to the extremes of the racial state. *Plessy v. Ferguson*, after all, initiated in 1892 in the Louisiana courts as a challenge to the 1890 state law restricting "colored races" to separate railway cars from "white races." Homer Plessy, a man classified in the 1890 US Census as "octoroon" but "negro" in the 1900 Census, was arrested for insisting on sitting in a first-class car reserved for whites. If the one drop rule can be said to have a place of baptism, Louisiana is a pretty strong candidate for its annunciation. But this nominating site of segregation is also a state of considerable racial ambivalence, revealed not least by the ambiguities in its legal administration of racial rule.

Thus, in 1908 the state of Louisiana had enacted an edict insisting "that concubinage between a person of the Caucasian or white race and a person of the negro or black race is . . . a felony" punishable by imprisonment not less than one month and not more than a year "with or without hard labor." Curiously, while cross-racial marriage had been outlawed by the state in 1894, cohabitation between white and black, "including even the pure-blooded negro," was "not forbidden

184

except in concubinage." "Proximity to negroes" was considered other-wise "unavoidable" in the public spaces of railway cars, whereas cross-racial cohabitation was a matter of private and so voluntary choice.

Octave Treadaway, a man characterized as "octoroon," and a white woman who revealingly remains anonymous were arrested for engag-ing in "concubinage." The lower courts acquitted them on grounds that the law did not apply explicitly to an octoroon person, and the District Attorney's office appealed to the Louisiana Supreme Court.[32] The sole question addressed by the Supreme Court was whether an octoroon is "a person of the negro or black race within the meaning of the statute."

The Court acknowledged that the "science of ethnology" at the time deemed a person "Caucasian or negro in the same proportion in which the two strains of blood are mixed in his veins." "Octoroon" accordingly would not count among "negro." The rule of hypodescent admittedly, thus, was not a scientific but a popular one, and the Court revealed via a comprehensive survey of dictionary and nation-wide popular and legal usage the identification of "colored" and so "octoroon" with "negro." This said, the Court admitted that the con-cubinage act, when originally presented to the Louisiana Legislature, had included a clause, explicitly struck by the Legislature as an outcome of its deliberations, defining "a person who is as much as one thirty-second part negro shall be . . . a person of the negro race." The Court concluded as a consequence that the Legislature intended thus to exclude "mulattoes" and "quadroons" from the scope of the con-cubinage act, no doubt because it might just apply to some of its own members or their relatives. The defendants' acquittal was upheld and, as Octave Treadaway's name ironically suggests, he walked away able to voice his freedom for another day at least where less fortunate "transgressors" of racial morality at the time had paid with their lives.

The State of Louisiana v. Treadaway et al. reveals not simply that the principle of hypodescent was hypocritical but that at most it was unevenly assumed and applied, and at least in contest with more ambivalent competing assumptions and applications concerning everyday racial interactions. This complexity in state racial conception and circulation was hardly restricted to Louisiana. Virginia, like states throughout the South, outlawed miscegenation, nevertheless legally allowing marriage "between a white man and a woman who is of less than one-fourth Negro blood though it be a drop less."

Gilbert Stephenson's comprehensive survey of state definitions of race throughout the US in 1909 reveals the checkered assumption and implementation of the one drop rule even in state regimes supposed most driven by its logic. Thus

> Alabama, Kentucky, Maryland, Mississippi, North Carolina, Tennessee and Texas define one as a person of color who is descended from a Negro to the third generation inclusive, though one ancestor in each generation may have been white. Florida, Georgia, Indiana, Minnesota, Missouri and South Carolina declare that one is a person of color who has as much as one-eighth Negro blood; Nebraska and Oregon say that one must have as much as one-fourth Negro blood in order to be classed with that race. Virginia and Michigan apparently draw the line similarly. (Stephenson 1909/1910: 43)[33]

Shortly after this Alabama nevertheless ruled that a person "descended on the part of the father or mother from negro ancestors, without reference to or limit of time or generations removed" would be Negro (Wallenstein 1994: 407). "Colored" of course was often, but not exclusively, used to exclude those of mixed racial descent from claiming whiteness.[34]

The application of hypodescent, as much socially as legally, however, is better understood as a pragmatic application of racial regulation than as an absolute requirement of racial rule. The supremacy of whiteness, viciously presumptive as it no doubt was for many, was not without its contradictions and contestations, its ruptures and restrictions, its self-doubts and slippages, its contrary desires and choices, responses and resistances. And these faultlines required the imposition of the state to mediate and manage, minimize and mask even their most minute manifestations.

Hickman herself (1997: 1227–8) cites a series of cases from 1885 to 1911 that bears out the dubitability of generalizing the one drop rule or taking it too literally. In 1885, Isaac Jones successfully appealed his conviction and almost three-year sentence for feloniously marrying a white woman on the grounds that he was less than "one quarter black" as required by the Virginia statute. The Court explicitly declared Jones a "mulatto of brown skin" and his mother "a yellow woman" while admitting his "blood quantum" amounted to less than that statutorily necessitated.[35] In North Carolina, a white man in 1910

186

tried to annul his marriage because his wife "was and is of negro descent within the third generation," thereby avoiding his spousal and child maintenance responsibilities. The Court ruled that the husband was unable to prove his wife was at least "one-eighth negro," as statutorily required, because he could not establish without doubt that her great grandfather "was a real negro of unmixed blood."[36] The following year, again in Virginia, two children were initially removed from a white mother on grounds that their stepfather was part negro. The man had married his white wife after the children's father had died, leaving the family destitute, and the defendant had cared well for his new family. The children were returned after her new husband's mother insisted that she was only one-eighth black and his father had been white, making the man at issue one-sixteenth black, too little for the law even if more than sufficient for the one drop rule.[37]

Thus, as the rights and privileges of citizenship were revised in the face of a perceived crisis of national identity and identification, not all would be able to qualify. Some "self-evidently" were not white, some clearly failed to qualify racially under the various naturalization laws and their amendments and found themselves forced into pained choices, many were deemed simply "racially unacceptable," and even when recognized as white some were positioned as less so than others. There were obviously tensions between state agencies – the immigration service, on one hand, running up against the judiciary on a range of cases, and lower courts in contrast with higher jurisdictions. One jurisdiction might be at odds judicially with another. Thus racial covenants might not be implemented in Manhattan while in Los Angeles in 1944 there were neighborhoods that legally prohibited occupancy by any "persons other than Caucasians'" (Hickman 1997: 1167).[38] Legal realism is intimately wedded to racial realism (cf. Bell 1995). In the end, the power of judicial (re)definition (in the hand of the upper courts especially) can be seen in the business of recreating and regulating the contours of whiteness, of continuing to massage the boundaries of national belonging and the definition of citizenship.

The reinvention of whiteness bridging the close of the nineteenth and opening of the twentieth centuries accordingly was not simply about the undertaking to maintain "a bulwark against undesirable Others without" and the "minimizing [of] perceived 'difference' among the varied peoples and races within," as Jacobson (1998: 233) would have it. This imputation so obviously blurs the sordidly subtle complexities of segregationism, the contradictions within the rule of hypodescent, and the checkered derogation assigned to racial distinction, as well as the ambiguous racially driven responses to immigration as to warrant no further comment. The sociolegal refashioning of whiteness upon which I have dwelled at length here was a response to the perceived threats of growing heterogeneity within that flowed from imperial and international engagement, and by the consequent challenges to the presumed supremacy of whites – in numbers and power, abilities and political domination, opportunities and access.[39] It was, in short, nothing more nor less than a transforming pragmatics of rule through and by race.

State Stocktaking

The modern state, I have argued, has been deeply implicated in composing, managing, and promoting racial distinction. Modern state rationality is disposed to racial classification schemas as modes of administration and social management. Such formalized distinction through racial classification has been central to the regulatory imperative of law's rule and administrative arrangements in modern states. Racial classification has informed the law of racial division and rule, even as such classification schemas were shaped by the commands of legal logic. Segregationism, as we have seen, was suggested and sustained by a complex and shifting set of racial terms. These profiles of racial distinction were conjured and circulated by state census apparatuses, as borne out variously in the United States and South Africa, among other places.

The bureaucracy of census taking is a central administrative technology – what I have elsewhere only half mockingly called racial administrology (Goldberg 1997: 31) – in managing the racial state. As a mechanism for national stocktaking at different historical moments, the state census is particularly revealing of how a racially managed state formation conceives and applies its racial comprehension and regulations, contrasting "majority" and "minority" in state formation (Appadurai 1996: 130–1). Activated in the shift from family, kinship, and local community as modes of social control to a focus on the abstraction of "population," modern census taking since the late

188

eighteenth century has presumed race, implicitly or explicitly, as its centerpiece in demographic accounting. Emerging out of colonial regimes, the modern census developed as a more or less comprehensive state mechanism to map population size, shape, distribution, quality and flow of labor supply, taxation and conscription pools, political representation, voter predictability, and the necessities of population reproduction. The census circulates revised and reworked popular categories of racial conception throughout the national population under the license of state authority. It thus lends the authority of the state to racial distinction while marking the "state imagination" (Appadurai 1996: 117) in deeply racial terms. A brief consideration of census taking accordingly may reveal shifts in racial nomination at different moments in national history tied to refashioned projections of population predictability and state stability, class order and political control.

I have written at length about the history of racial counting in the US census (Goldberg 1997), and I do not intend a detailed rehearsal of these arguments here. It is worth pointing out in light of the preceding section nevertheless the increasing proliferation in categories of blackness from the 1880 to 1890 censal counts. Thus the category of "Mulatto" that was listed beneath "Black" from 1850 to 1880 fractured into additional qualifiers of "Quadroon" and "Octoroon" in 1890, only to be collapsed into the singularity of an unqualified blackness in the interests of hypodescent by the 1900 enumeration. In 1910, however, the uncontainability of distinction in the face of undeniable population proliferation led to the reintroduction of "Mulatto." "Mulatto," in turn, was listed beneath the category "Black" until 1930, when both disappeared in favor of "Negro." It was perhaps in the face of these shifting designations along with Congressional concerns over immigration that the Census Bureau in 1923 explicitly redefined the categories of "white" and "Negro": "White," the Census Bureau insisted, "refers to persons understood to be pure-blooded whites." By contrast, "a person of mixed . . . white and Negro . . . is classified as a Negro . . . regardless of the amount of white blood."[40] Negro, in turn, object of the critical effects of Black Consciousness, gave way again principally to "Black" from the 1970 count.

Responding to demographic presence from the importation of "coolie" labor, "Chinese" first appeared in the 1870 Census and was joined by "Japanese" in 1890. A series of questions was added to the latter census about naturalization for those persons not born in the

United States. These questions were expanded in following census counts to include those about "mother tongue" and the ability to speak English. The 1929 instructions required enumerators to report a married woman as having the same citizenship as her husband. "Mexican," "Filipino," "Hindu," and "Korean" were added in 1930. Mexicans were initially presumed racially not to be white, unless explicitly and "accurately" claiming white descent. When both the Mexican government and the US State Department protested, this was altered to presumptive whiteness in 1940. The category disappeared altogether from the census count in 1950, to be replaced later by the supracategory "Hispanic," first appearing in the 1980 enumeration. "Hindu" and "Korean" disappeared after 1940, the latter alone to reappear from 1970.

We find in the example of these changing US censal categories of race one constant. This is the administrative imperative to track the threat of heterogeneity, and to massage the boundaries of whiteness and negritude, expanding or contracting them in response to the pragmatics of the perceived threat of demographic politics. Where the culture of whiteness – the norms and values, presuppositions and practices, the social and political order for which it stood – was considered threatened, racial administrology sought to soften the effects by contouring its boundaries, by "the illusion of bureaucratic control" (Appadurai 1996: 117). Throughout the history of US racial enumeration, whites have always been counted as a racially coherent and undifferentiated group. The concern invariably has been either to suppress the challenge by legally limiting its possibilities or to stave off the consequences by reshaping its grounds. The effects are most clearly evidenced in the shaping of voting districts (Guinier 1994; Peterson 1995).

Now racial classification schemas effected in the hand of the state are a species of "state speech". State speech authorizes not only what is and can be said and done but who are recognized as citizens, as agents of and within the state, and who simply are the objects of state action. The state census is a particularly effective instrument through which to effect these ends. For not only does the census nominate and elaborate the categories of recognition and authorization; by invading virtually every home the census circulates and advertises the categories state formation seeks to license. It thus serves as a medium in the (re)production of common sense. A brief history of South African census taking will serve to illustrate the general point.

Prior to the establishment of the Union of South Africa in 1910, census taking was conducted with checkered regularity under British colonial administration, mainly in the Cape and Natal. In 1879, concerned with issues of colonial administration, demographic distribution, and labor supply, a count only of "Natives" was conducted. In 1891, the British proceeded with a full count, introducing for the first time a range of racial definitions. The categories included "White, Coloured (sic) or Mixed," contrasted with "Other" ranging across "Chinese, Hindu, Mozambique and Malay," but also "Hottentot, Bushman, Bechuana (including Basuto) Fingu and Damara," as well as a separate category for "Kafir (Xosa, Tembu, Baca, Xesibe, and Bomvara)" (*Census Report* 1891/1892: xvii). ("Kaffir" later assumed derogatory connotation in South African parlance, equivalent to "nigger" in the US.) The undertaking was to furnish reliable information regarding urban and rural habitation, mapping relative population densities district by district, town by town.

The categories were streamlined by 1904 to include four general terms distinguished by color: "white, black, yellow, and coloured." Remarkably, the Census Bureau in the Cape admitted that "these groups are by no means scientific," that "as a result of . . . intermarrying – which is every year becoming less exceptional – the border line between the Race Groups is growing more and more confused and less easy to determine." It insisted, nevertheless, that race is still clearly distinguishable "as distinct classes" (*Census Report* 1904/1905: xxi). What emerged here was the concern that would dominate all future census taking in South Africa until apartheid gave way to its afterlife: the dramatic rates of increase in non-white populations relative to whites, most notably in urban areas. Once more, racial census taking was taken up as a tool to administer the perceived threats of racial heterogeneity, to structure demographic arrangements so as to minimize what were considered the degenerative biological, moral, and social effects of racial pollution. Fear of a black world was managed, so far as the perversity of racial logic would allow, by delimiting acknowledgment of its relative size.

The South African Act of 1909 incorporated the two British colonies of the Cape of Good Hope and Natal with the two independent Boer republics, the South African Republic (Transvaal) and the Orange Free State, defeated by the British in the Anglo-Boer War, into the Union of South Africa. The Act of 1909 mandated a census every five years, starting in 1911. Consistent with the 1904 Cape Census, the 1911 Union Census was careful to determine relative increase of the urban population in racial terms, celebrating the modest increase in relative percentage of "Europeans" as "an improvement" (*Census Report* 1911/1913: xxv). As in the US about this time, interestingly, Syrians were explicitly identified as white.

As a result of the Great War, the next census count was delayed until 1918 and covered only the "European population." The concern was focused explicitly and overridingly on whether whites were declining in numbers relative to "non-Europeans," difficult to do, no doubt, in the absence of tallying the latter. The next full census was reinstated in 1921. Here we find the Census Bureau consumed by a mentality of categorical neatness and scientistic precision, driven by its growing romance with statistics, as evidenced by adding the very term to its formal title. For the first time, graphs and charts supplemented tables throughout the reports, indicative of the "science of population management" being consciously applied to racial differentiation. Belying later characterizations of South African racial categorization as tripartite, the 1921 Census refined racial distinction into four prevailing categories that would dominate South African classification from that point forward: European or white, Coloured or mixed, Asiatic, and Native (Bantu) (in this order). Whites were defined as anyone of European descent; Asians as anyone of "Asiatic origin" and included Japanese, Chinese, Indians, Afghans, Arabs, and notably Syrians (all of whom but the latter had been included in 1911 under "Coloured"); "Natives" referred to "aboriginal tribes of the Bantu race"; and "Coloureds" were any mixed person not belonging to any of the other three racial groups and included "Bushmen and Hottentots" (*Census Report* 1921).

The presiding concern with relative size of the white population (*Census Report* 1921: vi) and "immersion" of whites in the "racial predominance" of non-Europeans "many generations behind the White race in the degree of its civilization" (18) determined prevailing censal concerns with calculations of population proportionality, increase, and decrease. Notable in this regard are the graphic predictions of comparative racial population growth from 1921 to 1971 on the basis of the rates over the preceding fifty years (28). Similarly, the census reports concerned themselves with area distributions, the feminizing of the European population relative to non-Europeans; with urbanization and population densities; as well as with relative group mobility as a result of railway travel with a view to labor supply. Questions regarding occupation and age as well as familial relationships were simplified for "Natives" on the insulting assumption that the "native mind" would be less familiar with or able to comprehend the complexity of questions generally posed to Europeans. And enumerators were instructed not to argue with those mistakenly insisting on a European form but simply to transfer the information offered later to the racially "applicable forms" (10).

The 1921 *Census Report* identified mixed "Asiatic-African" marriages as an area of concern, offering the potential for the emergence of a bourgeois political class that might challenge white domination. At the same time, on the basis of data available from the 1921 censal count, a report issued in 1923 warned of poor whites "perpetually on the margin of unemployment" (the South African equivalents of Phinehas McIntosh) as "constituting possibly an even greater danger to the State" than racial differentials or mixed marriages (23). Self-consciously harnessed by the Nationalist Party over the following decades, this was the class that constituted the basis for Nationalist electoral victory twenty-five years later and so too the formative class underpinnings for the institutional establishment of formal apartheid. So the 1923 Native (Urban Areas) Act marked the shift in racial concerns explicitly to urban space, seeking to limit influx of African people into the urban areas of South Africa strictly to actual employment and allocation of township housing accommodation in those areas (Posel 2000: 7). Application of this equation would require accurate and ongoing censal counts.

It is evident from later census reports that the Bureau was becoming increasingly statistically sophisticated, if strapped for cash in the depression years of the 1930s. A full account would be concerned to elaborate these sometimes fascinating details. For our purposes though, the next significant developments in census taking occurred after the Nationalist Party assumed power in 1948 and began systematically institutionalizing the specific structures of apartheid. Thus for the 1951 Census racial definitions alter to reflect not the South African Act of 1909 but the apartheid state's Population Registration Act of 1950. So where whites earlier had been defined as being of "pure European descent," now the definition becomes "those who in appearance obviously are, or who are generally accepted as, white persons."

This is taken to exclude persons who, although appearing white, are "generally accepted as Coloured persons." "Natives are those generally accepted as members of any aboriginal race or tribe of Africa"; and "Asiatics" are deemed "Natives of Asia and their descendants." "Coloureds" are defined by negation as those "not included in any of the other three groups." "Natives, Asiatics, and Coloured" are grouped as "non-whites," sometimes lumped together as a way to promote generalized exclusions, sometimes disarticulated, as convenient to state racial formation and control (*Census Report* 1951, 1: v). Racial definition, the categorical underpinnings of administrative apartheid, is reduced to appearance ultimately in the judgment of a government agent.

The intensification of separation in the formalization of apartheid after 1948 (Evans 1997; Posel 2000) can be understood in part as an extended response also to rising urbanization. If the censal counts can be believed, in 1904, 52 percent of "Europeans" lived in urban areas. By 1960 this number had jumped to 63 percent, mainly in the larger cities. In the same period, what was identified as the "Coloured" rate of urbanization increased from 50 to 68 percent, "Asiatic" from 36 to 83 percent, and "Bantu" from 10 to 37 percent. This effectively meant that in numerical terms more black people were living in urban areas than all the other groups combined, and almost twice as many as white people. The apartheid regime was concerned almost above all else with the racial dimensions of urban space, locating black townships very carefully in relation both to white cities and industrial sites. The concern was to maintain separation through "rational planning" of easy transportation access and maximizing the possibilities of police surveillance and control of urban environments (Evans 1997: 299–300). What followed by the 1970 Census count, in terms of group area formation and spatial distinction, were the ethnicization of "Coloured" and "Asiatics" into subgroups (Coloured or mixed, Malay, Griqua, Chinese, Indian, Pakistani) and "Bantu" into disaggregated "tribal" groups (Ndebele, Shona, Tswana, Xhosa, Zulu, Venda, etc.). What this exemplifies once more are the shifting concerns of state racial management increasingly driven by the panicked response to pressed and potentially explosive urban arrangements. In the face of projected population increases of whites at rates significantly lower than for "non-whites," racial administration increasingly concerns itself with the artifice of maintaining white homogeneity, the managed racial unity (and "purity") of whites no matter ethnic differentiation, and the ethnic disaggregation and dislocation of "non-whites."

The account I have sketched here of the administrative management of, by, and through racial states is not simply structural or functionalist, politicist or culturalist, determinist or discursive. These are academic distinctions social experience fails in the end to heed. As the examples of the naturalization cases and census taking reveal, race can be invoked by states – as also by individuals – at different moments and in different ways to promote power, privilege, and property. Race can be so mobilized precisely because social structure and modes of reference, political economy and culture, public and private spheres are already racially conceived and fashioned, shaped and ordered. Whiteness then refers to a structural condition, and (as Roediger notes in response to his critics, 1999: 185–90) is in no way meant to fix absolutely and disrespectfully in privileged and racist place the subject positions and experiences of every particular person classed as white. Race shapes social life as social conditions fashion racial arrangements. So race already offers a vocabulary available to – indeed, often fashioned formatively by – state-making. What race thus brings to state-making, to states that invoke its terms, are the (re)forming, fashioning, and intensifying of (relations of) power, privilege, and property. It provides a set of presumptions that is taken up as an understanding about "given" states of empowerment, impoverishment, and class status, naturalistically or historistically conceived, as well as ideological representations and rationalizations of their normative legitimation.

Racial states, then, are states that historically become engaged in the constitution, maintenance, and management of whiteness, whether in the form of European domination, colonialism, segregation, white supremacy, herrenvolk democracy, Aryanism, or ultimately colorblind- or racelessness. These are all states of white rule, where white governance and norms of white being and being white historically prevail. They are states, that is, where whiteness increasingly becomes the norm. Racial states, in short, are states ultimately where whiteness rules. They are states where whiteness is the rule, where the assumptions, norms, and orders for which it stands reign supreme. In historical terms they are states in which white rule prevails and is shored up by a world racial order of white dominance. White rule rules by going global: colonialism, imperialism, the Third Reich, anti-communism, globalization. It is the globalizing of white dominance, explicitly or implicitly, by design or structurally, economically, politically, legally, culturally. Whiteness, to put it summarily, stands socially for status and superiority, politically for power and control, and economically for privilege and property (C. Harris 1995), culturally for self-assertion and arrogance but also and dialectically for anxiety and a crisis in confidence.[41]

It follows that white states are states the design or effects of which are to (re)produce, manage, and sustain overall the conditions and structures across all dimensions of social, political, economic, legal, and cultural life of the relative power, privilege, and properties of whites. The constitution as singular groups of "Hispanic" in the United States, "Coloured" in South Africa, and "Gypsy" in Europe (Willems 1997) is a product in each instance of state racial management in interaction with group self-formation. This is not to say that particular people characterized as white will be in a position of power, privilege, and property in every dimension *vis-à-vis* those deemed not white. Class and gender (and indeed more recently legal, sociocultural, as well as economic) statuses interact with racial standings to produce particular social positions for individuals that do not necessarily conform to standard(ized) identity placements. Nevertheless, states reproduce as they represent the governing structure of power, privilege, and property in virtue of which white people as a rule (and white men in particular) occupy positions of power, privilege, and property in relation to those not white, locally or globally. The power, privilege, and property in and of white states are revealed in contrast to the relatively less privileged, powerless, and propertyless positions of those who might be considered not white in states of global arrangement not structured to privilege, empower, or property those deemed white. The possessive investment in whiteness (Lipsitz 1998) was not only state created and sustained in the face of transforming social conditions; the contours of whiteness itself were refashioned and reshaped sociolegally in the face of new challenges and charges, both global and local in cause and condition. White privilege reigns whether the social conditions it signifies are taken to be "non-white states" or (in some idealized normative sense) *raceless* states. It is the nature and implications of "raceless" states, then, that call now for consideration.

NOTES

1   Quoted in Furedi (1998: 34–5).
2   The pragmatics of segregationism are not inconsistent with assimilationism. Thus French colonial policy could accommodate assimilation of native elites – precisely by rendering them "less native" – while segregating the bulk of the colonized population.
3   Massey and Hajnal (1995: 529) define "exposure" as "the degree of potential contact between blacks and whites within geographic units." Exposure "measures the extent to which group members are exposed to one another by virtue of sharing a common area of residence."
4   Massey and Hajnal (1995: 529) define "evenness" as "the degree to which blacks and whites are distributed uniformly across geographic units." With evenness, "the black percentage of each geographic unit equals the black percentage as a whole."
5   By 1920 a majority of whites had been urbanized while only a third of blacks; by 1950 a majority of blacks were city folk, and by 1960 a greater percentage of blacks than whites lived in cities. Between 1920 and 1980 the blacks living on the land and working in agriculture declined 96 percent, and by 1981 this figure had almost disappeared to 1 percent (Hirsch 1993: 66–7).
6   *Plessy v. Ferguson* 163 US 537, 543, 16 S. Ct. 1138.
7   *Plessy v. Ferguson* 163 US 537, 543, 16 S. Ct. 1142, 1143.
8   *Plessy v. Ferguson* 163 US 537, 543, 16 S. Ct. 1142.
9   Consider the fascinating work on English panics, spanning at least the past century, regarding Continental invasion in considering construction of the Channel Tunnel (Darian-Smith 1999; Pick 1994).
10 See for instance the essays and reviews written between 1910 and 1930, and collected in Boas (1940).
11 As all generalizations go, this one has exceptions, as much in the differences between those bearing it out as in those exceptions proving the rule. Regarding the former, contrast Robert Park's empiricist sociology (Park 1950) with John Dollard's Freudian social psychology (Dollard 1937/1988). For the extent of the material in the social psychology of intelligence, attitudes, and prejudice from the 1920s on, see especially the bibliography in Richards (1997), as well as the analysis at ibid., pp. 65–159. Notable critics who theorize racism as systemic and sustained, "naturalized" and "normalized" conditions of modern political economies – like W. E. B. du Bois and Oliver Cromwell Cox, and even the more liberal centrist Gunnar Myrdal – are anomalies nevertheless proving the rule of the prevailing shift to an urban focus.

197

12 *Dred Scott v. Sanford* 60, 407; 1857 US.

13 This is not to deny that the renegotiation of whiteness in Britain intensifies after 1945, with the falling apart of classic colonial conditions. The crack in British colonial self-confidence, however, comes almost a century earlier with the Indian Rebellion in 1857, a crack that becomes a gorge in the wake of the Anglo-Boer War at century's turn. It took two world wars and a global economic depression to shatter that self-confidence completely.

14 *In re Sadar Bhagwab Singh* 246 F. 498, 499; 1917 US Dist., emphasis added. As Barrett and Roediger point out (1997: 22), this concern with the threat to homogeneity was not restricted to the courts. Unions like the American Federation of Labor (AFL) defended the admission of immigrant labor from Northern and Central Europe over "the scum" from the "least civilized countries of Europe" precisely because of the supposed implications for urban conditions.

15 *In re Cruz* 23 F. Supp. 774; 1938 US Dist.

16 *Ex parte Dow* 211 F. 489; 1914 US District.

17 *In re Saito* 62 F. 126; 1894 US App.

18 See petition of Easurk Emsen Charr to the Missouri District Court 273 F. 207; 1921 US Dist.

19 *In re Sadar Bhagwab Singh* 246 F. 499; 1917 US Dist.

20 Reaffirmed in 1922 by the Supreme Court in *Takao Ozawa* 260 US 178; 43 S. Ct. 65; 1922 US.

21 *In re Mohan Singh* 257 F. 213; 1919 US Dist.

22 *United States v. Bhagat Singh Thind* 261 US 204; 43 S. Ct. 338; 1923 US.

23 Or indeed in: Filipinos or "Porto Ricans" who provided military service to the US in times of war and were honorably discharged could be eligible for naturalization within a strict statute of limitations. *Petition of Easurk Emsen Charr* 273 F. 209; 1921 US Dist.

24 *In re Halladjian* et al. 174 F. 83; 1909 Cir. Ct. Franz Boas, among a litany of prominent anthropologists, gave supporting evidence in behalf of the successful petition of an Armenian woman the US government was seeking to denaturalize after eleven years. *United States v. Cartozian* 6 F. 2d 919; 1925 US Dist.

25 *United States v. Balsara* 180 F. 694; 1910 US App.

26 *In re Halladjian* et al. 174 F. 834 Cir. Ct. D.; 1909 Massachusetts; *In re Ellis* 179 F. 1002; 1910 US Dist. D. Oregon.

27 *Ex parte Shahid* 205 F. 812; 1913 US Dist.

28 *Ex parte Dow* 211 F. 489; 1914 US Dist.

29 *In re Dow* 213 F. 362; 1914 US Dist.

30 *In re Dow* 213 F. 366, 367; 1914 US Dist.

31 *Dow v. United States* et al. 226 F. 145; 1915 US App.

32 *State v. Treadaway* et al. 126 La. 300; 52 So. 500; 1910 La. The woman arrested with Octave Treadaway is referred to anonymously throughout, where referenced at all, as "et al." or "another."

33 Cited also in *In re Cruz* 23 F. Supp. 774; 1938 US Dist.

34 In his opinion, the judge in *Treadaway* actually cites Stephenson's survey of legislation (*State v. Treadaway* et al. 1910, 15ff.).

35 *Jones v. Commonwealth* 80 Va. 18 (1885).

36 *Ferrall v. Ferrall* 69 S.S. 60 NC (1910).

37 *Moon v. Children's Home Society* 72 S.E. 707 Va. (1911).

38 *Stone v. Jones* 152 P.2d 19 19 (Cal. Ct. App. 1944).

39 Leti Volpp adds complexity to these "fears of hybridity" (801) by surveying the juridical boundaries restricting miscegenation between whites and Asian Americans, most notably Filipinos in California, from 1870 onwards (Volpp 2000b).

40 Cited in Hickman (1997: 1187). Hickman mistakenly claims that the Census Bureau "stopped counting 'mulattoes'" in 1920, which did not in fact happen until 1930.

41 Literary exemplifications of these conflicted states of white being include the fine set of short stories by Alan Gurganus, *White People*, especially "Blessed Assurance" (Gurganus 1991), and John Coetzee's disturbingly insightful novel, *Disgrace* (Coetzee 1999).

8

RACELESS STATES

The Constitution of the United States . . . forbids, so far as civil and political rights are concerned, discrimination by the *General Government* or by the *States* against any citizen because of his race.

Brown v. Board (1954: 499, my emphasis)

[T]he proper constitutional principal is not, no "invidious" racial or ethnic discrimination, but no use of racial or ethnic criteria to determine the distribution of *government* benefits and burdens . . .

Posner (1974: 25, my emphasis)[1]

Police practices that . . . [attempt] to question every person in a general category may well have disparate impact on small minority groups . . . If there are few black residents [in a city], for example, it would be more useful for police to use race to find a black suspect than a white one. It may also be practicable for law enforcement to attempt to contact every black person, but quite impossible to contact every white person. If an area were primarily black, with very few white residents, the impact would be reversed. The Equal Protection Clause, however, has long been interpreted to extend to *governmental* action that has a disparate impact on minority groups *only* when the action was undertaken *with discriminatory intent*.

Brown et al. *v. City of Oneonta*, New York US Ct.
Appeals 1999, 98–9375: 5, my emphases)

[S]o far as white people are concerned, there is one simple rule for interracial projects: don't try to atone for the past. Forget the past and build for the future.

Halsey (1946: 156)

FOR RENT – Furnished basement apartment. In private white home.
The (Maryland) Courier, January 8, 1970[2]

In the rush from explicitly racial formation in contemporary politics and political theorizing, conceptions of colorblindness seem, if haltingly, to have become the public commitment of choice. The public discourse regarding raceless states has focused almost exclusively on whether and how they might be morally or legally imperative, with what sorts of compelling normative arguments might be offered for or against them (Collier and Horowitz 1991; Appiah and Gutmann 1996; Fair 1997). The moral and legal insistence on racelessness has tended to rest upon a historical narrative promoting it as the only fitting contemporary response to pernicious racist pasts (Sleeper 1997: 8). On this account, any contemporary invocation of race for policy purposes, affirmative or not, comes to be equated with the horrors of racist histories (cf. Eastland and Bennett 1979).

I am concerned here, in keeping with the prevailing narrative threaded through the book, not first and foremost with this play of normative argumentation concerning the appeal or lack of raceless states, though normative considerations lurk in the shadows of any thinking around these matters. My concern, by contrast, is with when and why the discourse of racelessness took hold of the political imagination in modern state formation, what interests the discourse represents and speaks to, what shaping of the state it offers in the face of racial histories. So the question with which I am concerned is not primarily whether racelessness is normatively justifiable. Rather, it is with why, for instance, colorblindness in the United States became explicit initially in the late nineteenth century seemingly as a countervoice to bald segregationism (witness Harlan's famous dissent at the close of the century in *Plessy*) (Carr 1997). To what, as Reva Siegel asks, did that commitment to colorblindness amount, and how has it served to articulate rather than erase racial commitments (Siegel 1998)? How, by way of comparison, has a "raced racelessness" emerged and become elaborated in Brazil as racial democracy, or more recently in Europe in the expression of ethnic pluralism, in Australia or Canada as state multiculturalism, and in South Africa as non-racialism? What are the connections between various assertions of state racelessness and the coterminous emergence of post-racial and "post-racist racisms" (Comaroff and Comaroff 2000a)?

I have argued in earlier chapters that *historicism* took hold, increasingly and increasingly assertively, as a counter-voice to *naturalist* racial presumptions from roughly the mid-nineteenth century on. For a century or so, these two paradigms of racial rule were in more or less sharp and explicit contest with each other, both between and within racially conceived and ordered regimes. Where naturalism underpinned the institution of slavery, historicist racial presuppositions mostly fueled abolitionist movements, proliferating as common sense in the wake of slavery's formal demise, promoted as civilized moral conscience in the face of insistent and persistent naturalist regimes. Sometimes, however, historicist assumptions were internalized, though never without conflict (see Balibar 1991b: 18; Memmi 1967: 90–118), even by those marked as less developed by such assumptions and in the name of resistance: witness, for instance, Alexander Crummell's "The Progress of Civilization along the West African Coast" (1861/1966).[3] By the close of the nineteenth century, naturalism found itself on the defensive before increasingly heterogeneous urban arrangements, intensified migrations between colonies and metropoles, and an emergent shift from biologically driven to culturalist conceptions of race. As (a set of) conceptual commitment(s), naturalism thus was challenged explicitly to defend – to rationalize – its claims in ways it had not hitherto faced. In short, by the mid-twentieth century, naturalism had shifted explicitly from the given of racial rule to the anomaly, from the safely presumed to the protested, from the standard of social sophistication to the vestige of vulgarity.

Given this shift, it might be asked why the discourse of "primitivism" emerged so vocally and influentially at just this moment. Was "primitivism" simply a holdover from naturalist commitment, the return of the repressed? Or could its fashionable flourishing as the nineteenth gave way to the twentieth century in fact be ascribed to the shift itself I have identified here? The projection of the "primitive" – the romantic fabrication of and longing for an original human subjectivity (Goldberg, Musheno, and Bower 2001), pristine in its representation – served precisely as a bridge in the Euro-shift from racial naturalism to historicism. The discourse of "primitivism" invoked, as Barkan and Bush (1995) so well formulate it, a modernist "prehistory of the future." The 1901 Pan-American Exposition in Buffalo, for instance, not unlike many others around the time, displayed a "native village" with the view to representing the "shift from the low levels of humanity to the higher ones" (Barkan and Bush 1995: 9). The "primitive" came to embody not so much an irrecoverable object of nature as the retrojection of civilization's own misty beginnings, the admission into human time of those yet considered inferior in contrast to freezing "them" in the irrecuperable past of geological time.

It will help to summarize the line of argument at play here with the view to revealing the historical transformations in dominant forms of racial governance. Naturalism increasingly gave way to the common sense of historicism, the violence of an imposed physical repression to the infuriating subtleties of a legally fashioned racial order. In modern constitutional terms, the law is committed to the formal equality of treating like alike (and by extension the unlike differently). This abstract(ed) commitment to formal equality, in turn, entails the color-blinding constitutionalism of racelessness as the teleological narrative of modernization and racial progress. Racelessness is the *logical* implication of racial historicism. It is the perfect blending of modernist rationality and the maintenance of de facto, if deraced, racial domination juridically ordered and exercised.

Centralizing State Racelessness

The formalized commitment to racelessness, I am suggesting, grows out of the modern state's self-promotion in the name of rationality and the recognition of ethnoracially heterogeneous states. Modern states, we have seen in earlier chapters, assumed their modernity in and through their racial elaboration. After abolition, in the face of growing self-assertion and the call for self-governance by the "despised races" in the late nineteenth century and alongside the shift from biology to culture in racial articulation, racial historicism increasingly challenged naturalism as the presumptive form of states of whiteness. Against this background, the modern state in the twentieth century came to promote its claims to modernization more and more through its insistence upon racelessness. That is to say, through its insistence upon rendering invisible the racial sinews of the body politic and modes of rule and regulation. Racelessness came to represent state rationality regarding race.

The displacement from naturalist to historicist discursive dominance as the prevailing common sense of racial presumption would take

203

almost another century of racist brutality and bestiality. I do not mean to suggest, however, that naturalism disappeared as a commitment of rule within and across all (or indeed any) racial states. Naturalist commitments, while representing now the extremes of racist expression, nevertheless continue to circulate at the social margins and beneath the surface, as exemplified by slips of the tongue by public figures. Similarly, the persistent climb to power in Europe of the likes of Haider or Le Pen, of the National Front in France, Freedom Party in Austria, Northern League in Italy, or the Vlaamse Blok in Belgium reveals the circumspect circulation of naturalism just beneath the surface of contemporary historicist discursive dominance. So the argument at play here does not rest on a claim to "progression" from less to more enlightened views, though historicism certainly has proclaimed itself in those terms. And it certainly does not follow that naturalism has withered and deceased. A rearticulated naturalism has asserted itself as the social position of marginalized "conscience" and "critic" of hegemony, the object of state repression while bearing the burden of social progress.

Like historicist regimes, then, naturalism also would claim to promote state modernization. If naturalists have sought state modernization in the past on the backs of racial exploitation and dehumanization, they now seek it through racial separation and restrictions on "racial" immigration. Historicists, by contrast, have sought modernization through "humanization" and the denial of the effects of racial significance (cf. Balibar 1991b: 21–3, and esp. n. 6). Thus, where naturalists continue to see *race* as deeply significant, historicists insist on its *historical effects* as ultimately altogether insignificant. It should be clear that the increasing ideological and administrative dominance of historicism in state modernization has displaced naturalism for the most part to the extreme, the antique, or the anomaly (cf. Essed 1996: 20–9). Witness the recent marginalization of white supremacist militias – in South Africa as in the US, in Germany as in France, in the Netherlands as in Belgium – as extremist or terrorist. They are groups that define themselves precisely as dismissive of the contemporary state seen as representative of the racial interests of those not white or European at the expense of those who are. Naturalism and historicism accordingly remain dialectically definitive, as they have been from the outset of their formulation, of each other's respective parameters of possible articulation.

204

If colonial empires were established for the sake of raw materials and minerals, space and land, profits and the exercise of power, slave labor made (materially) possible their initiation and maximization of their operability. As the implications of abolition and metropolitan industrialization were being realized, state modernization became the abiding concern. Towards the close of the nineteenth century, state modernization entailed and was promoted by centralization of administrative technologies and the nationalizing coherence of state identity. States sought to extend to themselves the coordinates of this centralizing coherence through national narratives. A common administrative apparatus promised the rationalizing efficiencies, in cost and effort, of expansive problem-solving capacities. Confidence in state administration "consisted (at least in part) in solving big national problems, through large-scale interventions, co-ordinated from the center. And the agent of social transformation was a much bigger, more powerful, more knowledgeable, state" (Posel 2000: 13). As states committed to the project of modernization, so state-ordered and ordained data collection expanded and intensified.

Rational, centralized states were considered capable of solving almost any problem placed before them, large or small. An imperious, rationalist, and universalist utilitarianism asserted control over all dimensions of social life, from capital formation and control to war-making. States sought in their deific drive to make themselves aware through their data-collecting agencies of social conditions in their totality. Knowledge enables power, as power produces knowledge, if they are not quite fully equated. While not equatable on other dimensions, various twentieth-century state projects, as Posel (2000) notes, were products of this imaginary: America's New Deal, the Stalinist Soviet experiment, Nazi Germany's Reich, Britain's post-war reconstruction, apartheid South Africa.

Despite the fact that since the 1930s race increasingly has been dismissed as a premodern marking, an ancient hangover, it is evident from these examples how central it has remained to the modernizing state. States sought through race to mediate and manage the tensions between economy and society, to maintain white privilege and power, to massage costs and controls. There is a marked distinction, however, between the kinds of modernization different racial regimes promoted. States sought to modernize themselves according to their existing needs and available resources, invoking varying forms of racial configuration in the process. Naturalist states modernized through expulsion and exclusion, denial and in the extreme the production of death of those defined as inherently inferior, as "naturally" not qualifying for citizenship. Historicist states sought to modernize by claiming to educate those regarded as less developed or lacking in progress, those historically less endowed with the capacities and rationalities of civilization, the mores and manners, values and virtues of democracy, most notably, the means to self-determination. And to marginalize surplus populations, intra- or internationally, by wharehousing or willing them away.

In their purest form, naturalist racial regimes entail the teleology of (a) uniracial state(s), the state of whiteness (under some more or less specific interpretation) as final solution. So naturalism aims for the racelessness, the racial hygiene, of white self-elevation through the spatial and ultimately physical removal of those considered non-white. No further need for racial definition where the state has been reduced to uniracial formation through eviction or obliteration. Historicists seek the racelessness of absorption and transmogrification of the racially differentiated into a state of values and rationality defined by white standards and norms, ways of knowing and being, thinking and doing. This is a state characterized in the final analysis as racelessness. It is achievable only by the presumptive elevation of whiteness silently as (setting) the desirable standards, the teleological norms of civilized social life, even as it seeks to erase the traces of exclusions necessary to its achievement along the way.

Racelessness, then, offers the conditions either for global force and power (the "thousand-year Reich") or for the globalizing circulation of untethered corporate capital (the likes of the World Bank and International Monetary Fund). Racelessness, it might be said, is predicated upon the reduction of all to the color of money. And as a matter of historical logic money, as the Brazilian characterization has long had it, *whitens*. Race becomes not so much reduced to class as rearticulated through it. The popularity in the 1980s of *The Cosby Show*, in the US and South Africa alike, hints at the redefinition of race through class mobility (Gray 1995).

By the mid-nineteenth century racial naturalism had helped to effect a global capitalism the conditions for the sustenance of which it conceptually contradicted. Naturalism thus gave way in the end to the insistence of and upon racial historicism by the contingent logic of historical "necessity." Modernization promoted the proliferation and intensification of global flows of human, social, and finance capital, both spatially and temporally. National borders were rendered increasingly porous if not altogether archaic, replaced or really displaced by the latter quarter of the twentieth century more and more to their local reinscription. These products of colonial conditions, but also the cause of their demise, have called for(th) novel racial dispensations in the name of a new racelessness. The Cold War closed with not only the constriction of communism but the death of formal apartheid. In the wake of these emergent shifts in global capital and cultural formations – from the colonial to the postcolonial, segregationist to desegregationist, apartheid to post-apartheid, nationalized to globalized – naturalism's intensely raced racelessness gave way *almost* hegemonically to the state of whitened colorblinding. The colorblinding state can be understood in this scheme of things as the ultimate victory of states of whiteness purged of their guilt and self-doubt, the language of race giving way to the lexicon of a bland corporate multiculturalism and ethnic pluralism.

To recapitulate then: naturalist racial regimes, modernizing states with (lingering) naturalist commitments, tended in their twentieth-century modernizing drive to segregationist racial formations (and their apartheid successors) (Posel 2000: 7). Historicist regimes on the other hand opted for racelessness as the mark of modernizing global commitment, burying the threads of their own racial articulation beneath the more or less vocal dismissals of naturalism as modernizing prehistory.

Segregationism, almost by definition, was a *regional* design seeking global reach. Regions were to be purged of racial distinction, conceiving states as racially discrete (at least in the purist fantasy if not quite the pragmatic version). Centralization in states predicated on purist assumptions of racial naturalism were committed to racist intensification, to forced racial removal for the sake of the artifice – the dangerous fantasy – of racial purity. The pragmatics of racial rule nevertheless sought to nuance what was possible in the wake of radical resistance and liberal caution to implement and effect. An intense struggle erupted, for instance, between the ideologues of a purist apartheid state (separation of races at all costs) and apartheid "realists" or pragmatists (a step-by-step implementation of apartheid policies determined by judgments of what could be achieved economically and politically).

The struggle was won ultimately – as it likely only could be – by the pragmatists, led ironically by Verwoerd:

> While on the one hand the policy of Apartheid has to be implemented at the same time it has to be done step for step in such a way that the country can bear the implementation of that policy. (House of Assembly Debates 1955, vol. 88, col. 3760. Quoted in Posel 2000: 14–15)

Like segregation, apartheid in the end was about the attempt to merge white supremacy (as ideology, as commitment, as enactment in all domains) with maintenance of elevated and intensified white economic prosperity. And white supremacy, premised upon the demands and imaginaries of white domination, realistically meant not complete absence of those defined as not white from the social formation but their controlled presence, their service of and obeisance to white order and oversight. White prosperity, like white supremacy, depended upon it. They depended not on the absence of "non-whites" from white space but their structured exploitation within it. After all, whites could measure their superiority and sense of racial self-worth only in the controlled presence of those not-white. Hence the strong surge of a qualified pragmatic racist "realism" (on "racial realism," cf. Balibar 1991b: 23). The assumption of power in the late 1980s of the "pragmatic" W. F. De Klerk was not so much an anomaly to Afrikaner political power as the logical resolution of its internal ideological struggles (against the background of "raceless" global capital and intensified internal urban ungovernability).

Segregationism and its apartheid aftermath proved in the end radically incapable, whether in South Africa or the United States or Israel, of coping with the dynamics of rapid and intense ethnoracially diverse urbanization. Urbanization in the first three decades of the twentieth century was fueled by a shrinking rural sector and expansive industrialization, and so by migration and immigration. It was prompted by a rapidly transforming mode of production, labor demands and desires, requirements and hopes, needs and fantasies as well as by political and legal shifts. The issues emerging as a result were considered much too complex for "local, uneven, ad hoc interventions" (Posel 2000: 11), and so were deemed to require more centralized, rationalized, national responses. Initiated by the fantasized fears flowing from urbanized social mobilities, segregationist and apartheid regionalisms actually conjured the very possibility of black self-determination naturalism was committed to denying. Exacerbated by the duplicate costs of segregationist maintenance and declining profitability, this implosion of the logic of naturalism thus devolved into historicist assumptions, more muted and less assertive, to be sure, but an emergent and ultimately pervasive common sense in any case. Here lies the foundation for the expression of racelessness as "a given" of racial resolution – as a way, the least invasive way, logically – out of the apparent impasse.

In the case of apartheid, Posel poses the implosive logic with considerable clarity:

> As apartheid evolved, the Nationalists aspired to a national information system which was impossible to produce – not least given the information technology of the day. . . . For an African to be in an urban area longer than 72 hours depended on meeting certain legal requirements in terms of Section 10 (1) of the Urban Areas Act: to work in an urban area depended on authorisation from labour bureaux; to get access to a house in an urban area depended on being legally resident. Everyone legally resident was supposed to be in authorised accommodation; information about how many people legally in the area were not employed was necessary to measure the size of the labour surplus. The knowledge required to implement the urban influx control policy, with the urban labour preference principle at its core, required a capacity to cross-reference and cross-check disparate batches of names on one hand (comparing lists of people with passes with people allocated housing as tenants and sub-tenants), and statistics on the other (comparing numbers of people allocated housing with numbers in employment). But the bureaucratic competence – let alone the information technology – required to do so was unavailable. (Posel 2000: 24–5)

Apartheid, like segregation, demanded an administrative apparatus impossible to develop in full, let alone sustain, not least in the face of intensifying moral doubts, geopolitical posturing, and critical resistance, local and global.

This implosion of naturalist logic and its racial regimes prompted two primary effects. The first was not the "progressivist" demise or denouement of racist expression so readily proclaimed. There was rather, as I have insisted, an emergent shift to (an emphasis upon) racial historicism, and at most a laborious meliorism committed to addressing racial "problems" in a piecemeal and mostly ambiguous manner. The second, relatedly, concerned the deflection of charges of racism from historicist presupposition. Racism, on this account, can be predicated only on naturalist assumption. It is deemed nothing other than the (irrational) claim of inherent, immutable, and so timeless racial (biological or moral) inferiority. Historicist racial meliorism – the claimed historical immaturity of those deemed racially undeveloped, and so admission of their developmental possibility – supposedly escapes the charge of racism by naturalist comparison. Racial historicism evades racism by definitional deflection. And in doing so it becomes the default position regarding late modern racial states.

That the distinction between naturalism and historicism regarding racism is overlooked, the latter camouflaged for the most part behind the former, explains also how liberals and conservatives alike (can) assert that racism is alleviated once naturalist articulation of it fades from view. Those committed to historicist conception accordingly can claim they are not racist but racial realists, sufficiently courageous "to call a spade a spade" (cf. D'Souza 1995). Thus racism persists behind the facade of a historicism parading itself as uncommitted to racist expression *in its traditional sense*.

Styles of State Racelessness

Retrospectively, World War II can be read as the ultimate contestation between competing visions of and conditions for racial globalization: the naturalist and historicist, white supremacist and white developmentalist or progressivist, the Aryan Reich and Anglo-American capital, millenarian colonialism and flexible postcolonial accumulability. The Global War accordingly represents the moment of acute social crisis, racially conceived. That the forces of Good won out over those of Evil was taken (in the spirit of ideology's demise) to promote the "end of racism," the limits of its irrational extremism (Malik 1996: 124; Barkan 1992: 1), thus at once camouflaging the shift in racial configuration and representation. Racial historicism could claim victory in the name of racelessness, sewing the assumptions of (now historicized) racial advancement silently into the seams of post-war and postcolonial reconstruction. Three-world theory, emerging as it did in the early 1950s, simply structured the tapestry in more precise terms. If apartheid was the ultimately doomed naturalist response to this crisis in racial representation, naturalism's seemingly last gasp (Derrida 1985), colorblindness furnished the historicist form of crisis management and containment, maintenance of racial configuration and control.

World War II was a moment of radical uprooting. It exacerbated existing population movements and gave rise to a wide range of new ones. Surviving Jews moved within and out of Europe in increasing numbers. East Europeans moved West in the face of creeping communism. Colonial subjects served without much fanfare in the Allied forces, settling in the wake of the war in Britain and France (Furedi 1998; Hesse 2000). It should come as no surprise, for example, that the Pan-Africanist Congress would hold its fourth international meeting in Manchester in 1945. In reiterations of the Black Atlantic, Black Americans, Africans, and Caribbeans moved in search of work from South to North, or from lower northern cities to more industrialized ones, and from East to West (as of course in another sense was the experience of Asians), fueling the war economy (Halsey 1946; Smith 1949). They gravitated in the wake of the war also, though in smaller numbers, from the likes of New York or Dakar, Bombay or Kingston, Lagos or Accra to London, Paris, Amsterdam, and Berlin to leave behind them the weight of American racial degradation or to seek higher education, as cultural producers or political critics. The anti-colonial independence movements soon manifested in a series of heady successes: India in 1947, China in 1949, Ghana in 1956, Algeria in 1961, and so on. Post-war reconstruction and economic boom in the North pulled postcolonial subjects into European and North American metropoles, as the United Nations condemned a naturalistic conception of racism as scientifically vacuous and anti-Semitism became the dominant intellectual measure of racial prejudice.

There emerge out of this increasingly heterogeneous worldly mobility of people numerous contrasting, oftentimes competing, conceptions of racelessness taking root in different sociopolitical and cultural milieus. In the United States colorblindness was crafted and codified in the contrast between desegregationism and integrationism; in South Africa non-racialism became the dominant counter to apartheid, most notably articulated in the Freedom Charter in 1956. In Europe especially emphasis on ethnic pluralism has occluded racial reference and displaced charges of racism to the margins of the "loony left," while

211

in Brazil public advocacy of racial democracy swept any attempted political organization around racial injustice behind a romanticized projection of racial – and so really a deracialized – peace.

Racelessness in its various explicit and implicit expressions thus gathered steam in the wake of World War II[4] and came to dominate public commitment in a variety of transnational settings from the 1960s onwards. Seen in this light, the expressed commitment to racelessness was really about the reshaping of the state in the face of civil rights, integrationist, and demographic challenges to privilege and power. Justice Harlan, himself a former slave owner, had already recognized this challenge colorblindness posed as the appropriate reaction a half-century earlier:

> The white race deems itself to be the dominant race in this country. And so it is, in prestige, in achievements, in education, in wealth, and in power. So, I doubt not, it will continue to be for all time, if it remains true to its great heritage and holds fast to the principles of constitutional liberty. (*Plessy v. Ferguson* 1896)

Thus, having established through racial governance and racist exclusion the indomitable superiority of whites – in prestige, achievements, education, wealth, and power – not as a natural phenomenon but as historical outcome, the best way to maintain it, as Harlan insisted, is to treat those de facto *un*like as de jure *alike* (Crenshaw 1998: 285). The reproduction of white supremacy, Harlan's historicism makes clear, requires labor, a fact obscured of course by naturalists. Illegitimate inequalities – historical injustices in acquisition or transfer, as Nozick (1974) would have it – are to be legitimized by laundering them through the white wash with the detergent of colorblindness. Colorblindness enables as acceptable, as a principle of historical justice, the perpetuation of the inequities already established. Harlan outstripped his peers by half a century in recognizing that colorblindness would maintain – should maintain, as he conceived it – white supremacy, as well as in being able openly to admit it (cf. Carr 1997: 116).

While speaking to their sociospatial and sociotemporal specificities, often as critical commitments, the appeals to "racial democracy" in Brazil, "non-racialism" in South Africa, "ethnic pluralism" in Europe, and state "multiculturalism" in the likes of Australia and Canada each

212

served to extend the racial status quo in and of those states (Bennett 1998). These various commitments to racelessness, fueled as they often were by a mix of guilt and moral enlightenment but also by a "racial realism" (Bell 1995; Balibar 1991b: 23) and realpolitik, served nevertheless invariably to renew white social control and to promote white power and privilege in the face of emerging challenges. In all these variations, racelessness was at once as much a refusal to address, let alone redress, deeply etched historical inequities and in-equalities racially fashioned as it was an expressed embrace of principles of a race-ignoring fairness and equal opportunity. Racial configuration anywhere, as I said earlier, is shored up by forms of racial configura-tion everywhere; and racial conditions everywhere are maintained of course by their reproduction in particular places.

Racial democracy became the public expression of choice in Brazil from roughly the late 1930s onwards. This banner of racial democrat-ization through the processes of *mestizaje* and *blanqueamiento*, of whitening through mixing, has been waved more widely throughout Latin America, most notably in Colombia and Venezuela, Argentina and Cuba (Taussig 1980, 1997; Skidmore 1990; Wade 1993; Whitten and Torres 1998, vols. 1 and 2).[5] Associated most insistently with the work of Gilberto Freyre, racial democracy denied the deeply marked racist past of Brazilian society, ideologically and materially (Fiola 1990; Fernandes 1998; Mitchell 1998; Levine and Crocitti 1999; Schwarcz 1999). Freyre had studied in the early 1920s with Franz Boas at Columbia University. From Boas he inherited a conception of the relation between race and culture (see author's introduction to Freyre 1946). This influence indicated a shift from presumptions of naturalism that had marked much of Brazilian thinking around race – medically and legally, socially and politically – throughout slavery more or less until abolition in 1888 (Schwarcz 1999) to culturalist assumptions consistent with historicism. From this culturalist commitment Freyre drew the central raceless implication that Brazil in the 1930s and 1940s was marked by no "racial problem." This racelessness, in turn, was bound up with Freyre's deeply questionable revisionist historical assumptions. These included claims of "soft slavery" (*escravidao suave*) and benign or "good masters" (*o bom senhor*), humane Portuguese colonialism, and "marvelous accommodationism" of "slave to master, black to white," a "luso-tropical gentleness" and "carefreeness" among the Portuguese colonizers.

213

Following abolition by the "Golden Law" in 1888 and the declaration of the Republic a little over a year later, Brazil was reconstructed discursively as a tropical racial paradise. It projected itself as the laboratory of racial modernity and democracy through miscegenizing mixture, most notably, as a result of Portuguese men's sexual attraction to "hot black women" (Fiola 1990: 4–7). Metissage was supposed to result in a sort of racelessness through *blanqueamiento* – genetic, economic, and sociocultural "elevation" following from the whitening of the body politic. The importation from Europe of those with superior and stronger "white blood" would eugenically purge Brazil of the less desirable African and Amerindian presence, producing in their place a "Latin" race (Fry 2000: 87). These "Law(s) of White Magic," as Antonio Collado has properly put it (Nascimento in Levine and Crocitti 1999: 380), fashioned the fairytale of a raceless Brazilian. This was supposedly a new race beyond classical racial conceptions, a raceless race each individual member of which uniquely melded European, African, and Amerindian biological and cultural heritage (Fry 2000: 90).

By the time of the various Vargas regimes from the 1930s through the 1950s, racial reference and politics, race-based organizations and mobilization had been outlawed in the name of a racial – really a race-denying and white-elevating – democracy. Thus immediately following abolition official documents pertaining to slavery were destroyed, and in the first century of the Republic census counts included "color" questions just three times. Indeed, by 1969 all studies documenting racial discrimination in Brazil were outlawed as subversive of national security (Fiola 1990: 17–19). Accordingly, no data categorized in racial terms were collected in the 1970 Census, though racial terms were reintroduced in the census count a decade later (Skidmore 1990: 27–8). Swept behind the veil of racelessness, the reification of deep historical inequalities, racially conceived and shaped with racial materials, had become untouchable and unspeakable. Marked by the interface of race and class, black people in Brazil today consequently live considerably shorter, less healthy and poorer lives, are less educated, face considerable employment discrimination in hiring and promotion including explicit racial restrictions on hiring in the private sector, as well as extensive police harassment and violence. White infant mortality in 1980 was 25 percent lower than that for non-white babies, and whites would live almost seven years longer. Four times as many whites had completed high school in 1990 and their income averaged twice as much as that of blacks and mestizos. The percentage of people of color in the prisons of large cities such as Rio and São Paulo was roughly double their respective ratios in the demographic compositions of those cities, and about half as many whites charged with crimes await trial on bail than do similarly charged blacks (Fry 2000: 92–3). Racist stereotypes have pervaded the population, reinforced by images in school textbooks and popular culture (Fiola 1990: 22–36). Racelessness in Brazil has fixed racial effects in place, rendering its material conditions seemingly inevitable and their historical causes largely invisible and virtually causeless (cf. Hanchard 1994; Fry 2000: 99–100).

It is important to emphasize that Brazilian commitment to racelessness historically, while intellectually initiated, has been for the most part extended through state commitment. I do not mean by this to ignore the relative surge in Brazilian race-consciousness over the past decade or so, prompted by a self-conscious campaign by activists to fashion a black racial identity in Brazil. This campaign has resulted in the modest introduction of some race-based policies, laws, and programs (Fry 2000: 99–100). All this notwithstanding, recent surveys in São Paulo and Rio de Janeiro reveal that while almost 90 percent acknowledged racial discrimination in Brazil, most respondents remained vehemently committed to the prevailing conception of racial democracy and declared themselves personally free of prejudice (Fry 2000: 94). These knotted considerations trouble deeply the claims made of late by Pierre Bourdieu and Loic Wacquant in a series of articles that globalization has generalized to the rest of the world through a form of pernicious cultural imperialism the prevailing structures of binary racial definition, (mis) comprehension, and order manifested in the United States (Bourdieu and Wacquant 1998).

Now though non-racialism in South Africa was prompted by a different, if not unrelated, set of circumstances, it has come to represent similar effects. Non-racialism emerged as the prevailing expression of anti-racism in the early 1950s, a seemingly reasoned if not radical response to the increasing institutionalization of formalized apartheid in policy and law, economy and society. If the state was being codified in the lexicon of race, if racially conceived and ordered culture was unavoidable and inevitable, its *raison d'être* rule by division, then resistance seemed to require at least the principled commitment to racelessness, to social arrangements that insisted on making no reference to race. The Freedom Charter of 1956, a document deemed by the apartheid state to be too subversive to be allowed to circulate, was fashioned through a remarkable coalition of the major liberal and socialist resistant groups united through their common opposition to apartheid. The coalition recognized, to its credit, that simple oppositionality would be insufficient to sustain the principled differences between them. Non-racialism became a coalitional cement, the common denominator between those committed to intensive land redistribution and nationalization of the mode of production at one end and the forces of a progressive liberalism based on a naively benign capitalism at the other.[6] The "Freedom Charter's terms," boasted Adam and Moodley (1986: 213–14),

> resemble the old-fashioned values of liberal democracies. They lack the ideological zeal of the classless society and the fascist rule of the master race. The Freedom Charter is a pluralist document: "national groups coexisting in equality with mutual tolerance . . . " In the liberal modesty of the nonracial opposition lies its justness and moral promise.

And yet, in the name of "national groups coexisting in equality," the Freedom Charter inevitably presupposes and reinstates the very racial configurations it is expressly committed to challenging. By extension, once sewn into the post-apartheid constitution non-racialism effectively reinstates prevailing racially figured class and in large part gendered formation as the status quo. Racelessness renders the material conditions of historically reified racial, and through them gendered, formations unreachable. Indeed, while opening up a window of opportunity to a small sector of especially black women at the elite end, it has done nothing to make significantly less privileged black women less vulnerable either to employment or sexual exploitation. Thus unemployment, rape, and the incidence of AIDS among poor black women have risen dramatically in the past decade. The structural conditions of apartheid have been displaced to the realm of private individuated experiences under post-apartheid. By the same token, the Truth and Reconciliation Commission, while importantly revealing how widespread were routine governmental abuses of black people throughout the era of apartheid, at once has had virtually nothing to say formally about widespread everyday racist expression in the same period. This everyday expression was structured by but also made possible state racist formation. The unintended implication has been to render apartheid the effect almost wholly of a governmentality run amuck, an anomaly somehow silently disconnected from the otherwise human decency of the general white populace.

The claimed commitment to colorblindness in the US, the rhetoric of racial democracy in Brazil, and the principled policy of non-racialism in South Africa each has had a triple effect. First, each has effected the relative silencing of public analysis or serious discussion of everyday racisms in the respective societies. Second, each has made it more or less impossible to connect historical configurations to contemporary racial formations. Margaret Halsey explicitly ties the prospect of integrative colorblindness to historical denial, as borne out by her words prefacing this chapter. Witness also the explicit denial of such connection on the US Supreme Court, with dramatic implications for the constitutionality of affirmative action.[7] And third, each instance of racelessness has displaced the tensions of contemporary racially charged relations to the relative invisibility of private spheres, seemingly out of reach of public policy intervention. As Reva Siegel (1998: 31) notes more narrowly in respect of colorblind constitutionalism in the US, racelessness is the state strategy to institutionalize prevailing racial privilege and power by protecting "historical race" (Gotanda 1995) from state intervention or interference. Judge Richard Posner's remarks prefacing this chapter provide ample evidence.

Now the European shift to the language of ethnic pluralism and the recent widening state invocation of multiculturalism over that of racial reference has had a triple effect too. For one, it has led to the relative disappearance from public debate of reference to European colonialism, its extensions, and its contemporary implications, thus reshaping the narrative of European history and memory (Werbner 1997: 261; Goldberg 2001a). As racial reference has given way to the insistent silences as a result of the shift to racelessness, ethnic subjectification has become more characteristic, or at least more noticeable (and noted), at Europe's historical edges: Bosnia, Kosovo, Chechnya, Somalia, Rwanda, East Timor, Fiji, the Moluccas, Quebec. Second, the ethnic (re)turn has rendered relatively awkward, if not impossible, direct critical reference to contemporary racism in European or even in settler societies. Witness, for instance, the persistence of the rule of "German blood" in defining German citizenship; and while Haider's anti-Semitic expression in Austria has been roundly condemned, the recent repeated beatings of people of color in Viennese subways by or with the collusion of the police has barely warranted a mention (Reisigl and Wodak 2000a). Referencing the Australian instance, Elizabeth Povinelli nevertheless captures the general logic at work. "Australian state officials," she writes,

> represent themselves and the nation as subjects shamed by past imperial, colonial, and racist attitudes that are now understood as having, in their words, constituted "the darkest aspect" of the nation's history and impaired its social and economic future. Multiculturalism is represented as the externalized political testament both to the nation's aversion to its past misdeeds, and to its recovered good intentions. . . . The nation would then be able to come out from under the pall of its failed history, betrayed best intentions, and discursive impasses. And normative citizens would be freed to pursue their profits and enjoy their families without guilty glances over their shoulders into history or at the slum across the block. (Povinelli 1998: 581–2)

The third effect of this shift to the framework of an ethnic pluralism identified with state multiculturalism has been to make more difficult the drawing of causal connections between colonial legacies and contemporary racial conditions in European or settler societies. The new managed multicultural Europe or Canada or Australia is taken to be the function of a new (neoliberal) world order that promotes immigration and refugees, criminalization and job competition, a world somehow connected, if at all, only marginally to their colonial histories.

As in Brazil, public institutions throughout Europe and European settler societies recently have been careful to espouse broadly explicit policies against racial discrimination with the view to being able to distance themselves from the phenomenon. But the effect of the World War II experience has been to narrow the concern over racism to its supposedly irrational and stereotyping expressions predicated on biological claims and so for the most part to limit contemporary racist expression to the extremes of neo-Nazi outbursts. Everyday racisms in private spheres proliferate behind the veil of their public disavowal in the name of ethnic pluralist and multicultural decency, on one hand, and the substitution of racial reference by the coded terms of policy concerns over immigration, criminalization, and the integrity of national culture, on the other (Essed 1996; Modood and Werbner 1997; Van Dijk 2000; Reisigl and Wodak 2000b).

Here the relatively explicit racial language in British public expression and certainly its proliferation of academic studies around race and racism reveal Britain as the European exception that largely proves the rule. The vigorous British academic debate in the 1980s indeed warned against privileging ethnicity to the relative occlusion of race and racism as the objects and terms of analysis (Solomos and Back 1996: 130). But Britain in any case remains Europe's anomaly in this, as in so much else. Those European studies on racism that do exist tend to be marginalized as disgruntled, if not extreme, voices in their own societies (Wodak 1991, 2001; Blommaert and Verschueren 1992; Essed 1993; Taguieff 2001; Solomos and Wrench 1993; Martiniello 1998a, 1998b; Wieviorka 1998; Van Dijk 1999/2001, 2001). The British academic focus on racisms, however, should not lead one to overemphasize official British openness concerning its recent racial record, however. The longstanding British denial of racism throughout its criminal justice system (Hall et al. 1978; Keith 1992), for instance, was underlined by the reticence regarding prosecution of the Stephen Lawrence murder and the subsequent furore over the state's investigation of Britain's long record of racist policing.

If non-racialism has left the materialities of racial distinction beyond reach, then critical multiculturalism has certainly prompted a radical rethinking of the exclusionary histories of racial structure. Nevertheless, the socially dominant conservative, liberal, and corporate versions of multiculturalism that have informed state practice – in Canada, Australia, the US, and Europe, to name but the leading formulations – have extended the *effects* of racelessness even if not quite so readily its refusal of any and all racial reference. In 1993, then Australian Prime Minister P. J. Keating claimed that the "new socially just multicultural society could be painlessly achieved with no serious costs or losses for... "we" non-Aboriginal Australians. [I]t would not challenge, threaten, or set into crisis the basic values of Australians (including "our" right to enjoy beaches and other recreation areas, including national parks)" (Povinelli 1998: 589). Under colonial assimilation colonizers sought to eclipse, if not erase, indigenous colonized cultures; under the managed multiculturalist turn, by contrast, the project has been to put to economic and political work the value of cultural distinction silently ascribed to racial difference (cf. Stratton and Ang 1998; Morris 1998). Think of the decade-long commercials for Benetton or Budweiser, Gatorade or Gap, Cisco Systems or Nike Sports.

In a Holland much the model of relative racial openness, marzipan and chocolate representations of "Zwarte Piet (Black Peter)," the colonial servant Sambo figure still so adored by white Dutch culture, adorn every shop window in the weeks leading up to Sinterklaas (St. Nicholas) Day each early December. Black Dutch people are forced into critical silence in the face of a Dutch repressive tolerance enamored annually with its national mascot not to mention tourist profit ("Oh, isn't he cute!") quietly conjuring the embarrassed riches of the golden age of empire (Pieterse 1992: 163–5). Britain faced its own version not too many years ago in the national(ist) battle over "Her Majesty's golliwog" representing Robertson's jam (cf. Pieterse 1992: 156–8). Thus racial distinction and derogation in the name of the nation are implicitly acknowledged to profitable purpose even as they are denied as a principled ordering frame of civil or political order. The (not-quite) postcolonial present is quietly reconnected to its colonial past through the weaving of (multi)cultural with commercial commitments. As Dutch society diversifies – its national football team is nearly half black, the population of Amsterdam fully one-third people of color and likely to become the majority over the next fifteen years – there are powerful reminders of the unbearable (but no longer so readily presumptive) whiteness of the Dutch state of being and control.

The foregoing line of analysis should not be taken to suggest that there are no relevant distinctions between American claims to color-blindness, Brazilian racial democracy, South African non-racialism, European ethnopluralist and Australian or Canadian multicultural maintenance. Each form of racelessness has been fashioned in the crucible of the conditions specific to their social, political, legal, and cultural conditions peculiar to their historical contexts of articulation.

One broad distinction, however, is worth noting here. Colorblindness and racial democracy are distinct from non-racialism and multi-culturalism, at least under one set of interpretations. The former were each fashioned explicitly as forms of political and social evasion, at least initially, while the latter grew out of critical commitments even as they quickly assumed more accommodating and so pacifying expression. It is true that invocation of both colorblindness and racial democracy could be read as attempts at a compromising social reconstruction, projects of reconciliatory nation-making or rebuilding in the wake of racially destructive histories. And indeed the codes of colorblindness in particular were taken up in the civil rights movement of the 1950s and 1960s as a coalescing of anti-racist forces. In the latter case, the investment in eliminationism was not first and foremost about conceptual erasure but a commitment to eliminating the material conditions racial characterization historically has referenced (Guinier and Torres 2001: ch. 1). Yet the accommodating compromises in the name of national reconciliation signaled both by colorblindness in the US and racial democracy in Brazil (and Latin America more broadly) exactly privileged, and in privileging reinforced, the relatively powerful and already privileged at the expense of the traditionally excluded. In short, they reinscribed a refurbished whiteness as the privileged, powerful, and propertied to the ongoing exclusions of those considered or classified not white. The legacies of non-racialism and multiculturalism, because fashioned in some sense to bring down "the house that race built," even as they have ended up as forms of redecoration, have perhaps been more checkered in their particular institutional effects.

Conditions and Codes of Racelessness

Racelessness is the neoliberal attempt to go beyond – without (fully) coming to terms with – racial histories and their accompanying racist inequities and iniquities; to mediate the racially classed and gendered distinctions to which those histories have given rise without reference to the racial terms of those distinctions; to transform, via the negating dialectic of denial and ignoring, racially marked social orders into racially erased ones. In rubbing out the possibilities of racial cognition and recognition in those societies historically marked by race – and which modern society has somehow not been so marked? – the classing marks of racist derogation and debilitation are rendered relatively invisible, histories reduced to pasts happily placed beneath the focus of memory, conveniently repackaged for commercial consumption and nostalgic renarration purged of historical responsibility (Goldberg 2001a). Proponents no doubt point to the virtues of this transcendence and forgetting, to the prospective leaving bygones behind and to the sort of optimistic hybridity reflected in Benetton's united colors.

221

But those colors of commercial unification linger with the now unaddressed (and perhaps unaddressable) presumptions of stereotypical distinction: those long characterized as non-whites whitened by
the classed color of money nevertheless bearing the distinctive birth-
marks of unaddressed because unaddressable inferiorized pasts ("never
quite" white, always "not yet," as Françoise Verges 2001, riffing on
Homi Bhabha, has reminded us).

Racelessness trades on collapsing in favor of the latter that distinction drawn in chapter 5 between racial states of governance and
states of being. The racial status quo – racial exclusions and privileges
favoring for the most part middle- and upper-class whites – is maintained by formalizing equality through states of legal and administrative science. These governmentalities of racial maintenance trade, as
I earlier pointed out, on treating non-like alike. They include instrumental implementation of principles such as equal treatment before
the law abstracted from socioeconomic or educational differentiations
and their affordability, or equal opportunity as process rather than outcome (dismissed deridingly as communist egalitarianism or quotas).
Behind the formalisms of such legally mandated equalities, lived inequalities of race, rendered informal and routinized, are extended as
the legitimate outcomes of private individual efforts generalized.

The forms of racelessness I have dwelt upon here – colorblindness,
racial democracy, non-racialism, ethnic pluralism, state multiculturalism
– each in their own way become the public naming of racial reference, a way of speaking about racial conditions in the face of their
unnameability or formal unspeakability. In so naming, one is at once
claiming racial conditions as unspeakable and yet spoken for; unmen-
tionable and yet spoken to; non-referenced and yet spoken about. If
racial reference is unavoidable as a state of being and yet as a form of
governance the state is required to be raceless, it means that the state
or state agencies are silenced. They are restricted more or less from
addressing, let alone redressing, the effects of racial discrimination.
Race supposedly could not even be discussed as a public policy concern save to render its expression off-limits to public political and
policy debate.

Take colorblindness, for instance. Colorblindness literally is concerned with being blind to color. In the historical ambiguity of the
failure of whiteness to recognize itself as a racial color, the implication
must be that colorblindness concern itself exclusively with being blind

to *people* of color. And through this blindness whiteness veils from itself any self-recognition in the traces of its ghostly power. Whiteness finds itself in colorblindness strung out on the gallows of Hegel's notorious dilemma of recognition. As a racial presumption, color-blindness continues to conjure people of color as a problem in virtue of their being of color, in so far as they are not white. As whiteness studies has so readily and rightly trumpeted as one of its central insights, whiteness remains unquestioned as the arbiter of value, the norm of acceptability, quality, and standard of merit. Color is considered a bruise, a blot on social purity, an unfortunate fact of life to be ignored, seen past yet still seen even if in blurred outline. Qua embodiments of whiteness, then, whites require for their own recognition as elevated those they take not to be their equals. So color-blindness presupposes a split disposition on the part of colorblind subjects, a doubled troubled consciousness. Racially understood, colorblindness is committed to seeing and not seeing all as white, though not all ever as quite, while claiming to see those traditionally conceived as "of color" *in* living color and yet colorless. It is as though the undertaking is to pick one out so as consciously not to pick one out. Either way, one is identified precisely in the default mode of racial terms. So, colorblindness fails as it succeeds, for even in announcing the end of racism it extends exclusion by another (if supposedly now nameless) name, by other (no longer meaningless) means.

This conceptual implosion of the colorblinding insistence reveals that each expression of racelessness conjures an excess of racial reference it is unable to contain. While reducing race to color, colorblindness can only awkwardly refuse a racial articulation that is not narrowly color-bound. (I have sometimes joked with my students that literally complete colorblindness would have people seeing only in terms of the codes of black and white.) Racial democracy conceptually opens itself to discussions of racially referenced political arrangements it seemed bent at once on denying. While perhaps the most completely negating of explicit racial range in thinking about social arrangements, non-racialism nevertheless can be read as leaving open the possibility of a racial analytics as an account and measure of historical and contemporary racisms. Ethnic pluralism is literally evasive of racial reference, while yet conjuring the possibility of a pragmatic if more or less quiet equation of race with ethnic identification. And state multiculturalisms reference race only to restrict it to a past better left behind, cut off from the present behind symbolic apologies lacking almost any material implication.

In its contemporary expression, racelessness is an attempt in the name of neutrality to reinstate by presupposing the normative appeal of a certain sort of homogeneity. Difference is deleted in the spirit of an assumption of transparency, a supposedly "see-through" sociality having immediate (i.e., unmediated) access to the content of people's character judged in terms of the prevailing norms of an Anglo-European moral tradition masquerading as modernizing universalism. Norms of whiteness are represented as the ideals of colorlessness and culture. Racelessness as a politics and culture is thus a belated attempt to reinstate the power of those values – and those representing those values – considered traditional. Historically, that is, of those who are white, or at least think the norms traditionally associated with whiteness are necessarily those by which social life ideally ought to be defined and refined. The dilemma is inescapable. Those who think they can avoid it by retreating to a neutral universalism evasive of racial reference do so only by veiling themselves in an ignorance of how racial histories continue to infuse all claims to value.

It should be unsurprising in light of this that racelessness effects implications at the level of individual consciousness also. At a recent international conference, an otherwise engaging panel on cultural transformation in South Africa was completely undone by the final intervention of a white North American panelist. Troubled by what she had taken initially as an all-white panel which turned out to be more mixed than she had read into the program, the panelist nevertheless repeatedly insisted that all white South Africans continue to see black South Africans as "kaffirs." She then proceeded to use this derogatory term emphatically in almost every other sentence subsequently uttered, insisting that the rest of the panel as well as the audience consequently were implicated in the reproduction of this referential racism (which indeed we ironically were by her repeated insistence). Called to task for her offensive and objectionable insensitivity by most everyone in the room (myself included), the panelist fell back on claiming white defensiveness in the face of her ridiculously radical critique. "I am married to a Sotho," she pronounced in defensive counter-attack, "I know a kaffir." The disturbed and disturbing ambiguity of this epistemological self-privileging, mimicking as it does the privileged form of colonial and apartheid insistence ("I know a _____ when I see one"), assumed its awful contemporary significance (the session ended with the one black South African panel member fleeing from the room wracked by sobs) in and through the arrogant white alchemy of racelessness. The misguided panelist arrogated to herself the capability of transcending her whiteness by becoming black in the megalomania of her own mind: "I married a Sotho, that makes me (tantamount to) a black South African."

Emptied of reference through racelessness, racial categories accordingly may be filled with any timeless or spaceless significance its proponents choose. There are many examples one could cite. The weekend inhabiting of American Indianness in the name of a rediscovered spirituality by Europeans or those of European descent is one. Another concerns the claims to pallid colorblindness of the white restaurateur or hotel receptionist in an historically white South African suburb in response to a mixed couple's complaints about blatantly disrespectful and discriminatory treatment even as (in the case of the restaurant) all black employees remained consigned to the kitchen and (in the case of the hotel) the cleaning and service staff remained completely black (Essed 2001). Hysterically troubled by their loss of racial control and feeling threatened as a result of their sense of Western abandonment, many white South Africans defensively fall back not so much on the old derogatory stereotypes but on a mimicked claim not to see race. A claim, of course, all too close to the (dis)comforts of apartheid.[8] America, the beautiful, land of the (race) free and home of the brave.

The political pragmatics involved in the raceless merging of states of racial governance and being are revealed most tellingly by those promoting governmental colorblindness and yet who openly invoke the language of race in "private" policy discussions to set strategy favorable to their political interests. Thus Republicans in the US committed to colorblindness in the public sphere strategize in private backrooms and boardrooms about voter redistricting to create all African American districts so as to guarantee Republican majorities in districts from which blacks were to be cartographically excised. The Republican National Committee appointed three co-chairs of its national nominating convention for its US presidential candidate in the 2000 election – a black Congressman, a white woman, and an Hispanic Congressman. The unashamed aim was to appeal not so much to "minority" voters as to "independents" (voting members of neither major party) who are known to favor greater diversity and whose votes turned out to be crucial to the prospects of the 2000 presidential election. Similarly, then-Governor of the State of Texas, George W. Bush emphatically opposed state-supported affirmative action in the name of colorblind commitments. He nevertheless rushed to speak at Bob Jones University in South Carolina to shore up a flagging political campaign in the presidential primary election against John McCain. Bob Jones University is a private self-professed Christian fundamentalist institution that refuses all public higher education subsidies. At the time the university proscribed cross-racial dating among students as immoral, a proscription George Junior pointedly refused to criticize in the name of the institution's freedom of private, unsubsidized commitment and his own profession of colorblindness. And throughout his presidential election campaign Bush was quite happy to parade in public his readily bilingual "little brown" nephew (the young man's mother, Bush's sister-in-law, is Mexican American) in calculated appeal to "Hispanic" voters.

The enormous historical inequalities manifest and managed under the rubric of racial naturalism everywhere European colonialism took root have been reincarnated postcolonially under the rationalizing rubrics of social, jurisprudential, cultural, and political racelessness. This reinscription at once obscures that history, re-members it purged of its debilities and of any responsibility in their reproduction. It is as if the inequities were natural, and so inevitable, outcomes of states of being, group character, civilizational characteristics (or their lack). To these ends, the Royal Belgian Museum for Central Africa to this day legitimizes itself as one of the most important institutions committed to "the scientific study of Africa." It claims to provide, as its pamphlet declares without the hint of irony or shame, "an impressive historic account of the explorations of Central Africa and of *the work of the Belgians in the former Belgian Congo*" (my emphasis). Peace through power, tranquility through strength, wellbeing through hard work, European virtue through rationality, civility and the civilizing mission by the presumption of racial naturalism and necessity.[9]

Here, in contrast to this public display, are some findings from the "secret documents" uncovered by "the investigating commission in the Congo state." This commission was a group appointed in 1904–5 by the Congo Free State's and Museum's founder, King Leopold II, as a form of public relations damage control in the face of critical attacks on his genocidal forced-labor policies in the Congo.

> Whenever the natives bring rubber to a post they are met by an agent guarded by soldiers. The baskets are weighed; if they do not contain the required five kilos, the man is immediately *rewarded* with 100 strokes with the *chicotte* [whip of hippopotamus hide]. Baskets that do contain the necessary weight are paid for with a length of cloth or with some other object. If there are a hundred men in the village and only fifty of them report with rubber, then these are held hostage while soldiers are sent to shoot the other fifty and to burn the entire village. (Quoted in Delathuy 1988: 529; Breman 1990: 93, my emphasis)

And again:

> We must beat them until they submit unconditionally or until they are all exterminated . . . You say to the owner of the first hut: here is a basket, go and fill it with rubber. Go into the forest at once, and if you are not back within eight days with five kilos of rubber, I shall set fire to your hut! – and you burn down as you have promised. The cudgel can be used to drive those men into the forest who do not want to leave the village. If you burn one hut after another, you shouldn't have to set fire to them all *to force* their obedience. (Quoted in Delathuy 1988: 519; Breman 1990: 89, my emphasis)

This is the "work of the Belgians" in the name of exploration and science, racial necessity and civilizing superiority, rubbed out in the Museum's representation of the historical record. If the brutes fail to deliver their quota, "exterminate all the brutes," as Conrad's Kurtz exhorts in the scribbled postscript to his Report to the International Society for the Suppression of Savage Customs (Conrad 1901/1991: 45–6). The brutishness is doubly deadened by this museographic excision.

Raceless states render the transparency of such racially driven violence and inequities private and opaque, a product of personal pre-ference and individualized imagination, and so irrepressible, unmarked and untouchable. Of the estimated 10 million indigenous Congolese exterminated – murdered and died by disease under Leopold's direc-tion and in the spirit of a civilization whose acts defy the label, half the area's population decimated between 1880 and 1920 – neither name nor a single word in the Museum's musing to self-proclaimed civilization. It is as though the natives failed to exist. Which in a sense, for the Belgians, they did, save as packhorses and instruments of labor, convenient but unfortunate occupants of the natural landscape, as readily a part of – reducible to – nature as the stuffed fauna and flora displayed in the Museum, and no doubt sometimes killed by the same weapons and at the same hands. No Western outrage here. The scientific study of Africa must go on, civilization's work undisturbed by memory, facilitated by raceless forgetting. No sanctions, moral or economic, for the host of NATO.

Expressly committed to race-blindness, that is, to a standard of justice protective of individual rights and not group results, raceless racism informally identifies *racial* groups so long as the recognition in question is no longer state formulated or fashioned. The possibility of racelessness publicly, and by extension of racial reference privately, trades exactly on an implicit and informal invocation of the sorts of massaged historical racial referents now denied in the public sphere. This in turn makes possible the devaluation of any individuals considered not white, or white-like, the trashing or trampling of their rights and possibilities, for the sake of preserving the right to *private* "rational discrimination" of whites. If the raceless *state* ought not to discriminate, it remains open to its citizens to restrict rental of their "private white apartments" to their self-defined kind. Such rational discriminators rationalize their avoidance of those not like themselves by appealing to statistical generalizations about groups intersectionally raced, gendered, and classed. By rational discrimination is intended that the discrimination is instrumentally valuable: "It is efficient, it makes economic sense," as D'Souza notoriously has put it (D'Souza 1995: 277). If discrimination in hiring, mortgage leasing, education, criminal justice, and consumption possibilities is mostly rational, the implication is that it ceases to be racist (Goldberg 1993: 14–40). The logical entailment of racelessness is the end not of racism but of its charge, its accusation and the bearing of its compensatory cost.

"Rational discrimination" is the handmaiden of racelessness. The values of efficiency and economy, the fundamental(ist) foundations of rational choice reason, assume the status of empirically established truth the force of which is unquestionable and so incontestable. Discrimination devolves, if not dissolves, into discretion. The disvalue of racist discrimination is discounted in the calculus of maximizing personal preference schemes. Not only are such preference-based racist exclusions, privileges, or distributions deemed acceptable in the private sphere, those racist configurations "that arise from differences in tastes or talents among racial groups" (Siegel 1998: 48) are rendered immune from state intervention. As Siegel points out, the concern of a raceless state agency shifts accordingly from redressing past and present racist exclusion to protecting the expression of private racial preference in the "racial marketplace" (Crenshaw 1998: 283) from state restriction.

Racelessness as Civic Religion

It is revealing to conceive of race in this context as constituting a "political religion" (Voegelin 1933/1997), a civic investment to create and promote a "political community" by the state in its absence. Here "whites" and "blacks" may be constituted as "communities," civic fraternities in the face of and giving face to an otherwise altogether anonymous and so threatened project of nation-building or national reproduction by the state. In so far as race can be conceived as a civic religion it is to be treated in a liberal democracy *as if* a religion. "What we need," insists D'Souza (1995: 545), "is a separation of race and state." So, if race is a religion or religion-like, then the state cannot be seen to express itself in favor of one rather than another in the public realm. But nor can the state interfere with *private* racial expression, much as it is precluded by US constitutionalism from interfering with religious speech. Racist discrimination thus becomes privatized, and in terms of liberal legality state protected in its privacy.

Racelessness accordingly sews the deep legacy of racial differentiation and distinction, material racial and social positions, into the social structures of their respective societies as the baseline, the given of social arrangements, the racial status quo as natural social order. Naturalism formalistically removed but its legacy, its structural implications, firmly reproduced through historical enactment. Racial naturalism and historicism, as I indicated earlier, trade on each other, and in multiple fashions. Committed to racelessness, those conditions that structure social formation today almost globally can no longer be addressed formally in racial terms. "States," as Carr puts it in the context of the US drive to colorblindness, "should not have segregated schools by law, and states should not integrate them either" (Carr 1997: 114). Thus the Republican Party Platform in the 1980 US general election stated:

> [E]qual opportunity should not be jeopardized by bureaucratic regulation and decisions that rely on "quotas," ratios and numerical requirements to exclude some individuals in favor of others, thereby rendering such regulations and decisions inherently discriminatory. (Quoted in Edsall and Edsall 1991: 144)

So historicism prevails in the struggle to provide the overriding interpretation of race as the civic religion because naturalism comes to be seen as too extreme, too intense, and so too at odds with intensifying heterogeneity. Naturalism is considered thus to become too disruptive. While naturalism served to intensify capital's interests and the dialectic of (in)security and freedom, capital's integration of the world, first through colonialism and then segregationism and apartheid, prompted renegotiation of racial orders, a rethinking of the fragile hold over and on homogeneity. Racelessness ultimately offered a reordering of racial rule without burden or guilt, responsibility or cost, in the face now not just of the rearticulation of capital – financial, economic, social, cultural – but intensified interaction of cultures and peoples.

The immediate effects of racelessness's referential repression are threefold. First, no longer racially addressable, racial inequities and inequalities are beyond the boundaries of racial redress. Second, racist inequality is magically transformed from its historical manifestations and effects perpetrated for the most part by whites against those who are not into the "reverse discrimination" against those whites supposedly suffering the exclusionary effects of "preferential treatment" or "positive discrimination" for those not white (Goldberg 1997; Fry 2000: 102–3). And third, the assumption of the raceless state identifies all race-consciousness as extreme, precisely because the modern liberal state trades on its own claims to neutrality. The assumption of racial reference as necessarily extreme equates by implication the likes of white terror groups such as the Ku Klux Klan with resistant black nationalist groups such as the Panthers or SNCC under Stokely, White Aryan Resistance with Negritude, the Third Reich with Pan-Africanism (cf. Peller 1995).

The combined implication of this effective trilogy is to fix in place as irreplaceable, as ahistorical, the inherited racist images of whiteness and blackness. Thus, where whiteness is taken to represent property, privilege, and power, blackness continues to represent devaluation – that loss of value, for instance, when blacks move into white neighborhoods (Williams 1998: 41). Blackness (and non-whiteness more generally) as social place-marker thus relatedly comes to represent surplus value, unusable or unproductive commodities, the remainder stock, the detritus of the global economy, an inhuman capital capable of producing profit on capital investment only by being treated as alien(able) objects, products to be traded in the marketplace of new racially driven economies.

The value of blackness on this account could only be a function of its devaluation. The more value socially, materially, and symbolically black people (qua black) are at the center of creating, the less valued they must be as (black) persons. Indeed, the value of blackness in the former senses is a function of black people's devaluation (qua black) in the latter, their devaluation in the latter a necessary condition for their value in the former. So, the more valuable blackness is deemed, the more worthless black people (qua black) are considered; the more civilized if not civilizing the supposed presumption of their employment or employability, the more barbarous they are rendered because assumed so; the more economically empowering the use of blackness, the more powerless black people (qua black) are required to be (cf. Marx 1975). On the one hand, this is a surplus value that allows world medical and political authorities to discount the devastating threat of AIDS to African populations until threatening to the West (the epidemic would depopulate a terribly overpopulated continent, predicted one happily callous American state strategist in the early 1990s) or to turn a blind eye to otherwise politically costly black genocides. On the other, this surplus devaluation is necessary to fueling the profit margins for otherwise marginal political economies, like the US prison industry, and so to renew otherwise flagging capitals, economic and social, political and cultural (Goldberg 2000b).

I do not mean by this line of critique to say there has been no "racial progress." A commitment to a meliorism and progressivism that produced none after all would be too crass an ideological subterfuge to rise to the claims of legitimation. But every form of racial progress thus predicated on white normativity is laden with ambiguity

231

and ambivalence, is undercut, qualified, and discounted, by the tinge of special treatment or exceptionalism, overcoming the odds despite one's birth(right), and so on. Thus I am emphatically not denying that throughout much of the world marked historically by colonial conditions, liberation struggles, and postcolonial transformation, racially predicated situations for peoples of color have markedly improved, de jure and de facto. But the necessity of such acknowledgment at once troubles the claim to progress itself by questioning the standards of judgment and the standpoint from which both those standards and the judgments presupposing those standards are made (cf. Scott 1998: 343). Progress for whom, measured against what? Sure, some things have improved, but determined against a yardstick already so debased it would be difficult not to demonstrate progress once that commitment was proclaimed. The measure of improvement has been the historical conditions colonially and racially established, not the presumptively elevated conditions of the privileged. That the privileges were racially predicated in the first place is already silently denied in the privileging of the standard of measurement to begin with. The standards are deemed objective, the standard bearers deserving of their achievements on their own merits, the standard of progress neutrally determined as rational judgments. Naturalistically racist assumptions give way via racial historicism to the neutral judgments of objective assessment the racial codes for which are nevertheless rendered imperceptible. Social seams remain sewn with racial threads now purged of all responsibility for their (re)production. Autogenerated, they are simply the way things are; social subjects abrogate responsibility for all but their own subjective expression guiltlessly enjoying at once the benefits of social positioning or suffering the slights of social subjection historistically fashioned.

This latter point must be complemented by pointing out nevertheless that the sort of social or judicial standards represented here hold out the possibility that they can be invaded, and at least sometimes and to some degree infused with new meaning. Consider, for example, the most effective instances of the Civil Rights Movement. Even in their most extreme racist manifestations, racial states do not fully determine or structure states of being, opportunity and possibility for state agents and objects of state structure. Rather, as extensions of racial states, raceless states set social agendas to which resistance is by definition a reaction. This is not to say that resistance is reactionary, but only to point out that agenda determination likely delimits the possibilities of conjuring, and certainly enacting, creative alternatives.

Racial states and their raceless extensions have maintained firm control over social resources by setting agendas for a wide range of social concerns. These include the shape of immigration and so the demographic profile of the nation; where people can live, and labor and under what sorts of social conditions; educational resources and access, that determine who gets educated and how, and who in turn is socially and politically mobile; and what counts as crime, who is marked as criminal, where criminal acts largely take place, and how they are punished. Raceless states thus silently extend the structure of social arrangements historically fashioned through race. The structure of racially skewed conditions are "diluted" through racelessness into class configurations (Takagi 1993, 1995). Liberal morality has long deemed class distinction more socially palatable precisely because one supposedly can be considered personally responsible for one's class position in ways one cannot be for racial determination, at least not on naturalistic assumption.

It is revealing, therefore, that in the conceptual collapse of race almost wholly into class that has accompanied the rise of that form of racial historicism I have identified as racelessness, apologists for colorblindness like Thomas Sowell have invoked the language of personal responsibility in charging African Americans with cultural poverty (Sowell 1995). Racelessness, as I have said, is the logical implication of racial historicism. Not only does it supposedly sweeten racial structure by diluting it in the substance of class formation; it renders individuals personally responsible – and so the agents of state-fashioned social structure literally irresponsible – for whatever racial distinctions linger. The politics of racelessness as a civic religion accordingly is bifurcated. It is not a politics of recognition but one of reconciliation and defensiveness, tolerance and dismissal (personal and positional) at the middle and upward ends of the social scale,[10] and of desperate survival and reconstruction, but also sometimes of resentment and recrimination, at the lower class ends. As such, racelessness is the war not on racism but on racial reference, not on the conditions for the reproduction of racially predicated exclusion and discrimination but on the characterization of their effects and implications in racial terms.

233

Raceless Worlds

It follows that conditions referenced as "racial" are always displaced elsewhere.[11] The racial conditions at the heart of raceless states are the most illustrative example. The problems characterized as "racial" are "inevitably" somewhere else: in the South for the North, the East for the West; in the cities for the suburbs, in the inner cities for the central business district, or in the suburbs for the cities; in the colonies for the metropoles, in Africa for Europe; in Muslims for Serbs, Romas for Central Europeans, or migrants for Western Europe; in Central America for the US, or in Chiapas for the PRI; on the West Bank for Israel or in the Aboriginal outback for white Australia. The "absent center of late modern life," its point of comparative reference, is the present place of race that we constantly displace to the stench of the not-so-well-placed or appointed or *resourced* backyard. It is the sense of race as there but not, to which we are blind but which we conveniently find always visible. In that sense, racial displacement is to an elsewhere that "just happens to be" the dumping ground of history but is actually someone's place of be-longing.[12] Our endless curiosity about the racial conditions racelessness would magically have disappeared reveals that, far from being a harbinger of some lost history, those conditions remain all about us, at the heart of defining or refining who we are and the states in which we live.

Racelessness thus represents a double displacement. It is first that guilt-shedding displacement from historical racial definition and conditions I have argued are central to modern state formation and states of being. But it is emblematic also of a displacement, a retreat from, a center modernity claimed to occupy but never quite did because its centeredness was always of its own fabrication. Greenwich is about as central an example as one could conjure. It is this latter displacement one might reference as the postcolonial condition. In the wake of its postcolonial fading, not only has Greenwich's meticulous time-keeping been tinkered with globally but its identity has shifted from the administrative heart of the British admiralty to tourist entertainment and recreational space, the home of the millennial dome. From one point of view, the postcolonial condition is experienced as a displacement circulating in the generalized politics of fear and ambiguity, ambivalence and sense of loss. These insecurities manifest in the tensions between terror and nostalgic longing in a world not so much out of control as one in which those formerly thinking they controlled the world of materiality or meaning no longer so clearly or firmly do.

Posed thus, issues of patriotism and patriarchy get raised anew. They too are about holding onto privileges and preferences in the face of insecurities over loss of old opportunities and control. But they are also about operating in those slippery spaces between lost securities and new possibilities, faded places and polities, hard-nosed rational choice calculations and feelings, persistent moralities and reinvented nostalgias whose holds nevertheless have become ever so tentative.

All this suggests that there is another form of displacement effected through racelessness, namely, from the state itself. The recent insistence on racelessness is at once commensurate and coterminous with the insistence on less government, on less state incursion into civil society. In the wake of civil rights and anti-colonial struggles of the 1960s, states as such were seen by those once thinking themselves in political control no longer as states of whiteness but as being *for* the racially identified poor and marginalized. States were seen to side for the most part with undoing racial privilege, most notably through affirmative action programs and anti-discrimination legislation and hate crime and hate speech codes.

Thus the attack on the state and the arguments for racelessness are of a piece. If state intervention is dramatically curtailed, the state of being will "naturally" carry forward those racial privileges historically reproduced by restricting active delimitation against racial privileges by the state order. This informal racial reproduction will be achieved in the name of protecting exactly those liberties that states have been willing to erode, namely, the liberty to associate with whom one will, to accumulate the wealth merited by one's talents and relatives, in short, in the name of the freedom to discriminate as one chooses. If we "naturally prefer our own kind" – and some "racial kinds" are inherently, naturally, better at some practices than others and these practices just happen to be the ones identified with social privilege, power, and accumulation of property – well, so be it. That's just the way the world "naturally" is, and a state that presumes to stand in the way of the state of nature is likely in the scheme of fitness to survive to find itself destined for the dustbin of history. Witness communist states. Indeed, so the argument might run to its logical conclusion, witness political states per se, as we have come to know them. Time for the private sphere and unregulated globalization to dictate terms to state formation. In racial terms, historicism returns to its naturalistic roots, though purged of explicit state implication.

This latter displacement from the state reveals moreover that racelessness and globalization are mutually implicated. The lunge to globalized frames of reference promotes the retreat from explicit racial reference; and the pull of racelessness disposes subjects to evacuate local racial terms. The more or less painless insistence on ending explicit formal racial reference in any place nevertheless is possible in the end precisely because of the ready circulation of racial states of being and informal, implicit racial reference in every (modern) place. Racial routinization and familiarity in the everyday breeds the possibility of formal racelessness in administrative and political ways.

Thus racelessness implies not the end of racial consciousness but its ultimate elevation to the given. The constantly moving, flowing racial images on the screen of representation are irreducible to any configuration of individuated raceless pixels the intersecting combinations of which manifest those images. The morphing liquidities of racial eliminativism, far from terminating the effects of the racial, assume racially invested identities and reproduce racially exclusive and exclusionary outcomes upon demand. Race, in and for the raceless state, is nowhere and everywhere at once, usable and discardable to whatever "productive" purpose those in command of production and the circulation of signification can sustain. At once sweated labor in Indonesia or Vietnam, the Maqiladoras or Monterey and faceless fiscal facilitators not to mention consumers in New York, London, Tokyo, or Chicago; diamond traders fueling wars in Sierra Leone and not quite faceless traders on the diamond exchanges of Antwerp or Amsterdam or Tel Aviv; natives of Europe and immigrants to Europe formerly identified as Natives of Africa or Asia or Latin America; purveyors of war in the Balkans or the South Pacific, the Caucasus or Central Africa and arms manufacturers and brokers in the US; "drug lords" in the South and East and "drug victims" in the North and West.[13] Racial images supposedly rendered raceless in global circulation; racelessly consumed as racially produced. Racial historicism naturalized as the world turns from modern racisms to the post-racist varieties, from racial configurations and racist exclusions state fashioned and facilitated to raceless extensions and meta-manifestations of racist configuration indelibly marking states of being. Worldly traces of modern racial states from which both state and race alchemically have been absented. We might call this globalization's will to the power of racelessness, and the late modern will to a superficially raceless and historically amnesiac power.

This post-racial routinizing of racial world-making poses acute conceptual and pragmatic challenges to anyone committed, as I am, to a politics of heterogeneities. I turn now in conclusion to face these challenges.

NOTES

1 Posner's article is quoted in support by the majority decision *in Hopwood* et al. *v. State of Texas* et al. 78 F. 3d (1996), fn. 33.

2 This advertisement is quoted in *United States v. Hunter* 459 F. 2d (1972), 205.

3 "But so far as contact with the elements of civilization is concerned, so far as the possibility of being touched by the mental and moral influences of superior and elevating forces is implied, Africa might as well have been an island as a continent. . . . A great ocean of sand has shut her off from that law of both national and individual growth, namely that culture and enlightenment have got to be brought to all new peoples, and made indigenous among them . . . the Christian and civilized world . . . has become both assured and helpful by the fact of an evident transitional state, in Africa, from her night of gloom, to blessedness and glory." Crummell's article is reprinted in Moses (1996: 169–87).

4 "British governmental thinking in the early 1940s came increasingly to emphasize the color-blind nature both of British colonial policy and public attitudes in Britain in general" (Rich 1986: 149; cf. Wolton 2000).

5 Racism in Colombia, Peter Wade writes, lies just beneath the surface, "often subtle, not systematic or thoroughgoing, but pervasive and occasionally blatant. To avoid the stigma to which blackness and black culture . . . are subject by the dominant nonblack world of whites and mestizos, black people may adopt the mores of that world. Alternatively, they may retrench for protection or due to rejection by the nonblack world. This is not simply a matter of choice about ethnic identity: the possibilities for either alternative are heavily structured, mainly by economic and political processes that circumscribe and indeed constitute the parameters of choice" (Ware 1993: 6). On the modern history of race in Peru, see De la Cadena (2000); in Guatemala, see Grandin (2000); in Argentina and Cuba, see Helg (1990); and in Mexico, see Gall (1998).

6　It was exactly over this question of non-racialism and the principle of race-transcending coalitions that black nationalist essentialists broke from the ANC in the late 1950s to form the Pan-African Congress.

7　"While there is no doubt that the sorry history of both private and public discrimination in this country has contributed to a lack of opportunities for black entrepreneurs, this observation, standing alone, cannot justify a rigid racial quota in the awarding of public contracts" (Sandra Day O'Connor's majority opinion denying the constitutionality of the affirmative action plan in Richmond, Virginia. *City of Richmond v. Croson* 109 S. Ct. 706, 724).

8　On the forms of everyday repression by which both domination and the dominated survive, see Barry Adam's all-too-readily overlooked analysis (Adam 1978).

9　Stephen Small has recounted to me how former slave plantations throughout the American South have established museums to generate local revenue, completely romanticizing the abject conditions under which slaves suffered in ways comparable to that portrayed in Ulrich Phillips's much criticized work or to Gilberto Freyre's representation of Brazilian slavery discussed earlier. Recently Spike Lee has complained about the complete evasion in the Hollywood blockbuster, *Patriot*, of reference to slave labor in the historical period covered by the film.

10　See Benjamin De Mott's (1995) trenchant critique of this deflation in the name of racial friendship, that "all you need is racial love."

11　I am grateful to Ann Stoler for a set of exchanges in light of which the following points became elaborated. See also Van Dijk (1999/2001).

12　Consider Supreme Court Justice Sandra Day O'Connor's choice words in *Shaw v. Reno* (1993), a reapportionment case concerning a majority black voting district in North Carolina: "Racial classifications of any sort pose the risk of lasting harm to our society. . . . Racial gerrymandering . . . may *balkanize* us into competing racial factions" (my emphasis).

13　Cf. Pat Williams (1991) on the racial experience of shopping at New York's Benetton and Arjun Appadurai's (1993) reflections on the wandering "heart of whiteness."

9

CONCLUSION: STATING THE DIFFERENCE

It is a vital concern of every State not only to vanquish nomadism, but to control migrations and, more generally, to establish a zone of rights over an entire "exterior," over all the flows traversing the ecumenon. If it can help it, the State does not dissociate itself from a process of capture of flows of all kinds, populations, commodities, money or capital . . . the State never ceases to decompose, recompose and transform movement, or to regulate speed.

Deleuze and Guattari (1986: 59–60)

Democracy was born in transgressive acts, for the demos could not participate in power without shattering the class, status, and value systems by which it was excluded.

Wolin (1996: 37)

Posing the Question of Post-racial States

Why, one might ask in retrospective conclusion, has modern state formation been predicated principally upon the artifice of homogeneity as an *idée fixe* in the ways I have suggested? Recall that in posing the challenge of state formation at the outset of modernity, Hobbes characterized the state of nature as driven by individualized force and fraud. Force and fraud framed the supposed sources of the natural condition, and in doing so revealed the "rational necessity" of modern state formation, namely, the capacity to make war and to develop capital's resources. Force and fraud, for Hobbes, are the *resources* of survival in the absence of state control, the abilities and facilities

239

rational choice would have us maximize in the absence of social security and in the drive to individualized survival. Well, if force and fraud are the virtues of presocial nature, comfort and control are the social conditions – the virtues of state formation – rationality would have the state maximize as (re)sources of establishing social security and abating the perceived need for individualized force and fraud. Comfort and control – comfort as a form of control, and social control as the underpinnings of social comfort – are to the modern state then what force and fraud are to lonely and threatened individuals in the state of nature: the virtues of survival, individuated and social. Comfort, feeling at ease with one's surroundings and so neighbors, is both presupposition and rational implication of commitment to minimized state intervention to sustain public security. And comfort, so the story goes, is most easily reproduced in the setting of those one best knows, kin and extended kin, family and friends, cultural brethren and common citizens.[1]

Race is taken to be the "natural" extension of this social narrative, questionable not least because, once the circle extends beyond those one literally knows, comfort becomes at best an artifice, in the intermediate a rationalization, and at worst the grounds of exclusion and expulsion, material and moral. And, of course, sometimes those one knows best, those closest to one, might make one feel the most uncomfortable. Homogeneity, and in particular racial homogeneity, thus is considered, not quite arbitrarily but altogether artificially, as among rationality's most effective means of social control, a key governing biotechnology in what Gramsci came to characterize as the reproduction of consent in one's social conditions and surroundings. What I have called racial naturalism as a prevailing mode of modern biogovernance grew out of this set of assumptions, giving way later, as we have seen, to the mandates and management of racial historicism.

A central question I have addressed throughout *The Racial State*, then, has concerned the kinds of state formation representative of the interests of racial homogeneity. My prevailing concern has been to map the racial contours and contents of modern states, both as a general state form and in their particular differences historically and spatially.

We can now ask, by contrast, what sort of state best represents the commitments of heterogeneities, demographically and culturally, politically and economically, socially and legally? A counter to the

240

sustained critique with which I have been engaged throughout is to consider the sort of social arrangements that mobilize from a central commitment not to the reproduction of homogeneity but to the generative possibilities of heterogeneities. What, in short, might be the shape of contemporary and future states, their principal modes of rule and representation, their social contours and lines of governance in the absence of and resistance to racist formation and in the aftermath of homogenizing logics? This is a question connected to but emphatically to be distinguished from that of the shape of *raceless* states.

One way of posing this question of post-racist states is to address what modern social formations might have emerged had they not been so racially conceived and weighted in the various ways mapped in this book. How, one might ask in other words, would modern states have formed but for race as an ordering principle? The shape of this question, however, as hinted in the close of the previous paragraph, is consistent with the presumptions of racelessness articulated in chapter 8, now universalized not just geographically but as a matter of nostalgic retrospection, historical memory in denial. The obvious response, if the question is taken on face value, is that class formation and exploitation would now be barer and balder, perhaps less mitigated, more intense on its own terms but precisely for that reason less sociologically defensible and defended. If that were so one could imagine that class conditions without the modalities and arrangements of racial configurations conceivably would have conjured more explicit, vigorous, sustained, and ultimately successful counters. But conceivably because balder and bolder and so more questionable and questioned, they also might have been tempered in ways making such class distinctions more palatable because less expressly and extremely exploitative, divisive, and exercised.

The deeper point here however is that it is impossible in the final analysis to tell which way it would have gone had race not so marked modern state and social formation. So the very call to imagine the alternatives to a history racially turned serves discursively to draw us away from the more compelling question of imaginative politics in the present and facing the future. Here the concern is not with what might have been but, given how we now understand what indeed has been and now is, with what the possibilities of transformation to social conditions and spaces of justice could yet be. So the question is not whether we can erase race – as we have seen, that only renders the structures of racist exclusion and derogation less visible – but with how we might be able to shape race and its social orderings in ways that are socially attractive and interactive. How, in short, can we transform racial configuration from the dispositions of homogenizing exclusion and exclusivity to the disposing towards heterogenizing openness and incorporation, social engagement and shaping to reflect the interests and conceptions of all?

I pose the question as one of general concern, one normatively confronting a plural subject, for two related reasons. The first is that we are all implicated, more or less deeply and directly, in responding to a set of social conditions and arrangements, locally and globally, that continues to be a central constitutive feature of the worlds we inhabit. If, as I have argued throughout, debilitating racial arrangements anywhere are sustained by and responses to racial arrangements elsewhere, if not most everywhere, then responses locally are both delimited by and have implications for racial conditions beyond the local. This is not to suggest that racial conditions everywhere and any time are alike, that racism (to use Stuart Hall's Gramscian formulation) is "everywhere the same – either in its forms, its relations to other structures, its relations or its effects" (Hall 1986/1996: 435). There are overlaps and similarities, intersections and influences between racial articulation and racist conditions locally and further afield. But, no matter the distinctions, critical responses to racist conditions beyond one's immediate location are likely in some basic and extended ways to affect and be affected by conditions locally also (cf. Klinker and Smith 1999; Dudziak 2000). Thus the identification in the emerging Cold War climate of the 1950s of the civil rights drive to "equality between the races" with a communist principle – and so the hysterical denunciation of the civil rights struggle as a communist plot (Carr 1997: 119) – rendered racial equality unAmerican. But then it at once admitted racist inequalities as quintessentially American, thus implicitly aligning the United States with the emergence of apartheid in South Africa, adding moral fuel to the civil rights fire in the United States.

Second, the plural invocation regarding responses to racial conditions indicates that effective interventions in relation to these conditions are a deeply collective commitment, and so responsibility. It bears emphasizing that effective critical transformation in respect to racist exclusions and discriminatory arrangements requires efforts, to be

242

sure, but always in some more extended spatial and temporal sense in concert with others, both those critically comprehending their consequential privileges and those disempowered by such conditions (Scott 1990). And this collective practice necessitates careful critical deliberation with each other. It involves at least a caring listening to the concerns of one's (potential) critical collaborators and thoughtful critics, a critically sensitive disposition. But it also requires a readiness to reasonable revision of axiological commitments and institutional structures and practices as a consequence of one's interlocutor's insights and interventions without reducing oneself to their imposed commands or demands.

To return directly to the principal question of heterogeneous states, of states premised upon commitments to heterogeneities, one might proceed as Philomena Essed urges us to do, by listing all the factors of institutional and individual privilege in a social formation, and all the factors of risk. Posed thus, it should become evident quickly enough how those factors of privilege and risk are distributed across population groups historically tied to racial conception and condition in radically uneven and inequitable ways. Given the ordering mechanisms in states of whiteness, these inequities are attributable for the most part not to personal capacities or inabilities of individualized group members but to the historical structures of racial states of rule and being. The question then becomes how best to address and redress these states of racial affairs, a question in which state arrangement, rule, and power to intercede are deeply implicated. This sort of formulation displaces the analysis from a narrow initial focus on groups to the inequitable benefits and burdens of privileges and risks, and of their social implications.[2]

In asking to what states without racism might amount, notice then that a number of concerns are being raised. First, what is being placed in question is the common contemporary call, at least as the first-level commitment, the causal condition, to erase race from our conceptual apparatus and frame of reference, from all state characterization and concern (Appiah and Gutmann 1996; Gilroy 2000; McWhorter 2000). It does follow from the line of analysis I have pursued in the book that the historical invocation of race by the state to exclusionary and discriminatory purpose or outcome ought to be eliminated from state design and practice, implicit or explicit. It does not follow from this critical commitment, however, that racial record-keeping for the sake of monitoring and redressing past and present forms of historical discrimination ought to be abandoned as a consequence, as Ward Connerly would do in the Californian context (Selingo 2000). The point is not so much the bald concern with racial reference and invocation, no matter the implications, but the purpose to which race is invoked and the work to which it is being put by and in the name of the state. The principal aim is – or ought to be – *states without racism*. Whether that commitment entails states without race will turn on whether race inherently or instrumentally causes or conspires to racist states, racist conditions of being and rule. So second, the principal concern is to withdraw the state from exclusionary racial definition and arrangement, to render state instrumentalities and instrumental state and institutional apparatuses unavailable to discriminatory racial usage. This entails, third, that it remains an open question whether and how race is usable or invokable outside of state force or enforcement, state determination or orchestration. Is it possible to engage racial arrangement, as Foucault suggested in his lectures on racism, sometimes as a counter-history (*contre-histoire*), a critical counter-history to dominating state formation, a mode of self-determining political and cultural resistance (Stoler 1995: 68–72), or indeed as a creative but non-exclusionary mode of cultural (re)formation? Or is racial arrangement, wherever and whenever, inherently an imposed mode of controlling governance and self-surveillance?[3]

Race and State Personality

Race, of course, could be violently invoked individually or institutionally outside of state purview, in the absence of state arrangement or engagement, in the face of explicit state commitments against discrimination. I do not mean to deny that in the absence of explicit state support individual or institutional racist expression – the exclusion or demeaning derogation of some by others in the name of race – can be debilitating, even devastating for those thus targeted. But I do mean to insist that state implication in racist expression exacerbates it in two related ways. The first is straightforward: the sustenance of such expression by explicit state support, by state arrangements encouraging racist expression or at least openly refusing to discourage it, magnifies the alienating exclusion well beyond its otherwise isolated moment. In short, the state imprimatur – explicit or implicit – extends the condition, institutionalizing it more deeply than it otherwise would be. State support transforms racial commitment from the relatively disconnected condition of individualized seriality into a sociocultural project, to use Sartrean terminology. The second and related form of state magnification is that state investment extends racist expression from the limited and more or less disconnected to its routinization in a state of social being. It marks the space of the social not just in racial colors but in a threatening hue by rendering the state of exclusions to what one might call the character, the "personality" of state condition itself. The state of social life takes on a particular character as a consequence, a disposition towards people defined as and in terms of population or group belonging. The state assumes accordingly a racial personality, setting the racial horizon of possibilities both for those falling within state confines and those outside its borders. The particular definitions of race by the state and articulations of racist exclusions through the modalities of class, gender, and national belonging characterize state personality, what the state "looks" and "acts" like, its very "demeanor." They offer the semblance of unity to institutional structures which, as we have seen (chapter 2), are often in contest with each other.

State personality is thus deeply connected to the ordering of *national character*, those popular philosophical portraits of eighteenth- and nineteenth-century state formation so printed in racial colors. Modern states fashioned a sense of identity, of character through culture, in terms of a racial palette. National belonging was produced institutionally in, through, and for the state, just as state institutions streamlined the terms of national belonging. Personal character and state personality were laced together through the cultural calling and recreation of citizens. Institutions, John Stuart Mill writes, "produce more effect by their spirit than by any of their direct provisions, since by it they shape the national character" (Mill 1861: 188–9; Lloyd and Thomas 1998). Cultural homogeneity outlined through racial markers inscribed the boundaries of access and standing economically and politically but also aesthetically and axiologically, representing in national and institutional terms prevailing conceptions of beauty and excellence, the right and the good.

Personality and "the national personality" (Balibar 1991c: 86) accordingly codified in sedimented form the racial commands of social destiny, biologically and sociologically, individually and institutionally. This identification of the racial and the governmental is straightforward in the case of naturalism, that state arrangement claiming to represent an eternal, fixed, unchanging, and organic condition, "natural" as much institutionally as individually. With historicism, the state – as the administrative structure of the nation – takes itself as developing rationally, progressing to ever more complete states of perfection, ever more direct and representative embodiments of the national will. This is the very will of the "the people" the state was instrumental at once in shaping (Lloyd and Thomas 1998: 3; Agamben 2000: 29–36). Citizens and sojourners, those belonging and strangers alike, see in the "person" of the state the generalized embodiment of some (central/ized) aspect of (national) character, the general will, a projection of (because fashioned to resemble) their own person-ality and its lacks, desires, and fears. So they recognize themselves – their own "personas" – in the personality of the state, "as [their] own," subject to a "common law," biological, political, civil (Balibar 1991c: 93–4). The distinction between public and private does not so much collapse but is sustained as the fiction, the *modern* state's self-narration laying the ground for the possibility of social production and generation, self-projection and representation.

Thus state personality, its purported character, is predicated on the character of state practices and what the state stands for. Consider the supposed exceptionalism of the Nazi state as the point of contrast with the racial invisibility of modern liberal democracies; or the racial baldness of the apartheid state contrasted with the post-apartheid state engaged in pursuit of commissioned truths in the name of reconciliation, of renewed nation-narration and (re)formation; or of raceless states pursuing the historicist politics of apologetics (Hartman and Best 2001). More than the obvious institutional character of the state, though, its personality references also, and relatedly, the sorts of personhood, individual and collective, for which the state is taken to stand and through institutional and cultural policies and practices to promote.

It is a central argument of *The Racial State* then that the sociocultural embeddedness of race – its forms and contents, modes and effects of routinization and penetration into state formation and order – has been basic to fashioning the personality of the modern state. Race has shaped modern social character as both a state of existence and forms

246

of rule. Race has circumscribed as it has codified for the modern state civil and governmental possibilities, its modes of privatized expression, its lines of rule and shape of power. In shaping the state's personality, racial configuration likewise molds the sorts of personhood rendered possible and permissible within the global frames and flows between modern states, though not in any narrowly deterministic sense. It offers the conditions of possibility for the enactments – what some have called the performativities – of personhood and subjectivity. It is in this latter sense that race is ultimately uncontainable by state formation. There is always the possibility for race to be mobilized as a counter-history, as counter-performativities and counter-practices to prevailing state design, though the social space for racial counter-performance is invariably contained and restrained. Racial terms are inherently delimited even as they are always open to leakage and seepage, the limits placed by the state around racial performativity invariably porous to some degree.

To take one instance of state configuration through racial articulation, what Balibar calls "crisis racism" becomes one mode for collapsing class distinctions within a nation-state. "Crisis racism" represents a common disposition to ascribe social threat to an outside, whether an internalized exterior, the alien within, or the stranger without. The ascription to externalities of the (invented) threat to state coherence and power – a war, or a war on drugs, for instance – assumes positivity in the implicit "transcendence" of class distinction in the name of a generalizing national character and state safety. State security buries class division beneath the symbolics of a common national character. This (re)generative tension between racial externalization and internal class transcendence for the sake of staving off threats to the state at the same time promotes the state maintenance of class distinction in the name of whiteness (Balibar 1991d: 219; Lowe 1996: 174; Agamben 2000: 36–44). In racial states, state emergencies invariably service white supremacy in the interests of controlling social classes. And yet the promotion of a national belonging over and against a threatening outside in moments of created crisis often becomes the most effective moment also for those racially identified within the national corpus as less privileged – as not white – to gain (civil) rights and civic standing. As Homi Bhabha remarks, "the state of emergency is also always a state of *emergence*" (Bhabha 1994: 41, emphasis in original). Hence the relation between national crises such as war (hot or cold, civil or global) and "racial progress" to which a number of authors have pointed recently (Bell 1995; Klinker and Smith 1999; Dudziak 2000). Such "racial progress" is qualified as a result always by its predication on the "dehumanization" of national threats, of those taken variably to fall outside of national belonging – Jews, Muslims, Palestinians, Moors, Africans, Caribbeans, Asians, Latin Americans, Southern Europeans, East Europeans, Balkans, and so on (Agamben 2000: 33).

The Race to State Homogeneity

One thing could be said with confidence, consequently, and this follows from the interface of the arguments in chapters 6 through 8: a state without *racism* would be one in and for which whiteness has retreated, has been fractured and fissured, has dissipated and dissolved. If, as I have argued, whiteness stands for the relative privilege, profit, and power of those occupying the structural social positions of whites in a hierarchically ordered racial society, racist states are states of whiteness. The elimination of such states accordingly must mean the demise of the associated privilege, profit, and power. But, it must be emphasized again, in light of the arguments in chapter 8, a state without racism in the wake of the long and vicious racist histories of the present cannot simply be a raceless state. Post-racist (in contrast to merely post-racial) states must be those for which state agencies, and most notably law, are vigorous both in refusing racist practice and in public representation of the unacceptability of all forms of discriminatory expression. I am not so naive or romantically utopian as to think this would amount to the end of all social privilege, power, and profit. But it would mean the end of a particularly vicious variety, the sort that has served both as modality of expression for and a kind of multiplier of class, gender, national and indeed state-based advantage and disadvantage. It would mean, in short, a very different sort of state personality, a different demeanor to those inside and outside the state cast(e), a different disposition to population definition and characterization, to law and law en*force*ment, to power and policy-making, to kith and kin, "legitimate" family and the shape of class, to sociospatial configurations and schooling, social engagement and accessibility, to national culture (most notably in and through

248

language, the "mother tongue") and historical memory (Balibar 1991c: 98–100).

States after racism would mean in short a deep transformation in state personality. Etienne Balibar is right thus to insist that "[d]estruction of the racist complex" requires "the transformation of the racists themselves" (though not just in *any* way), and so "the internal composition of the community created by racism" (Balibar 1991b: 18). Implicit within Balibar's imperative is more than just an exhortation to individuals to change their racist ways. Balibar here hints by extension at the social dynamics by which modern "community" is composed. And in the context of nation-formation, these dynamics bear the label, the (not so) hidden hand (Comaroff and Comaroff 2000a), of state juris-diction, of the forms and contents of legality and (in)justice, in national self-narration. But post-racist states would mean also very different dis-positions to other states, states of otherness, and state othering. Entailed would be not simply some extended circulation through racisms' polyvalent mobilities (Stoler 1995: 69), reinscriptions of racist modes and manners, racist "bearers" and "targets" mobilized from one crisis moment to another (Balibar 1991d: 219). They would mean, rather, a different set of global arrangements where racial dispositions or calculations no longer determined or set the formative background to international relations, no longer determined or even descriptively characterized the general flows of capital, commodities, workers and executives, refugees and im/migrants, or the radically uneven distribution of human and economic costs of AIDS and its treatment. It is these radically transfigured sets of assumptions and dispositions, characterizations and (institutional) arrangements, spatialities and chronicities that I mean to reference in urging the shift from prevailing presuppositions of homogeneity and fixity in state conception and personality to those of heterogeneity and flow.

Modern states, we have seen, by their (modern) nature systematically produce and reproduce "political and cultural homogeneity" (Parekh 2000: 184) as a matter of their institutional logic. The modernity of the state turns on the drive both to codify and to represent a general will, on the classification schemas invoked to order and administer (to) the population masses that make them up. This homogeneity is a function, by extension, of the bureaucratic insistence on formal equality sociopolitically and legally (though perhaps less so economically).[4]

States thus assume their modernity in and through producing and reproducing sameness, definitively squeezing out the different, the very heterogeneity which modernity's logic of spatio-temporal compression (Eagleton 1998: 50; Harvey 1989) has been instrumental paradoxically in effecting. In the name of justice, democracy, and equality – of a people with a common will, interests, and character – the modern state creates a population, a "community," cut from the same cloth.

Modern states administratively promote coherence of civil society and social structures, and through them the cohering of their populations. This coherence is ramified throughout the economy, polity, law, culture, modes of representation and social narratives. In this sense, the modern state is a form of institutional reinforcement, the enforcing mechanisms of institutional arrangements and conditions. The state thus conceived is a sort of conductor. It orchestrates but also serves as a conduit and symbol for the conduct – the disciplinary consistencies – of the institutions and individuals in virtue of which it is constituted, over which it ranges. But the state is also a conductor of culture – of institutional and social values and meanings, the generator and shaper of historical memory through schools, museums and monuments, public art and ceremonies, rituals and symbols. And as a conductor shapes the orchestra and arranges the score without necessarily making the music, so the state fashions citizens, those representative individuals at once able to play responsibly, by themselves but in concert (Lloyd and Thomas 1998). States accordingly are at once spaces and media of affiliation between governing bodies and populations. Race, as I have argued, is the oil between state and society, the black and white formal wear turning critical attention away from the players and towards enjoyment of the music, the social welfare of the "audience."

Homogeneity, it turns out, is the centralizing force, the grounding assumption, of modern state formation (Parekh 2000: 181–2, 184). David Lloyd has argued recently that representation, both as a signifying condition and in its political form, always involves a gap, a displacement: between the object represented and the representation of it, between subjects representing and objects represented, between sign and signified.[5] In its political form, the state undertakes to delimit the gap between those represented and those representing, to efface or diminish or overlay it into represent*able* subjects (through education and cultural socialization), into the (politically) represented. The subaltern – the socially marginalized, the colonized, the racially impoverished – are always by definition and "constitution" the outside of political representation as they are at the limit of signification. Just inside signification, so to speak, but (at) its margins, as the virtually unspeakable, subaltern subjects are the conditions of the possibility of speakability, indeed, of subjectivity itself (Spivak 1988). But speakability (or more broadly expressibility), the very possibility of representation, makes it necessary for the subaltern to be turned into representation, for the unspoken to be spoken for. I think here, for instance, of J. M. Coetzee's tongueless Foe (Coetzee 1988). The state, as a state of stating, of self-assertion, is driven by its own logic of representation to draw the extra-marginal subaltern back into representation. As modern state formation, politically speaking, takes itself as nothing other than the condition of representation, the modern state is logically challenged – necessitated, one should say – to bring into representation even those at the limits of state extension. It does so, among other means, by turning the condition of mourning identified with/as the subaltern condition, or that of grief (which all too often *is* the subaltern experience) into grievance (Cheng 2000). The modern state has a legacy of turning violence into injury (Brown 1995), historical wrong and its memory into legal redress, reconciliation, and reparations. Those states of unspeakable historical experience are metamorphosed at the hands of states and their agents into representable conditions, manageable states of affairs and affairs of state, through their reinscription in(to) the terms of legality. So the subaltern, as the limit of statability, represents the necessary condition of the state to speak itself. Formulated (one might even say represented) this way, the naturalistic representation of subalternity, of racial inferiority, in the history of modern state formation is prompted into the liberalizing mode of historicization in a sense as a condition of the possibility of state representation through law itself. The extension of representation, both as the condition of comprehension and the modern polity, is necessitated (ironically) as the condition of control, stability, and security. Subalterns become citizens (of existing or newly self-governing states) by "learning" to represent themselves in the terms of modernity.

Modern states, as I have argued throughout, are thus "structured in racial (and interactively in gendered and class) dominance" (Hall 1980).

So the state is not neutral but structurally reproduces and regulates the hierarchies it has helped institutionally to constitute. The liberal state professes neutrality between its members – between groups ethnoracially defined, between men and women, and members of social classes – and enacts laws and regulations predicated on such assumptions. It follows that state apparatuses such as law can be invoked to mobilize for more equitable treatment on the part of those the state hitherto has served to dispossess or disenfranchise, to disqualify from equal treatment or to disempower. In insisting on materializing what otherwise is projected as ideological rationalization, the marginalized are able to empower themselves though always subject to the limiting and homogenizing terms of state definition and design. Angela Davis (1998) comments that when those once actively resistant to state imposition, control, and definition of the political and socioeconomic arrangements later become representatives of state institutions – morphing in effect into state agents – there is something about the state apparatus, about its definition and functions, that delimits, constrains, and transforms the disposition and outlook of even the best intentioned. Thus, former Black Panthers or members of SNCC have become political representatives in Congress, and anticolonial revolutionaries such as Robert Mugabe, Kwame Nkrumah, or ANC leaders have assumed state power. They are constrained in their agency not just by the fact of their electoral representation but also by the institutional logic of state formation, agency, and incorporation into the modern world system.

Hence the inevitable ambiguities in modern state commitments. For instance, a commitment to freedom for all may be discounted by interpreting it as opportunity, not outcome. The expressed commitment to equality may be discounted as the formality of rights to speech or property with no attention paid to the substantive conditions rendering materialization or manifestation of those rights possible or even probable (cf. Waylen 1998). In insisting on equal treatment before the law, equal state promotion or resources, those subjected to state or social exclusions may advance their interests by invoking the neutrality principle of the liberal state in behalf of those not so readily benefited in the past. Of course, the formalism of state neutrality leaves it open equally to those hitherto in control or benefiting from the state of patriarchal whiteness to extend or redefine the structures of opportunity in their favor. The (at least implicit) characterizations

252

of the state as black or as representing the interests of those not white are deeply connected to the now common call for shrinking state power and influence. The contemporary insistence on state commitments to racelessness, I suggested in chapter 8, is a case in point.

Two points follow concerning characterization of modern racial states. The first is to note a distinction between strong racial states and weak racial states, or between strongly and weakly racist states. A state unambiguously committed to insistent and reductive racial definition, a state in which racial definition is routinized through its state apparatuses and penetrates its agencies, is likely a state committed to strongly explicit and enforced forms of racist exclusion. A state that is weakly racial – that may invoke racial classification in record-keeping, say, with an eye to tracking historical discrimination – does not necessarily promote racist exclusions, though it may sustain (at least by ignoring) a culture of racist derogation in civil society and social institutions. Obviously the particular shapes and expressions of racial and racist states run the gamut between these two poles.

Second, I do not mean to suggest that modern states lack all virtues. Unlike premodern states that rested on multiple sources of authority and rules applied differentially to various social classes, modern states at least in principle rest on a singular authoritative body and source of law applied equally to all citizens. Modern (at least liberal) states enshrine a unitary code of rights protecting all members positioned and placed in suitably similar ways. Individuals are both equally incorporated into the state and reasonably protected not just from each other but from state incursion. The so-called arbitrary characterizations of individuals – in group terms such as race, gender, class – are deemed at least juridically illegitimate considerations in state disposition and treatment of individuals. Goods and services, rights and powers, the distribution of burdens and responsibilities are to be open to all at least to compete (cf. Parekh 2000: 181–3). And modern liberal democracies seem more ready than most contrasting societies to tolerate if not to promote criticism, challenge, and revision, even if within implicit and definitive limits. There are accordingly wide and deep benefits of state modernization, both in the principles of arrangement and materially, that it would be silly and self-defeating to deny or to overlook. The virtues of liberal modernizing are real, to be sure, even as they are partial (Smith 1997: 10–11; Hall 2000: 228).

These virtues of modern states are considered to represent indices of progress over earlier state forms, and in many ways they can be considered to do so. And yet, the celebration of modernization also denies its inevitable burdens, either by ignoring them completely or discounting them as inevitable but limited costs of progress. Bearing this very consciously in mind, it must be pointed out that the claim to *racial* progress trades on a misconceived measure as a consequence. The state of racial progress – the progress of states *now* on race – is not to be measured against states of racist repression in the past.[6] That calculus too easily produces contemporary complacency and self-congratulation. The proper measure of "racial progress" – of the distance from racially fashioned or indexed exclusions – concerns assessment at the common historical moment ("the present") of the relative experience and conditions of each group racially defined and positioned, refined and conditioned against each other one. The historical contrast can only tell us how far we have come and convey a sense of what still has to be achieved, not that we have completed the task. Looking exclusively to the rear blinds us to seeing both how far there is to go or indeed to a reconsideration of what routes to adopt and signposts to pursue. Historical reconstruction and retrospection are crucial not as a fixation nor as contemporary celebration or rationalization but as indicating how we have come to the present, what the contemporary moment amounts to and on what it rests, and for revealing roadmaps to the future.

Counter-racial Questions

Given my characterization of the modern racial state as a will to power, as a particular sort of empowering self-assertion, the pressing question accordingly is not some version of the currently popular one in liberal circles, namely, whether a modern constitutional state can "recognize and accommodate cultural diversity" (Tully 1995: 1; Kymlicka 1996; Kymlicka and Norman 2000). That question presupposes as more or less given the very set of suppositions and structured ordering of the state marked so deeply by the histories of racial conception and formation. The question looks to embrace into the very fabric of social arrangements those hitherto excluded and denied, defined in cultural terms as "strange multiplicity," as outsiders or strangers. It leaves unquestioned the prevailing assumption of institutional and structural homogeneity, and the accompanying codification of existing racial powers and frames of reference. It manifests recognition of difference in speech and cultural expression, in "a just form of constitutional discussion in which each speaker is given her or his due" (Tully 1995: 6). But it is open to addressing only indirectly at best the institutional structures and material conditions shaping social possibilities and access, actual political arrangements and constitutive practices, and their long histories of constitution and reproduction. These histories have been marked constitutively for the most part by racially predicated exclusion and marginalization.

The counter-question, I am suggesting, from an assumption of radical and reiterative heterogeneity, of unsettlement and entanglement (Tully 1995: 11), is not simply one in the reactive frame concerning recognition and accommodation of and into the state's own historically limiting schemas. It concerns the grounds of its constitutive conditions themselves. Can a state be predicated on assumptions of heterogeneities? Can a state constitutively be open to the flows not simply of capital but of human beings recognized equally and with equal sensitivity, on and in equal terms, as belonging in their flows to the body politic, when both here and there, so to speak? Can heterogeneity in social arrangements coexist with the justice of the state and fair treatment of its citizens? What would state citizenship in a state so conceived come to look like? Indeed, what would such a state itself look like?[7]

Conceived thus, the question is less about belonging than it is about the state and its form. Or at least it is about the relation of citizenship to state form and shape. Is citizenship necessarily a condition – a *state* – of the state? Is the notion of belonging, both cultural and administrative, that citizenship implies tied inextricably to the structures of the state as we have come to know that institutional arrangement? For if it is so connected then there may be very distinct – indeed, undermining – constraints on a notion of "flexible citizenship" (Ong 1999). These limiting assumptions may pose sharp limits to the possibilities of conceiving citizenship predicated on flows rather than fixity, on mobilities (Urry 2000: 159–87) rather than on the given of modern stasis and the static implications of statehood. Is it possible, in short, to speak of citizenship in a robust sense in relation to multiple and intertwining ("entangled") commitments – social, familial, economic, cultural, political? And to what would such commitment amount institutionally, administratively, socially, personally?

The world(s) of race

To begin to map out some sort of reasonable response to this set of questions, one has to begin from the recognition that modern states become modern, as I have argued, by assuming racial reference and structure, though variably, by being drawn into a world system of racial states. This formulation accounts, for instance, for why former communist states after 1989 found themselves struggling with a variety of racist expressions – rabid anti-Semitism in East Germany, Russia, and Poland, anti-Roma sentiment in the Czech Republic, Slovakia, and Romania, ethnic cleansing in the former Yugoslavia, etc. – they had long sought to suppress. States in modernity are differentially located within the structures of racial globalities. Most commentators have understood racial configurations and racist articulations in contemporary states as anomalous, and racist states such as Nazi Germany or South Africa as extreme exceptions (e.g., Mann 1984; Kershaw 1989; Burleigh and Wippermann 1991). Rogers Smith (1997: 18) helpfully shifts the grounds of analysis by contrasting with the exceptional thesis a more nuanced characterization of the American polity as embedding "multiple traditions," both inclusivist and exclusivist. Both traditions, for Smith, are basic to – and competing for – American political foundations. Smith's revision importantly promotes a more nuanced critical theory of racial states in general, and of the US in particular.

I have been insisting throughout, however, on a deeper if connected point. Given the modernity of states as racially premised, the traditions of racial inclusivity are interconstitutive with and co-dependent upon the traditions of exclusivity. Modern states have ordered and arranged their racial inclusivities on the necessity of racist exclusivities. They have built their own fortunes on and through their deeply engrained entanglements with other states racially fashioned, both self-definitionally and as a matter of imposition. And the racial exclusions mounted and manifest in the name of racial states have been legitimated and tolerated by the citizenry precisely as a consequence of their incorporation into state structure and order, as the beneficiaries of state inclusion. States of whiteness, I have suggested in chapter 7, define themselves necessarily *in contrast to* and *against* those categorized not white, thus accounting for why in addition to the obvious material considerations colonialism was so integral to the modern European project of state formation (Balibar 1991d: 219). This deeply interactive tension between the inclusive and exclusive marking modern states[8] – a tension deeply imprinting upon citizenship, who belongs and who does not – therefore is also a product of and "resolved" by the global incorporation of modern states into a (transforming) world system of racially conceived and ordered states.

Race and colonial arrangement thus developed in a global geopolitics, historically variable and spatially materialized. Naturalism and historicism as I have articulated them throughout the book can be read as defining media or frames of interpretation for this European global stretch, initiating and developing acts and scenes in the staging of globalized and globalizing practice. We have watched the tensions between the two intertwine as forces to convene and reconstitute social order and determination through renewable definition of state formation – institutional arrangements and conditions of being – in the shifting and uncontainable logics of globalization. The more recent expression of race in fueling and in wake of contemporary globalizing articulations, I argued in chapter 8, expresses itself as racelessness. What I have referred to in previous chapters as the increasing internalization of race concerned the shifting siting and citation of race projected as the outside of or external to European or white societies to race as a constitutive and so internalized condition of social order. Over time this translated into racial division and divide being assumed as the given of social order, as the state of social being. In that sense the state ordering of race, the hidden hand of the state in promoting, maintaining, and managing racial order, could recede into the background. It could become less formal. The racial state gave way to the raceless one, the race-bound one to the supposedly race-blind one. But it could do so precisely because racial conditions and presuppositions penetrated social order so extensively, becoming routinized administratively and in everyday life. Racelessness, in short, traded on the fact that race became so readily, one might say universally, assumed.

Thus racelessness is at once product and purveyor of globalized neoliberalism. While the ethnoracial and gendered shaping of global markets is crucial to globalization historically and contemporarily understood, heterogeneous sensitivities entail that the marks of race can no longer be quite so explicit or intentionally imposed. Rather, they are structurally reproduced, routinized through otherwise "ordinary" and so seemingly "natural" and therefore supposedly unchangeable conditions. Racial configurations are no longer thinkable as moral or political imperatives, natural or historically evolutionary social conditions because the implications of such thinking are seemingly irreversible. The state of race has become global now in two new senses. First, in the race to "modernize," race has extended variably and more or less uncontainably across global geography. Uncontainably though not uncontrollably because race continues to be not just descriptive of worldly heterogeneity but a normative if changing order of its control. Second, race continues to register as a global concept in the sense of implicating all spheres interactively, though often in changing form and shape. Race accordingly continues to mark geopolitical, economic, cultural, legal, even biologically defined configurations in their renewed geonomic expression. In the latter sense, Philomena Essed (2001) has spoken provocatively of "cloning culture." These are the cultures (including the sociobiological) that promote reproduction of ethnoracial identities, the subjectivities of sameness. But they include as well those repetitive social practices that in their repetition regenerate the culture of cloning, the remaking of sameness as a "given" phenomenon, supposedly unchangeable and so seemingly unchallengeable. Racelessness and cloning culture are threads of the same, indeed related, social logic.

States of the racial state

Roughly speaking, then, we can identify three general modes of state racial management. The modern state principally was about the selective keeping out (save for mundane and manual labor) of the uncivilized and savage, the inherently inferior and the barbaric – in the colonies or the outhouse, and certainly from citizenship. As naturalism gave way dominantly to historicism, the high and the late modern states became more than committed simply to segregating *out* those racially characterized as less developed. Though at their apex modern states have traded on segre*gating* logics and reinscribed segre*gated* spaces – reserves, townships, or shanty towns at urban peripheries, job color bars, racially confined neighborhoods, gated communities, racially conceived immigration quotas and visa denial – later modern segregation has differed from its earlier twentieth-century forms. Where the earlier variety was state mandated and directed, the later variety has been predicated on personal preference schemas and racial routinization (Goldberg 1998). The late modern state has been concerned thus significantly with keeping *in* those regarded as especially racially unacceptable – locked into the inner city or locked up in prison houses. Here the carceral logics of political economy (Goldberg 2000b) are still those of containability, confinement, and control, location and restriction. In restricting for some, racial logic of course silently opens up possibilities for others, founding the freedom of whites upon the negating unfreedom of those not, as the contemporary focus on whiteness studies has revealed so informatively.

So we can distinguish between state policies and their attendant schemas of population classification that promote racially conceived exclusion and evacuation (the enemies without) and those promoting racially fashioned internment (strangers within). It follows that these two moments enact different prevailing logics of racially fueled order. The panoptical carcerality with which Foucault largely concerned himself defines the logic of modern state control. This is the logic of diffused internalized control through (self-)surveillance. By contrast, late(r) modern, racially managed regimes have enacted a new rationality of state control. This rationality is expressed through encapsulated containment. It enacts an evacuation of the space of those regarded as racially dangerous or threatening so long as the periphery of that space is fenced off by a "military cordon" (Taussig 1997: 56–7; Agamben 2000: 39–42). Because the boundaries are clearly cordoned off and ringed, militarized and policed, symbolically as much as materially, the interior for the most part can be abandoned to its own anarchic and self-destructive practices. "Both as container and as excluder," Sheldon Wolin reminds us,

> boundaries work to foster the impression of a circumscribed space in which likeness dwells, the likeness of natives, of an autochthonous people, or of a nationality, or of citizens with equal rights. Likeness is prized because it appears as the prime ingredient of unity. Unity, in turn, is thought to be the sine qua non of collective power. (Wolin 1996: 32)

Unity, as the motto of the South African state under apartheid would have it, is strength, power in the racial collective to exclude through containment.

The third logic, that of the new millennial or regulator state, has only very recently assumed coherence. The contemporary state has become one at least representationally of permanent crisis, the state of permanent crisis creation and risk management, of a cost–benefit corporatist politics in the interests of globalizing power, flexible accumulation, and localizing containment. The contemporary traffic cop or conductor state has come to be about regulating the flow of risks as a consequence of globalized penetration and access. It stands for the opening up of all (other) spaces potentially at least to the flows of opportunity and experience, social mobility and auto-mobility (Urry 2000: 190ff.), trade, travel, and tourism. The system of containerizing states under Fordist capitalism, state structures of governance and their worldly extensions more or less fully controlled the flows of capital, commodities, and labor within and between states. Regulator states of neoliberal millennial capitalism (Comaroff and Comaroff 2000b; Urry 2000: 163–4), by contrast, are confined increasingly to the "pastoral regulation" of social conditions and populations (Ong 1999: 22) strictly within states. This is a mode of regulation mediated more and more by extra-state institutional legalities and geopolitical economies. Classic colonialism, it might be said, traded on the practices of reaching, gazing, teaching, touching, and taking; postcolonial globaization, by extension, has enacted new modes and expressions of these practices. The container state, it is not too much of a stretch to insist, now services the possibility of the regulator state, becoming one among other of its modes of regulation. In this reconfiguration of the racial global, the imperatives to racelessness reengender race more or less exclusively as class, brokering the distinctions between the US and Brazilian racial models of social ordering (contra Bourdieu and Wacquant 1998, 1999). Here the blindfold of supposedly raceless justice falls from one eye just enough for discriminating judgment to "see race" while insistently denying it. The concern is to comprehend the points of racial reference and differentiation as a mode of discerning points of danger and distress, to negotiate its demands and challenges, its risks, while calculating how best to reap its benefits. The recent shift in approaching Harlem – from containable and avoidable danger, a polluting of the body politic (Goldberg 1993: ch. 8), to investment opportunity, unavoidable tourist site, and host to Bill Clinton's post-presidential affairs – is as good a representation as one might find of the transition from a logic of containment to one of regulation.

As the privileged travel, the sites to which they travel "upgrade" – even as they might and often do continue to conjoin sites that remain *de*graded. This repositioning of places and spaces in the calculus of risk and profit as they are stitched into the global reach of racial ordering suggests an inherently interactive logic of the upgraded and degraded. The latter are not just the measure and mark of the former but the very grounds of its possible elevation. As the disprivileged acquire mobility – they too fashion trade zones and diasporic networks, migrating cartographies and refugee routes – they furnish consumptive goods and "authentic" tourist performativities at devalued prices not otherwise available to those with disposable income (black markets and main street vending). But they provide also a labor force for menial work no local citizens feel compelled to undertake, and an unregistered surplus labor force holding down working wages in the face of "fully registered" or "legitimate" employment. Here privilege and disprivilege are marked in clear if redrawn racial terms, the flows of which are regulated by the traffic cop state.

In this scheme of things, racelessness offers a reshaping of the state, equal opportunities in law and name but inequalities and closed-off opportunities in fact, the shifts from race to class (racially molded). Racelessness is the effect (in part) of globalized migrations, movements, and mobilities, paradoxically perhaps their racial expression. Here, racelessness comes to represent the guiltless conditions through which globalized production, reproduction, and (re)distribution through sweated and child labor sites, tourist mobilities and flexible accumulation would flourish. Race has long been invoked in shaping geopolitical interests: from the importance of voyages of discovery and conquest to imperial competition; from colonial orders in global marketplaces and the fashioning of metropolitan modernities to racial reorderings in the wake of their demise; from world warrings to Cold War maneuvering racially configured. As globalization has assumed economic, political, and cultural ascendance – as local economies now serve and service globalizing masters rather than their modernizing inversion – racist explication has given way to raceless implication.

State racelessness, the absenting of *formal* racial invocation from state agency and state personality, nevertheless allows the marketplace to flourish through racial shaping and flows. The state is present through the structuring of its own racelessness, racially present in its traces even as it can claim absence and non-responsibility for the effects. Far from having its power wrenched from it as the result of globalization, the state through race and its claim to racelessness quietly, so much less intrusively, orders the shape and structure of globalized flows, their routes and loops, shades and colors, where capital touches down and to where it returns with most effect, where its investments – capital and human, corporate and social – are fleeting and where (relatively) long(er) term, foundational and fixed, where white and where never quite, where quiet and where overt, where almost irresistible and where noisily resisted. If colorblindness has served as the state of whiteness by another name, then racelessness projects whiteness as the ghostly power of world order, defining and refining access, circulation of citizens across states, the flow of capital, commodities, and consumers, labor and wealth, representations and significations between states.

Women, quite obviously and despite the checkered claims of gender equality, are positioned in racially marked globality differently than men, qualified by class and national origin. So peasant, lumpen, and refugee women from the East and South tend to end up as sweatshop workers, domestic labor, or sex workers, especially in the circulation of human capital to the West. Where they remain in their originating societies, they continue for the most part in traditional forms of production like subsistence agriculture, or move into global factories at radically diminished wages, or failing that take to streetwalking servicing mostly the tourist trade upgrade. Men by comparison tend to circulate as street traders or service workers in restaurants, low-paid laborers in factories or day laborers on construction sites (though of course young boys are also pressed into street trade). Racelessness, where it cuts affirmatively at all, tends to enable middle- and upper-middle-class women and men to seek similar opportunities as those in the North and West, by accessing higher education in more privileged universities and ultimately employment in high tech or finance sectors or in higher education. Racelessness, far from being the generation of equal opportunity or outcomes, paints deeply classed perspectives onto a canvas framed by states of whiteness. Race as class is fractured from its high modernist totalizations into micro-class formations.

Thus, at a certain historical moment – namely, that at which the norms and structures of white privilege have been enacted – explicit racial reference begins magically to evaporate. The maintenance, management, and sustenance of the classed privileges of power and exclusion to the benefits of whites no longer call forth explicit enforcement. Race and the elevations and devaluations for which it variously stands have so penetrated social life, have been so routinized in everyday reference and living that its calculus and metrics become taken-for-granted, taken up as a matter of course in everyday reference and arrangement. The privileges and preferences, profits and powers exercised through racial motivation or arrangement are assessed as a matter of course, in sizing up the moment, so to speak. Under racelessness, the state under formal racial erasure continues to be marked on the racial metric of global scales. Racial states, I suggested in chapter 5, are never complete, always needing to reassert themselves. They are interminably works in progress. The routinization of racial assumptions in state institutions thus makes it possible for contemporary states to express themselves racially without explicit recourse to racial terms.

So while it is conceptually possible to have a state enacting racial reference without enacting racial privilege, I want to insist on a form of racial reversal. The historical legacy of the world in which we live is one in which it should be evident that, though the state can claim formally to expunge racial reference, racist privilege, profit, and power are automatically reproduced and reenacted through the racial shaping of exclusions. Contemporary colorblind states are racist states absent race, post-racial but not post-racist, raceless yet racist. States that claim colorblindness, that insist on institutional racelessness, are able to do so by trading on the deep internalization of racial configuration in the states of being of their populations. Raceless states trade, in other words, on the social, economic, political, legal, and cultural conditions historically inscribing differentiated racial configurations and arrangements for their members and non-members alike.

Traceless Citizenships

Now *deracializing* concerns undoing the processes and structures of white dominance and rule through anti-racisms. It involves the unstitching of white rule, picking apart the fabric of worldwide white-ness, decolonizing global imaginaries of white dominance (Pieterse and Parekh 1995). And it calls for reimagining a world in which norms, standards, practices, relations, and structures fashioned his-torically by and associated with white dominance and dominating whiteness are no longer (conceived and ordered to be) singular. Deracializing amounts to dehomogenizing the state, heterogenizing forms of governance and being, loosening if not splintering the grip, the vice, of the racial imaginary on the state and of the state on racial configuration. So a state without racism(s) would be part of a global arrangement of states not marked by racial configuration. And this, it would follow, would be a world breaking dramatically with the global racial orderings of the past half-millennium, processes that began with decolonization a half-century ago in checkered and all too often checked ways. If a contemporary state without blackness (in the extended political sense) would be one subjected to a terrible holo-caust, biological or cultural, a state without whiteness would be one, in a worldly scheme of things, without racism as historically configured. It would not be a state in which black (or white) people necessarily would *not* be recognized as black (or white), nor one in which the norms of regulation and governance were set by and in terms of "black" interests, whatever they might amount to. Rather, such a state would be one in which people of color in general, like white people gener-ally, would be recognized as fully human (Fanon 1965: 250; Gordon 1995: 60). The salient point here is not the self-absorption of white-ness in its own demise, as is so much the case with whiteness studies, but the undoing of states of racial being and forms of governmentality in their global profusions. The aim is to deroutinize and desystematize interlocking worlds of race historically produced and the racially figured exclusions and derogations they entail.

In the latter sense, post-*racist* states would not only abandon state-prompted, based, or promoted racial taxonomies, categorizations, and censal classifications (save in the latter case for tracking discrimina-tion, past and present). States after racism would demand that the debilitating and distorting impacts of the histories of racial exclusions, institutional and individual, be transformatively addressed, with sensitivity and civility. Thus deracializing the state entails critically evaporating the hold of race on state powers over defining borders, the profiles of immigration, and on the body of citizenship. It requires undoing the hold of race on policing and incarceration as well as on the shape, scope, and implementation of law. And it means "eracing" the determinations of race on the space, place, and design of residence and education, work and recreation.

All this, in turn, presupposes a dramatically altered conception of citizenship. The question with which I am concerned thus becomes how we can conceive of state engagement and citizenship (of citizenship as state engagement and interaction rather than as state belonging and identification) outside of the constitutive oppositions identified above. Here citizenship is to be premised rather on openness and flows than on stasis and fixity, on heterogeneities rather than homogeneity. Aiwha Ong (1999) has begun usefully to theorize these concerns in a critical context as "flexible citizenship(s)."

Crossing borders must now be understood a staple both of social and economic arrangements and of political debates. Transnational population movements are engaged in a dynamic of sending and receiving, prompting new networks of demographic circulation and transformed conditions of existence at each end of the movement. These conditions include changing implications for settled communities as well as compressed impacts on lived conditions for those left behind in sending societies and hometowns. Lives are effected through job and service provision, the experiences of everyday racism in receiving societies, family formation and dissolution, community networks, and the composition of religious groups. Established social values are impacted dramatically, as well as material and lived cultures (Essed 1991; Hannerf 1996; Portes et al. 1999; Menjivar 2000). The new im/migration studies has offered valuable insight into the political conditions and impacts of these dramatic population movements in both sending and attracting societies, played out in debates concerning changing immigration law and conditions of settlement and movement, as well as policing practices and prison demographics.

The "push–pull" conditions of earlier migrations are no longer simple or simply unidirectional (Roberts et al. 1999). The political concern over transnational population movements in the past twenty years or so, in contrast if related to the economic considerations, principally has been about the composition of citizenship. It has concerned who properly belongs in and to the society and who does not, of the constitution of the social fabric and the implications for social formation. The modernist model considered people to belong statically to just one nation-state, to have interests in, obligations to, and principal political and economic rights in a single state. This national belonging was both predicated on and served to reify the underlying assumption that nation-states were institutional manifestations of cultural homogeneity, natural developments of an inherent commonality preexisting among groups imagined to have some extended form of kinship to and so common understanding of each other.

As we have seen, modern nation-states can no longer be considered homogeneously constituted, if they ever could. Heterogeneity is not new, only so much more dramatic and evident. Nation-states are made up more or less dramatically of various groups and cultures, ethnically and racially conjured and constituted, as the 2000 US Census data have begun to reveal, for instance. Groups and cultures are themselves internally dynamic and often at odds in assumption and practice, sometimes with multiple citizenship allegiances, constantly moving between countries and cultures (Faist 2000), if not individually certainly where the family, nuclear or extended, is taken to offer the basic social referent point. For two centuries now the state has fashioned as the license of national projection a conception of state personality as singular, as fixed fast. No longer can that myth be sustained.

Political theory and social thought of late have been consumed with reconsidering the bases of citizenship and political and cultural commitment. These renewed concerns are of course directly linked to concerns over globalization and the forms of transnational migratory mobilities, movements, and settlements thus prompted (Baubock 1994; Soysal 1994; Kymlicka 1996; Castles and Davidson 2000; Parekh 2000). The presumptions of homogeneity and stasis underpinning the modernist conception of citizenship have been undermined by the processes of intensified globalization and the spatio-temporal compressions fueled as a consequence. Questions of equal membership have become especially pressing in the face of the fact that globalizing economic, social, and geopolitical processes have so exacerbated the divides between the wealthy and the poor, not just on a global scale but within especially the wealthiest of nations such as the United States. These divisions have assumed even more complex ethnoracial composition than the old model dividing black from white.

What I have referred to as the container state of Fordist capitalism produced a conception of citizenship as inherited or insistent belonging. The modernist conception of citizenship, accordingly, has built

266

into it as a constitutive (if not foundational) condition the *identification* of individual citizen with the state. Implicit in this identification is a triple logic: first, of the disposition to frame citizenship in identity terms; second, of the state taken as a coherent, a singular entity; and by implication third, of citizen-members as settled and more or less statically located within the space of the state. Settlement was supposed the rule, movement and mobility exceptional, exciting, and excitable. National character equates with state personality in the figure of the citizen. The classic modern conception of citizenship, then, most effectively articulated in T. H. Marshall's famous lecture (Marshall 1950), concerns the claim to represent the social heritage of the nation-state. Citizenship in these terms is the abstract embodiment of the complementary right – liberty, interest, claim, empowerment – to participate in and benefit from social practices, collective benefits, and responsibilities of state belonging.

This classic conception of citizenship (what I have characterized as the modernist one) is predicated on stasis and state territorial sovereignty, on borders and interiorized burghers, spatial fixity and introspection. The modernist sense of citizenship is stat-ic, at basis immobile. It also, in a sense, bristles at its borders, antagonistically excluding those taken not to belong, not already a member. By contrast, I am asking with John Urry (2000: 167ff.) what a conception of citizenship (and by extension the state) – of civic engagement and commitment, interests and investments, powers and responsibilities – would amount to if taking as first principles social flow and flexibilities, mobilities and movements, transformativity and transition. What conception of citizenship and state fabric might one offer as an horizon of possibility for post-racist, post-regulator, post-regulated states on such assumptions?

Restrictions on capital movement and on the class of financial managers guaranteeing capital flows increasingly have evaporated. At the same time, traffic cop states have maintained more or less firm restrictions on the movement and mobility of those marked as ethnoracially different or threatening: "Muslim or Arab terrorists," "helpless (if not sometimes murderous) Africans," "economically challenged or trafficking Central Americans," "over-abundant Asians," and indeed any and all mis-taken for these cut-out characters. A post-racist cosmopolitanism will have to face up to open movements of people unhindered by ethnoracial restriction. Such open movement and mobility cannot be realized without the prospects of full sociomaterial, sociocultural, and sociopolitical participation locally and globally. This includes the prospects for developing vigorous social movements to represent general interests in the face of powerful opposition from those who continue to exercise the power to shape economic, political, legal, and cultural representation. Above and beyond all else, perhaps, the power of social movements serves as the limit to the self-arrogation of those commanding significant sociomaterial and political resources. Such concerns link up with interests in developing and sustaining relatively risk-free environments of habitation and work wherever people pass their lives. Where risks and dangers do exist they would be distributed as evenly and representatively (materially and demographically) across classes and powers as factors reasonably beyond control allow. This likewise necessitates a commitment to educational access, definition, encouragement, and the conditions for self-advancement for all wherever people might find themselves. And it presupposes openness about cultural expression without the privileging of some and the degradation of others, as well as mutual cultural interactions, engagement, and influence.

Here, English as a language and bearer of culture offers a revealing example of how parochial conditions can become generalized through "glocalization." In assuming the mantle of the lingua franca of globalization and increasingly of globally infused localization, English has become generalized as form and medium of (cultural and linguistic) imperialism, the cultivating medium of civilization, reason, and corporate success (Koundoura 1998). And yet, the in processes of globalizing medium, English becomes in-habited by local ethnoracial expressions of its projected differences, invaded linguistically and culturally by those taking on its terms and structures, thereby creatively transformed semantically and syntactically, but also culturally and politically.

So though "the openness of the linguistic community" may be "an ideal openness," hence "formally egalitarian," as Balibar quickly acknowledges it does "recreate divisions, differential norms," circles and cycles of civility and incivility. These differentiations and delimitations overlap largely with the sorts of divisions and distinctions I have been discussing (Balibar 1991c: 103). The utopian ideal of communicative openness much invoked in one qualified sense or another as the basis for multicultural democracy is a castle built on sand, for the very terms are not just disposed to shifting but to being shifted. Ambiguity is a constitutive condition of the terms of expression and their syntactic relation. Communication is colored by social factors such as political tensions or differences, nuanced by shortages of social goods whether socially manipulated or created by natural conditions, framed by the politics of place(ment) and positioning at both the expressing and receiving ends of communication. "The production of ethnicity," Balibar reminds us, "is also the racialization of language and the verbalization of race" (Balibar 1991c: 104).

Seriously civil commitments are now interwoven, as Urry indicates (2000: 174–5), with sets of global dispositions and commitments. For one, they presuppose a global or planetary in contrast with a parochial outlook and range (rather than frame) of reference. Risks and dangers as well as rewards and benefits, it follows, are to be considered on global and interactive scales rather than provincially and in isolation. Sources of meaningful information are increasingly diffuse and expansive regarding social impacts and implications of significant events, natural and social, and most every significant event now impacts well beyond the reach of its local occurrence. Ecological considerations necessitate, even from a local point of view, that resources be used sustainably and with planetary implications in consideration. The concerns in turn suggest as a presupposition that people individually and collectively consider each other with a sensitive respect whether in direct interaction or in extended and more distanced sociocultural reference.

Sensitivity within the circle of ethnoracial considerations, as more generally, is deeply intertwined with civility and trust. Social sensitivity, respect, and civility presuppose and promote trusting those with whom one interacts. Trust – especially ethnoracial trust historically located – has traditionally been localized to those in some more or less literal or abstract sense close to one, those about whom one has experience and those one takes to be like one, who speak the same language linguistically and culturally. The mobilities prompted by and (re)generating globalizing dispositions call forth expanded circles and cycles of civic trust by recognizing and acknowledging the (re)sources of their promotion. By contrast, we increasingly lose trust in states whose leaders express or convey ethnoracial disdain of one sort or another, for this disdain, if sustained, is often identified with state personality. Consider Yugoslavia under Milo˘sevi˘c.

It has been popular recently, as much in cultural as in commercial terms, to conceive of regional and transregional connectivities, net-works and lines of (inter)relation, to conjure, in short, nets that capture and captivate but also the open lines that work to instill sensitivity, civility, and trust. There are no magic pills here. Every disposition to closure and self-absorption threatens and is threatened by the lure of heterogeneous polyvalence. Every call to hybridity and the transformative is open to challenge in light of the limits of our collective visions and vocabularies, by existing structures and forms, and ultimately by the threat of the anarchic and formlessness.

The line of critical and promissory argument I have pursued throughout, then, leads not so much to anarchic conclusions, though the radical tensions between bald state terror and romantic anarchism offer always the limit cases that likewise require rethinking in the wake of global pressures. The state, as James Scott notes, "is the vexed institution that is the ground of both our freedoms and unfreedoms" (Scott 1998: 7). The response to racist states is as little a call to anarchism as it is to racelessness. Rather, it is the call to rethink again and again, without end or closure, the modern(izing) terms of social relation: of statehood and citizenship, of race and its intersected modalities, of democracies and public spheres; of freedoms and private spheres; of rights and responsibilities, civilities and incivilities.

Individuals as citizens of the state continue to be endowed racially (there is a sense in which as citizens they consensually are made to endow themselves as such, most notably under conditions of racelessness), just as racial configuration acquires individuated expression through the media of the state. What "modern" state does not conceive itself, or is not conceived by others, in ethnoracially tinged terms? It is this notion of self-endowment and self-regulation that raises the question of democracy in relation to racially conceived states and their global arrangement.

Democratizing race, heterogenizing democracies

Wendy Brown (1995) characterizes democracy as about governing together that we may govern ourselves. The (self-)regulation at the heart of governmentality is made obvious by inverting this neat formula: to govern ourselves so that we may govern together. That logic of (self-)regulation is already there, one might say and as Brown's book makes clear, in governing per se. So democracy is about ways of governing that (either) delimit the impositions of regulation or render governing acceptable – justifiable – precisely because more or less non-coercively (or uncoercively) engaged. I have expressed democratic governance thus without reference to self-governance (the imposition of governance upon oneself by oneself) not simply because of the difficulties in formulating a coherent conception of the self (Taylor 1992). Rather, it is because self-governance may be mediated – informed, encouraged, imposed – by externalities internalized, through the self on the self, so to speak, thus blurring the distinction between self-regulation and imposed regulation (cf. Butler 1997b).

Roughly speaking, a democratic state would be one where all the competing interests share state power, resources, and media of representation in a repeatedly renewable negotiation of balance (Dolan 1994: 55) without any one, or any alliance – racially or otherwise configured – dominating to the exclusion of or control over others. And a democratic state so conceived would be part of a global web of similarly conceived states. A totalitarian state involves the domination of all institutions and culture in and of the state by a single representative interest over all others. One could give similar readings, for instance, in conceptualizing authoritarian or fascist or racist states. A racist state would be one where a racially (self-)conceived group (usually the one controlling the terms of racial subjectification, including definition) dominates the power, resources, and representational media of the state to the relative exclusion, subjection, or subordination of other groups racially conceived. And, as we have seen, such a state is sustained by global networks of similarly ordered and ordering states, or at least of states easy with interactions with such states, what I have called "states of whiteness." A state engaged in racial configuring (a "racializing" state in the contemporary cliché) is one where groups within the state are racially conceived and defined especially by the state and its agents to various purposes and ends.

It is important to contextualize modes of democratic states in relation to relative access to and power over resources and voice, to the media to speak and be heard or listened to. There are many ways of being democratic, related in part to questions of how accessible are channels of expression, how even the distribution of resources and power, and how (how heavily and in what ways) such access and expressibility are mediated (Gould 2000; Mills 2000; Cunningham 2000). But there is also an outcome consideration that needs to be attended in considering the nature of democratic states that has to

271

do with what elsewhere I have conceptualized under the name of "incorporation" (Goldberg 1995). Here the question becomes whether and in what ways, thin or thick, less powerful interests and groups have been able to transform the principles, rules, norms, modes of organization, and terms of conception and expression – in short, the material culture – of state formation.

Instead of speaking of racial democracies, an anti-racist politics might better speak of democracies in more or less heterogeneous societies, of heterogeneous democracies. Homogeneous societies, I have argued, either are or certainly remain homogeneous via imposition, through enforcement in modern states not the least racially configured.[9] And so the question becomes how the definitions offered above can be tailored to reflect degree and kind of access and expressibility on the part of heterogeneous groups (sometimes racially characterized) and heterogeneous populations homogenized (through restricting racial configuration). More generally, how might democracy for hetero-geneous conditions be fashioned in non-foundational terms?[10] How do we think anew the shifting spaces and expressive conditions for democracy in ethnoracially heterogeneous societies? Democracy is understood to have no fixed foundations, no settled center, only the more or less unstable balance of shifting, negotiated, and revisable interests and powers within and beyond state purview, locally and regionally, state-bounded and globally. The constant negotiations, cultural and political, economic and legal, take place precisely in the wake and face of "split affiliations" and radical "undecidabilities" attendant to so much of everyday life in the "slipstreams of late capitalism" and the cross-sections of millennial regulator states (Bhabha and Comaroff 2001). Here the interests and powers are rendered more complex precisely in and through their racial making.

To these ends, I conceive of rights as generalizations of claims and interests, expressions of liberties and drives to powers of and from local customs and practices. As these generalizations face increasingly out-ward, as in their broadening they embrace more and more of the generally human (which is to say not the individual but the social characteristics of human being), I am suggesting that rights so conceived are projections outwards of the "human in us." And in return one could say the local and specific in part is the inward imbrication or instantiation of the general or generalizable, the specific embodi-ment of general social conditions. There are no absolute universals ontologically outside of abstraction from particulars, and no local instance (not even the radically idiosyncratic or idiolectic) completely cut off from representing manifestations of more generalized conception (Hall 2000: 234–5). The relation between the individual and the social, the social constitution of individuals and the social horizons of individuality, encourages as a result a conception of "cosmopolitan connection."

This picture amounts to a social citizenship constituted by a specificity and generalizability. It requires a connectedness both locally to those about one, to those sharing a culture more or less broadly ("cultural rights"), but also more and more outwardly to those linked together by the broadest of social – which is now at the very least to say global or planetary – conditions ("human rights"). So the insistence on rights locally, at least normatively, is at once also the realization of rights more generally, tentatively more globally. If rights are generalizations from local practice and local embodiments of generalized extensions, then my right – the right of those like me, of "my people" – at once contains the kernel of the rights (or their restriction and lack) for all. The challenge is to open up those self-interestedly invested in their own (restricting) rights to the claims, interests, liberties, and powers of others not just similarly situated but equally embodiments of extended social spaces of "overlapping, multiple and intersected modernities" (Ong 1999), developed and developing, we now call the planet.

I am pointedly not claiming that the connections and commitments I have identified here will magically reconfigure the state in their image, will open up the state to the erasure of its own bounded limits. State powers massage rights to their definition and purpose. I mention these rights and configurations as parameters of possibility. If we are to learn anything from reading in tension the likes of race critical theories (Essed and Goldberg 2001) and John Rawls (1971) together, it is that the available means are to be deployed to advance the interests of the most dispossessed and degraded in the society. In doing so, the very character, the personality, of state formation will be transformed. But it is also that the parameters, the "repertoires of meaning" (Hall 2000), no matter how diminished or expansive, are to be enlarged through collective and individual efforts against the grain, in the face of regulation and repression (Scott 1990). Throughout modernity those most dispossessed and degraded have tended overwhelmingly to be positioned as such through the stated configurations of race. And it is now undeniable that "society" has global reach,

273

and the global has local social embodiment. These efforts accordingly assume racial reference and global reach.

Rather than conceiving states as "pastoral regulators" committed to controlling social conditions and populations, is it possible to reconceive states as facilitators coping and coordinating social practices, as the nodal points and contact zones between flows? Can we think of states to be not as structures of imposed governmentalities but as the principal terrains in which social life is played out in all its cultural – what one might characterize as ethnoracial – thickness? In this context, flexible citizenship is not limited just to the case of "refugees and business migrants who work in one location while their families are lodged in 'safe havens' elsewhere" (Ong 1999: 214). What Aiwha Ong properly captures by this characterization is the ethnographic description of increasingly widespread practices prompted by and expressive of global lures and pushes. But the characterization requires an opening up to a more general set of conditions as a consequence of all sorts of flows, political and existential terror, commercial and work-seeking opportunity, and recreational lure. It raises the possibility of giving to the conception of "flexible citizenship" a valence of desirable because valuable normativity.

In this light, it is possible surely to be a part of and play a part in multiple sites of identification. Here the commitments would amount to respectful and sensitive consideration in the free flows and movements at and between each of those sites. Responsibilities and commitments as well as freedoms are (to be) exercised both at and between the point(s) of residence. Flexibility to date has been exercised more robustly by those economically best positioned to be mobile, as Ong points out. I am suggesting that the claims on, commitments in relation to, and responsibilities regarding citizenship are to be opened up to reflect the dramatically transformed conditions now facing much of the world's population. And to do this requires thinking in a different light, in more open(ed) and flexible forms, about both state and ethnoracial definition.

Modern political theory, at least in the social contract strain from Hobbes onwards, restricts heterogeneity to the state of nature (or in more contemporary terms, to one side of a veil of ignorance). The challenge this delimiting assumption poses is to find a form of social order excising what are perceived on the account as the dangerous challenges of the different. The resultant structure came to be understood

274

as the modern state, homogeneously fashioned. Much of contemporary liberal political theory regarding multicultural states has sought to open outwards the defining principles to make them responsive and responsible to what has been understood as the demanding diversity, the descriptive "multi-cultural" (Hall 2000: 209), of latter-day social life. I have been concerned throughout to challenge the very presuppositions of this picture. The principal questions with which I close the book, by contrast, concern whether it is conceivable to conjure social conditions – a "state" – against the formative background conditions of constitutive, contrasting, and fluctuating heterogeneities, of flexible citizenships, and mobile or "fugitive" democracies (Wolin 1996). And how far would these conceptions bring us towards not just post-racial but post- and renewably anti-racist states, public spheres and modes of governance?

It is apt to point this book towards an ending by posing the dilemma critical to the entanglements of ethnoracial and state formation I have discussed throughout. Against the thick hierarchical and exclusionary histories of racial configuration, potentially any invocation of race in state creation and formation is implicated in reproducing, extending, and renewing racist exclusions and derogations. As we have seen, against this background even raceless commitments ignore the history of racially predicated exclusions and the fact that contemporary racially skewed conditions were produced by such histories. Thus any undertaking to address these exclusions and the skewed conditions they (re)generate must be predicated on recognizing and redressing racially prompted and indexed exclusions. The seemingly paradoxical pursuit is that the "adjectival" (Hall 2000: 209) and causal categories of subjection and subordination are necessarily implicated, though as media of redirection, in the conditions of addressing and redressing the grounds of such subjection and subordination. A vigorous commitment to root out all forms of racist discrimination would be hard pressed to abjure any use of racial categories. Setting agendas by states in racial terms limits possibilities of conception and action to those terms, but absent those terms the programmatic address will tend to miss the mark. The terms accordingly seem to delimit possibilities even as the state's recognition of its own restrictions is a necessary condition for its transformation.

My concern then has not been with laying out the details of a counter-conception of fugitive or mobile cultures of democratic social arrangements. By fugitive democracies (Wolin 1996) I am suggesting democratic cultures in flight, in all of the complex meanings thus conjured. This includes flight from the histories of ethnoracial constraint; forms of social existence outside of the law of racial derogation and exclusion as well as from cloning cultures individually, biologically, and institutionally fashioned; mobilities between worlds of belonging and commitment, work and social relation that mark the histories of almost all in the world now. Fugitive democracies would seek sets of social arrangements hospitable to flight and flux, mobilities and motilities, multiplicities and "metis-friendly institutions" (Scott 1998: 352ff.), the complexities of counter-memories vested in cultures of the heterogeneous. "Democracy is a rebellious moment," Sheldon Wolin (1996: 43) rightfully insists, open to the transformative and unbounded, heterogeneities and uncontainability, and to limitless and reiterative negotiation (Hall 2000: 235).

I have been concerned consequently to shift *the space of presumption* in social conception, intellectual and material, from heterogeneity as state externality, as the outside of modern state formation, and homogeneity as the given, the infrastructure, in state grounding and foundation. My aim has been to reveal the racial forms of state erected upon those presumptions and the logics of modern political theory licensed in those terms. And to press the counter-question about the implications for social arrangements and political theorizing of the pervasiveness of heterogeneities as following from global flows and interfaces, of erasing the imposed boundaries between inside and externality, of group belonging and the spatial grounds for citizenship. How are we to conceive both formatively and substantively the shapings of heterogeneous social worlds beyond racial states without leaving racist states unaddressed? What will states and world systems of states amount to that are no longer regulated through race? How are we to elaborate social commitments and arrangements open to global flows, multiple and overlapping and interfacing modernities, "multi-identifications" (Essed 2000: 53–6), and flexible citizenships while sustaining trusting and respectful, sensitive and reasonable, just and equitable, free and fair social arrangements? For these are the marks and manifestations of the social beyond not just race but racist states. It is to engaged consideration of these sorts of questions that contemporary social and political theorizing should now be drawing us.

NOTES

1 Sheldon Wolin argues that already in Locke, homogeneity had been read back into the state of nature as an initiating assumption, but a homogeneity, he writes, that "turns out to have been the suspension of heterogeneity" (Wolin 1996: 40–1).

2 Philomena Essed is developing this productive line of analysis most helpfully in her book on gender, ethnicity, and leadership, currently in progress.

3 James Scott's terrifically insightful reading of the "public and hidden transcripts" of resistance to domination is suggestive of the various responses that might be made, individually and collectively, to racist imposition (see especially Scott 1990: 39–40). But the book leaves open a response to the questions I am raising here.

4 The variability and proliferation in the content of contemporary economic practices have taken themselves to require for their own sense of possibility and stability precisely the sorts of political and bureaucratic homogenization we are now witnessing. Contemporary economic practices in turn seem to transform the very cultural heterogeneities they seek out for new opportunities into the sorts of bland homogenization with which economic managers appear most comfortable.

5 Lloyd's point as well as the argument that follows are products of his very insightful talk on subalternity and representation at the University of California, Irvine in January 2001, and of our discussion following the talk. I am grateful to him for prompting the following paragraph.

6 Stephen Steinberg makes this point usefully in a thorough critique of American social science, from Booker T. Washington and Gunnar Myrdal to Orlando Patterson and the Thernstroms (Steinberg 1998: 70ff.).

7 James Tully (1995), to his credit, recognizes the contemporary manifestations of heterogeneity, albeit interpreted strictly in terms of cultural difference, and offers an account of constitutional transformation in post-liberal democratic societies vested solely in these terms.

8 "[T]he state has always been in a relation with an outside, and is inconceivable independent of that relationship. The law of the State is ... that of interior and exterior" (Deleuze and Guattari 1986: 15–16).

9 I suspect that this enforced imposition is quite deeply related to what Dolan (1994), following Lyotard, characterizes as the "'pietistic' theory of politics" and what by extension I might refer to as piety in modern state conception.

10 Dolan (1994) provocatively though in perhaps problematic historical terms calls this the "pagan" conception of the political.

BIBLIOGRAPHY

Acton, Lord 1862/1996: "Nationality," in Gopal Balakrishnan (ed.), *Mapping the Nation*. London: Verso, pp. 17–38.

Adam, Barry 1978: *The Survival of Domination*. New York: Elsevier.

Adam, Heribert and Moodley, Kogila 1986: *South Africa Without Apartheid: Dismantling Racial Domination*. Berkeley: University of California Press.

Agamben, Giorgio 2000: *Means Without End: Theory Out of Bounds*. Minneapolis: University of Minnesota Press.

Alexander, Jacqui and Mohanty, Chandra T. 1997: *Feminist Genealogies, Colonial Legacies, Democratic Heresies*. New York: Routledge.

Allen, Theodore 1994: *The Invention of the White Race: Racial Oppression and Social Control*. London: Verso.

Althusser, Louis 1971: *Lenin and Philosophy and Other Essays*. London: New Left Books.

Anderson, Benedict 1991: "Census, Map, Museum," in *Imagined Communities*, rev. ed. London: Verso.

Anderson, J., ed. 1986: *The Rise of the Modern State*. Brighton: Wheatsheaf Books.

Anderson, Perry 1974: *Lineages of the Absolutist State*. London: New Left Books.

Anthias, Flora and Yuval-Davis, Nira 1989: *Women–Nation–State*. London: Macmillan.

Appadurai, Arjun 1993: "The Heart of Whiteness," *Callaloo* 16 (4): 796–807.

Appadurai, Arjun 1996: "Number in the Colonial Imagination," in *Modernity at Large: Cultural Dimensions of Globalization*. Minneapolis: University of Minnesota Press.

Appiah, K. Anthony and Gutmann, Amy 1996: *Color Conscious: The Political Morality of Race*. Princeton, NJ: Princeton University Press.

Arendt, Hannah 1951: *The Origins of Totalitarianism*. London: Andre Deutsch.

Arendt, Hannah 1986: "Communicative Power," in S. Lukes (ed.), *Power*. New York: New York University Press, pp. 59–74.

Ashcraft, Richard 1972: "Leviathan Triumphant: Thomas Hobbes and the Politics of Wild Men," in Edward Dudley and Maximilian Novak (eds.), *The*

Wild Man Within: An Image in Western Thought from the Renaissance to Romanticism. Pittsburgh: University of Pittsburgh Press, pp. 141–82.

August, E., ed. 1971: *Carlyle, The Nigger Question and Mill, The Negro Question.* New York: Appleton Century Croft.

Baker, Lee 1998: *From Savage to Negro: Anthropology and the Construction of Race, 1896–1954.* Berkeley: University of California Press.

Bakhtin, Mikhail 1981: *The Dialogic Imagination: Four Essays.* Austin: University of Texas Press.

Balibar, Etienne 1990: "Paradoxes of Universality," in D. T. Goldberg (ed.), *Anatomy of Racism.* Minneapolis: University of Minnesota Press, pp. 283–94.

Balibar, Etienne 1991a: "*Es Gibt Keinen Staat in Europa*: Racism and Politics in Europe Today," *New Left Review* 187 (May–June): 5–19.

Balibar, Etienne 1991b: "Is There a Neo-racism?," in Etienne Balibar and Immanuel Wallerstein, *Race, Nation, Class: Ambiguous Identities.* London: Verso, pp. 17–28.

Balibar, Etienne 1991c: "The Nation Form: History and Ideology," in Etienne Balibar and Immanuel Wallerstein, *Race, Nation, Class: Ambiguous Identities.* London: Verso, pp. 86–106.

Balibar, Etienne 1991d: "Racism and Crisis," in Etienne Balibar and Immanuel Wallerstein, *Race, Nation, Class: Ambiguous Identities.* London: Verso, pp. 217–27.

Balibar, Etienne 1999: "Algeria, France: One Nation or Two?," in Joan Copjec and Michael Sorkin (eds.), *Giving Ground: The Politics of Propinquity.* London: Verso, p. 162.

Balibar, Etienne and Wallerstein, Immanuel 1991: *Race, Nation, Class: Ambiguous Identities.* London: Verso.

Barkan, Elazar 1992: *The Retreat of Scientific Racism: Changing Concepts of Race in Britain and the United States Between the World Wars.* Cambridge: Cambridge University Press.

Barkan, Elazar and Bush, Ronald, eds. 1995: *Prehistories of the Future: The Primitivist Project and the Culture of Modernism.* Stanford, CA: Stanford University Press.

Barrett, James and Roediger, David 1997: "In Between Peoples: Race, Nationality and the 'New Immigrant' Working Class," *Journal of American Ethnic History* (Spring): 3–44.

Baubock, Rainer 1992: *Immigration and the Boundaries of Citizenship.* Warwick, England: Center for Research in Ethnic Relations.

Baubock, Rainer, ed. 1994: *From Aliens to Citizens.* Aldershot: Avebury.

Bauman, Zygmunt 1989: *Modernity and the Holocaust.* Ithaca, NY: Cornell University Press.

Bauman, Zygmunt 1991: *Modernity and Ambivalence.* Ithaca, NY. Cornell University Press.

279

Bauman, Zygmunt 1997: "The Making and Unmaking of Strangers," in Pnina Werbner and Tariq Modood (eds.), *Debating Cultural Hybridity: Multi-cultural Identities and the Politics of Anti-racism*. London: Zed, pp. 29–45.

Bauman, Zygmunt 1998: *Globalization*. New York: Columbia University Press.

Baxi, Upendra 2000: "Postcolonial Legality," in Henry Schwartz and Sangeeta Ray (eds.), *A Companion to Postcolonial Studies*. Oxford: Blackwell, pp. 540–55.

Bayart, Jean-François 1993: *The State in Africa: The Politics of the Belly*. New York: Longman.

Bayart, Jean-François et al., eds. 1999: *The Criminalization of the State in Africa*. Bloomington: Indiana University Press.

Becker, Jerome 1887: *La Vie en Afrique: Ou trois ans dans l'Afrique centrale*, 2 vols. Brussels: J. Lebegue.

Bell, Derrick 1992: *Race, Racism and American Law*, 3rd ed. Boston: Little, Brown.

Bell, Derrick 1995: "Racial Realism," in K. Crenshaw et al. (eds.), *Critical Race Theory: The Key Writings that Formed the Movement*. New York: The New Press, pp. 302–12.

Benhabib, Seyla, ed. 1996: *Democracy and Difference: Contesting the Boundaries of the Political*. Princeton, NJ: Princeton University Press.

Bennett, David, ed. 1998: *Multicultural States: Rethinking Difference and Identity*. New York: Routledge.

Bentham, Jeremy 1820/1995: *Colonies, Commerce, and Constitutional Law: Rid Yourselves of Ultramaria and Other Writings on Spain and Spanish America*, ed. Philip Schofield. Oxford: Clarendon Press.

Berlant, Lauren 1991: *The Anatomy of National Fantasy: Hawthorne, Utopia, and Everyday Life*. Chicago: University of Chicago Press.

Bhabha, Homi 1994: *The Location of Culture*. London: Routledge.

Bhabha, Homi and Comaroff, John 2001: "Speaking of Postcoloniality, in the Continuous Present: A Conversation," in D. T. Goldberg and Ato Quayson (eds.), *Relocating Postcolonialism*. Oxford: Blackwell.

Blakely, Allison 1993: *Blacks in the Dutch World: The Evolution of Racial Imagery in a Modern Society*. Bloomington: Indiana University Press.

Blommaert, Jan and Verschueren, Jef 1992: *Het Belgische Migrantendebat*. Antwerp: International Pragmatics Association.

Blommaert, Jan and Verschueren, Jef 1998: *Debating Diversity: Analysing the Discourse of Tolerance*. London: Routledge.

Blyden, Edward Wilmot 1862/1996: "The Call of Providence to the Descendants of Africa in America," in Wilson Moses (ed.), *Classical Black Nationalism: From the American Revolution to Marcus Garvey*. New York: New York University Press, pp. 188–208.

Boas, Franz 1940: *Race, Language and Culture*. New York: The Free Press.

Bolt, Christine 1971: *Victorian Attitudes Towards Race*. London: Routledge and Kegan Paul.

Bonnett, Alastair 1998: "How the British Working Class Became White: The Symbolic (Re)formation of Racialized Capitalism," *Journal of Historical Sociology* 11, 3 (September): 316–40.

Bourdieu, Pierre and Wacquant, Loic 1998: "Les Ruses de la Raison Impérialiste," *Actes de la Recherche Sciences Sociales*: 121–2.

Bourdieu, Pierre and Wacquant, Loic 1999: "On the Cunning of Imperialist Reason," *Theory, Culture and Society* 16 (1): 41–58.

Bracken, Harry 1973: "Essence, Accident and Race," *Hermethena* CXVI (Winter): 81–9.

Bracken, Harry 1978: "Racism and Philosophy," *Philosophia* 8 (2–3): 241–60.

Brah, Avtar 1996: *Cartographies of Diaspora: Contesting Identities*. London: Routledge.

Brantlinger, Patrick 1995: "'Dying Races': Rationalizing Genocide in the Nineteenth Century," in Jan Nederveen Pieterse and Bhikhu Parekh (eds.), *The Decolonization of the Imagination: Culture, Knowledge and Power*. London: Zed, pp. 43–56.

Breman, Jan, ed. 1990: *Imperial Monkey Business: Racial Supremacy in Social Darwinist Theory and Colonial Practice*. Amsterdam: VU University Press.

Breuilly, John, ed. 1992: *The State of Germany: The National Idea in the Making, Unmaking, and Remaking of a Modern Nation*. London: Longman.

Brigham, John 1996: "The Other Countries of American Law," *Social Identities* 2, 2 (Summer): 237–54.

Broca, Paul 1860/1950: "On the Phenomena of Hybridity in the Genus Homo," in Earl Count (ed.), *This is Race: An Anthology Selected from the International Literature on the Races of Man*. New York: Henry Schuman, pp. 68–74.

Brown, Wendy 1995: *States of Injury: Power and Freedom in Late Modernity*. Princeton, NJ: Princeton University Press.

Buci-Glucksmann, Christine 1980: *Gramsci and the State*. London: Lawrence and Wishart.

Burleigh, Michael and Wippermann, Wolfgang 1991: *The Racial State: Germany 1933–1945*. Cambridge: Cambridge University Press.

Burrows, Guy 1903: *The Curse of Central Africa . . . With Which is Incorporated A Campaign Amongst Cannibals by Edgar Canisius*. London: R. A. Everett.

Butler, Judith 1997a: *Excitable Speech: A Politics of the Performative*. New York: Routledge.

Butler Judith 1997b: *The Psychic Life of Power: Theories of Subjection*. Stanford, CA: Stanford University Press.

Callaway, Helen 1987: *Gender, Culture and Empire: European Women in Colonial Nigeria*. London: Macmillan.

Callinicos, Alex 1993: *Race and Class*. London: Bookmarks.

Canny, Nicholas 1973: "The Ideology of English Colonization: From Ireland to America," *William and Mary Quarterly* 30 (October): 575–98.

Carlyle, Thomas 1843/1888: *Sartor Resartus: Lectures on Heroes, Chartism, Past and Present.* London: Chapman and Hall.

Carnoy, Martin 1984: *The State and Political Theory.* Princeton, NJ: Princeton University Press.

Carr, Leslie 1997: *Color-blind Racism.* Thousand Oaks, CA: Sage.

Cassirer, Ernst 1946: *The Myth of the State.* New Haven, CT: Yale University Press.

Castles, Stephen and Davidson, Alastair 2000: *Citizenship and Migration: Globalization and the Politics of Belonging.* London: Routledge.

Castles, Stephen and Miller, Mark 1998: *The Age of Migration: International Population Movements in the Modern World,* 2nd rev. ed. London: Macmillan.

Census Report of the Colony of the Cape of Good Hope 1891: Cape Town: W. A. Richards and Sons (printed 1892).

Census Report of the Colony of the Cape of Good Hope 1904: Cape Town: Cape Times Ltd. (printed 1905).

Census Report of the Union of South Africa 1911: Pretoria: Government Printing Office (printed in 1913).

Census Report of the Union of South Africa 1921: Pretoria: Government Printing Office.

Census Report of the Population of the Union of South Africa 1951: Pretoria: Government Printing Office.

Cheng, Ann 2000: *The Mourning of Race.* New York: Oxford University Press.

Claessen, H. J. and Skalnik, P., eds. 1978: *The Early State.* The Hague: Mouton.

Claestres, P. 1985: *Society Against the State.* New York: Zone Books (MIT).

Coetzee, J. M. 1988: *Foe.* New York: Penguin.

Coetzee, J. M. 1999: *Disgrace.* London: Secker and Warburg.

Cohen, Phil, ed. 1999: *New Ethnicities, Old Racisms.* London: Zed.

Cohen, R. and Service, E., eds. 1978: *Origins of the State: The Anthropology of Political Evolution.* Philadelphia: ISHI.

Colker, Ruth 1996: *Hybrid: Bisexuals, Multiracials, and Other Misfits under American Law.* New York: New York University Press.

Collier, Peter and Horowitz, David, eds. 1991: *Second Thoughts About Race in America.* New York: Madison Books.

Comaroff, John 1998: "Reflections on the Colonial State, in South Africa and Elsewhere: Factions, Fragments, Facts and Fictions," *Social Identities* 4, 3 (Fall): 317–25.

Comaroff, John L. and Comaroff, Jean 1997: *Of Revelation and Revolution: The Dialectics of Modernity on a South African Frontier,* Vol. 2. Chicago: University of Chicago Press.

Comaroff, Jean and Comaroff, John L. 2000a: "Naturing the Nation: Aliens, Apocalypse and the Postcolonial State," *HAGGAR: International Social Science Review* 1 (1): 7–40.

Comaroff, Jean and Comaroff, John L. 2000b: "Millennial Capitalism: First Thoughts on a Second Coming," *Public Culture* 12, 2 (Spring): 291–343.

Connolly, William 1984: *Legitimacy and the State*. New York: New York University Press.

Connolly, William 1991: *Identity/Difference: Democratic Negotiations of Political Paradox*. Ithaca, NY: Cornell University Press.

Conrad, Joseph 1901/1991: *The Heart of Darkness*, ed. Stanley Applebaum. New York: Dover.

Cookey, S. J. S 1968: *Britain and the Congo Question, 1885–1913*. London: Longman.

Coombe, Rosemary 1993: "Tactics of Appropriation and the Politics of Recognition in Late Modern Democracies," *Political Theory* 21, 3 (August): 411–33.

Coombe, Rosemary 1996: "The Demonic Place of the 'Not There': Trademark Rumors in the Postindustrial Imaginary," in J. Ferguson and A. Gupta (eds.), *Culture, Power, Place: Explorations in Critical Anthropology*. Durham, NC: Duke University Press, pp. 249–76.

Cooper, Frederick and Stoler, Ann Laura, eds. 1997: *Tensions of Empire: Colonial Cultures in a Bourgeois World*. Berkeley: University of California Press.

Cornell, Drucilla 1995: *The Imaginary Domain*. New York: Routledge.

Count, Earl, ed. 1950: *This is Race: An Anthology Selected from the International Literature on the Races of Man*. New York: Henry Schuman.

Crenshaw, Kimberle 1995a: "Race, Reform and Retrenchment: Transformation and Legitimation in Antidiscrimination Law," in K. Crenshaw et al. (eds.), *Critical Race Theory: The Key Writings that Formed the Movement*. New York: The New Press, pp. 103–22.

Crenshaw, Kimberle 1995b: "Mapping the Margins: Intersectionality, Identity Politics, and Violence Against Women of Color," in K. Crenshaw et al. (eds.), *Critical Race Theory: The Key Writings that Formed the Movement*. New York: The New Press, pp. 357–83.

Crenshaw, Kimberle 1998: "Color Blindness, History and the Law," in Wahneema Lubiano (ed.), *The House that Race Built*. New York: Vintage, pp. 280–9.

Crenshaw, Kimberle, Gotanda, Neil, Peller, Gary, and Thomas, Kendall, eds. 1995: *Critical Race Theory: The Key Writings that Formed the Movement*. New York: The New Press.

Crocker, Walter 1947: *On Governing Colonies: Being an Outline of the Real Issues and a Comparison of the British, French and Belgian Approach to Them*. London: Allen and Unwin.

Cross, Malcolm and Keith, Michael 1992: *Racism, the City and the State*. London: Routledge.

Crowder, Michael 1988: *The Flogging of Phinehas McIntosh: A Tale of Colonial Folly and Injustice, Bechuanaland 1933*. New Haven, CT: Yale University Press.

Crummell, Alexander 1861/1996: "The Progress of Civilization along the West African Coast," in Wilson Moses (ed.), *Classical Black Nationalism: From the American Revolution to Marcus Garvey*. New York: New York University Press, pp. 169–87.

Cunningham, Frank 2000: "Democratic Theory and Racist Ontology," *Social Identities* 6, 4 (December): 463–82.

Cunningham, George 1965: "The Italian: A Hindrance to White Solidarity in Louisiana, 1890–1898," *Journal of Negro History* 50 (January).

Dabydeen, David 1987: *Hogarth's Blacks*. Manchester: Manchester University Press.

Dabydeen, David 1992: "The Role of Black People in William Hogarth's Criticism of Eighteenth-century English Culture and Society," in Jagdish Gundara and Ian Duffield (eds.), *Essays on the History of Blacks in Britain*. Aldershot: Avebury.

Daedalus 1995: *States: A Special Issue* 124, 2 (Spring).

Dahbour, O. and Ishay, M., eds. 1995: *The Nationalism Reader*. New Jersey: Humanities.

Darian-Smith, Eve 1999: *Bridging Divides: The Channel Tunnel and English Legal Identity in the New Europe*. Berkeley: University of California Press.

Darity, William, Jr. 2000: "Give Affirmative Action Time to Act," *The Chronicle Review*, December 1, B18.

Darwin, Charles 1859: *The Origin of Species by Means of Natural Selection, or the Preservation of the Favored Races in the Struggle for Life*. London.

Da Silva, Denise Ferreira 1998: "Facts of Blackness: Brazil is not (Quite) the United States . . . and Racial Politics in Brazil," *Social Identities*: 201–34.

Davis, Angela Y. 1981: *Women, Race and Class*. New York: Vintage.

Davis, Angela 1998: "Reflection on Race, Class, and Gender in the USA: Interview with Lisa Lowe," in Joy James (ed.), *The Angela Y. Davis Reader*. Oxford: Blackwell, pp. 297–328.

Day, A. Grove 1955: *Hawaii and its People*. With illustrations by John V. Morris. New York: Meredith Press.

De la Cadeña, Marisol 2000: *Indigenous Mestizos: The Politics of Race and Culture in Cuzco, Peru, 1919–1991*. Durham, NC: Duke University Press.

Delathuy, A. M. 1988: *De Geheime Documenten van de Onderzoekscommissie in de Congostaat*. Berchem: EPO.

Deleuze, Gilles and Guattari, Felix 1986: *Nomadology*. New York: Semiotext(e).

De Mott, Benjamin 1995: *The Trouble with Friendship: Why Americans Can't Seem to Think Straight about Race*. New York: Atlantic Monthly Press.

Denton, Nancy 1994: "Residential Segregation: Challenge to White America," *Journal of Intergroup Relations* 21, 2 (Summer): 19–35.

Derrida, Jacques 1985: "Racism's Last Word," *Critical Inquiry* 12, 1 (Autumn): 290–9.

Dikötter, Frank 1992: *The Discourse of Race in Modern China*. London: Hurst.

Dolan, Frederick 1994: *Allegories of America: Narratives, Metaphysics, Politics*. Ithaca, NY: Cornell University Press.

Dollard, John 1937/1988: *Caste and Class in a Southern Town*. Madison: University of Wisconsin Press.

Dred Scott v. Sanford 1857: 60 US (19 How.).

D'Souza, Dinesh 1995: *The End of Racism*. New York: The Free Press.

Dubow, Saul 1995: *Illicit Union: Scientific Racism in Modern South Africa*. Johannesburg: Witwatersrand University Press.

Dudley, Edward and Novak, Maximilian, eds. 1972: *The Wild Man Within: An Image in Western Thought from the Renaissance to Romanticism*. Pittsburgh: University of Pittsburgh Press.

Dudziak, Mary 2000: *Cold War Civil Rights: Equality as Cold War Policy, 1948–1968*. Princeton, NJ: Princeton University Press.

Dumm, Thomas 1993: "The New Enclosures: Racism in the Normalized Community," in R. Gooding-Williams (ed.), *Reading Rodney King, Reading Urban Uprising*. New York: Routledge, pp. 178–95.

Dummett, Ann and Nicol, Andrew 1990: *Subjects, Citizens, Aliens and Others: Nationality and Immigrant Law*. London: Weidenfeld and Nicolson.

Dussel, Enrique 1998: "Beyond Eurocentrism: The World-system and the Limits of Modernity," in Frederic Jameson and Masao Miyoshi (eds.), *The Cultures of Globalization*. Durham, NC: Duke University Press, pp. 3–31.

Dworkin, Ronald 1988: *Law's Empire*. Cambridge, MA: Harvard University Press.

Eagleton, Terry 1998: "Five Types of Identity and Difference," in David Bennett (ed.), *Multicultural State*. London: Routledge, pp. 48–52.

Eastland, Terry and Bennett, William J. 1979: *Counting by Race*. New York: Basic Books.

Edsall, Thomas and Edsall, Mary 1991: *Chain Reaction: The Impact of Race, Rights and Taxes on American Politics*. New York: W. W. Norton.

Elias, Norbert 1982: *State Formation and Civilization*. Oxford: Blackwell.

Engel, David 2001: "Injury and Identity," in David Theo Goldberg, Michael Musheno, and Lisa Bower (eds.), *Between Law and Culture: Relocating Legal Studies*. Minneapolis: University of Minnesota Press, pp. 3–21.

Equiano, Olaudah 1789: *The Interesting Narrative of the Life of Olaudah Equiano, or Gustavus Vassa, the African: Written by Himself*.

Essed, Philomena 1990: *Everyday Racism*. New York: Hunter House.

Essed, Philomena 1991: *Understanding Everyday Racism*. London: Sage.

Essed, Philomena 1993: "The Politics of Marginal Inclusion: Racism in an Organizational Context," in John Solomos and John Wrench (eds.), *Racism and Migration in Western Europe*. Oxford: Berg, pp. 143–56.

Essed, Philomena 1996: *Diversity: Gender, Color, and Culture*. Amherst: University of Massachusetts Press.

Essed, Philomena 2000: "Beyond Antiracism: Diversity, Multi-identifications, and Sketchy Images of New Societies," in Martin Reisigl and Ruth Wodak (eds.), *The Semiotics of Racism: Approaches in Critical Discourse Analysis*. Vienna: Passagen Verlag, pp. 17–40.

Essed, Philomena 2001: "Diversity and Discrimination in Health Care: The Netherlands," presentation to the Center for the Study of Twentieth-century Health Sciences and the Department of Anthropology, History and Social Medicine, University of California, San Francisco.

Essed, Philomena and Goldberg, David Theo, eds. 2001: *Race Critical Theories: Text and Context*. Cambridge, MA: Blackwell.

Evans, Ivan 1997: *Bureaucracy and Race: Native Administration in South Africa*. Berkeley: University of California Press.

Fabian, Johannes 2000: *Out of Our Minds: Reason and Madness in the Exploration of Central Africa*. Berkeley: University of California Press.

Fair, Bryan 1997: *Notes of a Racial Caste Baby: Color Blindness and the End of Affirmative Action*. New York: New York University.

Fanon, Frantz 1965: *The Wretched of the Earth*, trans. Constance Farrington. Preface by Jean-Paul Sartre. New York: Grove Press.

Fanon, Frantz 1968: *Black Skin, White Masks*. London: Paladin.

Faist, Thomas 2000: "Transnationalization in International Migration: Implications for the Study of Citizenship and Culture," *Ethnic and Racial Studies* 23, 2 (March): 189–222.

Feldman, David and Steadman Jones, Gareth, eds. 1989: *Metropolis. London: Histories and Representations since 1800*. London: Routledge.

Ferguson, Kathy 1984: *The Feminist Case Against Bureaucracy*. Philadelphia: Temple University Press.

Fernandes, Florestan 1998: "The Negro Problem in Class Society, 1951–1960," in Norman Whitten and Arlene Torres (eds.), *Blackness in Latin America and the Caribbean*. Bloomington: Indiana University Press, pp. 99–145.

Fiola, Jan 1990: *Race Relations in Brazil: A Reassessment of the "Racial Democracy" Thesis*. Amherst: Latin American Studies Program, University of Massachusetts.

Fisk, Milton 1989: *The State and Justice: An Essay in Political Theory*. Cambridge: Cambridge University Press.

Fitzpatrick, Peter 1992a: *The Mythology of Modern Law*. New York: Routledge.

Fitzpatrick, Peter, ed. 1992b: *Nationalism, Racism and the Rule of Law*. Aldershot: Dartmouth.

Fitzpatrick, Peter 1999: "Passions Out of Place: Law, Incommensurability, and Resistance," in Peter Fitzpatrick and Eve Darian-Smith (eds.), *Laws of the Postcolonial*. Ann Arbor: University of Michigan Press, pp. 39–60, 61–88.

Fitzpatrick, Peter and Darian-Smith, Eve 1999: "Laws of the Postcolonial: An Insistent Introduction," in Peter Fitzpatrick and Eve Darian-Smith (eds.), *Laws of the Postcolonial*. Ann Arbor: University of Michigan Press, pp. 1–17.

Fitzpatrick, Peter and Hunt, Alan, eds. 1987: *Critical Legal Studies*. Oxford: Blackwell.

Ford, Richard 1986: *The Sportswriter*. New York: Vintage Books.

Foucault, Michel 1991: "Governmentality," in G. Burchell, C. Gordon, and P. Miller (eds.), *The Foucault Effect: Studies in Governmentality*. Chicago: University of Chicago Press, pp. 87–104.

Freyre, Gilberto 1946: *The Masters and the Slaves: A Study in the Development of Brazilian Civilization*. New York: Alfred Knopf.

Fry, Peter 2000: "Politics, Nationality, and the Meanings of 'Race' in Brazil," *Daedalus* (Spring): 83–118.

Fryer, Peter 1984: *Staying Power: The History of Black People in Britain*. London: Pluto.

Fryer, Peter 1988: *Black People in the British Empire: An Introduction*. London: Pluto.

Furedi, Frank 1998: *The Silent War: Imperialism and the Changing Perception of Race*. London: Pluto.

Furumoto, Kim Benita and Goldberg, David Theo 2001: "Boundaries of the Racial State: Two Faces of Racist Exclusion in U.S. Law," *Harvard Blackletter Law Journal*.

Gall, Olivia 1998: "The Historical Structure of Racism in Chiapas," *Social Identities* 4, 2 (June): 235–62.

Gerzina, Gretchen 1995: *Black London: Life Before Emancipation*. New Brunswick, NJ: Rutgers University Press.

Giddens, Anthony 1985: *The Nation-state and Violence*. Oxford: Polity.

Gilman, Sander 1990: "'I'm Down on Whores': Race and Gender in Victorian London," in D. T. Goldberg (ed.), *Anatomy of Racism*. Minneapolis: University of Minnesota Press.

Gilroy, Paul 1993: *Small Acts*. London: Serpent's Tail.

Gilroy, Paul 2000: *Against Race: Imagining Political Culture Beyond the Color Line*. Cambridge, MA: Harvard University Press.

Goldberg, David Theo 1993: *Racist Culture: Philosophy and the Politics of Meaning*. Oxford: Blackwell.

Goldberg, David Theo, ed. 1994: *Multiculturalism: A Critical Reader*. Oxford: Blackwell.

Goldberg, David Theo 1995: "The Prison House of Modern Law," *Law and Society Review* 29 (3): 541–51.

Goldberg, David Theo 1997: *Racial Subjects: Writing on Race in America*. New York: Routledge.

Goldberg, David Theo 1998: "The New Segregation," *Race and Society: Journal of the Society of Black Sociologists* 1,1 (May): 15–32.

Goldberg, David Theo 2000a: "Liberalism's Limits: Carlyle and Mill on 'The Negro Question,'" *Nineteenth Century Contexts* 22 (2): 203–16.

Goldberg, David Theo 2000b: "Surplus Value: The Political Economy of Prisons," in Joy James (ed.), *States of Confinement: Police, Detention, Prisons.* New York: St. Martin's.

Goldberg, David Theo 2002a: "Monuments to Memory: Relocating State Genocide," in Charles Briggs and D. T. Goldberg (eds.), *Discourses of Genocide.* Lanham, MD: Rowman and Littlefield.

Goldberg, David Theo 2002b: "The Power of Tolerance," in Tom Martin (ed.), *Racism and the Challenges of Multiculturalism.* Forthcoming.

Goldberg, David Theo, Musheno, Michael, and Bower, Lisa 2001: "Shake Yo' Paradigm: Romantic Longing and Terror in Contemporary Socio-legal Studies," in David Theo Goldberg, Michael Musheno, and Lisa Bower (eds.), *Between Law and Culture: Relocating Legal Studies.* Minneapolis: University of Minnesota Press.

Goodrich, Peter 1987: *Legal Discourse: Studies in Linguistic, Rhetoric and Legal Analysis.* London: Macmillan.

Gordon, Lewis 1995: *Fanon and the Crisis of European Man: An Essay on Philosophy and the Human Sciences.* New York: Routledge.

Gordon, Lewis 2000: *Existentia Africana: Understanding Africana Existential Thought.* New York: Routledge.

Gotanda, Neil 1995: "A Critique of 'Our Constitution is Colorblind,'" in K. Crenshaw et al. (eds.), *Critical Race Theory: The Key Writings that Formed the Movement.* New York: The New Press, pp. 257–75.

Gould, Carol 2000: "Racism and Democracy Reconsidered," *Social Identities* 6, 4 (December): 425–39.

Graham, Richard, ed. 1990: *The Idea of Race in Latin America, 1870–1940.* Austin: University of Texas Press.

Gramsci, Antonio 1971: *Selections from the Prison Notebooks*, ed. Quentin Hoare. London: Lawrence and Wishart.

Grandin, Greg 2000: *The Blood of Guatemala: A History of Race and Nation.* Durham, NC: Duke University Press.

Gray, Herman 1995: *Watching Race: Television and the Struggle for "Blackness."* Minneapolis: University of Minnesota Press.

Greenberg, Stanley 1980: *Race and State in Capitalist Development: Comparative Development.* New Haven, CT: Yale University Press.

Greenberg, Stanley 1987: *Legitimating the Illegitimate: State, Markets, and Resistance in South Africa.* Berkeley: University of California Press.

Grewal, Inderpal and Caplan, Karen 2002: "Postcolonial Feminist Scholarship: Theorizing Gender in a Transnational Way," in Philomena Essed, Audrey Kobayashi, and David Theo Goldberg (eds.), *Companion to Gender Studies.* Oxford: Blackwell. Forthcoming.

Guinier, Lani 1994: "[E]Racing Democracy: The Voting Rights Cases," *Harvard Law Review* 108: 137.

Guinier, Lani and Torres, Gerald 2001: "The Miner's Canary: Rethinking Race and Power." Manuscript in preparation.

Gundara, Jagdish and Duffield, Ian, eds. 1992: *Essays on the History of Blacks in Britain.* Aldershot: Avebury.

Gurganus, Alan 1991: *White People: Stories and Novellas.* New York: Alfred Knopf.

Gwynn, Sir Charles 1934: *Imperial Policing.* London: Macmillan.

Habermas, Jürgen 1986: "Hannah Arendt's Communications Concept of Power," in S. Lukes (ed.), *Power.* New York: New York University Press. pp. 59–74, 75–93.

Haggard, Rider 1902: *Rural England: Being an Account of Agricultural and Social Researches Carried Out in the Years 1901 and 1902.* London: Longman, Green and Company.

Hale, Grace 1998: *Making Whiteness: The Culture of Whiteness in the American South, 1890–1940.* New York: Pantheon.

Hall, Stuart, Critcher, C., Jefferson, T., Clark, J., and Roberts, B. 1978: *Policing the Crisis: "Mugging," the State, and Law and Order.* London: Macmillan.

Hall, Stuart 1980: "Race, Articulation and Societies Structured in Dominance," *Sociological Theories: Race and Colonialism.* Paris: UNESCO.

Hall, Stuart 1984: "The State in Question," in Gregor McLennan, David Held, and Stuart Hall (eds.), *The Idea of the State.* Buckingham: Open University Press, pp. 1–28.

Hall, Stuart, 1986/1996: "Gramsci's Relevance for the Study of Race and Ethnicity," in D. Morley and K.-H. Chen (eds.), *Stuart Hall: Critical Dialogues in Cultural Studies.* London: Routledge, pp. 411–40.

Hall, Stuart 1989/1996: "New Ethnicities," in D. Morley and K.-H. Chen (eds.), *Stuart Hall: Critical Dialogues in Cultural Studies.* London: Routledge, pp. 441–9.

Hall, Stuart 1996: "Introduction: Who Needs Ethnicity?," in Stuart Hall and Paul du Gay (eds.), *Questions of Cultural Identity.* London: Sage, pp. 1–17.

Hall, Stuart 2000: "The Multi-cultural Question," in Barnor Hesse (ed.), *Un/settled Multiculturalisms: Diasporas, Entanglements, Transruptions.* London: Zed, pp. 209–41.

Hall, Stuart, Critcher, C., Jefferson, T., Clark, J., and Roberts, B. 1978: *Policing the Crisis: "Mugging," the State, and Law and Order.* London: Macmillan.

Halsey, Margaret 1946: *Color Blind: A White Woman Looks at the Negro.* New York: Simon and Schuster.

Hammond, M. 1951: *City-state and World State in Greek and Roman Political Theory.* Cambridge, MA: Harvard University Press.

Hanchard, Michael 1994: *Orpheus and Power: The Movimento Negro of Rio de Janeiro and São Paulo, Brazil, 1945–1988.* Princeton, NJ: Princeton University Press.

Haney-Lopez, Ian 1996: *White By Law: The Legal Construction of Race*. New York: New York University Press.

Hannerf, Ulz 1996: *Transnational Connections: Culture, People, Places*. London: Routledge.

Harris, Angela 1995: "Race and Essentialism," in K. Crenshaw et al. (eds.), *Critical Race Theory: The Key Writings that Formed the Movement*. New York: The New Press.

Harris, Cheryl 1995: "Whiteness as Property," in K. Crenshaw et al. (eds.), *Critical Race Theory: The Key Writings that Formed the Movement*. New York: The New Press, pp. 276–90.

Hartman, Saidiya and Best, Stephen 2001: "Redress in Law, Literature and Social Thought," Proposal, Resident Research Group. University of California Humanities Research Institute. On file.

Harvey, David 1989: *The Condition of Postmodernity*. Oxford: Blackwell.

Haym, Ronald 1991: *Empire and Sexuality: The British Experience*. Manchester: Manchester University Press.

Hecht, David and Maliqalim, Simone 1994: *Invisible Governance: The Art of African Micro-politics*. New York: Autonomedia.

Hegel, George Wilhelm Friedrich 1821/1944: *Hegel's Philosophy of Right*. Translated with notes by T. M. Knox. Oxford: Clarendon Press.

Hegel, George Wilhelm Friedrich 1952: *Phenomenology of Spirit*. Oxford: Clarendon Press.

Hegel, George Wilhelm Friedrich 1821/1972: *The Philosophy of Right*. Oxford: Clarendon Press.

Hegel, George Wilhelm Friedrich 1975: *Lectures on the Philosophy of World History: Introduction, Reason in History*. Translated from the German edition of Johannes Hoffmeister by H. B. Nisbet, with an introduction by Duncan Forbes. Cambridge: Cambridge University Press.

Helg, Aline 1990: "Race in Argentina and Cuba, 1880–1930: Theories, Policies, and Popular Reaction," in Richard Graham (ed.), *The Idea of Race in Latin America, 1870–1940*. Austin: University of Texas Press, pp. 37–70.

Heng, Geraldine 2000: "The Romance of England: *Richar Cour de Lyon*, Saracens, Jews, and the Politics of Race and Nation," in Jeffrey Jerome Cohen (ed.), *The Postcolonial Middle Ages*. New York: St. Martin's, pp. 135–71.

Heng, Geraldine and Devan, Janadas 1992: "State Fatherhood: The Politics of Nationalism, Sexuality, and Race in Singapore," in Andrea Barker, Mary Russo, and Donna Summer (eds.), *Nationalisms and Sexualities*. New York: Routledge, pp. 343–64.

Hesse, Barnor 1999: "Reviewing the Western Spectacle: Reflexive Globalization through the Black Diaspora," in Avtar Brah, Mary J. Hickman, and Máirtín Mac an Ghaill, *Global Futures: Migration, Environment and Globalization*. London: Macmillan, pp. 122–43.

Hesse, Barnor, ed. 2000: *Un/Settled Multiculturalisms: Diasporas, Entanglements, Transruptions*. London: Zed.

Hickman, Christine 1997: "The Devil and the One Drop Rule: Racial Categories, African Americans, and the U.S. Census," *Michigan Law Review* 95 (March): 1161–1265.

Hirsch, Arnold 1993: "With or Without Jim Crow: Black Residential Segregation in the United States," in Arnold Hirsch and Raymond Mohl (eds.), *Urban Policy in Twentieth Century America*. New Brunswick, NJ: Rutgers University Press, pp. 65–99.

Hitler, Adolph 1990: *Hitler: Speeches and Proclamations, 1932–45*, Vol. 1, ed. Max Domarus. Illinois: Bolchazy-Carducci.

Hobbes, Thomas 1651/1968: *Leviathan*. Harmondsworth: Pelican.

Hochschild, Adam 1998: *King Leopold's Ghost: A Story of Greed, Terror, and Heroism in Colonial Africa*. New York: Houghton Mifflin.

Hodes, Martha Elizabeth 1997: *White Women, Black Men: Illicit Sex in the Nineteenth-century South*. New Haven, CT: Yale University Press.

Hoffman, J. 1988: *State, Power and Democracy*. Sussex: Wheatsheaf.

Hollinger, David 1995: *Postethnic America: Beyond Multiculturalism*. Basic Books.

Holloway, John and Picciotto, Sol, eds. 1977: *State and Capital: A Marxist Debate*. Austin: University of Texas Press.

Humboldt, Wilhelm 1969: *The Limits of State Action*. Cambridge: Cambridge University Press.

Huyler, Jerome 1995: *Locke in America: The Moral Philosophy of the Founding Era*. Lawrence: University Press of Kansas.

Ignatiev, Noel 1995: *How the Irish Became White: Irish-Americans and African-Americans in Nineteenth Century Philadelphia*. New York: Verso.

Jacobson, Mathew Frye 1998: *Whiteness of a Different Color: European Immigrants and the Alchemy of Race*. Cambridge, MA: Harvard University Press.

James, C. L. R. 1968: "The West Indian Intellectual," in John Jacob Thomas, *Froudacity: West Indian Fables by James Anthony Froude* (1889). London and Port of Spain: New Beacon Press, pp. 23–49.

Japin, Arthur 1997: *De Zwarte met het Witte Hart: Roman*. Amsterdam: Uitgeverij De Arbeidspers.

Jefferson, Thomas 1953: *Farm Book*, ed. E. M. Betts. Princeton, NJ: Princeton University Press.

Jefferson, Thomas 1781/1955: *Notes on the State of Virginia*, ed. W. Peden. Chapel Hill: University of North Carolina Press.

Jessop, Bob 1990: *State Theory: Putting the Capitalist State in its Place*. Oxford: Polity.

Jewsiewicki, Bogumil and Mudimbe, V. Y. 1995: "Meeting the Challenge of Legitimacy: Post-independence Black African and Post-Soviet European States," *Daedalus* 124, 3 (Summer): 191–207.

Joseph, G. M. and Nugent, Daniel, eds. 1994: *Everyday Forms of State Formation: Revolution and the Negotiation of Rule in Modern Mexico*. Berkeley: University of California Press.

Josipovici, Gabriel 1993: "Going and Resting," in David Theo Goldberg and Michael Krausz (eds.), *Jewish Identity*. Philadelphia: Temple University Press.

Kairys, David, ed. 1998: *The Politics of Law: A Progressive Critique*. New York: Basic Books.

Kant, Immanuel 1775/1950: "On the Different Races of Man," in Earl Count (ed.), *This is Race: An Anthology Selected from the International Literature on the Races of Man*. New York: Henry Schuman, pp. 16–24.

Kant, Immanuel 1764/1960: *Observations on the Feeling of the Beautiful and Sublime*, trans. John Goldthwait. Berkeley: University of California Press.

Kant, Immanuel 1970: *Kant's Political Writings*. Edited with an introduction by Hans Reiss. Translated by H. B. Nisbet. Cambridge: Cambridge University Press.

Keith, Michael 1992: *"Race," Riots and Policing: Lore and Order in Contemporary Britain*. London: UCL Press.

Kershaw, Ian 1989: "The Nazi State: An Exceptional State?" *New Left Review* 176 (July/August): 47–69.

Kershen Anne, ed. 1997: *London: The Promised Land? The Migrant Experience in a Capital City*. Aldershot: Avebury.

Kipling, Rudyard 1901/1913: *Kim*. New York: Doubleday.

Klinker, Philip and Smith, Rogers 1999: *The Unsteady March: The Rise and Decline of Racial Equality in America*. Chicago: University of Chicago Press.

Knight, Alan 1990: "Racism, Revolution and Indigenismo: Mexico, 1910–1940," in Richard Graham (ed.), *The Idea of Race in Latin America, 1870–1940*. Austin: University of Texas Press, pp. 71–114.

Knox, Robert 1862: *The Races of Men: A Philosophical Enquiry into the Influence of Race over the Destinies of Nations*, 2nd ed. London: Renshaw.

Koundoura, Maria 1998: "Multiculturalism or Multinationalism?" in David Bennett (ed.), *Multicultural States*. London: Routledge, pp. 69–87.

Kriegel, Blandine 1995: *The State and the Rule of Law*. Princeton, NJ: Princeton University Press.

Kymlicka, Will 1996: *Multicultural Citizenship: A Liberal Theory of Minority Rights*. Oxford: Oxford University Press.

Kymlicka, Will and Norman, Wayne, eds. 2000: *Citizenship in Diverse Societies*. Oxford: Oxford University Press.

Leckie, G. F. 1808: *An Historical Survey of the Foreign Affairs of Great Britain*. London: J. Bell.

Lee, J. M. 1967: *Colonial Development and Good Government: A Study of the Ideas Expressed by the British Official Classes in Planning Decolonization, 1939–1964*. Oxford: Clarendon Press.

Levine, Robert and Crocitti, John, eds. 1999: *The Brazil Reader: History, Culture, Politics*. Durham, NC: Duke University Press.

Lind, Michael 1996: *The Next American Nation: The New Nationalism and the Fourth American Revolution*. The Free Press.

Lincoln, Abraham 1863/1953: *The Collected Papers of Abraham Lincoln*, ed. Roy Baster. New Brunswick, NJ: Rutgers University Press.

Lindqvist, Sven 1996: *"Exterminate All the Brutes": One Man's Odyssey into the Heart of Darkness and the Origins of European Genocide*. New York: The New Press.

Lipsitz, George 1998: *The Possessive Investment in Whiteness: How White People Profit From Identity Politics*. Philadelphia: Temple University Press.

Litwack, Leon 1998: "The White Man's Fear of the Educated Negro: How the Negro was Fitted for his Natural and Logical Calling," *Journal of Blacks in Higher Education* 20 (Summer): 100–8.

Lloyd, David 1999: *Ireland After History*. Cork, Ireland: Cork University.

Lloyd, David and Thomas, Paul 1998: *Culture and the State*. New York: Routledge.

Locke, John 1824: *The Works of John Locke*, 9 vols., 12th ed. London.

Locke, John 1689/1960: *Two Treatises of Government*, ed. Peter Laslett. New York: Mentor Books.

Lorcin, Patricia 1999: *Imperial Identities: Stereotyping, Prejudice and Race in Colonial Algeria*. London: I. B. Taurus.

Lorimer, Douglas 1992: "Black Resistance to Slavery and Racism in Eighteenth-century England," in Jagdish Gundara and Ian Duffield (eds.), *Essays on the History of Blacks in Britain*. Aldershot: Avebury.

Lowe, Lisa 1996: *Immigrant Acts: On Asian American Cultural Politics*. Durham, NC: Duke University Press.

Lowe, Lisa and Lloyd, David, eds. 1997: *The Politics of Culture in the Shadow of Capital*. Durham, NC: Duke University Press.

Lugard, Lord Frederick 1922/1965: *The Dual Mandate in British Tropical Africa*. Hamden: Archon Books.

McClintock, Anne 1995: *Imperial Leather: Race, Gender and Sexuality in the Colonial Contest*. New York: Routledge.

MacKinnon, Catharine 1989: *Toward a Feminist Theory of the State*. Cambridge: Cambridge University Press.

McLaren, Peter and Torres, Rodolfo 1999: "Racism and Multicultural Education: Rethinking 'Race' and 'Whiteness' in Late Capitalism," in Stephen May (ed.), *Critical Multiculturalism: Rethinking Multicultural and Antiracist Education*. London: Falmer Press.

McLennan, Gregor, Held, David, and Hall, Stuart 1984: *The Idea of the Modern State*. Milton Keynes: Open University Press.

McWhorter, John 2000: *Losing the Race: Self-sabotage in Black America*. New York: The Free Press.

293

Magubane, Bernard 1990: *The Political Economy of Race and Class in South Africa*. New York: Monthly Review Press.

Magubane, Bernard 1996: *The Making of a Racist State: British Imperialism and the Union of South Africa 1875–1910*. Trenton, NJ: Africa World Press.

Majeed, Javed 1992: *Ungoverned Imaginings: James Mill's The History of British India and Orientalism*. Oxford: Oxford University Press.

Malik, Kenan 1996: *The Meaning of Race: Race, History and Culture in Western Society*. London: Macmillan.

Mamdani, Mahmoud 1992: *Citizen and Subject: Contemporary Africa and the Legacy of Late Colonialism*. Princeton, NJ: Princeton University Press.

Mann, Michael 1984: "The Autonomous Power of the State: Its Origins, Mechanisms, and Results," *Archives Européenes de Sociologie* 25: 188–90.

Mariscal, George 1998: "The Role of Spain in Contemporary Race Theory," *Arizona Journal of Hispanic Cultural Studies* 2: 7–22.

Marshall, T. H. 1950: *Citizenship and Social Class and Other Essays*. Cambridge: Cambridge University Press.

Martiniello, Marco 1998a: "Wieviorka's View on Multiculturalism: A Critique," *Ethnic and Racial Studies* 21, 5 (September): 911–16.

Martiniello, Marco 1998b: *Multicultural Policies and the State*. Utrecht: ERCOMER.

Marx, Anthony 1998: *Making Race and Nation: A Comparison of South Africa, the United States, and Brazil*. New York: Cambridge University Press.

Marx, Karl 1973: *Surveys from Exile: Political Writings*, Vol. 2. Harmondsworth: Penguin.

Marx, Karl 1975: "Economic and Philosophical Manuscripts," in *Early Writings*. London: Pelican.

Massey, Douglas and Denton, Nancy 1993: *American Apartheid: Segregation and the Making of the Underclass*. Cambridge, MA: Harvard University Press.

Massey, D. and Hajnal, Z. 1995: "The Changing Geographic Structure of Black–White Segregation in the United States," *Social Science Quarterly* 76, 3 (September): 527–42.

Memmi, Albert 1967: *The Colonizer and the Colonized*. New York: Beacon Press.

Menjivar, Cecilia 2000: *Fragmented Ties: Salvadoran Immigrant Networks in America*. Berkeley: University of California Press.

Merivale, Herman 1841/1928: *Lectures on Colonization and Colonies*. Oxford: Oxford University Press.

Merry, Sally Engle, ed. 1990: *Getting Justice and Getting Even: Legal Consciousness Among Working-class Americans*. Language and Legal Discourse. Chicago: University of Chicago Press.

Michaels, Walter Benn 1995: *Our America*. Durham, NC: Duke University Press.

Miles, Robert 1993: *Racism after Race Relations*. London: Routledge.

Mill, John Stuart 1861: *Considerations on Representative Government*. London: Longman.

Mill, John Stuart 1900: *Principles of Political Economy*. London: Longman.

Mill, John Stuart 1924: *Autobiography*. London: Longman.

Mill, John Stuart 1836/1963: "Civilization," in Gertrude Himmelfarb (ed.), *Essays on Politics and Culture*. New York: Anchor Books.

Mills, Charles 1997: *The Racial Contract*. Ithaca, NY: Cornell University Press.

Mills, Charles 1998: *Blackness Visible: Essays on Philosophy and Race*. Ithaca, NY: Cornell University Press.

Mills, Charles 2000: "Race and the Social Contract Tradition," *Social Identities* 6, 4 (December): 441–62.

Mitchell, Mark 1989: "Race, the New Right and State Policy in Britain," *Immigrants and Minorities* 8 (1 and 2).

Mitchell, Michael 1998: "Blacks and the *Abertura Democratica*," in Norman Whitten and Arlene Torres (eds.), *Blackness in Latin America and the Caribbean*. Bloomington: Indiana University Press, pp. 75–98.

Modood, Tariq and Werbner, Pnina, eds. 1997: *The Politics of Multiculturalism in the New Europe: Racism, Identity and Community*. London: Zed.

Moncrief, Gary 1991: "Gender, Race, and the State Legislature: A Research Note on the Double Disadvantage Hypothesis," *Social Science Journal* 28 (4).

Montaigne, Michel de 1946: *Essays: Selections*. London: Cassell.

Morris, Meaghan 1998: "Lunching for the Republic: Feminism, the Media and Identity Politics in the Australian Republicanism Debate," in David Bennett (ed.), *Multicultural States*. London: Routledge, pp. 225–51.

Moses, Wilson, ed. 1996: *Classical Black Nationalism: From the American Revolution to Marcus Garvey*. New York: New York University Press.

Murray, Charles and Herrnstein, Richard 1994: *The Bell Curve: Intelligence and Class Structure in American Life*. New York: The Free Press.

Nairn, Tom 1977: *The Break-up of Britain: Crisis and Neo-nationalism*. London: New Left Books.

Nedelsky, Jennifer 1990a: "Law, Boundaries and the Bounded Self," *Representations* 30 (Spring): 162–89.

Nedelsky, Jennifer 1990b: *Private Property and the Limits of American Constitutionalism: The Madisonian Framework and its Legacy*. Chicago: University of Chicago Press.

Needell, Jeffrey 1995: "History, Race, and the State in the Thought of Oliveira Viana," *Hispanic American Historical Review* 75 (1).

Nelson, Samuel 1994: *Colonialism in the Congo Basin 1880–1940*. Athens OH: Ohio University Center for International Studies.

Nott, Josiah 1843: "The Mulatto a Hybrid – Probable Extermination of the Two Races if the Whites and Blacks are Allowed to Intermarry," *American Journal of the Medical Sciences* 6: 252–6.

Nozick, Robert 1974: *Anarchy, State, Utopia*. New York: Random.

Omi, Michael and Winant, Howard 1995: *Racial Formation in the United States: From the 1960s to the 1990s*, rev. ed. New York: Routledge. (First edition published 1986)

Ong, Aiwha 1999: *Flexible Citizenship: The Cultural Logics of Transnationality*. Durham, NC: Duke University Press.

Outlaw, Lucius, Jr. 1996: *On Race and Philosophy*. New York: Routledge.

Palmer, Vance 1919: "The Empire and Asiatic Immigration," *Fortnightly Review* (July): 558.

Parekh, Bhikhu 1994: "Decolonizing Liberalism," in A. Shtromas (ed.), *The End of "Isms"? Reflections on the Fate of Ideological Politics after Communism's Collapse*. Oxford: Blackwell, pp. 69–84.

Parekh, Bhikhu 2000: *Rethinking Multiculturalism: Cultural Diversity and Political Theory*. London: Macmillan.

Park, Robert 1950: *Race and Culture*. Glencoe, IL: The Free Press.

Passavant, Paul 1999: "A Moral Geography of Liberty: John Stuart Mill and American Free Speech Discourse," in Peter Fitzpatrick and Eve Darian-Smith (eds.), *Laws of the Postcolonial*. Ann Arbor: University of Michigan Press, pp. 61–88.

Pateman, Carol 1988: *The Sexual Contract*. Princeton, NJ: Princeton University Press.

Pateman, Carol 1991: "'God Hath Ordained to Man a Helper': Hobbes, Patriarchy and Conjugal Right," in M. Shanley and C. Pateman (eds.), *Feminist Interpretations and Political Theory*. Oxford: Blackwell, pp. 53–73.

Peller, Gary 1995: "Race-consciousness," in K. Crenshaw et al. (eds.), *Critical Race Theory: The Key Writings that Formed the Movement*. New York: The New Press, pp. 127–58.

Peterson, Paul, ed. 1995: *Classifying by Race*. Princeton, NJ: Princeton University Press.

Pick, Daniel 1994: "Pro Patria: Blocking the Tunnel," *Ecumene* 1: 77–94.

Pieterse, Jan Nederveen 1992: *White Over Black: Images of Africa and Blacks in Western Culture*. New Haven, CT: Yale University Press.

Pieterse, Jan Nederveen and Parekh, Bhikhu, eds. 1995: *The Decolonization of the Imagination: Culture, Knowledge and Power*. London: Zed.

Poggi, G. 1978: *The Development of the Modern State*. London: Hutchinson.

Popkin, Richard 1978: "Pre-Adamism in Nineteenth Century American Thought: 'Speculative Biology' and Racism," *Philosophia* 8 (2–3): 205–39.

Porter, Roy 1995: *London: A Social History*. Cambridge, MA: Harvard University Press.

Portes, Alejandro, Guarnizo, Luis, and Landolt, Patricia 1999: "Introduction: Pitfalls and Promises of an Emergent Research Field," *Ethnic and Racial Studies* 22 (2): 217–37.

Posel, Deborah 1991: *The Making of Apartheid, 1948–1961: Conflict and Compromise*. Oxford: Clarendon Press.

Posel, Deborah 2000: "Modernity and Measurement: Further Thoughts on the Apartheid State," in Saul Dubow (ed.), *Science and Society in Southern Africa*. Manchester: Manchester University Press.

Posner, Richard 1974: "The DeFunis Case and the Constitutionality of Preferential Treatment of Racial Minorities," *Superior Court Review* 12.

Post, Robert C. and Siegel, Reva 2001: "Equal Protection by Law: Federal Antidiscrimination Legislation After *Morrison* and *Kimel*," *Yale Law Journal* (Winter): 101–86.

Poulantzas, Nicos 1969: *Political Power and Social Classes*. London: New Left Books.

Povinelli, Elizabeth 1998: "The State of Shame: Australian Multiculturalism and the Crisis of Indigenous Citizenship," *Critical Inquiry* 24, 2 (Winter): 575–610.

Prak, Maarten 1999: "Burghers into Citizens: Urban and National Citizenship in the Netherlands during the Revolutionary Era (c. 1800)," in Michael Hanagan and Charles Tilly (eds.), *Extending Citizenship, Reconfiguring States*. Boulder, CO: Rowman and Littlefield, pp. 17–36.

Pufendorf, S. 1678/1990: *On the Natural State of Men*, trans. M. Seidler. Lewiston: Edwin Mellon.

Rattansi, Ali 1998: "Racism, 'Postmodernism' and Reflexive Multiculturalism," in Stephen May (ed.), *Critical Multiculturalism: Rethinking Multicultural and Antiracist Education*. London: Falmer Press.

Rawls, John 1971: *The Theory of Justice*. Cambridge, MA: Harvard University Press.

Reisigl, Martin and Wodak, Ruth 2000a: "'Austria First.' A Discourse-historical Analysis of the Austrian 'Anti-foreigner Petition' in 1992 and 1993," in Martin Reisigl and Ruth Wodak (eds.), *The Semiotics of Racism: Approaches in Critical Discourse Analysis*. Vienna: Passagen Verlag, pp. 269–303.

Reisigl, Martin and Wodak, Ruth, eds. 2000b: *The Semiotics of Racism: Approaches in Critical Discourse Analysis*. Vienna: Passagen Verlag.

Rex, John and Mason, David, eds. 1986: *Theories of Race and Ethnic Relations*. Cambridge: Cambridge University Press.

Rich, Paul 1986: *Race and Empire in British Politics*. Cambridge: Cambridge University Press.

Richards, Graham 1997: *Race, Racism and Psychology: Towards a Reflexive History*. London: Routledge.

Roback, Jennifer 1991: "The Separation of Race and State," *Harvard Journal of Law and Public Policy* 14 (1).

Roberts, Bryan, Frank, Reanne, and Lozano-Ascencio 1999: "Transnational Migrant Communities and Mexican Immigration to the US," *Ethnic and Racial Studies* 22 (2): 238–66.

Roberts, Stephen 1929: *History of French Colonial Policy (1870–1925)*. London: P.S. King and Son.

Robinson, Cedric 1997: *Black Movements in America*. New York: Routledge.

Roediger, David 1991: *The Wages of Whiteness: Race and the Making of the American Working Class*. New York: Verso.

Roediger David 1999: *The Wages of Whiteness: Race and the Making of the American Working Class*, rev. ed. New York: Verso.

Rousseau, Jean-Jacques 1988: *The Basic Political Writings* (including *Discourse on the Origin of Inequality*, 1754, and *On the Social Contract*, 1759), ed. D. Cress. Indianapolis: Hackett.

Rude, George 1971: *Hanoverian London: 1714–1808*. Berkeley: University of California Press.

Sacks, Karen Brodkin 1995: "How Did Jews Become White Folks?," in Roger Sanjek and Steven Gregory (eds.), *Race*. New Brunswick, NJ: Rutgers University Press.

Sancho, Ignatius 1782: *Letters*. London: J. Dodsley.

Sartre, Jean-Paul 1960/1976: *Critique of Dialectical Reason*. London: New Left Books.

Saxton, Alexander 1992: *The Rise and Fall of the White Republic*. New York: Verso.

Schama, Simon 1997: *The Embarrassment of Riches: An Interpretation of Dutch Culture in the Golden Age*. New York: Vintage.

Schwarcz, Lilia Moritz 1999: *The Spectacle of the Races: Scientists, Institutions, and the Race Question in Brazil 1870–1930*. New York: Hill and Wang.

Scobie, Edward 1972: *Black Britannia: A History of Blacks in Britain*. Chicago: Johnson Publishing.

Scott, James 1990: *Domination and the Arts of Resistance*. New Haven, CT: Yale University Press.

Scott, James 1998: *Seeing Like a State: How Certain Schemes to Improve the Human Condition Failed*. New Haven, CT: Yale University Press.

Selingo, Jeffrey 2000: "Foe of Affirmative Action Seeks to Bar Colleges in California From Collecting Data on Race," *Chronicle of Higher Education*, February 14, 2001.

Shepherd, George and Penna, David, eds. 1991: *Racism and the Underclass: State Policy and Discrimination Against Minorities*. New York: Greenwood Press.

Siegel, Reva 1998: "The Racial Rhetorics of Colorblind Constitutionalism: The Case of Hopwood v. Texas," in R. Post and M. Rogin (eds.), *Race and Representation: Affirmative Action*. New York: Zone Books, pp. 29–72.

Siegel, Reva 2000: "Discrimination in the Eyes of the Law: How Color Blindness Discourse Disrupts and Rationalizes Social Stratification," *California Law Review* 88 (65): 77–118.

Skidmore, Thomas 1990: "Racial Ideas and Social Policy in Brazil, 1870–1940," in Richard Graham (ed.), *The Idea of Race in Latin America, 1870–1940*. Austin: University of Texas Press, pp. 7–35.

Sleeper, Jim 1997: *Liberal Racism*. New York: Viking.

Small, Stephen 2001: "Racisms and Racialized Hostility at the Start of the New Millennium," in John Solomos and David Theo Goldberg (eds.), *Blackwell Companion to Racial and Ethnic Studies*. Oxford: Blackwell. In press.

Smith, Anthony 1986: *The Ethnic Origins of Nations*. Oxford: Blackwell.

Smith, Lillian 1949: *Killers of the Dream*. New York: W. W. Norton.

Smith, Rogers 1997: *Civic Ideals: Conflicting Versions of History in U.S. History*. New Haven, CT: Yale University Press.

Solomos, John 1988: *Black Youth, Racism and the State: The Politics of Ideology and Policy*. Cambridge: Cambridge University Press.

Solomos, John and Back, Les 1996: *Racism and Society*. London: Macmillan.

Solomos, John and Wrench, John, eds. 1993: *Racism and Migration in Western Europe*. Oxford: Berg.

Sowell, Thomas 1995: *Race and Culture: A World View*. New York: Basic Books.

Soysal, Yasemin 1994: *The Limits of Citizenship: Migrants and Postnational Membership in Europe*. Chicago: University of Chicago Press.

Spinner, Jeff 1994: *The Boundaries of Citizenship: Race, Ethnicity, and Nationality in the Liberal State*. Baltimore: Johns Hopkins University Press.

Spivak, Gayatri 1988: "Can the Subaltern Speak?" in Patrick Williams and Laura Chrisman (eds.), *Colonial Discourse and Postcolonial Theory*. London: Harvester Wheatsheaf.

Stasiulis, Daiva and Yuval-Davis, Nira, eds. 1995: *Unsettling Settler Societies: Articulations of Gender, Race, Ethnicity and Class*. London: Sage.

Steadman Jones, Gareth 1971: *Outcast London: A Study in the Relationship Between Classes in Victorian Society*. Oxford: Oxford University Press.

Steinberg, Stephen 1998: "Up From Slavery: The Myth of Black Progress," *New Politics* 7, 1 (Summer): 69–81.

Stephenson, Gilbert Thomas 1909/1910: "Race Distinctions in American Law," *American Law Review* 43: 29–905.

Stewart, Maria 1835: *Productions of Mrs Maria Stewart, Presented to the First African Baptist Church and Society, of the City of Boston*. Boston: Friends of Freedom and Virtue.

Stoler, Ann Laura 1990: "Making Empire Respectable: The Politics of Race and Sexual Morality in 20th-century Colonial Cultures," in J. Breman (ed.), *Imperial Monkey Business: Racial Supremacy in Social Darwinist Theory and Colonial Practice*. Amsterdam: VU University Press, pp. 35–70.

Stoler, Ann Laura 1995: *Race and the Education of Desire: Foucault's History of Sexuality and the Colonial Order of Things*. Durham, NC: Duke University Press.

Stoler, Ann Laura 1997: "Racial Histories and their Regimes of Truth," in D. Davis (ed.), *Political Power and Social Theory*, Vol. 2. Ann Arbor, MI: JAI Press, pp. 183–206.

Stratton, Jon and Ang, Ien 1998: "Multicultural Imagined Communities: Cultural Difference and National Identity in the USA and Australia," in David Bennett (ed.), *Multicultural States*. London: Routledge, pp. 135–62.

Taguieff, Pierre-André 2001: *The Force of Prejudice: On Racism and Its Doubles*. Minneapolis: University of Minnesota Press.

Taiwo, Olufemi 1998: "Reading the Colonizer's Mind: Lord Lugard and the Philosophical Foundations of British Colonialism," in Susan Babbitt and Su Campbell (eds.), *Race and Philosophy*. Ithaca, NY: Cornell University Press.

Takagi, Dana 1993: *The Retreat from Race: Asian Admissions and Racial Politics*. Berkeley: University of California Press.

Takagi, Dana 1995: "We Should Not Make Class a Proxy for Race," *Chronicle of Higher Education*, A25.

Taussig, Michael 1980: *The Devil and Commodity Fetishism in South America*. Chapel Hill: University of North Carolina Press.

Taussig, Michael 1987: *Shamanism, Colonialism and the Wild Man: A Study in Terror and Healing*. Chicago: Chicago University Press.

Taussig, Michael 1997: *The Magic of the State*. New York: Routledge.

Taylor, Charles 1992: *Sources of the Self: The Making of the Modern Identity*. Cambridge, MA: Harvard University Press.

Thomas, John Jacob 1889/1968: *Froudacity: West Indian Fables by James Anthony Froude*. London and Port of Spain: New Beacon Press.

Thomas, Laurence 1993: *Vessels of Evil: American Slavery and the Holocaust*. Philadelphia: Temple University Press.

Tilly, Charles 1994: "The Time of States," *Social Research* 61: 269–95.

Tilly, Charles 1994: "Entanglements of European Cities and States," in Charles Tilly and Wim Blockmans (eds.), *Cities and the Rise of States in Europe: A.D. 1000–1500*. Boulder, CO: Westview, pp. 1–27.

Tilly, Charles and Blockmans, Wim, eds. 1994: *Cities and the Rise of States in Europe: A.D. 1000–1500*. Boulder, CO: Westview.

Tocqueville, Alexis de 1843: "L'Emancipation des esclaves," in *Oeuvres complètes*. Paris: Gallimard, 1951–89. Tome 3, vol. 1, pp. 79–111.

Todorov, Tzvetan 1984: *The Conquest of America*, trans. R. Howard. New York: Harper Colophon.

Todorov, Tzvetan 1993: *On Human Diversity: Nationalism, Racism, and Exoticism in French Thought*. Cambridge, MA: Harvard University Press.

Tully, James 1995: *Strange Multiplicity: Constitutionalism in an Age of Diversity*. Cambridge: Cambridge University Press.

Unger, Roberto Mangobeira 1986: *The Critical Legal Studies Movement*. Cambridge, MA: Harvard University Press.

Urry, John 2000: *Sociology Beyond Societies: Mobilities for the 21st Century*. London: Routledge.

Van Dijk, Teun 1999/2001: "Denying Racism: Elite Discourse and Racism," in Philomena Essed and David Theo Goldberg (eds.), *Race Critical Theories: Text and Context*. Cambridge, MA: Blackwell.

Van Dijk, Teun 2000: "On the Analysis of Parliamentary Debates in Immigration," in Martin Reisigl and Ruth Wodak (eds.), *The Semiotics of Racism: Approaches in Critical Discourse Analysis*. Vienna: Passagen Verlag, pp. 85–104.

Van Dijk, Teun 2001: "Reflections on 'Denying Racism: Elite Discourse and Racism,' in Philomena Essed and David Theo Goldberg (eds.), *Race Critical Theories: Text and Context*. Cambridge, MA: Blackwell, pp. 481–5.

Verges, Françoise 2001: "Post-scriptum," in Ato Quayson and David Theo Goldberg (eds.), *Relocating Postcolonialism*. Oxford: Blackwell.

Voegelin, Eric 1933/1997: *Race and State. Collected Works*, Vol. 2, trans. Ruth Hein. Baton Rouge: Louisiana University Press.

Voegelin, Eric 1933/1998: *The History of the Race Idea. Collected Works*, Vol. 3, trans. Ruth Hein. Baton Rouge: Louisiana University Press.

Volpp, Leti 2000a: "Righting Wrongs," *UCLA Law Review* 47, 6 (August): 1815–37.

Volpp, Leti 2000b: "American Mestizo: Filipinos and Antimiscegenation Laws in California," *UC Davis Law Review* 33, 4 (Summer): 795–835.

Wade, Peter 1993: *Blackness and Race Mixture: The Dynamics of Racial Identity in Colombia*. Baltimore: Johns Hopkins University Press.

Wallenstein, Peter 1994: "Race, Marriage, and the Law of Freedom: Alabama and Virginia, 1860s–1960s," *Chicago-Kent Law Review* 70: 370–1.

Wallerstein, Immanuel 1974–89: *The Modern World System*, 3 vols. San Diego: Macmillan.

Walker, David 1830: *An Appeal in Four Articles; Together with a Preamble to the Colored Citizens of the World, but in Particular, and Very Expressly, to those of the United States of America*, 3rd ed. Boston: David Walker.

Warren, Samuel D. and Brandeis, Louis D. 1890: "The Right to Privacy," *Harvard Law Review* 193.

Waylen, Georgina 1998: "Gender, Feminism and the State: An Overview," in Vicky Randall and Georgina Waylen (eds.), *Gender, Politics and the State*. London: Routledge, pp. 1–17.

Weiner, Michael 1994: *Race and Immigration in Imperial Japan*. London: Routledge.

Weisberg, D. Kelly, ed. 1993: *Feminist Legal Theory: Foundations*. Philadelphia: Temple University Press.

Werbner, Pnina 1997: "Afterword: Writing Multiculturalism and Politics in the New Europe," in Tariq Modood and Pnina Werbner (eds.), *The Politics of Multiculturalism in the New Europe: Racism, Identity and Community*. London: Zed, pp. 261–5.

Werbner, Pnina and Modood, Tariq, eds. 1997: *Debating Cultural Hybridity: Multi-cultural Identities and the Politics of Anti-racism*. London: Zed.

301

West, Cornel 1982: *Prophesy Deliverance! An Afro-American Revolutionary Christianity.* Philadelphia: Westminster.

West, Shearer, ed. 1996: *The Victorians and Race.* Aldershot: Scolar Press.

Wheatley, Phyllis 1773: *Poems on Various Subjects, Religious and Moral.* London: A. Bell.

White, Hayden 1972: "The Forms of Wildness: Archaeology of an Idea," in Edward Dudley and Maximilian Novak (eds.), *The Wild Man Within: An Image in Western Thought from the Renaissance to Romanticism.* Pittsburgh: University of Pittsburgh Press.

Whitten, Norman and Torres, Arlene, eds. 1998: *Blackness in Latin America and the Caribbean,* Vols. 1 and 2. Bloomington: Indiana University Press.

Wiegman, Robyn 1995: *American Anatomies: Theorizing Race and Gender.* Durham, NC: Duke University Press.

Wieviorka, Michel 1998: "Is Multiculturalism the Solution?" *Ethnic and Racial Studies* 21, 5 (September): 881–910.

Willems, Wim 1997: *In Search of the True Gypsy: From Enlightenment to Final Solution.* London: Frank Cass.

William, Sir Henry, ed. 1935: *The High Commission Territories Law Reports: Decisions of the High Court and Special Courts of Basutoland, the Bechuanaland Protectorate and Swaziland, 1926–53.* Maseru.

Williams, Patricia J. 1991: *The Alchemy of Race and Rights: Diary of a Law Professor.* Cambridge, MA: Harvard University Press.

Williams, Patricia 1998: *Seeing a Color-blind Future: The Paradox of Race.* 1997 BBC Reith Lectures. New York: Noonday Press.

Williams, Raymond 1981: *Marxism and Literature.* New York: Oxford University Press.

Williamson, Joel 1995: *New People: Miscegenation and Mulattoes in the United States.* New York: New York University Press.

Winant, Howard 1994: *Racial Conditions.* New York: Routledge.

Wodak, Ruth 1991: "Turning the Tables: Anti-Semitic Discourse in Post-war Austria," *Discourse and Society* 2: 65–84.

Wodak, Ruth 2001: "Reflections on 'Turning the Tables: Anti-Semitic Discourse in Post-war Austria,'" in Philomena Essed and David Theo Goldberg (eds.), *Race Critical Theories: Text and Context.* Cambridge, MA: Blackwell, pp. 486–92.

Wolin, Sheldon 1996: "Fugitive Democracy," in Seyla Benhabib (ed.), *Democracy and Difference.* Princeton, NJ: Princeton University Press, pp. 31–45.

Wolpe, Harold 1988: *Race, Class, and the Apartheid State.* London: J. Currey.

Wolton, Suke 2000: *Lord Hailey, the Colonial Office and the Politics of Race and Empire in the Second World War: The Loss of White Prestige.* London: Macmillan.

Wood, Donald 1964: "Brief Biography," in John Jacob Thomas, *Froudacity: West Indian Fables by James Anthony Froude* (1889). London and Port of Spain: New Beacon Press, pp. 9–22.

Young, Robert 1995: *Colonial Desire: Hybridity in Theory, Culture and Race*. London: Routledge.

Yuval-Davis, Nira 1987: "Women, Nation, State: The Demographic Race and National Reproduction in Israel," *Radical America* 21 (6).

Zubaida, Sami, ed. 1970: *Race and Racialism*. London: Tavistock.

INDEX

Lightning Source UK Ltd.
Milton Keynes UK
UKOW06f0416240117

292731UK00002B/211/P